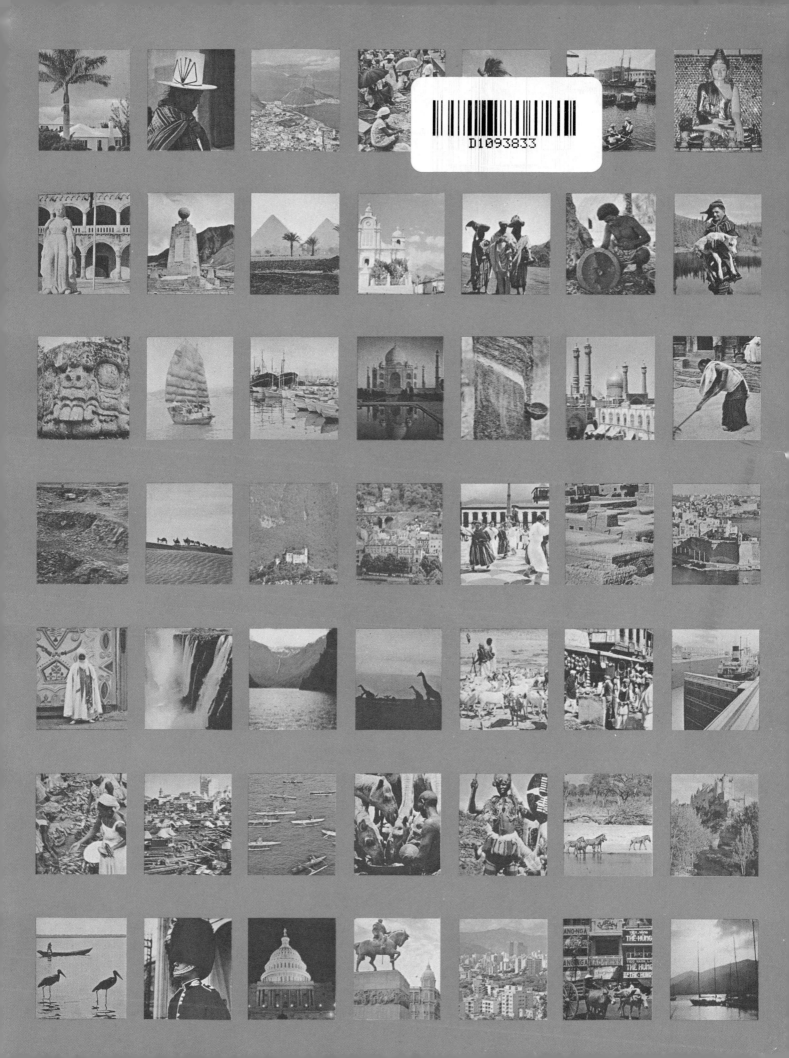

# THE WORLD AND ITS PEOPLES

*Macedonian dancers.*

# YUGOSLAVIA RUMANIA BULGARIA ALBANIA

GREYSTONE PRESS / NEW YORK

*Library of Congress Catalog Number: 65-26559*

*Cover and Book Designed by Harold Franklin*

MANUFACTURED IN THE UNITED STATES OF AMERICA

# THE WORLD AND ITS PEOPLES—EDITORS AND CONTRIBUTORS

# Table of Contents

YUGOSLAVIA

RUMANIA

BULGARIA

ALBANIA

*The Gulf of Kotor on the Dalmatian coast.*

# YUGOSLAVIA

The Roman bridge over the Neretva River at Mostar, 50 miles southwest of Sarajevo. Mostar is the chief city of Herzegovina and lies in a wine-producing and cherry-growing region. Apart from its Roman bridge — reconstructed in 1556 on the site of the original structure — Mostar possesses the remains of Roman fortifications and has many Turkish mosques. These latter tell of the leading part Turkey has played in the history of the city.

## AREA AND BOUNDARIES

YUGOSLAVIA, WHICH OCCUPIES THE northwestern and central parts of the Balkan Peninsula, is the largest and most complex of the Balkan countries. It has a mountainous, well-forested terrain, and is inhabited by people of a number of different races, with a population estimated at 19,292,000 in 1964.

Yugoslavia covers an area of 99,082 square miles. It is situated approximately between longitude 46°53′ N., at the meeting point of the Yugoslavian, Austrian and Hungarian frontiers, and 40°51′ N., at Lake Prespa in the extreme south. Its westernmost point is at latitude 13° 23′ E., to the northeast of Udine, in Italy, and its easternmost point is around 23°0′ E., in eastern Macedonia.

Yugoslavia is bordered to the north by Austria and Hungary; to the northeast by Rumania; to the east by Bulgaria; to the south by Greece; to the southwest by Albania and the Adriatic Sea; and to the west by Italy. The country's Adriatic coastline extends for about 450 miles.

## ORGANIZATION OF THE STATE

### Administrative Divisions

THE SOCIALIST FEDERAL REPUBLIC OF Yugoslavia is composed of six republics: Bosnia-Herzegovina; Croatia;

Macedonia; Montenegro; Serbia (including the two autonomous territories of Vojvodina and Kosovo-Metohija); and Slovenia. The six republics and two autonomous territories are subdivided into 40 districts and 577 communes.

## The Constitution

The Constitution of April 7, 1963, replaced the constitutions of Jan. 31, 1946 and Jan. 13, 1953.

Under the present constitution, legislative and executive power is wielded by the Federal Assembly, a body of 670 members divided into five Chambers: Federal, Economic, Education and Culture, Social Welfare and Health, and Organizational-Political. Each has 120 members, and in addition the Federal Chamber has a further 70 members who are elected by the six federal republics and two autonomous territories to represent their particular local interests.

On a lower level than the Federal Assembly are the assemblies of the six socialist republics, with a total membership of 2274; the assemblies of the two autonomous territories, with a total membership of 540; the assemblies of the 40 districts, with a total membership of 4000; and the assemblies of the 577 communes, with a total membership of 42,907.

The members of all these legislative bodies are elected for a four-year term, a half of each assembly being renewed every two years. Suffrage is universal for all citizens over 18 years of age.

The Federal Assembly elects the president of the republic, the vice-president of the republic, and its own president and vice-president. These officers are elected for a four-year term. The president of the republic may be re-elected for only one further four-year term, but this rule does not apply to President (Josip Broz) Tito (1892-    ), the leading political figure in the creation of modern Yugoslavia.

### THE FEDERAL EXECUTIVE COUNCIL

The Federal Chamber, the premier chamber of the Federal Assembly, is responsible for the election of the highest executive body, the Federal Executive Council. This consists of 12 members of the Federal Chamber, together with the presidents of the executive councils of the republics, the federal state secretaries for Foreign Affairs and Defense, the federal secretaries and the secretary of the Federal Executive Council.

### Justice

Justice is administered by courts ranging in importance from the county tribunals, through the district courts and the supreme courts of the republics and autonomous territories, to the Supreme Court of the Federal Republic, situated in Belgrade.

In the county tribunals and district courts judges are accompanied on the bench by lay assessors, appointed by the Federal Assembly.

### Religion

The Yugoslavian Constitution guarantees freedom of worship to all citizens. There is no established State Church, but the predominant church is the Serbian Orthodox, to which, in 1953, about 41.4 per cent of the population belonged.

The Serbian Orthodox Church is ruled by a Holy Synod, which consists of the Patriarch and four bishops, and a council of all the bishops, both of which meet once or twice annually. There are 23 Serbian Orthodox bishoprics in Yugoslavia, and around 2000 priests.

### ROMAN CATHOLIC CHURCH

The Roman Catholic Church, to which about 31.8 per cent of the population belong, has four archbishoprics; there are also seven bishoprics directly dependent on the Holy See. Yugoslavia has not had established diplomatic relations with the Vatican since 1952.

### OTHER RELIGIONS

Moslems, who make up approximately 12.3 per cent of the population, are under the direction of the *Reis-ul-Ulema,* which has its seat at Sarajevo. The Protestants, mainly Lutherans with small bodies of Reformed Church members, Baptists, Adventists and Methodists, amount

*The caves (the largest in Europe) of Postojna, a village in Slovenia, 23 miles southwest of Ljubljana. The cavern in the foreground is one of the most complete and spectacular examples of underground erosion of limestone caused by a watercourse —in this case the Piuca. In the* Sala da Ballo *(ballroom) grotto a ball is held on each Whit Monday, when the grotto is brilliantly illuminated.*

# YUGOSLAVIA, RUMANIA, HUNGARY, AND BULGARIA

Statute Miles

Kilometers

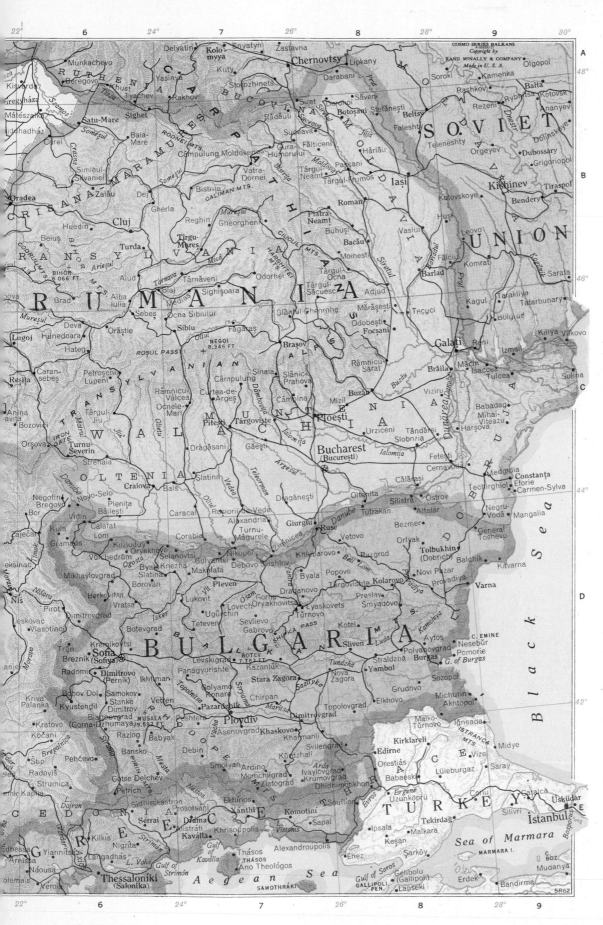

**RUMANIA**

**Principal Cities**

Arad . . . . . . . . . . B 5
Bacău . . . . . . . . . B 8
Baia-Mare . . . . . . . B 6
Bârlad (Bîrlad) . . . . B 8
Bistriţa . . . . . . . . B 7
Botoşani . . . . . . . . B 8
Brăila . . . . . . . . . C 8
Braşov (Oraşul-
   Stalin) . . . . . . . C 7
Bucharest
   (Bucureşti) . . . . . C 8
Buzău . . . . . . . . . C 8
Călăraşi . . . . . . . . C 8
Cluj . . . . . . . . . . B 6
Constanţa . . . . . . . C 9
Craiova . . . . . . . . C 6
Focşani . . . . . . . . C 8
Galaţi (Galacz) . . . . C 9
Giurgiu . . . . . . . . D 7
Hunedoara . . . . . . . C 6
Iaşi . . . . . . . . . . B 8
Lugoj . . . . . . . . . C 5
Lupeni . . . . . . . . . C 6
Mediaş . . . . . . . . . B 7
Oradea . . . . . . . . . B 5
Petroseni . . . . . . . C 6
Piteşti . . . . . . . . C 7
Ploeşti . . . . . . . . C 8
Reşiţa . . . . . . . . . C 5
Roman . . . . . . . . . B 8
Satu-Mare . . . . . . . B 6
Sibiu . . . . . . . . . C 7
Sighet . . . . . . . . . B 6
Suceava . . . . . . . . B 8
Târgovişte . . . . . . . C 7
Tecuci . . . . . . . . . C 8
Timişoara . . . . . . . C 5
Tulcea . . . . . . . . . C 9
Turda . . . . . . . . . B 6
Turnu-Severin . . . . . C 6

**YUGOSLAVIA**

**Principal Cities**

Banja Luka . . . . . . C 3
Bečej . . . . . . . . . C 5
Belgrade (Beograd) . C 5
Bitola (Bilolj) . . . . E 5
Celje . . . . . . . . . B 2
Karlovac . . . . . . . C 2
Kikinda . . . . . . . . C 5
Kragujevac . . . . . . D 5
Kumanovo . . . . . . D 5
Leskovac . . . . . . . D 5
Ljubljana . . . . . . . B 2
Maribor . . . . . . . . B 2
Mostar . . . . . . . . D 3
Niš . . . . . . . . . . D 5
Novi Sad . . . . . . . C 4
Osijek . . . . . . . . C 4
Pančevo . . . . . . . C 5
Peć . . . . . . . . . . D 5
Pirano . . . . . . . . C 1
Prilep . . . . . . . . E 5
Priština . . . . . . . D 5
Prizren . . . . . . . . D 5
Pula (Pola) . . . . . . C 1
Rijeka (Fiume) . . . . C 2
Šabac . . . . . . . . . C 4
Sarajevo . . . . . . . D 4
Senta . . . . . . . . . C 5
Skopje (Skoplje) . . . D 5
Sombor . . . . . . . . C 4
Split . . . . . . . . . D 3
Subotica . . . . . . . B 4
Tetovo . . . . . . . . D 5
Tuzla . . . . . . . . . C 4
Vršac . . . . . . . . . C 5
Zagreb . . . . . . . . C 2
Zenica . . . . . . . . C 3
Zrenjanin
   (Petrovgrad) . . . . C 5

Conic Projection
SCALE 1:4,000,000    1 Inch = 63 Statute Miles

*Crno Jezero (Black Lake) is a small, picturesque lake of glacial origin. It lies in the mountainous, fir-clad hills on the northeastern side of the Durmitor massif between the Tara and Piva rivers. It is situated three miles northeast of Bobotov Kuk, the highest peak of the massif.*

### Language

Yugoslavia has three official languages: Serbo-Croatian, Macedonian and Slovenian. By far the greater part of the population speak Serbo-Croatian, which is written in Latin script in Croatia but in Cyrillic script elsewhere. Macedonian is written in Cyrillic characters, while Slovenian is written in Latin characters.

### Currency and Measures

The basic unit of currency in Yugoslavia is the *dinar,* which is subdivided into 100 *paras.* Since the end of World War II, all banking has been nationalized, and the main bank is now the National Bank of Yugoslavia. Coins are issued to the value of 50 *paras* and 1, 2, 5, 10 20 and 50 *dinars,* and notes to the value of 100, 500, 1000 and 5000 *dinars,* the total amount in circulation in 1962 being 283,797 million *dinars.*

On Jan. 1, 1952, the *dinar* was revalued as being worth 2.96223 milligrams of gold. Its current official rate is 750 *dinars* to the U.S. dollar.

The metric system of weights and measurements has been in official use since 1883 in the regions which now comprise Yugoslavia.

to about 10,000. The Jewish minority have a Grand Rabbi in Belgrade. It is estimated that about 13 per cent of the population profess no religion.

### Education

Education in Yugoslavia is free and compulsory between the ages of seven and 14. A considerable increase in the number of educational institutions of all kinds, particularly technical institutes, has taken place in recent years. In 1962 there were 14,568 primary schools; 275 senior secondary schools; 1272 technical colleges; 108 teachers' training schools; and a number of special schools of various kinds for national minorities.

Yugoslavia has five universities. These are situated at Belgrade, Ljubljana, Sarajevo, Skoplje and Zagreb, and offer a very wide range of faculties, particular emphasis being placed on scientific subjects.

---

## PHYSICAL GEOGRAPHY

YUGOSLAVIA IS A RUGGED AND MOUNtainous country, some 75 per cent of its area being covered by hills. However, these elevations rarely reach any great height, the major peak being Mt. Triglav (9393 feet). Although the country's formation is complex, it can be divided into three basic areas: the lowlands of the north; the Morava and Vardar basins of the east; and the Dinaric Alps.

### The Northern Lowlands

The northwestern corner of Yugoslavia is occupied by the eastern European Alps, which split into a number of ranges to enclose the head of the Sava River. The first range is the

*The Crnojevica River flows out of the northern end of Lake Scutari (the largest lake on the Balkan Peninsula, situated on the Albanian-Yugoslavian border) and runs at a leisurely pace through low-lying marshland down to the Adriatic Sea.*

Karawanken Alps, composed of limestone and, further west, of ancient crystalline formations.

They are divided into a number of groups which have an average elevation of 6000 feet. The highest group is the Savinja Alps, which possess the tallest peak, Mt. Grintavec (8390 feet).

Further east, the valleys of the Sava and Drava rivers are separated by the ancient outcrops of the Papuk (3126 feet) and the Fruska Gora (1768 feet). This area is rich in well-watered, fertile valleys and plains, rarely exceeding 1000 feet in elevation. This is predominantly agricultural country, but the northeastern part of the area is characterized by steppes, areas of sand dunes, and widespread areas of wind-borne loess.

### The Morava-Vardar Region

The greater part of eastern Yugoslavia consists of the Morava River basin in the north, which comprises most of Serbia, and the Vardar River basin in the south.

The northern Morava basin is characterized by low, terraced formations, while in the southern basin broad, flat valleys are separated by older rock formations such as the Kopaonik range, which has an average elevation of 6000 feet.

The Vardar is canalized in its lower course. This basin is a fertile area and produces, among other things, cotton, wine and vegetables.

### The Dinaric Alps

The Dinaric Alps, which run along the eastern coast of the Adriatic Sea, consist of a number of limestone formations, interspersed with ancient crystalline rock formations. In general, the peaks do not exceed 6000 feet in elevation. They are interspersed with barren, semi-desert plateaus formed by the erosion of limestone rocks.

### The Coast

The Adriatic coast of Yugoslavia is broken by many small bays and inlets. It is also characterized by a large number of long islands, running parallel to the coastline, formed by the summits of submerged formations of the Dinaric system. The largest of these, from north to south, are the islands of Krk, Cres, Pag, Dugi Otok, Brac, Hvar, Korcula and Mljet.

### Rivers

The main watercourse of Yugoslavia is the Danube (Dunav), the second longest river in Europe (the Volga is the longest). Within Yugoslavia the Danube receives some 40 tributaries in a course of just over 360 miles. The most important of these are the Tisza, Drava, Sava and Morava rivers. In the plains, the Danube has an average width of about a mile, but below Belgrade, in the gorge known as the Iron Gate, this narrows to around 400 feet in places, creating excellent conditions for production of hydroelectricity.

#### THE LONGEST RIVER

The longest river with its complete course in Yugoslavia is the Sava (583 miles). It rises between the Karawanken and Julian Alps and flows near Ljubljana and Zagreb to join the Danube at Belgrade. The greater part of its length is navigable since its gradient is mainly slight. Its main tributaries spring from the Dinaric uplands and include, from north to south, the Kupa, Una, Vrbas, Bosna and Drina rivers.

#### TO THE DANUBE

The Drava enters Yugoslavia through the Klagenfurt Basin in Austria and part of its 193-mile course through Yugoslavia marks the Yugoslavian-Hungarian border. Its main

Above: *Bobotov Kuk (8272 feet), the highest point of the Durmitor massif, in northern Montenegro.* Below: *An aerial view of the mouths of the Gulf of Kotor, in southwest Yugoslavia. Yugoslavia's coastline is steep and rocky, and is often deeply indented by such inlets, which follow the line of the mountain ranges.*

*The National Assembly building in Belgrade, built between 1928 and 1934. Since the end of World War II, it has been the meeting place of the Assembly of the People's Republic of Yugoslavia.*

the Zrmanja (33 miles), the Mirna (30 miles), and, most important, the Neretva (135 miles). The Neretva forms the only natural line of communication between Bosnia-Herzegovina and the Adriatic, and has a wide, marshy delta, which has been rendered navigable by much canalization.

### TO THE AEGEAN

With the exception of the Strumica River, the Yugoslavian rivers which empty into the Aegean belong to the Vardar system. The Vardar's main tributaries are the Treska, the Lepenac, the Bregainca, and the Crna Reka.

## Lakes

Yugoslavia has many lakes, but few of them are of any notable size. The majority are lakes of ancient glacial origin which are concentrated in the Alpine ranges on the higher slopes of the Dinaric ranges. The Alpine lakes on Mt. Triglav are particularly well known. Other glacial lakes are found in the Sar Mountains and in Montenegro. The two largest are in Slovenia. These are Lake Bohinj (two miles long and one mile wide), 35 miles northwest of Ljubljana, and Lake Bled (one-and-a-half miles long and one mile wide).

### MANY SPRINGS

A number of lakes, both permanent and temporary, are formed on the plateaus and on the limestone ridges of the Dinaric ranges. Often, the many springs of these regions flood the surrounding areas, creating marshes. The largest lake of this area, and the largest completely within the borders of Yugoslavia, is Lake Vrana (eight miles long and one to two miles wide), which lies near the Adriatic coast between Zadav and Sibenik.

### THE BIGGEST LAKE

The biggest lake in the Balkan Peninsula is Lake Scutari, lying on the Yugoslavian-Albanian border, which is 29 miles long and fairly shallow. A number of rivers run into Lake Scutari, whose major outlet, which flows into the Adriatic, is the Bojana.

Two large lakes formed by the movement of the earth's crust are situated in the extreme south of Yugoslavia on the Albanian and Greek borders. These are Lake Ochrida and Lake Prespa (see *Albania: The Land*).

## Climate

Although Yugoslavia is situated nearly as far south as Italy, its climate

tributary, before it flows into the Danube, 11 miles east of Osijek, is the Mur.

The Tisza River flows southward for about 120 miles through Yugoslavia, a great part of its course being parallel to the Danube, which it joins 25 miles northwest of Belgrade.

### IN SOUTHERN SERBIA

The Morava (227 miles) is formed from two main branches, the Southern Morava, which rises in the Macedonian Hills, and the Western Morava, rising in the Stari range. The two join downstream from Krusevac, in southern Serbia, and flow north to join the Danube below Belgrade. The main tributary of the Western Mo-

rava is the Ibar (150 miles), and the main tributary of the Southern Morava is the Nisava (100 miles).

### TO THE ADRIATIC

The rivers flowing from the Dinaric Alps into the Adriatic are mainly short, due to the narrowness of the coastal strip. They are few and have separate systems without important tributaries. Their upper courses are marked by waterfalls and rapids, while their lower reaches are generally wide and navigable, due to the lack of silting caused by the absence of alluvial deposits in the limestone hinterland.

Among the rivers emptying into the Adriatic are the Krka (46 miles),

is not characterized by the hot, dry summers and wet, humid winters which typify the Mediterranean countries. The mountainous terrain, and the considerable width of the peninsula, mean that only the southern Adriatic coast and Macedonia are much influenced by Mediterranean conditions.

The climate of the greater part of Yugoslavia is characterized by a wide difference between summer and winter temperatures. Belgrade has an average January temperature of 29°F. and an average July temperature of 72°F., with an average annual temperature of 52°F.

### THE WARMEST AREAS

The warmest areas are found in the Danubian Plain and in the Morava Valley, to the north, where summer temperatures often exceed 80°F., except on high ground. The high regions of the south, such as the Sar Mountains, have average temperatures of up to 20°F. colder than those of the valleys and snow remains all the year in sheltered, high places.

### NORTHERN WINDS

In spring and autumn the cold air leaving the mountainous areas creates a low-pressure area to the south, giving rise to northerly winds. Cold northerly winds are also common during the winter, caused by cold air flowing from continental Europe.

### RAINFALL

Rainfall in Yugoslavia is generally moderate, varying between 30 and 60 inches annually. The Morava and Vardar regions and the area north of Belgrade receive less than average rainfall. But on the northeastern Adriatic coast the rainfall is sometimes as high as 180 inches annually, the highest in Europe. The driest area is in the extreme south, which sometimes receives less than 20 inches annually. In general, the summer is the wettest season and the winter the driest.

The main snowfalls in the mountainous regions usually occur in January and February.

### Vegetation

Vegetation in Yugoslavia may be divided into three main types; Mediterranean, steppe and central European.

Mediterranean vegetation is confined to the Adriatic coast, the lower Vardar valley and the off-shore islands. The coastal strip is character-

*Sarajevo, the largest city and capital of Bosnia-Herzegovina. The town consists of two distinct parts: the lower, new town has wide streets and modern buildings; while the upper, old town (illustrated), situated on hills, is Oriental in character, with a network of narrow alleys. It was in Sarajevo that the Archduke Francis Ferdinand of Austria was assassinated on June 28, 1914.*

ized by a profuse growth of maquis (thick, copse-like shrub), together with such trees and plants as the wild olive, cypress, broom, myrtle and strawberry. The lower slopes of the Dinaric ranges also have a thin covering of maquis, interspersed with thyme and tamarisks, up to about 1200 feet. The forested slopes have now been mainly cleared of timber, and junipers predominate.

### GRASSLAND AND POPLAR TREES

In the area of the Danubian Plain steppe-type vegetation predominates. The drier areas, where loess and black earth predominate, are now largely devoted to the production of cereals, while in the better watered areas there are large tracts of grassland interspersed with groves of poplar.

### BIRCH, BEECH AND SILVER FIR

In the other main regions of Yugoslavia, vegetation of the central European type predominates. Uncultivated areas less than about 2000 feet in altitude are rich in shrubs of all kinds, together with oak, ash, maple, hornbeam and other deciduous trees, while maple, oak, birch, beech and silver fir are found between 2000 and 4000 feet.

### MOUNTAIN PINE AND BILBERRY BUSHES

Above 4000 feet conifers predominate, with large areas of fir and pine, especially in the more inaccessible elevations of the Dinaric ranges. Above 7000 feet typically Alpine vegetation is found, with mountain pine, rhododendrons and bilberry bushes.

The animal life of Yugoslavia is similar to that of other European countries, the lower slopes of the mountains being particularly rich in wild life, notably goats.

## HUMAN GEOGRAPHY

### History of Settlement

BECAUSE OF THE CUSTOM OF CREMATing their dead practiced by the very early inhabitants of the territory which is now Yugoslavia, very little is known of their racial type. Iron Age remains discovered at Glasinac, in Bosnia, show that they were of a Nordic type; and it is probable that the Dinaric type, to which the majority of modern Yugoslavians belong, is basically descended from a Nordic people, modified by contact with the Slavs who settled the territory from the 6th and 7th centuries A.D. on.

### FIERCE INDEPENDENCE

The Slav races, entering from the Carpathians, had the same fierce independence which characterizes the modern Yugoslavians. They tended to settle in tribal and racial groups: the Slovenians in the north, the Croatians in the central area and the Serbians in the south. The achievement of national unity in Yugoslavia was a long and arduous process, succeeding only after centuries of internecine troubles and oppression by foreign invaders. Indeed, the greatest unifying force has been the need to unite against a common enemy, a need which found full expression in World War II and resulted in the creation of the modern state.

### Composition of Population

The marked differences between the various groups that make up the Yugoslavian population make the organization of the country into autonomous federal republics and territories, in which each area is able to retain a great deal of its ancient character, a particularly suitable one.

There are five main national groups in the present population together with a number of smaller national and religious minorities. Out of the present population of 18,549,251 (1961) it has been estimated that 40 per cent are Serbians; 22 per cent Croatians; 8 per cent Slovenians; 5 per cent Macedonians; and 3 per cent Montenegrins. In addition there are Albanian, Hungarian, German, Rumanian, Bulgarian and Italian minorities.

### Distribution and Density

The average density of the Yugoslavian population in 1961 was estimated at around 116 per square mile. The average density of the constituent republics varies as follows: Serbia and the autonomous territories of Vojvodina and Kosovo-Metohija, 138; Slovenia, 126; Croatia, 118; Bosnia-Herzegovina, 103; Macedonia, 88; Montenegro, 55.

### THE SEVEN CITIES

There are only seven cities in Yugoslavia with over 100,000 inhabitants, the largest being Belgrade, the capital, with over half-a-million. The second biggest is Zagreb, in Croatia, followed by Sarajevo, Skoplje, Ljubljana, Novi Sad and Rijeka.

The proportion of urban dwellers throughout the country is not high, but it is likely to increase rapidly with the growth of industrialization.

## Regions and Cities

### SERBIA

Serbia is now a federal republic of Yugoslavia. Together with the autonomous territories of Vojvodina and Kosovo-Metohija it occupies the eastern part of Yugoslavia. Serbia proper has an area of 21,514 square miles and, in 1961, a population of 4,823,274.

### BELGRADE *(pop. 598,346)*

Belgrade, the capital of Yugoslavia and of the federal republic of Serbia, is situated in northeastern Yugoslavia at the confluence of the Danube and Sava rivers. Founded as a Celtic settlement in the 3rd century B.C., it became a Roman stronghold on the route to Byzantium under the name of Singidunum.

Belgrade has had an eventful history. It has been the site of many battles and has been occupied often by foreign invaders, including the

Greeks, Bulgarians, Hungarians and Turks.

Nearly one-quarter of the city was destroyed by bombardment in World War II and, after postwar reconstruction, little of the ancient town survives, though traces of a Turkish fortress on a slope overlooking the Sava River are preserved as a public park.

Belgrade is an important cultural center, with a university and notable museums, art galleries, libraries and theaters. As the seat of government it is also a communications center, with an airport at nearby Zemun. Its industries include textiles, chemicals, brewing and food processing.

## NIS *(pop. 84,741)*

Nis, the second city of Serbia, is situated on the banks of the Nisava River some 125 miles southeast of Belgrade. It was an ancient Roman fortress, under the name of Naissus, and has been the site of many battles because of its position on two valleys, which provide the most convenient communication route between central Europe and the Aegean Sea. Remains of the old Turkish fortifications survive on the north bank of the river, while the modern town lies to the south.

Because of its geographical position, Nis is an important center of road and rail communications, and was a major military establishment in World War II. In World War I it was for a time the seat of the Serbian government. The industries of the modern city include railway workshops, an iron foundry and food processing.

### VOJVODINA

Vojvodina is an autonomous territory of Yugoslavia, situated in the extreme northeast of the country, with a population in 1961 of 1,854,965 and an area of 8683 square miles.

## NOVI SAD *(pop. 110,877)*

Novi Sad, the capital of the autonomous territory of Vojvodina, is on the left bank of the Danube River, 45 miles northwest of Belgrade. The city was founded after 1690 and was for many years a center of Serbian nationalism and of many political and cultural movements.

The modern city is a center for the marketing of agricultural produce and for wine making.

## SUBOTICA *(pop. 75,036)*

Subotica, situated in the extreme northeast of Yugoslavia on the Hungarian border 100 miles northwest of

*General view of Dubrovnik, a major port of Dalmatia, and the off-shore island of Lokrum. The old town covers a small, rocky peninsula and is still enclosed by its original walls, while the newer district of Gruz has grown up along the slopes of the hills that overlook the town. During the Middle Ages, when Dubrovnik was an important center of international trade, the city was named Arragosa.*

Above: *Dubrovnik, due to its fine position on the Adriatic, is both a major trading port and a popular vacation resort.* Below: *Panoramic view of Sarajevo, which lies on both banks of the Miljacka River, in the heart of rugged, mountainous country. Sarajevo is the fifth largest city of Yugoslavia.*

Belgrade, is an important center for marketing agricultural produce and for stockbreeding. It is also an expanding industrial center with railway workshops, footwear factories and plants for the manufacture of cast-iron ware.

### KOSOVO-METOHIJA

Kosovo-Metohija, situated in southern Yugoslavia on the Albanian border, is an autonomous territory of the Yugoslavian republic with a population, in 1961, of 963,988 and an area of 3997 square miles.

## PRISTINA *(pop. 38,593)*

Pristina, the capital of Kosovo-Metohija, is situated 150 miles south of Belgrade. It is of great historical importance, having been the center of the Serbian government under Stephen Nemanya (1114-1200), the founder of the first Serbian dynasty. In 1389 the Turks established their domination over the Serbians after their victory at the nearby Kosovo Polje (Field of Blackbirds). Among the many remains at Pristina are a number of notable mosques and a 14th-century monastery with ancient frescoes. The modern town is a center for the production of sugar and coffee.

### CROATIA

Croatia, the second largest of the federal republics of Yugoslavia (21,611 square miles), is situated in the north and west of the country, and includes the greater part of the Adriatic coastline. It had, in 1961, a population of 4,159,696.

## ZAGREB *(pop. 457,499)*

Zagreb, the capital of Croatia and Yugoslavia's second city, is situated on the Sava River 230 miles northwest of Belgrade. The older part of the city, consisting of the *Gradac* (the aristocratic quarter) and the *Kaptol* (the ecclesiastical quarter), lies on the slopes of the Medvednica Hills, while the modern town spreads out over the plain.

Although it is thought to have been a Roman settlement, Zagreb's history dates from the founding of the Roman Catholic bishopric in 1093. A number of historic buildings still remain, including the archbishop's palace, which has a 13th-century chapel, and the Gothic cathedral (13th-15th centuries). Zagreb also possesses a university founded in 1669 and is the site of the Yugoslav Academy of Science and Arts, a nuclear energy institute, and many fine libraries, art galleries and museums.

The industrial development of Za-.greb began in the 19th century. It is now a center for the production of textiles, chemicals, paper and asbestos. It has engineering workshops and is also an important communications center, possessing an airport.

## DUBROVNIK *(pop. 22,961)*

Dubrovnik is a major port of Dalmatia on the Adriatic, 360 miles southwest of Belgrade.

Greek refugees fleeing from invading Slav tribes founded the town around 614 and named it Ragusium (hence its Italian name, Ragusa). Dubrovnik later became a well-known asylum for exiles, one of the most notable of which was Richard I of England.

In the 16th century, it developed into an important commercial center, trading with India and the Americas. Dubrovnik is also a popular tourist and holiday resort.

## OSIJEK *(pop. 73,125)*

Osijek, a port on the Drava River 130 miles east of Zagreb, was an important fortress in Roman times. It is now a center for the distribution of agricultural produce and a flourishing industrial city producing timber products, wines, textiles, leather goods, silk and glassware.

## RIJEKA *(pop. 100,989)*

Rijeka, formerly an Italian provincial capital known as Fiume, is Yugoslavia's leading seaport, and is at the head of the Kvarner Gulf on the Adriatic. Its older quarter contains a Roman triumphal arch dating from the 3rd century A.D. and a cathedral founded in 1377. It has had a checkered history during this century, being in turn Hungarian territory, Italian, a free state, Italian again, split between Italy and Yugoslavia, and eventually, in 1947, Yugoslavian territory.

The modern port of Rijeka, with the suburb of Susak, handles around 2.5 million tons of goods annually. The city is also a center of industrial development, with oil refineries, to-

bacco and chemical industries, and a hydroelectric power station.

## SPLIT *(pop. 93,386)*

Split is a good natural harbor in the center of Yugoslavia's Adriatic coastline. It is an important tourist center and is best known as the site of the remains of the great palace built by the Roman emperor Diocletian about 295 A.D. The ruins of the palace enclose the old quarter of the town, built from the 7th century onward. Notable buildings include the Temple of Aesculapius, now a chapel with a Romanesque campanile dating from the 14th-15th centuries, and the 9th-century cathedral.

Split is Yugoslavia's main fishing port and is also an important industrial and commercial center, with a

large cement works. It produces wine, olive oil and bauxite.

### SLOVENIA

Slovenia is a federal republic of Yugoslavia and is situated in the extreme northwest of the country. It has an area of 7796 square miles and, in 1961, a population of 1,591,523.

## LJUBLJANA *(pop. 157,412)*

Ljubljana, the capital of Slovenia, is situated in central Slovenia on the Ljubljanica River, 70 miles northwest of Zagreb. It was the site of a Neolithic settlement and in the 1st century B.C. became the Roman colony of Emona. It was destroyed by the Huns in the 5th century and was under Austrian rule—except for a short period as part of Napoleon's

*View of one of the Plitvice lakes, a group of 16 lakes in western Croatia 65 miles southwest of Zagreb. These beautiful lakes (some up to three miles long) are situated in wooded hills and are connected by waterfalls which are sometimes 250 feet high. The area is a popular vacation and tourist resort and is noted for its trout fishing.*

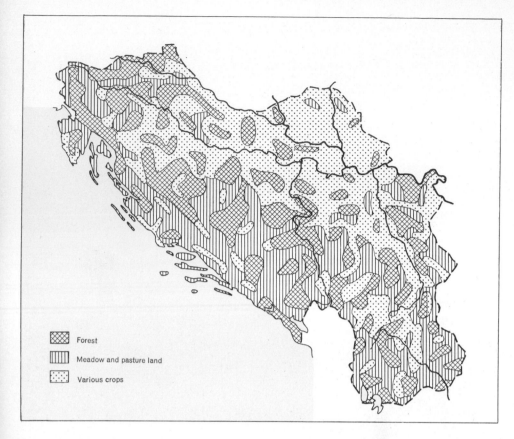

Forest

Meadow and pasture land

Various crops

*Utilization of the soil.*

Illyrian kingdom—from 1277 to 1918.

The old city of Ljubljana, damaged by a number of earthquakes, especially by that of 1895, is the site of a Romanesque cathedral, several notable churches, a medieval castle, a university (1596) and many learned institutions. It is an expanding commercial and industrial city with textile, pottery, footwear, chemical and engineering industries, and is also a leading road and rail junction.

## MARIBOR *(pop. 85,144)*

Maribor, on the Drava River near the Austrian border, 65 miles northeast of Ljubljana, has been a settlement since Roman times. The modern city was founded in the 10th century and was of considerable importance during the 12th and 13th centuries. It is the site of a much-restored 12th-century cathedral and a 15th-century castle.

Maribor is now a popular tourist center and a prosperous market for the distribution of the agricultural produce of the district. It produces footwear, iron and tin ware, oil, wine and timber products.

### BOSNIA-HERZEGOVINA

Bosnia-Herzegovina, a federal republic of Yugoslavia, situated in the center and south of the country, has an area of 19,909 square miles and, in 1961, a population of 3,277,948.

## SARAJEVO *(pop. 198,914)*

Sarajevo, the capital of Bosnia-Herzegovina, is situated in the center of the country on the Miljacka River, 125 miles southwest of Belgrade. It was founded by Hungarians in the 14th century and has had a stormy history, having been the site of many battles and having been several times destroyed by fire. It has been mostly rebuilt since 1878, but among the remaining historic buildings are a 14th-century church, the oldest in Bosnia, with contemporary religious paintings, and a picturesque Moslem quarter including the Begava Djamia mosque. In 1914 Sarajevo was the scene of the murder of the Archduke

*Some of the terraced vineyards of the small Dalmatian island of Susac in the Adriatic Sea, 80 miles west of Dubrovnik. Although wine production flourishes throughout the country, particularly in the hills and plains of Serbia, the most highly prized wines come from Dalmatia. Yugoslavian wines are exported to many parts of Europe.*

*Zagreb is Yugoslavia's second largest city and the capital of Croatia. Situated 230 miles northwest of Belgrade on the Sava River, it is a major industrial center. This aerial view shows the great electrical engineering works on the outskirts of the city.*

Francis Ferdinand of Austria (1863-1914) by Serbian extremists, an action which precipitated World War I.

Sarajevo is a prosperous commercial and cultural center with a university founded in 1946. Its industries include textiles, brewing, carpet-making and tobacco and there is a flourishing craft tradition of hand-weaving.

## MOSTAR *(pop. 35,242)*

Mostar, the chief city of Herzegovina, lies among rugged mountains on the Neretva River between Dubrovnik and Sarajevo (50 miles to the northeast); it is connected to both towns by a railroad. At the time of Austrian rule (1878-1918), Mostar was an important center for Serbian patriots.

The city is noted for its tobacco, wine, fruit (especially cherries) and vegetables. There are bauxite and anthracite deposits nearby, which have recently been exploited.

## TUZLA *(pop. 53,008)*

Tuzla, situated 50 miles north of Sarajevo, is a religious center and the seat of an Orthodox bishopric. It is a market for the agricultural produce of the area, particularly fruit, and the site of important deposits of petroleum, lignite and salt.

### MACEDONIA

Macedonia is a federal republic of Yugoslavia situated in the extreme south of the country, with an area of 10,229 square miles and, in 1961, a population of 1,406,003.

## SKOPLJE *(pop. 171,893)*

Skoplje, the capital of Macedonia, lies in a wide plain on the Vardar River, 210 miles southeast of Belgrade. In Roman times it had an aqueduct; it was in Turkish hands from the 14th to the early 20th century. It is a university city and a center for agricultural produce. Industrialization has been rapid in recent years.

On July 26, 1963, one of the worst earthquake disasters of recent years devastated the city of Skoplje. More than 1000 people were killed and 75

*Main mineral resources and processing industries.*

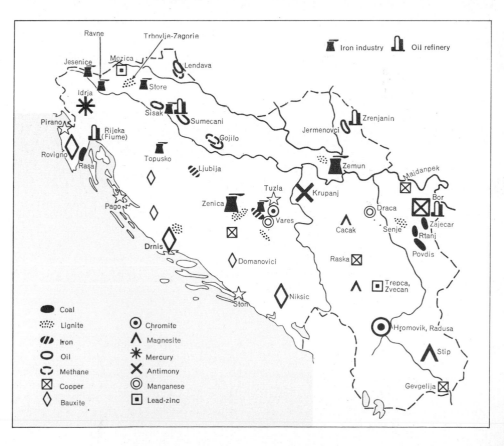

per cent of the city's population were rendered homeless. Nearly all public buildings, including the university, were destroyed. Since that date, international aid from all parts of the world has assisted in the rebuilding of the city.

### MONTENEGRO

Montenegro, situated in the extreme southwest of Yugoslavia, is the smallest of the federal republics, with an area of 5343 square miles, and, in 1961, a population of 471,894.

### TITOGRAD (pop. 30,659)

Titograd, formerly called Podgorica, the capital of Montenegro, is in the south of the country, near the Albanian border, on the Moraca River. The city was formerly a center of Turkish influence, and there are many Turkish remains, including fortifications. It is now the chief commercial center of Montenegro.

---

### ECONOMIC GEOGRAPHY

SINCE THE END OF WORLD WAR II the new economic system attendant upon the establishment of Communist rule in Yugoslavia has seen extensive nationalization of industry and col-

lectivization of land, together with increased planning for industrial expansion. Some scope has, however, been left for private enterprise, though this is limited in most fields.

In 1961, Yugoslavia's total labor force was estimated at 8,340,000 of which 1,181,700 people were employed in nationalized industries.

## Agriculture

In spite of increasing industrialization, more than half of Yugoslavia's total labor force is employed in agriculture. Since 1953 private land holdings have been limited to 25 acres each and the bulk of the land is now worked by peasants' cooperative organizations, of which, in 1962, there were 2882, with 1,397,465 members. Altogether, over 25,451,000 acres of land were under cultivation in 1962.

### CEREALS

The main crop is maize, which is grown mainly in Slovenia, Vojvodina and in the fertile Sava, Danube and Morava valleys. Production in 1964 amounted to 5,380,000 tons. Other cereals include wheat (4,143,000 tons), barley (524,000 tons), oats (345,000 tons) and rye (156,000 tons).

Potatoes are an important food crop and are grown throughout the

country, 2,020,000 tons being produced in 1962. Other vegetables, notably beans, are also grown wherever conditions are suitable.

Industrial crops include tobacco (46,000 tons), grown mainly in Herzegovina, Macedonia and Vojvodina; hemp (40,000 tons), grown in Slovenia and northern Croatia; and sunflower seed (231,000 tons), for edible oil.

### PLUMS, GRAPES AND WALNUTS

Fruit growing is also important, the main crop being plums (979,000 tons), grown in the Drina, Sava and Morava areas. A great part of this crop is distilled to make wine, as is the grape harvest (1,122,000 tons). About 114 million gallons of wine were produced in 1962. Serbia and the Dalmatian coast are the main wine-producing areas. Apples (280,000 tons), pears (113,000 tons), olives and walnuts are also widely grown.

The forest belts of Yugoslavia also contribute to the economy, for timber is one of the country's main exports. In 1962, 321,230,000 cubic feet of timber were cut, the greater part being beech, oak or coniferous wood.

## Stockbreeding and Fishing

Cattle breeding predominates on the pasture lands of Slovenia, Croatia and Vojvodina, while on the Dinaric ranges and in Macedonia, where the country is more rugged, sheep and goats predominate. Pigs are raised in regions with extensive oak woods, while poultry is kept throughout the country.

In 1963 the total livestock was estimated at 10,100,000 sheep, 5,400,000 cattle, 5,000,000 pigs, and 1,180,000 horses.

Freshwater fishing is concentrated upon the Sava, Drava and Danube rivers, and on Lakes Scutari and Och-

rida. The catch in 1962 amounted to 13,370 tons.

Sea fishing, which is of greater importance, is concentrated on the Adriatic, where there is a flourishing canning industry. In 1962 Yugoslavia had a fishing fleet of 207 motor vessels with a gross tonnage of 7497 tons, and 3573 sailing and rowing craft. The saltwater catch, mainly mackerel, sardines and tunny, amounted, in 1962, to 20,861 tons.

### Mineral Resources

Yugoslavia is rich in mineral deposits. Iron is mined at Vares, Ljubija and Prijedor in Bosnia, and at Topusko in Croatia. Production in 1963 amounted to 2,297,000 tons. The chief mines for copper ore (5,678,000 tons) are at Bor in Serbia. Lead and zinc (2,508,000 tons) are mined at Trepca and Mezica, while chrome ore (94,000 tons) is found at Skoplje and

Kumanovo in Macedonia and also in southern Serbia. Podrinje and Kupranj are the sites of the chief deposits of antimony (123,000 tons). Bauxite (1,285,000 tons) is found along the Adriatic coast.

Fuel deposits include lignite (26,085,000 tons mined in 1963), found north of Zagreb in Slovenia; in the upper Sava region, near Senje, in Serbia; and around Sarajevo and Zenica in Bosnia. Coal (1,287,000 tons) and petroleum (1,610,000 tons) come mainly from eastern Serbia. In addition, hydroelectric power stations produced 13,534,000,000 kwh in 1963.

### Industry

The main centers for smelting and processing are situated in Slovenia and Kosovo-Metohija. Production figures in 1963 included 1,588,000 tons of crude steel; 1,060,000 tons of pigiron; 76,755 troy oz. of gold; and 4,083,345 troy oz. of silver.

The engineering and chemical industries are mainly concentrated upon the larger towns of northwestern Yugoslavia. Among the most important products (here given with production figures for 1962) are sulphuric acid (321,000 tons); nitric acid (45,700 tons); fertilizers (712,320 tons); iron castings (227,000 tons); and steel castings (31,710 tons).

The textile industry, centered in Slovenia and Croatia, produced

## YUGOSLAVIA AREA AND POPULATION

| FEDERAL UNIT | AREA (Sq. miles) | POPULATION (1961) |
|---|---|---|
| Bosnia-Herzegovina | 19,909 | 3,277,948 |
| Croatia | 21,611 | 4,159,696 |
| Macedonia | 10,229 | 1,406,003 |
| Montenegro | 5343 | 471,894 |
| Serbia (with Vojvodina, and Kosovo-Metohija) | 34,194 | 7,642,227 |
| Slovenia | 7796 | 1,591,523 |
| TOTAL | 99,082 | 18,549,291 |

A section of the Danube River. For a large part of its middle course the Danube flows through Yugoslavia. Some of its more important tributaries are also in Yugoslavia. These are: the Drava, which joins the Danube eight miles east of Osijek; the Tisza, which meets it between Novi Sad and Belgrade; the Sava, which joins it at Belgrade; and the Morava, whose confluence with it is at Devin.

*Location of major industries.*

373,152,000 square yards of cotton; 51,428,000 square yards of woolens; 26,312,000 square yards of rayon; and 8,511,000 square yards of hemp.

In addition, rapid development is taking place in the rubber, leather, glass, tobacco, soap and distilling industries.

### Foreign Trade

Yugoslavia's exports consist mainly of timber and timber products, agricultural produce and non-ferrous metals. The main countries to which these exports are sent are, in order of importance, Italy, West Germany, the U.S.S.R., the U.S.A., and the U.K.

The total value of exports in 1963 amounted to approximately $790 million.

Yugoslavia's imports consist mainly of machinery, metal products, textiles, chemicals and foodstuffs. The main countries from which these goods are imported are, in order of importance, the U.S.A., Italy, West Germany, the U.S.S.R., and the U.K.

The total value of imports in 1962 amounted to approximately $1,056 million.

### Communications

In 1962 Yugoslavia's road communications network totaled 4840 miles of macadamized road, and 31,616 miles of cindered road. In that year vehicles included 99,130 automobiles and 37,606 trucks and buses. In the same year the country's railroad system covered 7400 miles of track.

The Yugoslavian merchant fleet in 1962 consisted of 342 vessels of 907,000 gross tonnage. In addition there were 1210 river craft. The country has 1152 miles of navigable rivers and 119 miles of canals.

The national airline, Jugoslovenski Aero Transport, carried, in 1962, 226,681 passengers on internal flights and 81,490 passengers on international flights. The chief airports are situated at Belgrade, Zagreb, Ljubljana, Sarajevo, Skoplje, Dubrovnik and Titograd.

*The Velebit Mountains, part of the Dinaric Alps. Falling sheer to the Adriatic, they run parallel with this sea for about 100 miles. The highest peaks are: Vaganjski Vrh (5766 feet) and Rajinac (5432 feet). Interspersed with barren plateaus and crossed by a few narrow and tortuous roads, the Velebit Mountains are extremely arid.*

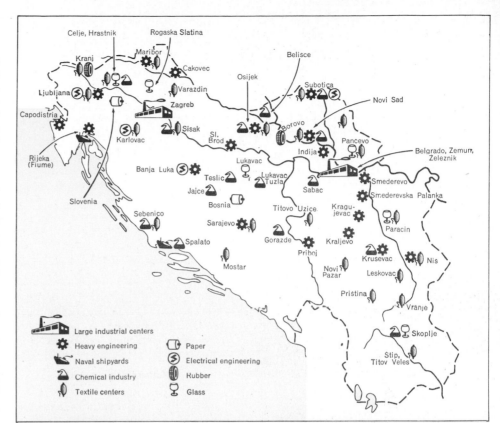

*Many old Yugoslavian traditions are kept alive by the efforts of folklore societies. At a folklore meeting in Belgrade a group of men and women display the traditional costumes of their region. The colors of the men's white kilts, black belts and red bodices are echoed in the red and black, fringed aprons of the women and their white sheepskin jackets.*

## CONTRASTS IN CHARACTER

THE COUNTRY OF YUGOSLAVIA, AS AN entity, is a political and geographical simplification. It is, in fact, an amalgamation of six previously independent republics: Slovenia, Croatia, Serbia, Bosnia-Herzegovina, Montenegro and Macedonia. The population of each of these republics is strongly individual in its traditions, its religion and the external influences to which it has been subject.

The people of Yugoslavia cannot, therefore, be treated as a homogeneous national group. A sketch of the main characteristics of the people of each of the republics provides a good illustration of the varied nature of Yugoslavia as a whole.

### The Slovenians

Slovenia is the most northwesterly region of Yugoslavia. Its people have been greatly influenced by the Western European way of life, particularly that of Germany.

The Slovenians are most at home in the mountains, which cover a large area of Slovenia. Their general character is contradictory; they combine a fierce energy and application to hard work with the dreaminess and lyricism generally considered to be typically Slavic characteristics.

The people of Slovenia are the most literate in Yugoslavia. Even the peasants buy and read many books.

### The Croatians

The Croatians are, for the most part, plains-dwellers, as opposed to the mountain folk of Slovenia. Any external influences once again come from the West. The general character of the people reflects their environment, and is quite distinct from that of the Slovenians.

The Croatians are slow and persevering and are capable of great self-control. They are also courteous and hospitable. Two qualities which help the Croatians to take their place in modern life are a flair for business and a taste for efficiency.

### The Dalmatians

Dalmatia is politically a region of Croatia, but the way of life is very different from that found in the rest of Croatia.

The region forms a narrow strip on the west coast of Yugoslavia. The people are traditionally sailors and display the qualities frequently found

*A group of girls, in national dress, pose for their photograph during a festival in the region of Skoplje, in northern Macedonia. The aprons and bodices of their festive costumes are richly embroidered in traditional designs based on lozenges and zigzags. The dominant colors are red, black and white.*

among seafaring folk; they are gravely serious and deeply religious.

Physically they are vigorous, hardy and long-lived.

Their many contacts with foreign countries, particularly Austria, Italy and—more recently—America, have given these people questioning and versatile minds and a broader outlook than is common in other regions.

## The Serbians

The Serbians are the most numerous of the national groups of Yugoslavia. Their territory covers a large area in the east of the country.

In contrast to the more stolid Slovenians and Croatians, the Serbians are a gay, uninhibited people. They could be described as the country's "Bohemians," for they have a tendency to combine irreverence, sensuality and intellectuality in their actions and conversation.

## The Bosnians

Bosnia-Herzegovina is one of the central regions of Yugoslavia. The character of the people is less individualistic than is found in the populations of the other regions.

Where the province approaches the coast the people have many of the characteristics of the Dalmatians. In the interior, however, the influence of the Orient is stronger, as it is in Macedonia. The Mohammedan religion is widespread throughout Bosnia and this may explain the severity of many customs and ideas.

### The Montenegrins

Racially the Montenegrins are the most undiluted of the Serbians, but the harshness of their environment has given them a unique character which wholly distinguishes them from the Serbians of Serbia.

Their basic characteristic is masculinity. Women are not rated highly: in reckoning the number of her children, a woman will discount the girls. The Montenegrins are patriotic, warlike and proud. In the past they were the greatest warriors among the southern Slavs. This tradition persists in the survival of ancestral feuds.

As well as being men of action, the Montenegrins are poets and their poetic gifts are manifest in the national epics.

### The Macedonians

The people of Macedonia are distinct from the Serbo-Croatians. They have a language of their own, which is closer to Bulgarian than to Serbo-Croatian.

Macedonia is another province in which the Mohammedan and Christian religions are practiced side by side. The atmosphere is, in general, that of a Moslem country. The people are characterized by a slowness and lack of ambition which contrasts them to the more energetic Serbians and Slovenians and the warlike Montenegrins. They are taciturn and reserved and are also very superstitious. The province is rich in survivals of ancient customs and beliefs.

### FAMILY LIFE

#### The 'Zadruga'

THE TRADITIONAL FAMILY ARRANGEMENT of the southern Slavs was that of the large family, or clan, forming a self-sufficient community. This is called a *zadruga*. The *zadruga* continues to exist, in its original form, in the mountainous regions of Serbia and Macedonia. Otherwise, this type of family community has ceased to exist.

The name, however, is used now for the Yugoslavian version of the collective farm, which runs on the same communistic principle as did the old family communities.

#### MALE DOMINANCE

The head of the *zadruga* was usually the oldest responsible male member, who was, in practice, a clan chieftain.

He ruled together with his wife,

*This scene in the market place of Ulcinj, southern Montenegro, appears timeless. There is an air of inertia—or serenity—which suggests a pace of life quite different from that of the more progressive west. The veiled woman on the left is particularly representative of the conservative element in Yugoslavian life, for the veil is no longer compulsory for Moslem women.*

whose function was to oversee the work of the women. Next in order of authority were the men; they had the right to speak in the family council. Women and children had few rights within the family circle. Marriages among the members of the family were forbidden.

The patriarch exercised absolute authority in the domestic community. He administered the finances, dealt with the village authorities, distributed and supervised all work, planned family feasts and was the judge in all family controversies.

The women lived in the background. They were not allowed to sit down at table with the men; they ate only when the latter had finished their meals. In married life it was the wife's duty to serve her menfolk and to wash and kiss their hands.

Hereditary possessions, houses, outbuildings, tools, furniture and animals were all held in common. Only the dowry of a woman remained her own property and, at her death, it passed to her sons. In the *zadruga* only men had real hereditary rights; women could inherit only if there were no men in the line of inheritance.

The *zadruga* occupied a specific sector of the village and this sector was then known by the family name. Sometimes the whole family lived together in one very large house. This is now extremely rare. Where the old *zadrugas* continue to function, each section of the family has a separate dwelling and these are all grouped around the main farm.

## Collective Farms

Forced collectivization of the land has been abandoned in Yugoslavia. A certain number of collective farms do, nevertheless, exist. Sometimes the farm comprises the whole village, which may perhaps house 750 families. The standards of housing are high. The average house has three to four rooms, out-buildings and a cellar. It is comfortable and clean and is often attractively color-washed.

## Slovenian Villages

Slovenia is the most advanced and prosperous province of Yugoslavia. The Slovenian villages reflect this state of affairs. The standard of living is closer to that of Central Europe than to that of the Balkans.

The main building material is wood. Houses are substantial and are similar in appearance to the Alpine type of house which has its most familiar form in the Swiss chalet.

## Croatian Peasant Life

The villages of the Croatian plain take a form which is only possible in regions where land is rich and abundant. The houses are built along a village street which sometimes runs for a considerable distance over the plain. This ribbon formation contrasts with the compact form of the Serbian *zadruga* villages.

In the villages of the plain, houses are single-storied and surrounded by various outbuildings. They are usually wooden and are solid and substantial. The living room, on the ground floor, is large. Upstairs there are two bedrooms. Sometimes, when the family is large, the boys sleep in the barn.

## Bosnian Villages

Some Bosnian villages show very strong Turkish influence. There are very rare remnants of *čifluks*. These were a type of manorial settlement in which the peasants' huts were arranged around the house of the *bey*, the tribal head or the governor.

### MOSLEM VILLAGES

The usual Moslem villages are centered around a small square which contains the mosque, the bakery and the fountain. The houses are Turkish in type. They have inner gardens, which cannot be seen from outside, and wide, overhanging balconies.

Some of the older villages contain *kulas*, which are fortified houses. The lower stories are constructed of loop-holed stone and it was here that the cattle were kept in troubled times. The upper story, which is built of wood, contains the family's quarters.

### CHRISTIAN VILLAGES

In the forest and mountain districts, where the population is Christian, there are many hamlets, consisting of only five or six houses scattered over a wide area. These houses are wooden and are built according to a pattern handed down for generations. Some houses still have the old type of hearth with a central stove for warmth and light and a hole in the roof through which the smoke can escape.

Bosnia is not altogether backward. Since World War II many neat modern villages have been built to replace those destroyed in the war.

## The Stone Houses of Montenegro

There is a popular legend which tells how, on the Day of Creation,

God brought two sacks, one filled with earth and the other with stones. As He passed over the land which was to become Bosnia and Montenegro, the bag containing the stones burst and scattered its contents on the land beneath. This is how the Montenegrin peasants like to explain the origin of their region's landscape. The houses they build blend perfectly with this landscape, since they make use of the predominant building material, stone. In contrast to the wooden houses of the more northerly provinces, which are square or rectangular, the Montenegrin stone houses are round.

## Macedonian Houses

Macedonia, like Bosnia, retains a few remnants of the old *čifluks*.

The usual dwellings, however, are built on the mountain sides and seem to cling to them. They are roughly built of sun-baked brick and gleam white against the rock. The kitchen is also used as a living-room.

## RELIGION AND BELIEFS

OVER THE CENTURIES THE PEOPLES of Yugoslavia have been subject to many different influences and this is reflected in the complexity of the religious scene.

The north and west of the country, which have always been most strongly influenced by Central Europe and Italy, are predominantly Roman Catholic. Further south and east, in southern Croatia, Serbia, Bosnia-Herzegovina, Macedonia and Montenegro, the Christians are Orthodox. The effect of the long Turkish rule in Bosnia (from the 15th to the 19th century) is apparent in the large number of Moslems in this province. Islam is also practiced in Macedonia and Montenegro.

### The Bogomils

Most Bosnian Moslems are descended from followers of the Bogomil

*Skoplje, capital city of Macedonia, was severely damaged by an earthquake on July 26, 1963. This view of the outskirts of the city, taken before the disaster, shows the co-existence of the old and the new which is so typical of Yugoslavia. Modern blocks of buildings take their place among the pointed towers of the minarets.*

heresy. Originally the Bogomils were a Christian sect and from the 10th to the 15th century they were widespread in the Balkans. They believed that the visible, material world was created by the Devil.

## Superstitions

It is possible that the Bogomil doctrine of the material world as the work of the Devil may have contributed to a general belief in the many devils who live in water, forests and fields.

These devils are terrifying beings who lie in wait for men at night.

Their favorite haunts are crossroads and it is dangerous for anyone who forgets this fact and stops at a crossroads. The most dreadful of the devils is a species of werewolf with long claws. He attacks people who linger in the darkness. Draped in a shroud, he strangles them and then sucks their blood.

### THE 'VILE' MAIDENS

Men are in constant danger of falling victim to supernatural beings. Sometimes, as in the case of the *vile*, the danger is one of seduction rather than attack. The *vile* are young and very beautiful maidens who wear a star on their foreheads and let their hair flow loose about their shoulders. They live in the air, on earth and in the water, and are present in the colors of the rainbow, in the scent of flowers and in running water. Their voices are soft, tender and bewitching. Often they fall in love with heroes and handsome young men. If a man falls under the spell of the voices and the beauty of these sirens he may be abducted by them. They will lure him into a deep whirlpool and he will disappear without trace.

### VAMPIRES

The most terrifying of all the vindictive beings created by the Yugoslav popular imagination is the vampire. A vampire is usually a man who has died a violent death. But there is also danger that a person who has died a natural death may become a vampire, if insufficient care is taken to see that no cat or chicken walks over the corpse before burial.

On the 40th day after burial the corpse rises from the grave. Completely invisible, it passes through the village sucking human blood, hoping, thereby, to recover life. If it is not detected at this stage, the vampire gradually becomes stronger; its body develops until, to all outward appearance, it is a man again. It takes up some respectable occupation and continues its nightly attacks without arousing suspicion.

There are two clues to the identity of a vampire. On Saturday—the day of the dead—the vampire becomes a corpse again and its house or shop remains closed. The second clue is provided by the threads of clothing which stick between the teeth of the vampire when it bites its victim.

### THE CULT OF THE DEAD

Among Yugoslav peasants the relationship between the living and the dead is often one of fear. They dread the return of the dead as devils. In this form they are a threat to the peasants' lives, houses and crops. To conciliate them it is a common practice for peasants to take gifts to the graves of their dead.

*The reinforced concrete buildings and the Gothic architecture of the old church combine with the conventional European clothes of the passersby to give this street scene in Novi Sad a distinctly West European air. This blending of the strictly functional in architecture into the traditional was accelerated throughout Europe by the damage inflicted on many cities during World War II.*

**Right:** *Dubrovnik, once the old republic of Ragusa, is one of the most popular Yugoslavian holiday resorts, as well as being one of the country's most historic cities. The narrow, stepped, cobbled street, lined by stone houses with tiled roofs, typifies the old city, which is built on a tiny promontory.*

### Folk Customs

For the Yugoslav peasant, there are customs and rites to be observed on every important occasion of his life. The most significant moments of life —birth, marriage and death—are often surrounded by strict ritual.

In some parts of Yugoslavia, barren women who want a child enact a certain ritual on the vigil of the feast of St. George. At night they place an unworn nightgown on a fruit tree. The nightgown is examined next morning before dawn. If a living creature is found upon it, this is a sign that the woman will have a child within the year. She puts the nightgown on in the belief that she will become fruitful, like the tree on which the garment has lain.

In Macedonia, near Skoplje, barren women go, in spring, to a mountain known as the "mountain of the snakes." Here they wait for a snake to crawl over their skirts and, if this happens, they will have a child.

### CHILDBIRTH AND GUNS

In Herzegovina, to hasten labor in childbirth, peasants open and close the breech of a gun. This act is thought to have magic properties

*In a street market in one of the Dalmatian islands peasants in black or in sober-colored traditional costumes mingle with the gaily clad tourists, who are ready to photograph anything which strikes them as picturesque. Despite the influx of foreign visitors, the old way of life continues.*

which will hasten the passage of the child into the world.

In other regions, if a birth is slow, guns are fired in the room. This is a more practical custom, since it is intended to startle the mother into giving birth quickly.

### THE THREE FATES

As he grows, the child is submitted to a series of magical rites. The first of these takes place on the third day after birth. That night, the newborn child is visited by the three Fates, who foretell his future. To propitiate the Fates the parents bake a bun which they crumble on the window sill.

### BLACK PEARLS AND THE EVIL EYE

To protect the child against the evil eye, a black pearl is placed around his neck. This attracts and neutralizes any envious or evil looks. As an even greater precaution, the child is often given amulets to wear or small bags filled with blessed objects.

If, in spite of every precaution, the evil eye lights upon a child and he becomes an epileptic as a result, there is only one cure. The child must be given a new name. The evil remains with the old name, for the child is considered to be a different person.

## Courtship and Marriage

Magic and ritual play an important part in matters of love and marriage.

To attract the man she loves, a girl may begin by collecting some of the earth on which he has walked. She puts the earth into a pot and plants a marigold, the flowers of which are never supposed to fade. She hopes that, as the golden flowers blossom, grow and never die, the love of the young man will similarly blossom.

In Serbia, an engagement to marry is accompanied by a special ritual. The father of the young man, carrying a cake and a basket of flowers, pays a formal call on the fiancée's family. During the visit he is given a meal. The proposed marriage is discussed in private by the bride's family, although it has been already settled.

After the discussion, the bride kneels before her future father-in-law and kisses his hand. He gives her the flowers, she kisses his hand again and thus the engagement becomes official.

### MARRIAGES IN SERBIA

A peasant marriage in Serbia is an occasion of great ceremony. Before the wedding all the guests meet at the bridegroom's house and then set out, in procession, for the bride's house. The procession is headed by the "clown," who carries a large cask of drink to offer to passersby.

At the bride's house, the men wait while the women dress the bride. Before leaving for the ceremony she kneels in front of the lighted stove in the kitchen and kisses the earth. She then bows to her parents, kisses their hands and asks their blessing.

### THE BRIDE AND A BABY

After the church ceremony the procession leaves for the bridegroom's house. The bride performs certain ritual acts as she leaves her carriage. She must walk over a sack of oats and a plow which have been placed on the threshold of the house. There she is greeted by a woman who hands her a baby which she must lift high into the air and kiss. After this she may enter her new home.

In the kitchen of her new home the bride's mother-in-law leads her three times round the stove and hands her a small shovel with which to make a pile of coal. This last task accomplished, the wedding ritual is completed and the company is free to eat, drink, sing and dance.

### MARRIAGES IN MACEDONIA

The date for a Macedonian wedding is very carefully calculated. It must always take place at the full moon, to encourage fertility.

During the first two weeks in July an unusually large number of couples are married in Galicnik, a village in the mountains of northeast Macedonia. This custom arose at a time when the men of the village migrated to the towns to work, returning to their village only for two weeks.

## Death Rites and Customs

Like all the Balkan Slavs, the Yugoslavians begin their preparations for a funeral long before a person is actually dead. Coffin and winding sheets are prepared, as are the napkins and towels for the funeral guests. Wine is provided for the mourners to drink "to the health of the good soul."

### SERBIAN FUNERAL CUSTOMS

When Serbian peasants go to the funeral of a friend or relative they make their way to the cemetery by deserted streets and paths, hoping

Moslem orders; many of them used to be nomadic and their way of life resembles, in some ways, that of the members of Christian monastic orders. They have the power, granted by Mohammed, to heal many ills. The activities of the dervishes are now very limited, and their healing powers are discredited.

### THE DERVISH'S BREATH

If the dervish diagnosed the illness as caused by the evil eye, the cure would be carried out in the presence of the whole village. The process of healing was a magical one. After questioning the patient the dervish would breathe all over his body. He would then write a few mystical words on a piece of paper, picking out and encircling certain of the letters. Into each of these circles he would then hammer a nail and at the end of this performance the patient would proclaim himself cured.

### THE STARS AND SUGAR WATER

If the illness is caused by the patient's having passed through a cursed spot, the cure is more complicated. The dervish must identify the cursed spot and, for this, he requires time to consult the stars. Once he has discovered the correct place he immediately sprinkles it with a mixture of sugar, water and various other more mysterious ingredients. The dervish then gives the sick man a linen string to wear around his wrist. After a few days the illness disappears.

### THE BUILDING SACRIFICE

The ceremony of the building sacrifice was still carried out until a few years ago in some Macedonian villages. When a new church was almost complete a girl was chosen for the sacrifice. It was felt to be a great honor for the family for one of the daughters to be selected.

The priests wore their best vestments and the villagers put on their festive costumes for the ceremony. All surrounded the new church. The girl, dressed as a bride with gold coins about her forehead and her neck, stood with her back to a niche in the

---

they will be seen by nobody. By doing this they hope to deceive the corpse into thinking he is still alive.

### WINE ON THE CORPSE

At the cemetery, the priest reads the prayers and pours a mixture of red wine and olive oil over the corpse in the form of a cross. The coffin is then buried.

### Funeral Rites in Macedonia

Certain Macedonian deathbed customs rest on a belief in vampires. During the final moments before death the family and friends of the dying person make a tight circle around the deathbed. This is to prevent a cat or chicken from walking over the body, for if this occurs the dead man will become a vampire.

### SOULS ATTRACTED BY WATER

The actual burial is a hurried affair. Great care must still be exercised, even during the desperate rush to the cemetery. The soul is attracted by water. When the funeral procession is passing a house the inmates, therefore, cover any receptacle containing water. The soul might otherwise be drawn to the water.

### The War Against Evil

The Yugoslav peasant feels himself to be constantly menaced by evil in various forms. Many traditional customs are concerned with his defense against these threats to his life.

### ILLNESS AND THE EVIL EYE

Illnesses are popularly believed to be caused either by the evil eye or by the frequenting of a cursed spot. Even today, in the most backward regions, people resort to sorcery and magic formulas to cure illness.

There are certain traditional healers among the Yugoslavians. Gypsy magicians are popular healers, but the most spectacular cures used to be performed by dervishes.

Dervishes are members of various

wall. When the sun was at its height and the girl's shadow very short, the chanting priest pretended to cut the shadow off at the ankles. The niche was then quickly walled up. The girl's shadow which, in this case, was identified with her soul, was thus captured within the walls of the church. Almost every church in Macedonia bears traces of a walled-up niche.

## FESTIVALS

THE YUGOSLAVIAN PEASANTS ARE NOT morbid, as their preoccupation with fighting evil may suggest. Their festivals, some of which are quite pagan, show them in a lighter mood.

### The 'Slava'

The most important feast in the Yugoslav year is that of the family patron saint. It is called the *slava*. Even avowed Communists, who scorn all other religious festivals, will observe the *slava*.

The *slava* is a Serbian institution, although it is also celebrated by Catholic and Orthodox Christians in other parts of Yugoslavia. It has its origin in the time of the Slav conversion to Christianity, and is thought to celebrate the day when the ancestral tribe was converted to Christianity.

The ritual of the *slava* is still strict-ly kept in rural areas. It lasts for three days and is a time of feasting and hospitality. As part of the religious ritual, the members of the family are anointed on the forehead with holy oil by the priest. Before the feast each member of the family must eat a spoonful of *zito*, which is a type of ritual cake of flour, sugar, nuts, vanilla and lemon.

### Christmas Rites

Although Christmas is a Christian festival, many of the Yugoslavian peasant customs observed at this season have pagan roots.

One of these customs is the burning of the yule log, which was originally a ceremony of purification carried out at the winter solstice (the time when the sun is at its furthest point south from the equator). The ceremony begins a few days before Christmas, when Serbian peasants go into the woods to choose a young tree. They fell it, with just three blows of the axe, so that it falls toward the east. As they strike they recite a magic formula, exhorting the log to bring them prosperity. At home, the log is burned. It is believed that the calves, lambs, piglets and kids to be born in the coming year will number as many as the flying sparks.

### Seasonal Festivals

The first important event of the peasant's year is the arrival of spring. Celebrations usually take place during the first days of May. The rites are frequently intended to ensure fertility. In one Serbian village, the women throw handfuls of maize on to the sloping roof of the church and, as they do so, imitate the bleating of sheep. The grain bounces off the roof into the open mouths and outspread aprons of the women. It is believed that anyone who swallows some of the grain will have large flocks of sheep and many children, and that anyone catching some in her apron will have a good maize harvest.

All over Yugoslavia there are propitiatory ceremonies to celebrate the new season. Death, in the form of a doll, is expelled to symbolize the end of winter, the harsh season.

The spirit of reviving vegetation is *Zeleni Jurij* (Green George). In Slovenia, Green George takes the form of a boy dressed in leaves and flowers. He goes into the fields, carrying a lighted torch in one hand and a

*Conversation is very much enjoyed in Yugoslavia, especially by the people of the central regions. Four old men sit around a table in Mostar, in central Herzegovina, and set the world to rights. Almost as much is said with the hands as with the mouth. Here the long co-existence of people of different races and religions has brought about an attitude of mutual respect and toleration.*

cake in the other. A crowd of girls follows him singing. A ring of fire is made with flaming branches and, inside this ring, the cake is shared out among all those taking part in the ceremony.

### CEREMONY OF THE RAIN

The peasant is dependent for his well-being on nature. Thus the arrival of spring, the season of new growth, is immensely important. Rain to ensure the continuance of growth is also vital to agricultural communities. The Serbian peasants have a rain-making ceremony, in which the main figure is a small girl known as the *dodola.* She is dressed entirely in grass and flowers which cover even her face. Together with a procession of other little girls, she walks through the village, stopping in front of every house and dancing. The other children sing a song (the refrain of which is "ah dodo, ah dodo le") and the housewife pours water over her.

### FIELDS AND FAMILY

The Yugoslavian peasant, despite a profound religious faith, retains many traces of the faith of his pagan ancestors in traditional customs. Like theirs, his life is centered on his fields and his family. He feels the necessity for practical measures to ensure the warmth and moisture necessary to make the crops grow and the stock flourish and to ward off supernatural dangers which threaten him.

## SONGS AND DANCES

TWO TRADITIONAL YUGOSLAVIAN PAS-times are those of singing (or listening to songs) and dancing. These are more than mere recreations. Songs and dances are an essential part of everyday life, accompanying such events as weddings and funerals.

Yugoslav folksongs are generally classified as masculine or feminine.

### Masculine Songs

The so-called masculine songs are heroic. They are sung by one voice to the accompaniment of a *gusla*—a one-stringed fiddle. The *guslar* (minstrel), who frequently was blind, was a common entertainer in earlier times. The words of his songs were passed down, by word of mouth, from generation to generation. Traveling from village to village, he would recite the poems celebrating great events or heroes of the past. The oral tradition is now dying. A few blind minstrels were still active in Bosnia 30 years ago, but today they are rare.

### HEROIC BALLADS

The home of the Yugoslavian heroic ballad is Serbia. The Serbians are a gay, resilient people who have kept alive their national consciousness through centuries of oppression. One means by which they have done this is by cherishing their heroic songs. In them they kept alive the memory of events and heroes of the past. The most famous of such events is the Battle of Kosovo, and the most popular hero is Marko Kraljević.

*The Battle of Kosovo* is an epic cycle dealing with the defeat of the Serbs at the hands of the Turks in the Battle of Kosovo (1389). The leader of the Serbs, Tsar Lazar, has a vision of St. Elias before the battle. He is given the choice of an earthly or heavenly crown and chooses the

*Shopping in a Yugoslavian street market is a leisurely affair; there is time to gossip and to haggle over purchases. At this stall, in a Zagreb market, paprika (ground red peppers) and garlic, which give many Yugoslavian dishes their strong and spicy flavor, are sold along with eggs and vegetables.*

*After the grain has been harvested the stalks are not wasted. They are loaded onto carts and taken down to the river to be washed, before they are made into brooms and sold in the town markets. The ox-drawn carts are of a primitive simplicity, consisting of a flat, wooden bottom attached to two sloping, slatted sides.*

latter. The Serbs are prepared to die and do so bravely.

### HISTORY AND FANTASY

The cycle of *Marko Kraljević* contains history intermingled with fantasy. The real Marko was a vassal of the Turks who died fighting for his Turkish overlords. In the epic, Marko is a mighty figure of a man, striking fear into evildoers— particularly into the Turks. He rides on a wonderful horse, Šarac, with which he shares his red wine. The Marko of the legend is the embodiment of Serbian patriotism and the spirit of revolt against oppression.

### DEFEATING THE TURKS

In Montenegro, too, the epic songs deal with the struggle against the Turks. They are unusual for the fierceness of their tone and the patriotic pride they express.

One description of a battle with the Turks tells how 300 Montenegrins fight 5000 Turks. A count of the dead is taken and it is found that 4000 of the Turks lie on the field,

but only three of the Montenegrins are missing: "one had gone for water, one for bread and the handsomest was stretched out beside his gun."

### Feminine Songs

The feminine songs are lyrical and, in the main, are love songs. They can be sung by one or two voices and are often unaccompanied.

They have a great variety of rhythms and tunes and an equal variety of tone in the contents. Some are lyrical outpourings of the heart, full of ardor or melancholy. Others take the form of witty dialogues.

### Dance Accompaniments and Dances

The dances and songs of Yugoslavia are sometimes closely linked, as when songs are the accompaniment to dances. These songs are sung either by small groups or a solo female voice.

Sometimes the songs are general in character and express the thoughts

and feelings of the whole community. Occasionally the words of a song express respect for the old, austere, patriarchal society. In such songs sensuality is suppressed. Woman is seen as upright and pure, calm and obedient. Usually, however, there is more freedom of expression. The main theme is sensual love in its many aspects: its violence, its vicissitudes and its triumphs.

### Dances in the Villages

Yugoslavian folk dances, which have retained their own national character, date back to the period between the 11th and 14th centuries.

### THE NATIONAL DANCE

The national dance is the *kolo*, an intricate, circular dance with a set harmony of gestures. It comprises hundreds of different steps and has a quick and varied rhythm.

The accompaniment to the *kolo* can be instrumental or vocal, or it

*A Montenegrin peasant, dressed in the breeches, cummerbund and pill-box hat typical of male attire in this region, sits beside the central hearth of his house. In these primitive dwellings, where the open fireplace is sunk into the center of the floor, the smoke has to escape through a hole in the roof.*

broken by the ecstatic leaps or rushing attacks of isolated groups of dancers.

Montenegro has more war-dances than any other region of Yugoslavia. The steps of these dances are heavy and are accompanied by gun-shots and by the shouts of the men and the shrieks of the women.

## Silent Dances

Some of the most beautiful Yugoslavian dances are silent; they have neither instrumental nor vocal accompaniment. The rhythm is kept by the steady beat of heels pounding the ground or by the jangling of jewelry.

According to legend the silent dance originated in Bosnia during the Turkish occupation. The peasants and shepherds took refuge in the forest to dance undisturbed by the invaders and there they improvised dances with no musical accompaniment. `

## The 'Moreška'

Sometimes the dances take on so elaborate a form that they become veritable dramas. The best known of these dramatic dances is the *moreška*, which takes place on Korcula Island (one of the Dalmatian islands) on June 29, the feast of St. Theodore. The dance re-enacts the battle between the Moors and the Turks for the possession of the city of Korcula.

Half the inhabitants of the town are dressed in red and represent the Moors, while the rest, dressed in black, represent the Turks. All the dancers carry swords. Two men play the parts of Moro, the Moorish king, and Osman, king of the Turks.

### DUEL OF KINGS

The dance takes the form of a general battle followed by a duel between the two kings. Although the movement is, at first, slow and stately, the dance gradually gathers speed. The sword-play is tremendously skillful and requires long training.

The outcome of the battle is determined in advance. The Moorish king and his army are finally defeated.

may consist of rhythmic gestures.

The *kolo* is the one dance common to all the peoples of modern Yugoslavia. It demonstrates the fundamental cultural unity of the national groups, which are so different in language, religion and temperament.

### PISTOL-SHOT ACCOMPANIMENT

The *kolo* danced in Montenegro combines violence with lyricism; it is often accompanied by pistol shots which the young men fire into the air. In front of almost every house in a Montenegrin village there is a small flint-paved square for dancing. The spectators sit on stone benches around the sides. An epic singer may sometimes prepare the atmosphere for the dance by singing of heroic deeds long past. The recitation is followed by the various figures of the *kolo*: the circle of spinning dancers is sometimes

*In Yugoslavia, a wedding is an occasion of celebration and strict ritual. The actual engagement is sealed by the ceremonial visit to the bride's family by her future father-in-law. On the wedding day, the bridegroom must call at the bride's house. In this illustration a Macedonian bridegroom is cheerfully greeted by the relatives of the bride.*

### Ritual Dances

Some of the more backward regions of Yugoslavia still retain survivals of ritual dances once widespread among the ancient Slavs.

In the Djevdjelija region of southern Macedonia, it is believed that fairies sometimes cause devils to enter the bodies of women. To exorcise these a magic dance is performed.

The dance is circular in formation like the *kolo*. The possessed women whirl themselves into a state of trance-like ecstasy in which they utter meaningless words. The ceremony ends with the intervention of a further group of girls, who perform a dance of purification, chanting magic words to restore the possessed to their senses.

### The Fire Dance

In some parts of Macedonia, a sect of the Orthodox Church celebrates the feast of St. Constantine with the pagan rite of the fire dance. The ceremony begins, early in the afternoon, with a banquet. A large pile of gasoline-soaked wood is erected in the village square and set alight. A drum begins to beat, accompanied by a three-string viola, and the obsessive rhythm is kept up until nightfall.

As darkness falls, a few men spread the flaming embers to make a carpet about four inches thick. As the drum and viola beat out the monotonous rhythm, first one person, then more and more people begin to dance on the glowing embers. The dancers finally drop to the ground in exhaustion. The soles of their feet are not even blistered. This is a mystery which doctors are unable to explain.

## RECREATIONS

The traditional entertainments of Yugoslavian country people are songs, dances and story-telling. But in this more sophisticated age the traditional pastimes are disappearing —except in the more backward regions—in favor of such popular entertainments as soccer.

### The 'Korzo'

The rhythm of life in the towns of Yugoslavia differs from that of the country.

Yugoslavian town-dwellers generally work from seven in the morning until two in the afternoon. After lunch a siesta is taken until five o'clock, when it is time for the evening walk, the *korzo*. The *korzo* is an

*At a wedding breakfast in Slovenia, women and children sit around a laden table. The Yugoslavians love family occasions—such as a wedding—as opportunities for wearing their festive costumes, for dancing and for eating and drinking. Sometimes the bride's family will stint themselves for a whole year in order to provide a sumptuous feast at the daughter's wedding.*

occasion for meeting friends and exchanging greetings, jokes and gossip.

The practical value of the *korzo* is that it arouses the appetite for the solid evening meal.

### Hunting and Fishing

Yugoslavia, with its contrasts of landscape and peoples, provides a variety of outdoor activities.

Yugoslavia is a mountainous and wooded country, which makes it excellent terrain for hunting. The variety of animals hunted is extremely wide. Croatia has many thousands of stag and roebuck; great red deer roam the forests of northeastern Serbia.

More unusual game is provided by the vegetarian jackals in the Peljesac Peninsula of Dalmatia and on Korcula Island. Bears are hunted in the forests of Bosnia-Herzegovina and southern Macedonia, and in the mountains of western Macedonia there are still a few lynx.

Yugoslavia is also a country of fishermen. Notable among the many excellent fishing grounds are the Drina River of eastern Bosnia, with

its great salmon, and Ochrida Lake, on the Yugoslavian-Albanian border, which contains a unique type of pink-fleshed trout.

On the Adriatic coast, underwater fishing is a popular leisure activity.

### Winter Sports

The Slovenians are active mountaineers and expert skiers. They are the only people—except for the Scandinavians—to possess their own words for skis and skiing.

At weekends and holiday times special excursion trains leave the large Slovenian towns, such as Ljubljana, for the mountain resorts of the province. Thus the town-dwelling Slovenians are still able to indulge the national passion for skiing.

### Soccer

The only truly national sport of Yugoslavia is soccer, which is popular all over the country.

The season begins in spring and lasts until autumn. Matches are usually played on Sundays and are atten-

Left: *The flat, green landscape in which these two peasant women are standing typifies the fertile Croatian plain. The placid, contented appearance of the women, emphasized by the wimple-like effect of the white head-cloths framing the faces, reflects the general prosperity of the region, which contains the richest agricultural land in Yugoslavia.*

are used as receptacles—are grown throughout the Balkans. Before they are quite dry the gourds are engraved, and the cut-out pattern colored by means of certain acids. The rest of the surface of the gourd is blackened over.

### Glass Painting and Beehive Boards

There are two traditional Slovenian peasant crafts which are now unfortunately dying out.

One of these is painting on glass, which was carried out in gay colors by a lasting process so that the pictures could survive in the smoky atmosphere of the peasant's cottage. The motifs are religious.

Another exclusively Slovenian craft is the painting of the wooden boards placed across the front of beehives. The motifs of these paintings are, again, frequently religious, but there are also scenes from everyday life and illustrations of proverbs.

### Women's Costumes

Traditional costumes are still worn throughout Yugoslavia although, in many regions, they are worn only on festive occasions.

Costumes vary greatly from region to region and even from village to village. It is therefore impossible to give more than a general picture of Yugoslavian peasant costume, with a few particular regional peculiarities.

In the south and west of the country the essential basic garment for women is a long dress. This is replaced, in the north and east, by a bodice and skirt. A woolen belt, usually brightly colored, is worn in all regions. The commonest type of footwear are *opanči*, which are sandals consisting of a leather sole curved at the toe.

Festive costumes are decorated

Right: *A Bosnian Moslem, wearing the characteristic red fez, performs his ritual ablutions before entering the mosque. Bosnia has the highest percentage of Moslems of all the Yugoslavian provinces. Many of them are fair and European in appearance, because their ancestors were Slav Christians who were converted to Islam when the Turks invaded Bosnia in the 14th century.*

ded by large crowds. The Belgrade soccer ground holds 60,000 seats.

## CRAFTS AND COSTUMES

CARPETS ARE AN IMPORTANT PART OF the furnishing of a Yugoslavian house, but it is only in Moslem houses that they are used as floor covering. Elsewhere they are hung on walls or laid over chests and beds.

Carpets are either flat-woven or piled (clipped). The flat carpets are woven on a vertical loom and are made especially in the Pirot region of eastern Serbia. The designs are delicate and complicated, often comprising plant motifs.

Piled carpets may have either a long or short pile. In both types the designs are essentially geometric, with motifs of hooks, lozenges and zigzags. The carpets with a long pile have sparse designs in few colors.

### Embroidery

Much of the Yugoslavian woman's skill goes into her embroidery.

Embroidery is sometimes worked from a pattern drawn on the material.

In this case a variety of stitches is used. The other common technique is that of tapestry, in which stitches are counted. The usual stitch used here is cross-stitch.

Designs are generally abstract, but plant motifs also occur.

### Wood Carving

Wood carving is a very ancient craft, seen at its best in Montenegro, Bosnia and Slavonia (in Croatia). Many different techniques are used, including cutting out, relief work and the inlaying of color with sealing wax.

Wood carving is used to decorate the façades and roofs of peasant houses. It is also used on such everyday articles as spoons, boxes, drinking vessels and cradles.

The decorative motifs are mainly abstract, with variations and combinations of zigzags, triangles and circles.

In Moslem areas, the style shows Oriental influence and many plant designs are used to decorate furniture.

### Gourds

The techniques of wood-working are extended to gourd-decoration.

Gourds—fruit which, when dried,

*Metal-working is not a peasant craft in Yugoslavia, but in certain areas—particularly Montenegro—the traditional male costume is often embellished with beautifully decorated swords, daggers or even guns. The inspiration for these pieces comes from the East.*

Headdresses are very varied and are often elaborately constructed out of metal wire, silk threads, flowers and other ornaments.

## Men's Costumes

The Yugoslavian male peasant's costume is generally simpler and less colorful than that of the woman, but there is great regional variation.

Very few Croatian men now wear national costume but when they do it consists of homespun trousers gathered inside elaborate boots, a linen shirt with cross-stitch-embroidered front and a sheepskin jacket with appliqué designs in dyed leather.

### RED TOP FOR BLOOD

One of the most distinctive traditional costumes is that of the men of Montenegro. They wear bright blue breeches, a pale blue coat and red waistcoat. The black sides of the pill-box hat commemorate the Battle of Kosovo, its red top represents blood and its gold flash is symbolic of independent Montenegro.

The costume of the Macedonian man is less colorful than that of the woman. It consists of a short jacket and baggy trousers in brown, woolen homespun. Over these he wears a sheepskin jacket and on his head he wears a high pill-box hat with striped sides. Macedonian dancers frequently wear a short white kilt over white trousers tucked into gay, woolen stockings.

## FOOD AND DRINK

YUGOSLAVIAN CUISINE IS RICH, OILY and highly flavored. Each region shows traces of foreign influence in some of its dishes: many dishes from Serbia, Bosnia and Macedonia have been influenced by Oriental cooking; Croatian and north Serbian cuisine reveals Hungarian influence; and Slovenian cooking has been influenced by Austria. Despite all these in-

with metal badges, pendants, coins, chains and jewels. In the case of unmarried girls, these ornaments represent their dowries. Fashions change, and many girls now wear bags of bank notes about their necks.

### MOTHERS AND WIDOWS

Croatian festive costumes are very elaborate, with multiple skirts, frills, lace insertions and embroidery. Here the decorations often have a special significance. The stripes on a woman's sleeve indicate the number of her children. A certain pattern, embroidered in blue and green, shows that the wearer is a widow prepared to take a second husband.

In Bosnia, an area much influenced by the Turks, white linen baggy trousers are worn with tight jackets.

### SHEEPSKIN WAISTCOAT

A Macedonian woman's Sunday costume consists of a loose white cotton dress worn under a black woolen knee-length dress, which is gaily embroidered. The waist is encircled by a broad red belt. An open, sleeveless waistcoat of dyed sheepskin, also elaborately embroidered, is worn over the rest of the costume.

*Many of the dances of Yugoslavia require very skillful footwork. In this Slovenian dance, a dagger is plunged into the ground and the dancer spins and leaps around it to the accompaniment of very fast music. She is wearing* opanči, *hand-sewn sandals which are attached around the ankles with thongs.*

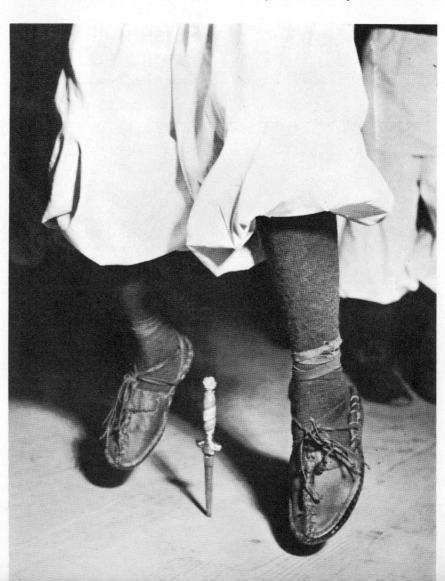

*Songs and dances are part of the everyday life of Yugoslavian peasants. In Macedonia the instrumental accompaniment to a song or a dance may be provided by bagpipes of the type being played by this man, who wears the characteristic short, white kilt and gaily colored stockings of the region.*

fluences from abroad, Yugoslavian cooks have created their own independent cuisine with specific Yugoslav specialties.

## Soups and Hors d'Oeuvres

In Yugoslavia soup is rarely eaten in the evening, but is reserved for the heavier midday meal.

*Govedža supa* is beef soup, *brodet* is fish soup and *pileča čorba* is chicken soup. These are the three basic types of soup. The chicken soup is often a rich dish, containing whole joints of chicken, to which thick cream and lemon juice are added.

A type of thick soup, known as *kačamak,* is a traditional peasant dish. It resembles porridge more than soup, since it consists of maize cooked with milk or cream. It is eaten with corn bread.

### JELLIED GOOSE AND SUN-CURED HAM

The hors d'œuvres eaten in Yugoslavia are generally excellent. *Piktije* is jellied goose or pork and *pršut* is dried meat cut into very thin slices.

Montenegrin dried ham is treated in a special way. It is cured in the sun, then built into a limestone wall where it is left for at least six months.

### RED AND BLACK CAVIARS

Two types of caviar are obtainable in Yugoslavia. Genuine black caviar, obtained from sturgeon, comes from Kladovo, in eastern Serbia. A poorer quality red caviar comes from Ochrida, in Macedonia.

A popular Yugoslavian hot dish, sometimes eaten before the main course, is *gibanica*. A paste, made from white flour, cream and eggs, is cooked with layers of *kajmak*, which is Serbian cream cheese. *Kajmak* is made from the top of the milk, boiled and flavored.

*Pita* and *burek* are the basis of other paste dishes. *Pita* is a paper-thin paste, while *burek* is thicker and is usually cut into segments. In Bosnia it is made into long rolls. The paste is filled with sweet or savory fillings. The usual savory fillings consist of soft cheese or minced meat.

## Spit-Roasted Dishes

Yugoslavian cooks are at their best when cooking meat and the most characteristic tool of their trade is the spit.

Two of the most popular Serbian dishes are *ražnići* and *čevapčići.* *Ražnići* are small pieces of pork, sometimes alternating with pieces of veal, threaded on a skewer and roasted over a charcoal grill. They are served with chopped raw onion or cubes of roasted bread.

A related dish is *čevap.* This consists of pieces of pork—cut larger than is the meat for *ražnići*—which are marinated with onions and spices and grilled.

### MINCED PORK, BEEF AND RAW ONION

*Čevapčići* are small balls of minced pork and beef roasted over a charcoal grill. Like *ražnići* they are usually served with raw onion, but a true gourmet enjoys them served with *kajmak.*

A variant of *čevapčići* is *pleska-*

*vica.* This consists of minced pork, beef and lamb grilled, in small rissoles, with onions and hot peppers.

### SUCKLING PIGS AND YOUNG LAMBS

Yugoslavian cooks specialize in spit-roasted whole suckling pig or young lamb. The lamb or pig is prepared the day before cooking. The entrails are removed through a slit in the stomach and the kidneys through two small holes in the back. The inside is well salted and rubbed with lemon. After this the stomach opening is sewn up and the spit is pushed through, along the spinal column and out through the center of the head. The outside of the carcass is rubbed with lemon and salt and it is then ready for roasting.

The cooking, over a charcoal grill, takes several hours. The spit is continually turned and the distance from the fire decreased as the roasting continues.

When cooked, the flesh of these young animals is white and tender.

### Salads

All spit-roasted meats may be served with salads of various kinds.

A Serbian salad, *ajvar,* is made of cooked sweet peppers and eggplants mixed together and served with hot peppers, vinegar, oil and garlic.

A winter salad is made from beans cooked in olive oil and water and mixed with chopped garlic and onion.

### Casserole Dishes

Many Yugoslavian casserole dishes depend on the vegetables in season. They are generally cooked with cream or beaten eggs.

*Leco* is made from fried sausages, assorted meats (frequently veal or chicken), peppers and tomatoes which are all stewed together. The egg yolks are stirred in at the last minute.

A very rich and tasty dish is *djuveč.* This is a thick rice stew with a basis of pork or, more rarely, game or fish. Peppers, tomatoes, eggplants and string beans are added and the whole is flavored with hot paprika.

*Bosanki ponac,* or Bosnian stew,

*In Yugoslavia lace-makers of the country regions bring their wares into the larger towns where they are sold at very high prices. Industrialization has not killed the old crafts, but the greater affluence in the towns, together with the influx of foreign visitors, has caused many peasant handicrafts formerly practiced for domestic use to become highly commercialized.*

is made from mutton cooked with potatoes and whole heads of garlic.

### Sarma and Moussaka

Two of the most popular Yugoslavian dishes, *sarma* and *moussaka,* are of Oriental origin. *Sarma* usually consists of sour cabbage leaves stuffed with rice and minced pork. These are cooked slowly with smoked gammon and ribs of pork. *Sarma* is generally served hot with yoghurt or sour cream, but it can be served cold.

### STUFFED VINE LEAVES

A variant of *sarma* is made from vine leaves stuffed with mutton, rice and onion. It is cooked in thick tomato and paprika sauce. This is a seasonal dish, since the vine leaves must be tender and not yet have developed the hard fibers which appear later in the year.

*Moussaka* is a dish of Turkish origin. A mixture of minced mutton and eggplants is topped with a thick sauce of beaten eggs and sour cream. Sometimes marrows or potatoes are added. It is cooked in the oven.

### Fish

The versatility of Yugoslavian cooks seems to be expended on their meat dishes, and little imagination is shown in the cooking of fish.

On the Dalmatian coast, which has a great variety of seafood, fish is usually simply cooked in unrefined oil, which gives it a distinctive flavor. Some fish are very good grilled and the Dalmatian cooks are masters of grilling. Tuna, mullet and mackerel are among the most popular fish, but the dentale, caught in the Adriatic, is considered a great delicacy.

### Desserts and Cakes

The most popular dessert in Yugoslavia—as elsewhere in the Balkans—is *baklava.* The basis of this is a paste of the *pita* type. Numerous layers of the wafer-thin pastry are brushed with melted butter; and between the layers there is filling of blanched, chopped walnuts and cinnamon. The whole is cut into squares and baked for one-and-a-half hours. While it is cooking, a syrup of honey, sugar, water and lemon juice is prepared. While still boiling, the syrup is poured over the cooled *baklava.* The dessert is then left for a few minutes before serving.

Other sweet fillings for pastry are apples, dark cherries or pumpkin.

*Slatko* (preserved fruits) in syrup

are eaten both as a sweet and as an accompaniment to chicken.

Yugoslavia is not particularly individualistic in its cakes, which tend to be variations of Austrian and Hungarian pastries. One such specialty is a very rich layer cake, flavored with almonds, walnuts or chocolate. It is filled with cream and nuts.

*Potica,* a Slovenian specialty, is a coffee layer cake with nut fillings, while *duboš,* a cake of Hungarian inspiration, is garnished with coffee and caramel.

### Drink

Coffee with milk or cream is almost unobtainable in Yugoslavia except in hotels catering for tourists. The coffee drunk by Yugoslavians is the Turkish variety, which is made from very finely ground coffee, sweetened and boiled up two or three times. The brew is very strong and very sweet.

### RAKIJA

If the Yugoslavians have a national drink it is *rakija,* a very strong and volatile spirit. The commonest type is *slivovica,* a liqueur which is distilled from plums. Other types are *travanica,* a local Dalmatian *rakija* distilled from mountain herbs, and *klekovaca,* yellowish in color, which is distilled from juniper.

The Yugoslavs drink *rakija* throughout the day. It is best drunk before a meal with light snacks such as *pršut* (dried meat).

### WINES

Much of Yugoslavia is vine-growing country, but the chief wine districts are Dalmatia and Slovenia.

Yugoslavian wines are classed as *belo* (white), *crno* (black) or *ružica* (rosé). A great variety of wine is produced, including dry, sweet and sparkling wines.

Three of the best Dalmatian wines are produced in the islands. From Vis Island come *Viško crno,* a heavy, red wine which is excellent with meat dishes, and *Vugava* which is golden-yellow in color. *Grk,* from Korcula Island, is an amber-colored wine.

The standard Slovenian wine is *Cviček,* a slightly acid vin rosé. The best-known Slovenian wines are those from the Ljutomer region and the Slovenian-Austrian border. These are mostly dry, white wines, but the Ljutomer region also produces a sparkling white wine sold under the name *Duc de Slovénie.*

*George Petrović (c. 1766-1817), known as Karageorge, was the founder of the first Serbian dynasty. He led the Serbians when they drove out their oppressors (1804-07). When the Turks overran Serbia again in 1813, Karageorge fled to Hungary. He returned home in 1817, but was murdered in his sleep.*

## EARLY HISTORY

THE LARGEST ETHNIC GROUP IN THE Balkan Peninsula is the Southern Slavs, who form the dominant part of the populations of both Bulgaria and Yugoslavia, "the land of the Southern Slavs." The Slavs, thought to have originated in the upper regions of the Dnieper River, first began to scatter from the 1st century A.D. onward; during the following centuries some went east to Russia, others west to Poland and Czechoslovakia, while other groups moved south to the Balkans. But probably they did not arrive there in large numbers before the beginning of the 6th century A.D., after the collapse of the Western Roman empire under the assaults of the barbarians.

The whole of the Balkans had been under Roman rule, those regions now forming Yugoslavia constituting the province of Dalmatia and parts of the provinces of Pannonia, Moesia and Macedonia.

When the Slavs came, unlike the Goths before them, they came to stay. They spread widely throughout the Balkan Peninsula.

In time they were assimilated into Greece, while the country in and around modern Albania became the only part of the Balkans in which the earlier native Illyrians, Macedonians and Thracians still predominated. Elsewhere, by the early 7th century the Slavs were in general possession, even where, as in Bulgaria and in Balkan regions effectively controlled by the Eastern Roman or Byzantine empire, it was as a subject race.

### Religious Differences

The Serbians and Croatians, who between them constitute around 62 per cent of all Yugoslavians, in the proportion of about two Serbians to one Croatian, speak the same language; but their histories have been quite different until recent times. While the Serbians occupied the center and east of the country, the Croatians settled in the lands bordering on the Adriatic and in the regions of the Sava River. Thus, while the Serbians (and the Macedonians to their south) fell under the influence of the Byzantine Empire and the Orthodox Eastern Church, the Croatians (and the Slovenians to the north of them) were more affected by the power of Rome, and, later, of Hungary and Austria.

Today, the Croatians and Slovenians are mostly Roman Catholic, the Serbians and Macedonians mostly Orthodox, and while Serbo-Croatian is one language, the Croatians write it in Latin characters, the Serbians in Cyrillic.

The Croatians were converted to Christianity in the 7th century. At about the same time, Latin priests started missionary work among the Serbians, but their wholesale conversion to Christianity toward the end of the 9th century was a political act, and Constantinople, not Rome, became their spiritual as well as their temporal overlord.

The Serbians, threatened by the expanding power of the Bulgarian state, acknowledged the overlordship of the Byzantine emperor in return for his protection—a submission they were to make again and again in similar situations during the next three centuries. The most enduring consequence of their act was their adherence to the Orthodox Church.

### First Serbian Kingdom

At that time the Serbians were organized in clans under more or less independent chieftains called *zhupans*. During the relatively short periods of supremacy enjoyed by one or another of these *zhupans* over his neighbors, the dominant ruler would call himself *Veliki Zhupan* (Grand Zhupan). Not until Stephen Nemanya (1114-1206) became Grand Zhupan in 1159 was a stable, independent Serbian state created.

Serbian nationalism was greatly strengthened by the work of Stephen Nemanya's youngest son, Rastko, who under the name of Sava became the first archbishop of Serbia. Besides consolidating the position of the Orthodox Church in his country, as a patron of education Sava helped to civilize the Serbians, who venerate him as their patron saint.

### STEPHEN DUSHAN

The Serbian kingdom reached its greatest extent under Stephen Dushan, Nemanya IX (c. 1308-55). In 1331 he strangled his father and seized the throne. He embarked on a career of conquest that was to bring Albania, western Bulgaria, and most of Macedonia under his rule; on Easter Day 1346 he was crowned as tsar of the Serbians and Greeks. Acutely conscious of the weakness of the Byzantine Empire, he hoped to resist the Turkish invasion of the Balkans by uniting Slavs and Greeks under his leadership; but when he died in 1355 his empire broke up.

The last chance that the Serbians would overcome the invaders perished on the field of Kosovo on June 15, 1389, along with the flower of the Serbian nobility. Among the slain were the last Serbian tsar, Lazar, and the Turkish sultan, Murad I.

### TURKISH SUBJUGATION

For 70 years after this disaster Serbia's rulers (under the title of "despots," conferred on them by the Byzantine emperor) maintained a precarious hold on a shrinking country by alliances with Constantinople, Venice and Hungary, at the same time treating with the Turks. But in 1459 the remnants of independent Serbia were swallowed up by the Ottoman Empire. Four years later the same fate befell the separate Serbian kingdom of Bosnia. When the adjoining territory of Herzegovina was taken by the Turks in 1482, the only regions to retain their independence were the Ragusan Republic of Dubrovnik (which survived as an autonomous state until the French destroyed it during the Napoleonic Wars) and Montenegro, which had split off from Serbia on the disintegration of Stephen Dushan's empire.

### Rise and Fall of Croatia

The Croatians, living in regions more exposed to pressure from other states, developed centralized political organizations more rapidly than the Serbians. The two Croatian duchies of the 8th century, one in Pannonia, the other in Dalmatia, were absorbed respectively by the Frankish and Byzantine empires in 812; but soon

*A fresco by Petar Lubarda (1907- ), depicting the Battle of Kosovo (June 15, 1389) at which the Serbians were overcome by the Turks. This battle, which marked a turning point in Serbia's history, has been a constant source of inspiration to artists and poets. Both Lazar I, the last Serbian tsar, and Murad I, the Turkish sultan, were killed at Kosovo, and the Serbian nobility was practically wiped out.*

they shook off foreign rule and united under Branislav, who reigned as duke from 879 to 892.

In 925 one of his successors, Tomislav, was crowned king of Croatia by Pope John X. This first kingdom of the Southern Slavs reached the height of its power under Petar Kresimir. Not long afterward, in 1097, the last Croatian king, Petar Svacic, fell in battle against the invading Hungarians. Five years later the Croatian kingdom was united with that of Hungary, under the rule of the Hungarian King Kálmán (1070-1116). Croatia retained its own parliament, but was dominated by its more powerful partner until Hungary herself was crushed by the Turkish victory at Mohacs in 1526.

Most of Croatia was overrun by the Turks, while the region round Zagreb became an outpost of the Austrian empire.

### TURKISH RULE

The Turks ruled over their Slav subjects with a combination of savagery and cunning. They bled the peasants white by imposing heavy taxes and conscripting not only men but boys for the subjection of their own people. They destroyed the aristocracy except where, as in Bosnia, it embraced Islam to hang on to its feudal privileges. Thus, while Christianity was tolerated, the only way to escape from serfdom was through apostasy.

Hundreds of thousands of Serbians and Croatians fled north to the shelter of the Austrian empire; many other Serbians settled in Russia. Henceforth Serbian and Croatian recruits constituted a major force in the wars of Austria and Russia against the Turks.

### THE SERBIANS' STRUGGLE FOR INDEPENDENCE

THE FIRST MAJOR ACTION OF THE SUBject Slavs on their own was a rising of the Serbians in 1804. Under the leadership of George Petrović (c. 1766-1817), the peasant patriot known as Karageorge (Black George), they took Belgrade in December 1805

and cleared the Turks from their country. But after the Russo-Turkish War of 1806-12 was concluded by the Treaty of Bucharest (under which Russia was officially recognized as a protector of Serbia, which was to have a measure of autonomy), the Turks, taking advantage of Russia's involvement in the war against Napoleon, entered Serbia in force in the summer of 1813, crushing all resistance. Karageorge and many of his followers fled to Hungary.

### Miloš Obrenović

Two years later, stung to madness by the cruelty of the Turks, the Serbians rose again. Miloš Obrenović (1780-1860), a Serbian leader who had helped the Turks to reimpose control over the country, put himself at the head of the rebels. Faced with the danger of an uncompromising war of liberation, the Turks tacitly accepted Miloš as "Supreme Chief" of Serbia, when Serbian leaders gave him that title in 1817.

Shortly before his elevation to hereditary prince, his old chief Karageorge returned to Serbia. He was betrayed to the Turks, probably by Miloš himself, and murdered in his sleep. The blood feud between the two families, begun with the suspected poisoning of a half-brother of Miloš by Karageorge, was to dominate Serbian politics for 100 years.

During the reign of Miloš, the alliance of Russia, Britain, and France which helped the Greeks gain their independence also secured greater autonomy for Serbia. But Miloš's rule was so despotic that in 1824 there was an uprising against him, which, however, was suppressed.

In 1835 a conspiracy compelled him to grant a new constitution (which was never implemented), and finally, in 1839, he was forced to abdicate. His son, Milan Obrenović II (c. 1819-39), succeeded him, but died a month later. Milan's younger brother, Michael Obrenović III (1825-68), reigned until 1842, when he was forced into exile.

The *Skupština* (parliament) unanimously elected Alexander (1806-85), third son of Karageorge, to succeed him. Notable progress in education and law reform was made during his reign; while under the Treaty of Paris (1856), which ended the Crimean War, the Western powers rewarded Serbia for her neutrality by guaranteeing her autonomous status. But internal intrigue continued, and in December 1858 Alexander was deposed and the throne restored to Miloš Obrenović.

### Michael and Milan Obrenović

On the death of Miloš in 1860 his son Michael returned to the throne. The withdrawal of the last Turkish garrisons from Serbia in 1867 did not satisfy Michael Obrenović's high ambitions. He negotiated an alliance with the independent Balkan states of Greece, Rumania, and Montenegro, and planned with Bulgarian and Croatian nationalists the creation of a nation of all the Southern Slavs. His dreams were cut short by his murder in 1868; but his assassins failed in their aim of restoring the Karageorgević dynasty to power. The throne was given to Michael's cousin, Milan (1854-1901), who reigned as Milan Obrenović IV.

The most notable event of Milan's reign was the insurrection, in 1875-77, of the Serbians of Bosnia-Herzegovina against their Turkish masters. In 1876 both of the independent Serbian states, Serbia and Montenegro, went to their aid; but the Turks defeated them and they were forced to sue for peace. The Bulgarians had also revolted in 1876 and been ruthlessly repressed.

The following year the Russians went to war on behalf of their fellow Slavs. But the Russian rulers were more interested in establishing an independent Bulgaria than in the Serbians, and had secretly agreed with the Habsburgs to support their claim to the enslaved Serbian territories as the price of Austro-Hungarian neutrality.

Russia defeated Turkey in a ninemonth campaign. The Congress of Berlin (1878), at which the other powers imposed a settlement on the combatants, recognized the new Bulgarian state (though it was made much smaller than the state Russia had forced Turkey to agree to), but placed Bosnia-Herzegovina under the administration of the dual monarchy of Austria-Hungary; and while Montenegro emerged from the war and the peace settlement almost doubled in size, Serbia gained very little for her pains. However, her complete independence was acknowledged, and in 1882 the *Skupština* proclaimed Serbia a kingdom.

### Dominance of Austria-Hungary

Disillusioned with Russia, Serbia's rulers turned to Austria-Hungary, who now completely dominated the northwest Balkans. King Milan fell completely under the Habsburg thumb, and the disgust evoked by his humiliating foreign policy (which had also featured a futile war with Bulgaria in 1885) and his scandalous personal affairs eventually drove him from the throne. In a last-minute bid for popularity, Milan granted a more liberal constitution in January 1889. The bid failed, and two months later he abdicated in favor of his son Alexander (1876-1903).

After dismissing his regency council in 1893, before coming of age, Alexander ruled in as arbitrary a fashion as his father had, suspending and changing constitutions, rigging elections, imprisoning opponents, and wavering between subservience to Austria-Hungary and subservience to Russia. With his assassination in 1903 the Obrenović line was extinguished.

The *Skupština* gave the crown back to the Karageorgevićs. Peter I (1844-1921), eldest son of the Prince Alexander who had been deposed in 1858, proved to be Serbia's wisest and most selfless ruler. Under him, Serbia made considerable constitutional and economic progress; but her latent conflict with Austria-Hungary became an open, all-out struggle. In 1906, to destroy a customs agreement between Serbia and Bulgaria, Austria-Hungary banned the import of Serbian goods into all the territories she controlled. This attempt at economic strangulation failed; but, in 1908, with the ban still in force, Austria annexed Bosnia-Herzegovina, which was still nominally under Turkish suzerainty. Russia expressed her support for Serbia's bitter protest and a European war was narrowly averted by Russia's backing down before a German ultimatum.

### The Balkan Wars

To prepare for a conflict that now seemed inevitable and to try to ensure that no outside power should again step into the vacuum caused by Turkey's declining power in the Balkans, Serbia made secret alliances with Bulgaria, Greece and Montenegro that included agreements on the

*The palace of Diocletian (245-313 A.D.), Roman emperor from 284 to 305, formed the nucleus of the town of Split in the Middle Ages. Diocletian built the palace, whose construction began in 295, for his retirement. Despite extensive damage, the palace is generally considered to be one of the finest remaining examples of Roman architecture in Yugoslavia.*

division of the Turkish territories they hoped to capture. A bid for freedom from Turks by the Albanians, whose country three of the allies wished to partition, impelled the Balkan League to go to war with Turkey in October 1912. They were swiftly victorious both in Macedonia and in Albania, but the conference of powers which began sitting in London on Dec. 16, 1912 thwarted Serbian aims at expansion through Albania to the Adriatic, by agreeing to the establishment of an independent Albania.

Apart from fixing Turkey's frontier with Europe, the London Conference left the victors to share the spoils among themselves. On June 1, 1913, Serbia and Greece formed an alliance, with the object of increasing their shares at Bulgaria's expense.

### DEFEAT OF BULGARIA

On June 29 Bulgaria attacked her former allies, but was beaten back, while on July 11 Rumania, in pursuance of her claim to southern Dobruja, invaded Bulgaria from the north. On the following day Turkey broke the Treaty of London by attacking the Bulgarians in Thrace. By the end of the month Bulgaria was forced to sue for peace. She lost land to all her enemies, and the resentment she harbored against Serbia caused her to join the other side in the great conflict that was coming.

### The Events that Led to World War I

Despite the bitter discords among themselves, the unity of all Serbians was their deepest aspiration; they could never accept Austria's annexation of Bosnia-Herzegovina, and this blow in their face was to lead to the immediate cause of World War I.

On June 28, 1914, the Austrian Archduke Francis Ferdinand (1830-1914), heir to the Habsburg throne, and his consort were assassinated by a Serbian student while they were on a visit to Sarajevo, capital of Bosnia. On July 23 Austria-Hungary presented an ultimatum to the Serbian government, accusing it of inciting the murder at Sarajevo and demanding that all activity directed against the dual monarchy should cease. Serbia's reply was very conciliatory, but she refused to accept the demand that Austro-Hungarian delegates should be allowed to take part in an inquiry into anti-Austrian movements in Serbia. The rulers of Austria-Hungary considered Serbia a threat to the Habsburg empire and had deliberately made their ultimatum unacceptable so that its rejection would give them an excuse for destroying Serbia's independence. On July 28 Austria-Hungary declared war on Serbia.

Three times the Serbians drove the Austro-Hungarian forces from their soil. Not until the fall of 1915, after they had suffered a terrible typhus epidemic and Bulgaria had entered the war against them, were the Serbians overcome by an offensive led by the German general Mackensen. The remnants of the Serbian army escaped through Albania and were evacuated to Corfu, where a government-in-exile was set up.

## 'LAND OF THE SOUTHERN SLAVS'

IN JULY 1917 A YUGOSLAVIAN committee composed of Serbian, Croatian and Slovenian leaders declared for the union of their peoples, and after the war, in December 1918, the new state came into being under King Peter I of Serbia (1844-1921). The name Yugoslavia was adopted in 1929, during the reign of his son, Alexander I (1888-1934).

### Between the Wars

The years between the two world wars were marked by bitter strife between Serbians and Croatians. The Croatians refused to submit to a centralized administration dominated by Serbians. The Croatian Peasant party, led by Stefan Radić (1871-1928), advocated a system of federal states with a substantial measure of autonomy. In 1928, Radić and two other Croatian representatives were assassinated in the assembly by a Montenegrin representative. The Croatian Peasant party and the Independent Democrats boycotted the assembly, and in the following year Alexander dismissed parliament and set up a dictatorship.

Under the cloak of national unity, the political parties were suppressed and criticism was stifled, elected local authorities were dissolved and judges removed from office. But opposition was only driven underground and an extreme separatist group of Croatians known as the Ustachi organized the assassination of Alexander on Oct. 9, 1934, while he was on a state visit to France.

### THE REGENCY

A regency headed by Alexander's cousin, Prince Paul, held the reins

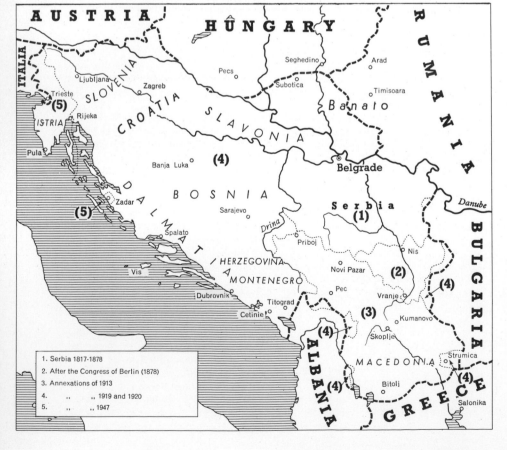

*Stages in the formation of Yugoslavia from 1817 to 1947.*

1. Serbia 1817-1878
2. After the Congress of Berlin (1878)
3. Annexations of 1913
4.     ,,     ,, 1919 and 1920
5.     ,,     ,, 1947

of power from 1934 to 1941, during the minority of Alexander's son, Peter II (1923- ). The dictatorship was eased and serious efforts were made to reconcile the Serbians and the Croatians; but during those critical years in international affairs Yugoslavia's rulers pursued a policy of friendship with the Fascist governments of Italy and Germany. On March 25, 1941, they signed a pact with the axis powers. Two days later the government and the regency were ousted by popular demonstrations and a military conspiracy.

### Under the Nazi Heel

German troops invaded Yugoslavia on April 6, and within 11 days they had overcome the resistance of her ill-prepared forces. Most of the country was partitioned by Germany, Italy, Bulgaria, and Hungary; but the axis powers recognized the so-called Independent State of Croatia set up by Croatian separatists, led by the Ustachi chief Ante Pavelić (1889-1959).

The territory nominally under the control of Pavelić's puppet state included Bosnia, and it was here that, within a few months of Yugoslavia's collapse, the first armed resistance to the Fascists broke out again. The Ustachi answered with a massacre of Serbians; but thousands escaped to the hills and forests.

Meanwhile, in Serbia itself, Draza

Mihajlović (1893-1946), an army colonel, had organized a guerilla force known as the Chetniks. Shortly afterward the Communist party, led by the Croatian peasant Josip Broz, known as Tito (1892- ), also formed guerilla bands. The hard core of the Chetniks were ardent royalists and Serbian nationalists; Tito's partisans, though led by Communists, held many different viewpoints and were drawn from all the peoples of Yugoslavia.

For a time the rival forces cooperated; but the Chetnik leaders became more and more concerned with fighting the Croation nationalists, and their opposition to Communism finally led them to collaborate with the invaders against the partisans. Allied aid (mostly British), which up to March 1943 had been given exclusively to the Chetniks, was all transferred to the partisans in May 1944, and in June King Peter's government-in-exile in London was persuaded to abandon Mihajlović.

## COMMUNIST YUGOSLAVIA

IN OCTOBER 1944, RUSSIAN TROOPS and Bulgarian divisions under Russian command entered Yugoslavia. With the partisans, they had liberated the whole of Yugoslavia by April 1945. In January 1945 King Peter had transferred his powers to a regency, and although some political leaders returned from exile, power was now effectively in the hands of the Communist party. When elections were held in November 1945, there was a single list of approved candidates.

### The Federal Constitution

The new assembly deposed King Peter and proclaimed a republic on Nov. 29, 1945, and on Jan. 31, 1946, it adopted a federal constitution. This divided Yugoslavia into six constituent republics—Bosnia-Herzegovina, Croatia, Macedonia, Montenegro, Serbia and Slovenia—and set up

*The town hall of Trogir, situated west of Split on the Adriatic coast, was built during the 15th century. The town, center of a Roman Catholic bishopric since the 10th century, has a 13th-century cathedral as well as 15th-century castles and Renaissance palaces. Originally a Greek colony, Trogir's other foreign rulers included Romans, Venetians, Hungarians and Austrians.*

for collaborating with Pavelić's Fascist state, but Pavelić himself, who had fled in May 1945 to Austria and afterward to Argentina, was never brought to justice. On March 8, 1947, Peter II and the other members of the Karageorgević dynasty were deprived of their nationality and their property was confiscated.

### Break with Russia

At first Yugoslavia's relations with Soviet Russia and the other Communist states were very close. But there was an important difference between the Communist party of Yugoslavia and its sister parties in Eastern Europe. The Yugoslavian Communists had established their military and administrative organs themselves. They had built up the strongest resistance movement in Europe and fought with invicible courage for their country's independence. They were not prepared to accept direction from outside and quickly grew impatient with Stalin's arrogance.

In June 1948 Stalin launched a violent attack on Tito for his alleged betrayal of Communist principles.

The leaders of the Communist satellite states joined in the attack and the Yugoslavian Communist party was expelled from the Communist Information Bureau (Cominform), which had been set up in Belgrade in 1947 to co-ordinate the activities of the Communist parties in different countries.

The total economic boycott that followed forced Yugoslavia to turn to America and Western Europe for trade and aid, and in March 1953 Tito made a state visit to Great Britain. Yugoslavia's relations with her non-Communist neighbors also improved. On Aug. 9, 1954, she signed a pact with Greece and Turkey, and on Oct. 5, 1954, she settled her dispute with Italy on how the territory of Trieste should be partitioned. Tito also found that Yugoslavia's independence from the Soviet bloc increased his prestige with Arab and Asian leaders and in the United Nations, and in September 1961, he acted as host to a conference of "neutralist" leaders in Belgrade.

### Changing the Face of Communism

More important, Yugoslavia played a major role in changing the apparently rigid face of Communism. Though for a time the brand of "Titoist" was used with deadly effect

within the Serbian republic two autonomous regions, Vojvodina and Kosovo-Metohija, where Albanians are in a majority. Theoretically, the republics were given a large measure of autonomy, but in fact authority remained centralized in the hands of Tito and the Communist party bureaucracy.

Old scores were settled by the Communists. Among those who paid the penalty were Mihajlović and Aloysius Stepinac, the Roman Catholic archbishop of Zagreb. Mihajlović, captured on March 13, 1946, was charged with treason and war crimes which included the massacre by Chetniks of more than 100,000 Moslems. He was sentenced to death and shot in Belgrade on July 17, 1946. Stepinac was sentenced on Oct. 11, 1946, to 16 years' imprisonment

in purges of Communists in other countries, the poisonous propaganda directed against Tito failed in its main aim of splitting the Yugoslavian Communist party. On the contrary, Yugoslavia's example of bold independence encouraged other satellite countries, notably Poland, Hungary and, later Rumania, to strike out on their own "roads to socialism."

For some time after the death of Stalin, in March 1953, Russia remained very hostile to Yugoslavia; but in May 1955 Nikita Khrushchev, as first secretary of the Communist party of the Soviet Union, visited Belgrade with Nikolai Bulganin, the Soviet premier, and publicly apologized for Russia's treatment of Yugoslavia.

However, the manner in which the Hungarian uprising was suppressed at the end of 1956 caused a further breach between Russia and Yugoslavia, and although relations have improved since, Yugoslavia has consistently refused to give up her independent status as a neutral between the armed camps of East and West. China and Albania, who have never accepted the changes in Russian policy since the death of Stalin—changes to co-existence in foreign affairs and greater flexibility in the interpretation of Communist doctrines at home—consider the Yugoslavian Communists to be "tools of the Imperialists" and "revisionists" whose distortions of "Marxism-Leninism" have corrupted even the fatherland of Communist revolution.

### NEW POLICY OF DECENTRALIZATION

The policy of the Yugoslavian Communists certainly revealed important differences in outlook between their party and the parties of other Communist states. 'From the beginning they looked upon the peasants as, in Tito's words, "the most stable foundation of the Yugoslavian state." In 1951 they abandoned forced collectivization, at that time embracing 36 per cent of farmland, and two years later they gave up state requisitioning of cereals and allowed the peasants to sell their produce on the open market.

Having vested the control of virtually all of the country's industries in the state, they suddenly resolved to snatch them out of the grasp of bureaucrats and to allow elected workers' councils to have some say in the way they were run and in the distribution of their incomes.

Similarly, they decided to decentralize the machinery of government, setting up a framework of 1500 communes, each with elected repre-

*Josip Broz, called Tito (1892-    ), with another resistance fighter during World War II. During the course of the war Tito's partisans established ascedancy over Draža Mihajlović (1893-1946), the royalist leader of a rival guerilla force, known as the Chetniks, which was supported by the Yugoslavian government in exile. Tito became premier of a Communist-controlled republican government in March 1945. Since 1953 he has been president, and in 1963 his tenure of this office was made one of unlimited duration.*

### OUTBURSTS OF REPRESSIVE MEASURES

These Yugoslavian Communists' decentralization measures have been punctuated by outbursts of repressive measures against dissenters. The most notable case was the trial of two of Tito's closest associates, Milovan Djilas and Vladimir Dedijer, who were given suspended sentences in January 1955 for making propaganda hostile to the state. Djilas wished Yugoslavia to go both further and faster toward a free socialist society, and continued to write articles highly critical of the regime. Following the publication in an American periodical of an article praising the Hungarian revolution, he was given a three-year jail sentence, and after his exposé of Yugoslavia's new oligarchy, *The New Class*, had been published in New York in August 1957 he was tried again. However, a marked feature of his trials was the boldness of the defense and the ill-ease of the prosecution, and although he was given a seven-year sentence, he was released from prison in February 1961.

A major consideration in these and other political trials in Yugoslavia was the sensitivity of her leaders to the charge that they had split the Communist camp and were putting the country back on the road to capitalism. It was seen again in the trial of Mihajlo Mihajlov in May 1965 under a law making it a criminal offence to insult a friendly state. Mihajlov was prosecuted for stating in an article that the Soviet Union had had "death camps" before Nazi Germany and for making highly critical remarks about her present regime. He was sentenced to nine months' imprisonment.

### Constitutional Changes

Yugoslavia's constitution has been changed twice since the adoption of the first republican constitution in 1946. The 1953 constitution was heralded as a return to Marxist principles, which had been perverted in the Soviet Union into state capitalism. It introduced one unique institution, a Council of Producers, representing industrial workers, artisans and peasants; but this was abandoned in 1963 in favor of councils representing citizens engaged in every kind of work.

An important feature of the 1963 constitution is that no office except that of president of the republic can be held by the same person for more than four years. The president can be re-elected for a second four-year term. Tito, who was premier up to 1953 and has been president since, was exempted from this restriction.

| FUNDAMENTAL DATES | |
|---|---|
| **925 A.D.** | With the crowning of Tomislav as king of Croatia, the first Southern Slav kingdom is founded. |
| **1331-55** | Under Stephen Dushan the Kingdom of Serbia expands into an empire. |
| **1389** | The Turks break Serbian resistance at the Battle of Kosovo and during the following century bring most of the Balkans under their rule. |
| **1804** | Karageorge leads first successful insurrection against the Ottoman Empire. |
| **1829** | Serbia obtains autonomy. |
| **1878** | Serbia's complete independence is confirmed by the Congress of Berlin. |
| **1912-13** | The Balkan Wars. |
| **1914** | Archduke Francis Ferdinand of Austria is assassinated on June 28. |
| **1918** | The creation of the Kingdom of the Serbians, Croatians and Slovenians is formally announced. |
| **1929** | The country is given the official title of Yugoslavia. |
| **1941** | Germany invades Yugoslavia. The country is partitioned among members of the axis. |
| **1945** | Tito becomes premier. |
| **1946** | Yugoslavia proclaimed a federal republic. |
| **1948** | Tito's policy is denounced by the U.S.S.R., and Yugoslavia, expelled from the Cominform, turns to the West. |
| **1953** | Tito becomes president. |
| **1954** | Alliance between Yugoslavia, Greece and Turkey. |
| **1963** | The Yugoslavian republic adopts its third constitution. |

sentatives to handle local government administration and to advise on economic goals for its area. The work of the communes is co-ordinated in the assembly and executive council of each constituent republic, whose work is, in turn, co-ordinated in the federal assembly and the federal executive council. In these and other ways a much greater degree of participation by the people in the machinery of government has been achieved in Yugoslavia than in the other Communist countries.

*Fragment of a terra-cotta vessel found in Bosnia. Made during the late Stone Age (20,000-3000 B.C.), the dish is covered with a spiral design characteristic of prehistoric ornamentation in this area. The decoration is related to, and perhaps derives from, contemporary Grecian art. The same type of spiral motifs were also used to enhance vessels, belts and jewelry made in Bosnia during the Bronze Age (3000-1000 B.C.) and early Iron Age (which began in 1000 B.C.).*

the application of small figures (see left); those of Serbia by white painted ornamentation in geometric or spiral patterns; and those of the extreme south by Greek influences. One of the earliest centers of artistic activity was the Sarajevo area, where the remains of Bronze Age (3000-1000 B.C.) dwellings have been uncovered.

### The Iron Age

The early Iron Age in Bosnia began in 1000 B.C. A large number of burial mounds date from this period. They are rich in arms, ceramics and ornaments, including belts and bracelets with both Thracian-Sumerian (a blend of ancient southeast European and Mesopotamian cultural influences) and Illyrian (from eastern Adriatic coastal regions) decorative motifs.

### The Illyrian Tribes

The culture of the peoples of the Adriatic coast, the Illyrian tribes, was much influenced by the well-developed sea communications between them and the east coast of Italy.

#### FINDS IN BURIAL MOUNDS

In Yugoslavia, the Illyrians developed a flourishing bronze and iron industry and a system of military fortifications.

Finds made in burial mounds include household ceramics, imported Greek artifacts, amber articles from the Baltic area, Egyptian and Phoenician glassware and artifacts of local manufacture, such as weapons and buckles.

### Greek and Italian Influences

The Celtic invasion, which touched the extreme south of the area around 500 B.C., left little trace, but from the 6th century B.C. onward there are ample signs of Greek influence, stimulated by the existence of Greek trading colonies on the Albanian and Dalmatian coasts.

Greek influence was particularly strong, as might be expected, in the Macedonian area. Notable finds have been made at the burial sites near

---

## INTRODUCTION

IT IS OBVIOUS THAT THE ARTISTIC development of communities situated on main communication routes, on the Danube, Sava, Morava and Vardar rivers or on the Adriatic coast, necessarily differed from that of the more isolated areas, which were mountainous and less open to outside influence.

During the Middle Ages three distinct artistic trends developed simultaneously: in Dalmatia, the Italian influence prevailed; Slovenia and Croatia were influenced by Central European styles; and in Serbia and Macedonia, the atmosphere of the Byzantine Middle East was dominant. From the beginning of the 14th century to the second half of the 19th century the art of Dalmatia, Slovenia, and Croatia developed along similar lines under the influence of the European Baroque style. At the same time, the art of Serbia and Macedonia continued under Byzantine influence. It was not until 1850 that the art and architecture in all areas of present-day Yugoslavia became uniform in style.

## PREHISTORIC ART

THE EARLIEST ARTISTIC REMAINS FOUND in Yugoslavia consist of small, roughly carved figures and bowls dating from the late Stone Age (20,000-3000 B.C.).

### The Bronze Age

The ceramics of Bosnia are distinguished by spiral decorations and

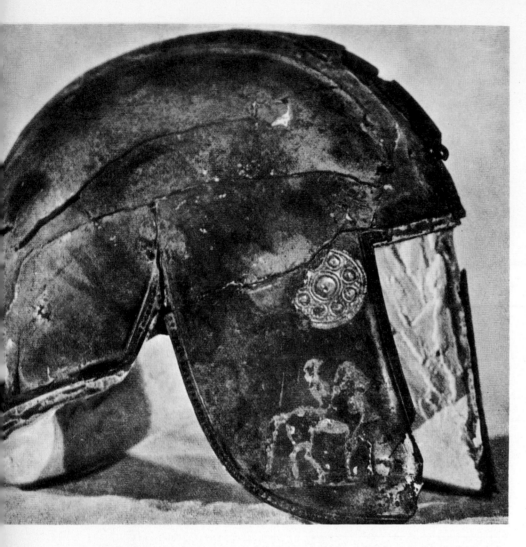

and spiraled adornments and friezes of vine branches and birds.

At Ptuj, east of Celje, is the large funerary monument known as the Orpheus Pillar. The monument was surmounted by a bearded head flanked by two lions, and the sides bore scenes in relief of Venus and Adonis, Cupids with torches, and Orpheus in the underworld with Pluto and Proserpine, separated by friezes of animals, birds and dancers.

The museums of Belgrade and Zagreb are rich in funeral monuments with representations of everyday scenes, like that discovered at Kostolac, which depicts the collection of taxes. In addition, there are carved female figures with carefully sculpted drapery, and sarcophagi.

## DALMATIA

### Late Roman and Early Christian Art

DALMATIA (NOW A REGION OF CROatia) figured prominently in the cultural life of Illyria during the late Roman and early Christian periods. Its capital was Salona, now Solin, near modern Split.

The major buildings included a temple with a pillared portico, a colonnaded theater, an amphitheater, built in the 2nd century A.D., with two tiers of arches supported by Tuscan and Ionic columns, a public bath-house, a courthouse and an aqueduct.

From the 3rd century onward, with the coming of Christianity, Solin became a religious center, with oratories, a basilica built in the 4th century, a baptistery and a bishop's palace. Fine mosaics in the basilica date from the 5th century, while a further basilica, with an octagonal baptistery, has also been excavated.

The invasions of the Huns, Avars and, finally, the Slavs, which began in the 6th century, caused the inhabitants of Solin to take refuge within the walls of nearby Spalato, now called Split. Here the Roman Emperor Diocletian (245-313) began the erection of a great palace, to

Lake Ochrida. These include artifacts found in the tombs of Greek soldiers, among them a large bronze drinking cup (see page 57), decorated with figures of horsemen in very high relief, with spiral handles worked with gorgons' heads, resting on a tripod also carved with figures and bronze ornamented helmets (see above).

To the west, the Etruscan and Venetian cultures of Italy influenced the Illyrian cultures. An example of this may be an urn found at Vace, now in the National Museum, Belgrade. But there is some doubt as to whether this, and similar examples found in Slovenia, is of local workmanship or of imported Italian origin.

## THE ROMAN OCCUPATION

ROMAN PENETRATION BEGAN AS A COMmercial enterprise in the 3rd century B.C. and developed into a military conquest in the following century. In the 3rd century B.C. the Romans had established trading centers in Illyria and had assumed the protection of the coastal Greek trading centers. By the beginning of the Christian era much of the territory that constitutes modern Yugoslavia had been incorporated into the Roman Empire.

### Roman Art and Architecture

In many centers, Roman architectural and applied arts became fused with earlier Greek influences. This is apparent at Stobi (Gradsko). For example, the great marble amphitheater, located there, was adapted by the Romans to house gladiatorial combats and wild beast shows.

The development of figurative art in the Roman period can be traced by the study of funerary monuments. At Celje, in Slovenia, the more traditional forms are fused with Roman elements. Statues and reliefs in local marble, executed for tombs, include representations of gods and heroes, hunting scenes and scenes from mythology, set within frames with arched

which he retired on his abdication in 305.

### DIOCLETIAN'S PALACE

The great palace built by Diocletian on the plan of a Roman camp covers an area of around ten acres and its massive fortifications still enclose part of the modern city of Split.

The whole concept is carried out on a monumental scale and embodies architectural principles based on both Greek and Roman forms which were to be most influential on Yugoslavian architecture up to the Middle Ages.

### SCULPTURE

In addition to the many remains of the original Roman structures, Split is rich in sculpture carved in relief. Scenes represented include mythological subjects, and, later, biblical subjects. Both Roman and early Christian remains are preserved in the Split Archaeological Museum and City Museum.

## The Middle Ages

The Slav tribes who are the ancestors of the modern Yugoslavians arrived in Dalmatia in the 7th and 8th centuries A.D. They brought no artistic traditions with them, but instead turned for inspiration to the late Roman models which already existed.

Thus the arts of Dalmatia differ from those of eastern Croatia and Slovenia, which were influenced by the Germans and Magyars. The Croatians who settled in the Dalmatian region were cut off from the Balkan world and attached to the neo-Latin cultures, which resulted in an artistic tradition which has always been basically Italian.

### ARCHITECTURE

The origins of medieval architecture in Dalmatia lie in the late Roman and early Christian periods, and the influence of Solin and Split was felt far down the Adriatic coast, and even penetrated into Slovenia and Bosnia.

The earliest buildings of the me-

dieval period were often constructed on or around existing Roman structures. Thus, the 9th-century church of St. Donat at Zadar was based upon the Roman forum, and use was made of Roman stonework in its construction. Similarly, the present 12th-century cathedral of St. Triphon at Kotor is in the Romanesque style and was built on the foundations of an earlier church of the 9th century (see page 69).

### A DALMATIAN STYLE

In the 7th century, Bishop John of Ravenna transformed Diocletian's mausoleum at Split into a cathedral. His example was followed by the converted Croatian princes, who first began building in the area of Solin. Their buildings demonstrate the way in which Lombardian structural innovations were fused with the Romanesque to produce a truly Dalmat-

*Bronze drinking cup and tripod rest (5th or 4th century B.C.) found in a Macedonian tomb near Ochrida. It is most likely that both vessel and stand are Macedonian copies of Greek works of art that had been imported into the area during the 5th century B.C. Decorative motifs include the high-relief sculptures of horses and riders in a frieze at the top of the cup, the heads forming the handles, the mythological figures which encircle the tripod, and the horses' hoofs at the base .*

*Terra-cotta statue of a woman (5th century B.C.) found near the Bitolj Plain in Macedonia. The sculpture was made in Tanagra, part of central Greece, from where it was taken to southern Italy and then, during the 2nd or 1st century A.D., to Macedonia. The subtle design includes a complex of curves and counter-curves and forms a balance between a realistic and an idealistic representation.*

ian style, which may be seen in the small 9th-century church of St. Cross, in Nin.

### ITALIAN MONKS

In the 11th century, further innovations were introduced by Italian Benedictine monks, who introduced porticos flanked by towers, a distinct division of the interior into three naves and three apses, and established the architectural proportions of monuments.

Thus between the 12th and 14th centuries Dalmatia steadily developed its own architectural traditions, not far removed from the mainstream of Italian architecture. Among the finest buildings of the period are the cathedral of St. Lawrence at Trogir, a Romanesque basilica with three naves (see page 60); the cathedral of Sibenik, begun by Italian architects and completed by one George of Dalmatia in a modified Gothic style (see page 63); and the cathedral at Rab, with its fine belfry.

### SCULPTURE

In the field of sculpture, Italian influence is also dominant. There is little difference between works produced on the Italian mainland and those produced in Dalmatia, and Italian sculptors are known to have been exclusively employed in the ornamentation of Dalmatian churches.

Among the finest examples of Romanesque sculpture in Dalmatia are the decorations of the cathedral of St. Lawrence at Trogir, mentioned above. The main door is flanked by figures of Adam and Eve, supported by lions, executed about 1240 by the Master of Radovene, and by columns showing figures of the apostles and saints interspersed with imaginary animals and grotesque figures (see page 60). Over the doorway are carved scenes from the Nativity, while the supporting arch is carved with scenes from the Annunciation and other episodes from the Gospels.

Equally distinguished are the carvings in the cathedral at Split. Those on the main door, which were executed about 1214, are the work of the Dalmatian Andrea Buvina and depict scenes from the life of Christ in relief.

## PAINTING

In painting, with a few exceptions, Italian tradition was also followed. Illuminated manuscripts of the period were inspired by the productions of the school of Monte Cassino (11th-13th centuries) and later by the School of Bologna (14th century). Likewise, the frescoes in the 13th-century church of St. Krsevan at Zadar are reminiscent of those found in Aquileia.

## The Gothic Period

### ARCHITECTURE

Dalmatian Gothic architecture was particularly influenced by the decorated Gothic of the Venetian region, combined with late Romanesque and early Renaissance elements. It was mainly limited to the northeastern and coastal regions, making its first appearance in the 13th century and flourishing particularly in the 14th in a more advanced form.

Early Gothic elements are fused with the Romanesque and Renaissance features in the clock tower of the cathedral of St. Lawrence, Trogir, with its slender columns and small shrines, while the cloisters of the 14th-century Dominican convent of Dubrovnik are in the same style (see page 65).

The simpler Gothic style was soon supplanted by the more decorated

*Temple of Augustus built 2-14 B.C. by Roman inhabitants of Pula on the Adriatic Sea. In almost perfect condition, the temple includes three undecorated façades and the colonnaded west front illustrated here. The columns are decorated with Corinthian capitals, a form commonly used in Roman architecture. The triangular pediment once contained sculpture which is now in the Pula Museum of Ancient and Medieval Antiquities.*

and flamboyant Gothic of Venetian origin. Many examples of this kind exist throughout Dalmatia. Among them are the Clock Tower (1445), and the Rector's Palace, built in the 15th century, both in Dubrovnik; the façade of the Town Hall and the Cipiko Palace, at Trogir; and the Town Hall, now a museum, at Split.

### SCULPTURE AND PAINTING

An example of Gothic sculpture, in Dalmatia, is the fine porch of the Franciscan church at Dubrovnik, executed in 1498. Many fine examples of religious artifacts of this period are preserved at Zadar, including the silver sarcophagus of St. Simeon.

The major Dalmatian painter of the Gothic period was Juraj Culinovic (1436/7-1504), often known by his Italian name of Giorgio Schiavone (George the Slav). Culinovic studied in Padua and appears to have worked mainly in that city, before retiring to Sibenik in around 1477, although he is known to have been commissioned to provide an altarpiece, no longer extant, for Sibenik Cathedral in 1489.

His works, which include a polyptych of ten panels in the National Gallery, London, England, showing figures of the Virgin and Child and the saints, worked in a carefully modeled, detailed style, were influenced by the Italian masters Fra Filippo Lippi (c. 1406-69), Francesco Squarcione (1394-1474), and Andrea Mantegna (1431-1506).

## The Renaissance

### ARCHITECTURE

During the 15th century a number of Italian architects were responsible

*Marble head of a young man (1st century A.D.) made in Slovenia by Roman inhabitants. The carving was found at Ptuj, one of the largest Roman sites in the territory of present-day Yugoslavia. Like the sculpture carved in Italy at that time, the head is naturalistic in style. It is even possible that the work was executed as a portrait bust (Ptuj, Museum of Art).*

for introducing the Renaissance style into Dalmatia. Notable among these was Niccolo Fiorentino (Nicolas of Florence), who completed Juraj Dalmatinac's work on Sibenik Cathedral, and designed a richly decorated memorial chapel for the cathedral of Trogir (1468-72). His work at Sibenik is distinguished by the use of rounded arches and of octogonal drums set on square bases.

Another Italian was Andrea Alessi, from Durres in modern Albania, who introduced the use of fluted pilasters, shell-shaped wall niches and friezes of classically inspired *putti,* or wingless cherubs, in his work on the baptistery at Trogir. Renaissance architecture also flourished on the island of Hvar, which has a Renaissance cathedral with a fine belfry, a Franciscan convent from the same period, and a loggia designed by the Veronese architect Michele Sanmicheli (1484-1559).

### SCULPTED LIONS

Sanmicheli, with his assistants, was also responsible for the fortified walls and gates, with sculpted lions, at Zadar. A number of fortifications in the Dalmatian area, especially in those parts occupied by the Venetian Republic, date from this period, when the Turkish threat of invasion was ever present.

Earlier in the Renaissance period,

*St. Lawrence Cathedral at Trogir in Dalmatia. Built during the first half of the 13th century, the cathedral of St. Lawrence was decorated in about 1240 by the architect-sculptor the Master of Radovene (today in Bulgaria). The sculptural details from the western façade, illustrated above, include the figures of Adam and Eve which rest on lions' backs. Not visible are the carvings over and around the doorway representing scenes from the Nativity and the Annunciation. The sculpture and architecture, similar to other works of art produced in Dalmatia during the 13th century, are Romanesque in style.*

duction of religious artifacts in gold and silver, and excellent collections of these, together with art treasures imported from Italy, including paintings by Titian and Raphael, are preserved in the Historical Museum, the cathedral and the state archives. The most distinguished Dalmatian sculptor of the period, however, was Johannes Dalmata (c. 1440-c. 1509), who worked mainly in Hungary.

Like Johannes Dalmata, the greatest Dalmatian painters of the Renaissance left the country to gain wider recognition. Luciano Laurana (c. 1422-80), a painter and architect, was trained in Venice and worked mainly in Urbino, where he was responsible for much of the work on the Ducal Palace (c. 1465-80), which had begun in the Gothic style, and was the teacher of the Italian architect Bramante (1444-1514). He is also thought to have designed the Ducal Palace at Gubbio (1474-80).

### ITALIAN INFLUENCE

Andrija Medulic (Andrea Meldolla, c. 1515-63), sometimes called Schiavone like his predecessor mentioned earlier, came from Zadar. Few facts are known of his life, but he is believed to have studied in Venice, where most of his work was executed for private patrons. The influence of Titian and later of Tintoretto are to be seen in his paintings, which include two compositions of mythological subjects in the National Gallery, London, and *The Flight Into Egypt* in the Art Institute of Chicago.

### PAINTERS AT DUBROVNIK

A school of painting also flourished in Dubrovnik, where the local artists were influenced not so much by Venetian art as by the work of the Italian Carlo Crivelli (1430-95), who worked mainly in Padua and the Marches. Kotor, further south, was more Venetian in character. The Venetian painter Vincenzo di Bíagío Catena (c. 1470-1531), the pupil of

the great Florentine architect Michelozzo di Bartolommeo (1396-1472) had worked in Dubrovnik, where he rebuilt the Rectors' Palace after a fire in 1464. Dubrovnik is one of the best preserved examples of a Renaissance city. Among the many fine buildings dating from the period is the church of St. Saviour, designed by the Andrijic brothers, the most

distinguished native architects, after 1520; and the Sponza Palace, a combination of the Gothic and Renaissance styles erected by the Dalmatian architect Milicevic in the century (see page 62).

### SCULPTURE AND PAINTING

In the Renaissance period, Dubrovnik was a center for the pro-

Giovanni Bellini and associate of Giorgione, is said to have worked there, though some modern critics maintain that the painter in question was a certain Vincenzo dalle Destre, from Treviso.

## CROATIA AND SLOVENIA

### The Middle Ages

THE ARTS OF CROATIA AND SLOVENIA, before the Baroque period, are relatively undistinguished compared with those of Dalmatia. Many of the most important artistic manifestations in the area were destroyed in the Tatar invasion of the 13th century, but a few buildings are worthy of note.

#### ARCHITECTURE

Of the Romanesque buildings, the best preserved is the Cistercian monastery at Sticna, in Slovenia, which dates from 1136 and contains a number of interesting illuminated manuscripts, while the more ancient buildings of Zagreb have lost their original character after extensive damage caused by earthquakes and fire.

Gothic architecture in Croatia is better preserved, since buildings in this style continued to be erected until the 17th century. Many of the earlier examples are now in ruins, but the churches of Sveti Primoz and Ptujska Gora are still in a moderate state of preservation. The monastery of Lepoglava, which later developed into Yugloslavia's first university, was founded in the early 15th century, while there are later Gothic churches at nearby Krapina and at Zagreb (the church of St. Mark, partly rebuilt).

#### PAINTING AND SCULPTURE

The sculpture of the period in Croatia and Slovenia is of little importance. Most of the Gothic work in the churches of the region is in the tradition of peasant wood carving, notably the figures in the church of St. Mark, Zagreb.

Painting is of more importance, since there are interesting examples of medieval frescoes in some Gothic churches of the region. In Croatia, the most important examples are to be found in the church of St. Mary at Beram, built 1474. The frescoes there depict *The Adoration of the Magi* and *The Dance of Death,* the latter a common medieval composition showing people of all classes of society being led in a procession by the figure of Death. These frescoes, executed by a master known as Vincent of Kastav, are in the Gothic tradition, but already display a knowledge of Renaissance innovations.

#### FRESCOES IN GOTHIC CHURCHES

A number of Gothic churches also contain frescoes. The earliest of these is the composition depicting *An Angel,* executed in the mid-14th century, in the church of Turnisce. Of a later date are the compositions showing *The Virgin and Child with St. Joseph,* dating from the mid-15th century, in the church of Cerngrob, and the remains of a depiction of *The Last Judgement,* in the church of Visoko, also dating from the mid-15th century, and executed by the Gothic master Janez of Ljubljana. Finally, in the church of Mace, built in 1467, there is a composition depicting *The Adoration of the Kings,* executed by an anonymous late-Gothic master.

In the Croatian and Slovenian regions the Gothic style developed gradually but directly into the Baroque. The Renaissance had some influence on individual artists but left no important monuments, since the

*Gracanica Monastery Church (1321) at Pristina, Serbia. The Byzantine style, which determined the design of this monastic church, dominated Serbian ecclesiastical architecture from the end of the 13th to the beginning of the 19th century. The Byzantine features in the church of the Gracanica Monastery include the Greek Cross plan which is inscribed within a square, and the five cupolas, four over the corners of the block and one over the crossing.*

northern part of Yugoslavia had more contact with central Europe, both geographically and politically, than with Italy.

## DALMATIA, CROATIA AND SLOVENIA

### The Baroque Period

THE BAROQUE STYLE, STEMMING IN architecture from the work of Giovanni Lorenzo Bernini (1598-1680) and his associate Francesco Borromini (1599-1667) and in painting mainly from the work of Michelangelo da Caravaggio (c. 1565-1609), became the predominant style throughout western Europe during the 17th century. In addition, this was the period of the Counter Reformation, a time of great artistic activity, particularly in Catholic countries.

### ARCHITECTURE

Baroque architecture in Yugoslavia made its first appearance in Dalmatia, when a disastrous earthquake at Dubrovnik in 1667 led to a great deal of rebuilding. The cathedral was restored by the Italian Andrea Ruffalini starting in 1671, while the church of St. Blaise, the patron saint of the city, was completed in the early 18th century by the Venetian architect Mario Gropelli. The Jesuit church, from the same period, was designed by Andrea dal Pozzo (1642-1709), a Jesuit from Trent, who had come to Yugoslavia in 1700 to draw up plans for the cathedral of Ljubljana.

### MANY SMALL CASTLES

The Roman—and Venetian—inspired Baroque style of Dalmatia soon spread into Croatia and Slovenia and into Vojvodina, in north Serbia, taking on a slightly different form in the last-mentioned area, due to Austrian influence. An interesting trend in the lay architecture of the time was the erection of many small castles, especially in Croatia and Slovenia. Among these were the Statenberg Castle, near Makole, now converted to a hotel, and the castles of Skofja Loka, now a museum, and the castles of Lasko and Toplice.

### BAROQUE VILLAS, CHURCHES AND A CONVENT

The most important buildings of the Baroque period are, however, religious foundations. In Ljubljana, where the remains of the old town contain a number of Baroque villas in the Austrian style, the church of St. James, the Franciscan church, and Pozzo's Cathedral are all Baroque structures, while the Ursuline Convent is basically a Baroque structure but with overtones of the Rococo.

### BAROQUE MANSIONS

In Croatia, Varazdin preserves a number of fine Baroque buildings, among them the Franciscan and Jesuit churches. The church of St. Catherine in Zagreb is also a Baroque structure. In Slovenia, there are a number of well-preserved Baroque mansions at Piran, while the cathedral and castle of Maribor have numerous Baroque additions, both internal and external, to their original design.

### SCULPTURE AND PAINTING

In sculpture, the Baroque style retained many traces of the Gothic. Italian sculptors were prominent, among them Francesco Robba (1698-1757), who worked in Ljubljana, where, in 1715, he executed a marble fountain in front of the Town Hall (see page 64) and a number of other decorative commissions. Robba also worked in Zagreb, where he executed

*Sponza Palace at Dubrovnik in Dalmatia. The palace, begun during the late 15th century and completed during the 16th century, is basically Venetian-Gothic in style. This is especially evident in the shape of the windows on the second floor and in the elaborate decoration above the roof. The colonnaded portico, which was constructed during the 16th century, is built in an Italian Renaissance style.*

an altar in the 17th-century church of St. Catherine and a stuccoed ceiling for the convent library.

In Slovenia and Dalmatia the principal formative influences on the painters of the time were exerted by Italians, among them Giulio Quaglio, a follower of Correggio, who executed frescoes in Ljubljana Cathedral, and Trifone Cocoglia (1661-1713), who executed a number of fine altarpieces and whose major work is the frescoes in the shrine of the Madonna of the Chisel, on a small island in the Bay of Kotor.

Among the most important of the native artists who were influenced by Italian painting during the Baroque period were Francis Jelovsek (1700-58), a follower of the Italian Nicola Grassi (1682-1749), and Valentine Mencinger (1699-1759), who was much influenced by the fusion of Venetian color and dramatic lighting effects in the work of Giovanni Battista Piazzetta (1682-1754).

Further east, in the Vojvodina region, the spread of Italianizing influences, centered on Novi Sad, caused local artists to move further away from the hitherto predominant Byzantine tradition. The influence of the Austrian Baroque was also strong in this area. Many monasteries in the region have series of fine Baroque frescoes and even the icon painters, bound by centuries of tradition, showed signs of Baroque influence.

Among the important painters of the region were Theodor Krachun (d. 1781) and Theodor Ceshliar (1746-93), who painted religious works and some portraits and whose use of delicate color presaged the advent of the influence of the Rococo and Neo-classical styles.

However, the most important Yugoslavian master of the late Baroque and Rococo periods was the Dalmatian Federico Bencovich (c. 1667-1756), who is sometimes known as Federighetto. Like Mencinger, Bencovich was much influenced by Piazzetta. He studied in Bologna under Carlo Cignani (1628-1719), but was also influenced by the elegant and dramatic compositions of his fellow pupil, Giuseppe Maria Crespi (1665-1747).

## The Early Nineteenth Century

After the decline of Venetian power, Italian influence on Yugoslavian art was not entirely superseded in the regions under discussion, but continued to exist alongside Austrian influence. The artistic center of the

*Sibenik Cathedral in Dalmatia. The cathedral, begun in 1430, was completed during the last decade of the 15th century. Italian architects were responsible for the initial plans and construction of the church; it was completed by the Italian-trained architect George of Sibenik. While the overall appearance resembles early Italian Renaissance architecture, some parts, such as the west façade, have been modeled on specific 14th-century Venetian buildings.*

area, however, moved from Dalmatia in Croatia, to Zagreb, where the Neoclassical style continued to dominate architecture in the area until the various eclectic movements of the 19th century, common to most European countries, were responsible for the erection of many undistinguished buildings in the major towns.

### AUSTRIAN MODELS

The main trend in painting during this period was toward the academicism of the Austrian painters of genre and history subjects, such as Friedrich von Amerling (1803-87), Peter Krafft (1780-1856), and Ferdinand Georg Waldmüller (1793-1865). This trend is illustrated by the work of Konstantin Danil (1798-1873), a painter of religious subjects and portraits. In portraiture, however, a simpler and more sincere style, though still based on Austrian models, was achieved by Djura Jaksic (1832-78) and Dimitrije Avramovic (1815-55).

---

### ART IN SERBIA

#### Byzantine Rule

THE DEVELOPMENT OF THE ARTS IN Serbia and Macedonia differs considerably from that of the regions which have already been discussed. The Slav tribes who had occupied the Balkan Peninsula around the 7th century A.D. had formed separate political and ethnic groups, whose independence gradually increased in accordance with the decline of the power of the Byzantine Empire.

The country of Serbia evolved from the mountainous Raska region, in the area of the Ibar River, and was originally little more than a collection of tribal groups, each under the rule of a *Zhupan* (a chieftain). These tribes acknowledged the supremacy of a *Veliki Zhupan,* who was, in turn, subservient to the Byzantine ruler. By the reign of the *Veliki Zhupan* Stephen Nemanya (1114-1206), Serbia had achieved a measure of independence, and Stephen Nemanya's son, Stephen "The First Crowned" (ruled 1196-1228), was able to assume the title of King of Serbia in the first year of his reign.

Serbia subsequently became an empire early in the 14th century. Its decline began toward the end of the 14th century, when it became a principality, and culminated in the Turkish occupation, which lasted from 1459 to 1804.

Serbian culture may be said to

have flourished in the medieval period, to have reached its peak in the in the 14th century and, after the Turkish occupation, to have been reduced to an almost purely monastic art. Throughout this period, the artistic center of the area often changed, and Serbian art is, therefore, less a single line of artistic development than a series of different movements emanating from various centers.

### EFFECT OF TURKISH DOMINATION

Serbian medieval art was an artistic development separate from that of the rest of Yugoslavia; isolated and without continuity, and it is only in fairly recent years that its true nature has been explored. The long period of Turkish domination rendered the monuments of Serbia and Macedonia more or less inaccessible to Western scholars, and modern research dates only from the beginning of the present century.

## Roman and Early Christian Art

The origins of Christian art in Serbia are vague when compared with the clearly defined Roman tradition established in Dalmatia. The techniques of Roman architecture, however, left traces in Serbia, as throughout the whole Balkan region. Throughout the early Christian period the basilican plan remained in use for both churches and lay structures, and Byzantine principals were common throughout Serbia and Bulgaria, two closely related regions both historically and culturally.

### THE BYZANTINE STYLE

During the 9th and 10th centuries the dominant form of architecture in both regions was the central plan in the strict Byzantine style, though

certain local developments made their appearance. These included the use of internal pilasters to support the dome, deeply set into the walls in Bulgaria, but projecting further in Serbia. Thus it may be seen that the Byzantine tradition afforded a basis for differing kinds of development, further stressed by the fact that in Bulgaria the decoration of external surfaces with colored stones tended to correspond to the internal decoration and to reflect its motifs, while in Serbia interior and exterior decoration were completely independent and the decorative elements of both had intrinsic value.

## The Raska School

The buildings of the Raska school, in northern Serbia, the majority of which date from the 12th-14th centuries, were mainly based on the simple plan of a single vaulted nave surmounted by a cupola. Even the earliest buildings of the school, however, showed divergences from the Byzantine model, often in the support of the cupola which was sometimes based upon a square tambour and sometimes, as in the church of St. Luke (1195), at Kotor, supported on pointed arches.

The Byzantine use of a square

*Left: The Fountain of the Three Rivers (1715) in Ljubljana. This Baroque fountain was created by the Italian sculptor Francesco Robba (1698-1757). Made of marble, the sculpted figures which encircle the obelisk represent the rivers Sava, Ljubljanica and Krka. Italian Baroque carvings, especially works by Giovanni Lorenzo Bernini (1598-1680), acted as the major source of inspiration for Robba's creation. Right: Cloisters of the Dominican monastery at Dubrovnik (14th century). Built in a Venetian-Gothic style, the cloisters' most interesting features, derived from the architecture of Venice, include the slender columns, the elaborate decoration within the archways and the design of the balustrade above.*

and a drum to support the cupola is found in the Church of the Virgin at Studenica (1183). In this church, as in many others of the school, the nave and portico are covered by a single roof, the portico, together with the side chapels, being an addition made in 1230.

Although the spatial organization of the Church of the Virgin is Byzantine in form, the exterior shows signs of the influence of Dalmatian Romanesque, not only in superficial decoration but also in the disposition of architectural proportions. This is more evident in the church at Zica, the center of the first Serbian archbishopric. The church is basically built on the Romanesque cruciform plan, with the addition of two small side-chapels, each with its own cupola. The connection of the drum of the main cupola with the inner walls and the sweeping line of the façade are evidence of Italian influence by way of Dalmatia.

An even more complex variation is found in the monastery at Sopocani (c. 1255), where the building narrows in three flights toward the summit (with a portico and tower added during the 14th century).

### THE CHURCH AT DECANI

The largest and most lavishly decorated of the Raska churches, however, is the church at Decani, built from 1327 to 1334. In this building, designed by the Franciscan Fra Vita, also known as Vid of Kotor, Italian influences predominate over the Byzantine.

The church at Decani consists, broadly speaking, of three interlocked basilicas rising gradually to a central cupola supported on a square drum. It has a high transept with five naves and two apses, while the influences of the Lombard style are clearly apparent in the rib-vaulting of the narthex and in the elaborate sculpted decorations of the interior and exterior. The church is similar to Italian structures, notably Siena Cathedral, in its polychrome exterior of layers of pink and gold marble.

### CHURCH INTO MOSQUE

Other important buildings of the Raska school include the church of St. Akilja (1295) at Arilje; the church at Banjska (1312-18), converted into a mosque during the Turkish occupation; the monastery of Djurdjevi Stupovi (1220) at Ivangrad; the church at Karan (1332-37); the church of St. Mary (1220) at Kotor;

Moses, *a detail from a carving by Ivan Mestrović (1883-1962). Mestrović, one of Yugoslavia's most outstanding modern sculptors, was born in Dalmatia. He studied carving in Italy and France before he moved to the United States in 1947. The most important sources for Mestrović's style include works by Michelangelo (1475-1564), Aristide Maillol (1861-1944) and François Rodin (1840-1917). Mestrović produced various types of sculpture, especially monumental religious and mythological works, portrait busts, medals in relief and decoration on vases.*

the group of buildings which make up the monastery at Pec (1317-24); and the churches at Mileseva (1234-35) and Moraca (1252).

## The Macedonian School

The architecture of southern Serbia, or Macedonia, the culture center from about the end of the 13th century onward, is much more closely connected to Byzantine forms. The basic form of structure is known as the cross-in-square plan, and consists of a cruciform structure imposed upon a square ground plan, surmounted by a central cupola. A variation of the Macedonian style is seen in the buildings of the so-called Kosmet school, in which small cupolas are added to each corner of the square structure, in addition, to the cupola.

### LINKING THREE MAIN CHURCHES

The main buildings of the Macedonian school proper include the small churches at Andres (1389), Budisavci and Crna Gora, the last-named being the site of several small churches dating from the 14th century. One of the group of churches which makes up the monastery complex at Pec, mentioned earlier, was built in the Macedonian style in 1330, when a narthex was also constructed to link the three main churches of the complex.

### SCHOOL CHURCHES

There are a number of interesting Macedonian school churches at Ochrida, including Sancta Sophia, converted from its original basilican form in the 10th century, transformed to a mosque during the Turkish occupation, and currently being restored to its 14th-century state. Also at Ochrida is the church of St. Jovan Bogoslav (14th century), which has an octagonal cupola with gables.

Other notable Macedonian churches are those of Konca (1366); the church of St. Arhandjeli at Lesnovo (1340-49); the Church of the Bogorodica (1371) at Matka; the Church of the Bogorodica at Musutiste (1315); the church of St. Nikola (1329) at Banja, near Priboj; and a number of churches at Prilep, including those of St. Nikola, St. Dimitri and St. Arhandjeli.

### THE MONASTERY CHURCH AT GRACANICA

The finest example of the buildings in the style of the Kosmet school, mentioned above, is the Gracanica Monastery Church at Pristina, built in 1321 (see page 61). It is built of alternate layers of stone and brick, with brick arches, and has a central cupola with smaller cupolas at each of the four corners, giving a general impression of soaring height.

Other churches of the Kosmet school include St. Djordje (1313-18) at Nagoricano; the church of Bogorodica Ljeviska (1307-15) at Prizren, based on a basilican original and reconverted after serving as a mosque during the Turkish occupation; and the Church of the Holy Apostles (1320) at Salonika.

### The Morava School

The third school of Serbo-Macedonian architecture is the Morava school, which flourished, as its name suggests, in the Morava valley in the later part of the 14th century. The buildings of this school are characterized by their rich decorations, both of sculpture and polychrome brickwork and are mainly built on a trefoil pattern, with apsidal branches at the east, north and south, and a high central cupola.

The earliest building of this type, constructed originally in 1186, and added to up to the end of the 14th century, is the monastery of Chilan-

dari, on Mt. Athos, in Greece, which was influential on church architecture throughout the Yugoslavian region. The most important architect of the period was Rade Borovic, whose signature is found incised in the stonework of the Lazarica, or Palace Church (1370-74), at Krusevac, and the church at Ljubostinja (1394-95).

The finest example of the Morava school of architecture is the monastery church at Manasija, a fortified and moated structure of stone with a central cupola and smaller cupolas on the four corners, built in 1407-18. Other important buildings of the school include the church at Kalenic (1413-17); the monastery churches at Ravanica (1381), Ruděnice (1395), Smederěvo (1440) and Veluce (1395).

### Sculpture and Painting

Sculpture, in Serbian churches of all schools, fulfilled a decorative function with its style closely related to that of the architecture it embellished. In the Raska churches it appears to have been modeled on Romanesque, Byzantine and Gothic examples impartially, for traces of all three styles can be found in the carvings of the church at Gradac, founded in 1270. Among the finest of the decorative carvings of Raska churches are those round the doors and windows of the church at Decani, whose polychromed marble decora-

*Stall Holder (1957), a painting by the contemporary Yugoslavian artist Gabrijel Stupicha. It is clear that modern European works of art, especially those by German and Austrian painters, have helped to create Stupicha's style. The* Stall Holder *is decorative in color and design but the feeling of gaiety is modified by the expressionistic depiction of the figure, most evident in the treatment of her face.*

tions have already been mentioned.

Byzantine and Caucasian elements predominate in the sculptural decorations of the buildings of the Macedonian and Kosmet schools, particularly fine examples being found at St. Arhandjeli, Lesvono; St. Demetrije, Prilep; and the convent of St. Demetrije at Titov Veles.

Decorative sculpture reached its highest point of development in the buildings of the Morava school. As in Macedonia, Byzantine elements predominate, and plants, animals and intertwined geometric patterns are the most common motifs, although human figures sometimes appear in carved lunettes. The finest examples of decorative carvings are to be found in the churches of Kalenic, Rudenice and Veluce.

### MEDIEVAL PAINTING

Perhaps the most important manifestation of art in Serbia was that of medieval mural paintings, whose artistic value has only recently been fully appreciated. The frescoes of Croatia and Slovenia have already been discussed, but those of Serbia are both more numerous and artistically superior.

### ABRAHAM AND THE APOSTLES

The earliest examples are the work of Byzantine painters. Restoration work in the 9th-11th-century church of St. Sophia at Ochrida has brought to light frescoes dating from about 1058, where part of a frieze depicting angels has been uncovered. These very early works are distinguished by well-balanced composition and an intensely spiritual quality, achieved through a severity of style linked with strongly drawn features. The subjects depicted include scenes from the life of Abraham and representations of the Church Fathers and the Apostles, the whole cycle terminating in a representation of Christ in Glory, and they are rendered in deep, luminous colors.

### IN SOFTER COLORS

Of a slightly later date are the frescoes in the chapel of St. George, near Kurbinovo, where the scenes from the life of Christ and of St. Cosmas and St. Damian are executed in a slightly more restrained style, probably dating from the middle of the 12th century. From the same period are the frescoes in the church of St. Pantelejmon at Nerizi, near Skoplje, which are in a more intimate style, depicting scenes from the life of Christ in softer colors and with a deep emotional quality.

### DECLINE IN QUALITY

After the fall of Constantinople the unity of the Serbian-Macedonian style was shattered by the breakdown of communications. The dramatic qualities of the early style degenerated, in Macedonia, into the rather monotonous style of various provincial and traditionalist masters. In Serbia, on the other hand, the consolidation of the Nemanya rule gave rise, as has already been discussed, to the founding of great religious establishments.

### RELIGIOUS AND SECULAR

The major monasteries and churches contained the mausoleums of the kings and the nobility, and important evidence of both political and artistic history is provided by the secular frescoes in these mausoleums, portraying scenes from the lives of their occupants. These frescoes, together with those purely religious compositions in the monasteries and churches, were executed by Serbian court painters from the late 12th century until the Turkish occupation.

### PURELY SERBIAN

The churches of the Raska school, with their relatively simple construction, lent themselves particularly well to the first phase of Serbian painting. The oldest purely Serbian examples date from the 12th century, notably the frescoes in the church of St. George at Rasa, where the saint is depicted in a monumental style derived from Hellenistic models.

### THE EARLIEST FRESCOES

The finest examples of early Serbian painting are to be found in the monastic Church of the Virgin, at Studenica, in the monastery of Mileseva; and in the monastic church of Sopocani. At Studenica the oldest frescoes date from about 1208, and the monumental representation of the Crucifixion displays both Byzantine and Italianate elements. At Mileseva the earliest frescoes were executed before the middle of the 13th century by two masters known as George Dimitri and Christophorus, whose work has a realistic though spiritual quality and betrays a definite penchant for portraiture. Once again, both Byzantine and Italianate elements are present, as they are also at Sopocani, where the frescoes date from 1258 to 1265.

### DEVELOPMENT IN MURALS

The early part of the 14th century showed a further development in mural painting, expressed in the work of the painter Astrapa and his pupils Michajlo and Eutichije. Astrapa's work, notably the frescoes in the Church of Our Lady, Prizren, is characterized by strongly drawn figures, marked contrasts of light and shade, and by the skillful use of vivid color. Michajlo and Eutichije were together responsible for frescoes in the church of St. Clement, Ochrida, the church of St. Nikita, near Skoplje, and the church of St. George at Staro Nagoricino. In their work, a trend away from the monumental qualities of earlier frescoes toward a more dramatic, intimate attitude is particularly evident.

### SMALLER FRESCOES

In the 14th century the growing sophistication of interior design of churches led to a modification of painting styles. Frescoes became smaller and were divided horizontally into cycles, each having a symbolic connection with the part of the church in which it was placed. Dramatic qualities were emphasized by the use of imaginative architectural backgrounds and expressive atmospheric qualities, while a literary element was emphasized by the addition of inscriptions giving sources for the scenes depicted.

### THE APOCALYPSE

However, in spite of the Western trend toward humanity and drama, frescoes such as those in the Gracanica Monastery, executed by followers of Michajlo and Eutichije, and in the monastery of Decani, executed by a group of painters including one Segije Gresni, are still basically Byzantine in their stylization, though illuminated by Serbian humanism. The paintings at Decani are particularly interesting since, though of uneven quality, they present a unity of more than one thousand compos-

*The cathedral of St. Tryphon, in the village of Kotor, in western Montenegro. It was built during the 12th century, on the foundations of the original 9th-century structure. The late Romanesque style which characterizes it was derived from Italian Romanesque architecture. The practice of using the Italian mode was common in Montenegro, and nearby Dalmatia, during the medieval period.*

Seated Woman *by Radimir Stojadinović. This contemporary piece of cast bronze sculpture and its dramatically modern setting seem somehow to symbolize Yugoslavia's postwar industrial and social revival. The difficulties for artists in any country so young, with few national artistic roots, are gradually being overcome .*

One interesting result of Hegedusic's theories has been the emergence of a school of primitive art based on the village of Hlebine. Influenced by Hegedusic, who worked there in 1929, a group of peasants, headed by Ivan Generalic (1913-    ) and including Mirko Virius (d. 1943), Franjo Filipovic, Dragan Gazi, Tereza Posavec and Marija Matina, began to produce works in a colorful, stylized manner reminiscent of the paintings of Douanier Rousseau, the French primitive, or the American, Grandma Moses. The work of his school is now known throughout Europe, and an exhibition of their paintings was held in London in 1965.

Abstract painting has also firmly established itself in Yugoslavia, where it is not discouraged as it is in a number of other Communist countries. Among the best-known nonfigurative painters at present working in Yugoslavia are Michelangelo Conte (1913-    ), Pierre Omcikus (1926-    ), and Ivan Picelj (1924-    ).

### Sculpture

The best-known sculptor of modern Yugoslavia is undoubtedly Ivan Mestrović (1883-1962), whose work has been honored by exhibitions all over the world. Mestrović had studied the works of the great Italian masters, such as Michelangelo, in Rome, and was also influenced by the work of Antoine Bourdelle (1861-1929) and Aristide Maillol (1861-1944). His work, which is represented in most leading museums in America and Europe, is characterized by its monumental qualities allied with lyrical passion (see page 66). He lived in the United States of America, where he taught at the University of Syracuse and at Notre Dame from 1947 until his death.

A number of younger Yugoslavian sculptors have also achieved international reputations. Among them are Vojin Bakic (1915-    ), Dusan Dzamonja (1928-    ), who is represented in the Museum of Modern Art, New York, Olga Jancic (1929-    ), Olga Jevric (1922-    ), Ivan Kozaric (1921-    ), and Drago Trsar (1927-    ).

itions forming part of a cycle depicting the Apocalypse.

With the decline of Serbian power toward the end of the 14th century, the art of fresco also underwent a decline, taking on a more provincial, traditional quality. Notable among the later products of Serbian artists are the frescoes in the church of St. Andrew, near Skoplje, executed in 1389 by Jovan Zograph and the monk Georgije. These frescoes, like other late works in the monastery church at Kalenic, are characterized by a lack of emotional force, expressed in a decrease of linear boldness.

---

## MODERN YUGOSLAVIAN ART

### Painting

BEFORE THE UNION OF THE SOUTHERN Slav peoples into a single community, at the end of World War I, various groups of artists flourished independently in the area and in the artistic centers of Europe. As in other countries, many artists were attracted to the great centers of Paris, Munich, Düsseldorf and Vienna, and worked in one or other of the eclectic styles of the 19th century.

Modern painting in Yugoslavia may be said to have been influenced mainly by the post-Impressionist movements and particularly by Expressionism, with the main centers of artistic development at Belgrade, Zagreb and Ljubljana. One of the major figures of 20th-century art in Yugoslavia is Krsto Hegedusic (1890-    ), the founder of the Zemblja movement, who advocated a style of painting based on traditional Slav models but much influenced by both Expressionism and Primitivism.

The peoples of Yugoslavia can today be divided linguistically into three main groups: the Serbo-Croatians, the Slovenians and the Macedonians. While it is only recently that the Macedonians have begun to use their own language for literary purposes, the Serbo-Croatians and Slovenians can proudly claim relatively ancient traditions in this field.

# SERBO-CROATIAN LITERATURE

UNTIL THE FOUNDATION OF THE KINGDOM of Yugoslavia after World War I, the Serbians and Croatians had two distinct literatures. The first stage of these literatures lasted until the beginning of the 16th century, and the quality of its output was unimpressive. The earliest Serbian and Croatian documents were written in Old Slavonic. The texts are mostly liturgical, biblical or moralistic, and it was not until a relatively late date that occasional versions of Byzantine stories, lives of saints and, finally, legislative documents of Italian derivation, such as the Croatian *Zakon Vinodolski* (Law of Vinodol) 1288 and the Serbian *Zakonik Stefana Dušana* (Code of Stephen Dushan)1349, also began to appear.

## Croatian Literature

Certain Croatian Glagolithic manuscripts (i.e. those written in the old Slav alphabet) of the 14th and 15th centuries have a certain interest since they contain, besides religious verses, the occasional profane poem and—very important as historical sources—some lives of Serbian kings and bishops. These include the *Život sv. Simeuna* (Life of St. Simeon), a biography of the founder of the Nemanya dynasty, written by his son, St. Sava (d. 1236?).

Throughout the Renaissance the coastal towns of Dalmatia had a flourishing and varied literature written in three languages: Latin and Italian for historical, philosophical and scientific works; Croatian, Italian and Latin for poetry and drama.

The first signs of this Dalmatian branch of Croatian literature appeared almost simultaneously in the cities of Split and Dubrovnik and in the island of Hvar. Marko Marulić (d. 1524), a native of Split, wrote many treatises in Latin and a religious poem in Croatian, *Judita* (Judith) 1501. Hanibal Lucić (1485-1553) of Hvar, an erotic poet whose work was inspired by Ovid, wrote the romantic courtly drama *Robinja* (The Slave Girl) 1520, and Peter Hektorović (d. 1572), also of Hvar, made his name with an amusing fishing eclogue (1555).

### DUBROVNIK

In the 16th and 17th centuries, it was Dubrovnik which assumed the leading role in the literary life of the Dalmatian coast and, although it was always open to Italian influence, it did produce some original works.

Notable authors include Andrije Čubranović (d. 1530?) who wrote carnival poems, one of which is *Jedjupka* (The Gypsy-Woman) 1599, Mavro Vetranić (1482-1576), who wrote the allegorical-philosophical poem *Putnik* (The Pilgrim) and the idyll *Rèmeta* (The Hermit); and Marin Držić (1508-67), known especially for his skillfully written little comedies, which are very reminiscent of Sienese rustic farces. They include *Novela od Stanca* (The Tale of Stanac) and *Dundo Maroje* (Uncle Maroje). During the second half of the 16th century there existed a flourishing group of lyric poets inspired by the Italians Pietro Bembo (1470-1547) and Torquato Tasso (1544-95); they include Dinko Ranjina (d. 1607) and Dominko Ziataric (d. 1609).

Seventeenth-century literature in Dubrovnik was completely dominated by three great writers: Ivan Gundulić (1588-1638), who wrote the pastoral drama *Dubravka* (1628) and the epic poem *Osman* (1621 or 1622), modeled on Tasso; Ivan Bunić (d. 1658), a writer of serene and joyful lyrics which recall the poetry of the Italian Gabriello Chiabrera (1552-1637); and Junije Palmotić (1606-57), who was a prolific and versatile writer, especially of plays, which include tragedies on mythological and classical themes, tragi-comedies and romantic works. This was the peak of Dubrovnik's literary achievements; from this time on, form and content grew trivial.

### THE COUNTER REFORMATION

The Reformation had very little influence in Croatia; but, on the other hand, the Counter Reformation did. The promoters of Counter Reformation literature in Croatia were the Jesuits and Franciscans, and they were soon supported by local collaborators such as Bartolomej Kasić (1575-1650), the Bosnian Matija Divković (1563-1631), the Croatians Juraj Habdelić (1609-78) and Juraj Križanić (1618-83), and the Slavonian Antun Kanižlić (1700-77). The main work of these writers was the compilation of books of moral education and philology.

From the beginning of the 17th

*Primoz Trubar (1508-86), portrayed in this engraving of 1578, was a Protestant preacher who developed the Slovenian literary language. His self-imposed task was, by translation, to supply the Protestants of Slovenia with the most essential of the sacred books. He translated the Bible and wrote epistles.*

century until the mid-18th century religious themes predominated, although the first works of profane literature in Croatia also date from this time. These were often written by members of noble families, such as Petar Zrinyi (1621-71), who wrote a Croatian paraphrase of a poem written in Hungarian by his great-grandfather Miklós, about the heroic defense of Szigetvar; Fran Krsto Frankopan (1643-71), a lyric poet; and Pavao Ritter-Vitezović (1652-1713), an ardent student of history.

### ILLYRIANISM

The most important manifestation of Croatian Romanticism was Illyrianism, a movement inspired by Janko Drasković (1770-1856) and continued by Ljudevit Gaj (1809-72). The aim of Illyrianism was the political and cultural unification of all the southern Slavs. Although the Illyrian movement did not fulfill its most ambitious aims, it achieved a certain measure of success, particularly in giving the Croatians a single literary language and freeing them from the cultural tutelage of the German- and Hungarian-orientated bourgeoisie.

A few notable writers emerged out of the general mediocrity of the Illyrianist writers: Stanko Vraz (1810-51), a Slovenian poet who began writing in Slovenian dialect but was later influenced by the ideas of Ljudevit Gaj and adopted Croatian as his language; Petar Preradović (1818-72), a lyric poet; the Greek Dimitrije Demeter (1811-72), author of a tragedy, *Teuta* (1844), later to become celebrated; and Ivan Mažuranić (1814-90), who wrote a dramatic short poem, *Smrt Smail Age Čengića* (The Death of Smail-Age Čengića) 1846, inspired by the struggle between the Montenegrins and the Turks.

### ABSOLUTISM AND AFTER

The absolutist regime of Alexander von Bach (1813-93), the Austrian prime minister during the 1850s, finally put an end to Illyrianist hopes, and the generation which grew up between 1850 and 1860 produced no literary personalities to compare with those of the previous generation.

With von Bach's dismissal, the decade of absolutism was over and Croatian culture flowered again. It had the particular support of the bishop Joseph Georg Strossmayer (1815-1905), a great patron of the arts, who in 1866 founded the Yugoslav Academy of Science and the Arts in Zagreb. A celebrated poet and dramatist of the time was Franjo Marković (1845-1914), but the period as a whole was dominated by the work of August Šenoa (1838-81), a lively story-teller, whose work combines both romantic and realistic elements; among the best-known works of this prolific writer are the short story *Prosjak Luka* (Luka the Beggar) 1879 and the novels *Zlatarevo zlato* (The Goldsmith's Gold) 1871 and *Seljačka buna* (The Peasants' Revolt) 1877.

### REALISM

During the last 20 years of the 19th century, realism entered into Croatian literature. Its main exponents were Evgenij Kumičić (1850-1904), the author of short stories and novels on social and historical themes; Vjenceslav Novak (1859-1905), who wrote, with deep understanding, of the lives of people on the Croatian littoral and in Zagreb, a Croatian city; Ante Kovačić (1854-89), who composed poetry but was mainly a short-story writer and novelist; Ksavor Šandor Djalski (the pseudonym of Ljuba Babić Gjalski, 1854-1935), a sympathetic chronicler of the unsophisticated society of Zagora (a region of western Croatia) and its destruction by social progress; and Josip Kozarac (1858-1906), who focused his attention on the problems of the countryside.

One of the best of the late-19th-century poets was Silvije Strahimir Kranjčević (1865-1908), who wrote contemplative lyric verse.

*The law courts at Capodistria in Trieste. They were built while Capodistria was under Venetian rule and this is reflected in the design of the windows at the far right and the towers which flank the façade. Begun in the 13th century, the law courts were constructed on a Romanesque plan, but during the 14th and 15th centuries early Gothic features were added.*

A bronze sculpture of a 10th-century archbishop, Gregory of Nin, by Ivan Mestrović (1883-1962), a leading Yugoslavian sculptor. Nin, in western Croatia, was a medieval bishopric. The statue is located in a park at Split, the leading city of Dalmatia. Mestrović studied in Paris and the statue shows the influence of two great French sculptors: Aristide Maillol and Emile Bourdelle.

### THE EARLY TWENTIETH CENTURY

At the beginning of the 20th century in Croatia, as elsewhere in Europe, 19th-century themes began to be superseded. Under German, French and Italian influences, Croatian literature was now moving toward modernism as writers attempted to discard patriotism and didacticism.

At this time the most productive literary centers in Croatia were Dalmatia and Zagreb. Some well-known Dalmatian writers were: Ante Tresić-Pavičić (1867-1949), a Neoclassicist poet whose work recalls that of the Italian poet Giosuè Carducci (1835-1907); Milan Begović (1867-1948), a sensual lyric poet similar to the Italian Gabriele D'Annunzio (1863-1938) and, later, a writer of vivid dramas and of stories; and Vladimir Nazor (1876-1949), the greatest poet of his generation and chief literary personality until his death.

Among the well-known writers of the time who were born or settled in Zagreb are Antun Gustav Matoš (1873-1914), a critic and theorist whose ideas left their mark on the whole epoch, and Vladimir Vidrić (1875-1909), the author of a book of poems, *Pjesme* (1907), which, although few, are profoundly felt and rich in ideas.

## Serbian Literature

Toward the end of the 17th century groups of Serbians left their native towns and villages and fled to southern Hungary to escape Ottoman domination. A hundred years later these people had advanced considerably, both in their standard of living and in their cultural activities. They had struck up close relations with other countries and cities, notably Russia, Venice, Budapest and Vienna.

At the time of the benevolent reforms of Holy Roman Emperor Joseph II (1741-90), in the second half of the 18th century, the cultural life of the Serbians living in the Habsburg Empire developed further. The first publications in Serbian were printed in Vienna; and from then on men of letters such as Jovan Rajić (1726-1801), Zaharija Orfelin (1726-85) and Dimitrije Obradović (1742?-1811) could begin to educate their fellow Serbians.

### ROMANTICISM

Serbian literature was very rich in popular poetry, particularly epic poems. These were subdivided into various cycles, such as those which dealt with the Battle of Kosovo, with the national hero Marko Kraljović and with the brigands and fugitives known as the *Haiduks* and *Usoks*. It was not known when or where they were composed.

The romantic trend represented by this popular poetry had a famous supporter in Vuk Stefanović Karadžić (1787-1864), who made vast collections of popular verse.

Of the first generation of Serbian Romantic writers, the most important were Jovan Sterija Popović (1806-56), an excellent prose-writer and the

"Father of Serbian Drama;" Sima Milutinović (1791-1847), who tried to combine his natural tendency toward Classicism with a more popular approach; and Petar Petrović Njegoš (1813-51), author of the dramatic poem *Gorski Vijenac* (The Mountain Wreath) 1847.

Most of the second generation of Romantic writers came from the Backa and Banat—regions of Serbia which had been exposed to Hungarian and German influence—and were members of the democratic and nationalistic Young Serbia movement. This current produced Jovan Jovanović (1833-1904), a prolific and extremely well-read poet.

### REALISM

The last quarter of the 19th century saw a reaction against Romanticism and the beginning of a trend toward Realism. The most important theorist of this movement was Svetozar Marković (1864-75), a positivist socialist and a follower of the Russian

*The prince-bishop of Montenegro, Petar Petrović Njegoš (1813-51), is considered Serbia's greatest poet and is sometimes described as "the Shakespeare of Montenegro." His best work, Gorski vijenac (The Mountain Wreath) 1847, is a dramatic poem based on a historical theme. The poem is both a reflection of life in the Montenegro of Njegoš' own day and a study of human destiny.*

*Ivo Andrić (1892-    ) is the leading prose writer of modern Serbia. In 1961 he won the Nobel prize for literature. His work includes novels, short stories, essays and literary criticism. His fiction is set in Bosnia and usually displays shrewd psychological observation. He is considered an immaculate stylist.*

revolutionary Nikolai Chernyshevski (1828?-89).

Two writers of Croatian Dalmatia who wrote in Serbian were Stjepan Mitrov Ljubiša (1824-78), who described the folklore and customs of Dalmatia and Montenegro; and Simo Matavulj (1852-1908), whose novels, short stories and plays contain vivid pictures of various regions, from the Adriatic coast to Belgrade.

Two Serbian-born writers were Milovan Glišić (1847-1908), a dramatist and short-story writer; and Laza Lazarević (1851-90), a subtle observer of the society around him, which he depicted in his short stories.

### MODERNISTIC TRENDS

Various Serbian authors writing at the end of the 19th century anticip-

ated that abandonment of pure realism that has marked most European literature of this century. Two such writers were Vojislav Ilić (1862-94) and Svetolik Ranković (1863-99), whose collection of short stories *Slike iz života* (Images of Life), and novels *Gorski car* (The Tsar of the Mountain) 1897 and *Porušeni ideali* (Shattered Ideals) 1900, were characterized by a marked interest in psychology.

The first definite signs in Serbia of the modernistic trends which originated in France and were already rife throughout the rest of Europe began to appear at the beginning of the 20th century in the field of poetry. The most important poets of this modernist movement were Aleksa Šantić (1868-1924), a rather vague lyric poet, and Jovan Dučić (1874-1943) and Milan Rakić (1876-1938), who were both preoccupied by verseforms and who believed in a purely aesthetic, self-sufficient literature which need not concern itself with national, political or social problems.

Serbian prose writing, however, remained, during the first two de-

nojlović (1883- ) were Expressionists and Rastko Petrović (1898-1949), Rade Drainac (1899-1943), Milan Dedinac (1902- ) and Aleksandar Vučo (1897- ) were Surrealists.

Ivo Andrić (1892- ), an important prose writer of the period and winner of the Nobel prize for literature in 1961, is a perfect stylist. Three of his most striking novels are *Gospodica* (The Young Girl) 1945, *Travnička kronika* (Chronicle of Travnik) 1945 and *Na Drini ćuprija* (Bridge on the Drina) 1945, the first being a subtle psychological portrait of the heroine while the other two are based on themes from Bosnian history.

### CROATIAN WRITERS

Of writers from Croatia during this same period the most important, for his extraordinary versatility, was Miroslav Krleža (1893- ), whose tremendous body of work includes lyrical works, drama, narrative prose and critical writings.

Post-World War I poets from Croatia include Antun Branko Simić (1898-1925); Gustav Krklec (1899- ), a lyric poet who wrote verse of intense feeling; Dobriša Cesarić (1902- ), who was concerned with social problems; Vladimir Kovacić (1907-

cades of the 20th century, largely free from experimentation and modernism and was basically realistic. An important fiction writer was the highly original Borisav Stanković (1876-1927), whose novels include *Nečista krv* (Tainted Blood), considered not only his finest book but also one of the most significant works of the time.

### The Merging of the Two Literatures

The birth of the kingdom of Yugoslavia, after World War I, made closer contact between Serbians and Croatians possible. As a result, their literatures grew ever closer, until, now one speaks not of Serbian or Croatian but of Serbo-Croatian literature. New movements—Futurism, Expressionism, Surrealism— reached Yugoslavia from abroad and aroused great interest there.

#### SERBIAN WRITERS

Of writers from Serbia, Stanislav Vinaver (1891-1955) and Todor Ma-

*The old theater at Hvar (Dalmatia), built in 1612. One of the oldest theaters in Europe, it was the first to be built in Yugoslavia. Plays by many of the most important Dalmatian writers were staged here, including those of Junije Palmotić (1606-57), who wrote comedies and tragicomedies, mainly on mythological themes.*

); and Vjekoslav Majer (1900-   ), a quiet, reflective poet.

Perhaps the most significant poetic work, however, was produced by Vladimir Nazor (1876-1949), an extremely prolific and versatile writer. His principal collections are *Lirika* (Lyrics) 1910, *Hrvatski kraljevi* (Croat Kings) 1912, and *Pjesme* (Poetry) 1942. The important Croatian prose writers were Slavko Batusić (1902-   ), writer of travel diaries and novels; and August Cesarec (1893-1941), who wrote novels and short stories.

### CONTEMPORARY LITERATURE

Most contemporary Serbo-Croatian writers have been concerned with the problems arising out of World War II and the struggle for recovery. The most important of these writers are Ivan Goran Kovačić (1913-43), a short-story writer and lyric poet; Jovan Popović (1905-52), who wrote of social struggles and partisan activity; and Oskar Davico (1909-   ), who was known first as a poet and later as an excellent prose writer and whose novel *Pesma* (Ballad), set in Belgrade during the German occupation, is particularly well-known.

## SLOVENIAN LITERATURE

### From the Earliest Times to Romanticism

UNTIL THE FIRST HALF OF THE 16TH century, cultural life in Slovenia was very restricted, and literary activity was confined to the monasteries, where it was limited to the modest works of copyists and illuminators. Up to the 15th century, texts written in Slovenian, such as the *Brižinski Spomeniki,* or Freisingen Monuments, of the second half of the 10th century, were all biblical or ecclesiastical.

#### PROTESTANT REFORMERS

It was not until the Reformation that Protestant writers began to use Slovenian for literary purposes. One such writer was Primož Trubar (1508-86) who translated the New Testament and wrote various epistles and polemical works. Other notable Protestant writers were: Adam Bohorić (c. 1520-1600), a pupil of the great German religious reformer Melanchthon (1497-1560), and author of a first, though faulty, grammar of the national language; Hieronymus Megiser (c. 1553-1618), a German historian and lexicographer; and Jurij Dalmatin (c. 1530-89), author of a classic Slovenian version of the Bible.

#### THE COUNTER REFORMATION

Slovenian literature was, at first, little affected by the Counter Reformation. Signs of the Baroque and of Italian influence do not appear until toward the end of the 17th century and the beginning of the 18th.

#### THE ENLIGHTENMENT IN SLOVENIA

In Slovenia, as in Serbia, the reforms of Joseph II encouraged a broader development of literary activity and of culture in general.

The first writer to spread the ideas of the Enlightenment was a monk, Marko Pohlin (1735-1801). Later, the "Academia Operosorum" of Ljubljana, the capital of Slovenia, sponsored works of philology and grammar, as well as artistic and scientific works.

The most interesting writers at the time of the Enlightenment were Valentin Vodnik (1758-1819), educator and poet; and Anton Linhart (1757-95), founder of the Slovenian drama. One of his works is a version (1790) of the French playwright Beaumarchais' *Marriage of Figaro* (1784).

Napoleon's creation, in 1809, of the Illyrian provinces, with Ljubljana as capital, gave further encouragement to literary activity in Slovenia, since it was a step in the direction of cultural and national unity, the ideal which lay behind the Romantic movement in Yugoslavia.

The spiritual mentor of the Romantic generation was Matija Čop (1797-1835), and its main exponents were Stanko Vraz (1810-51) who, after a promising poetic debut in his mother-tongue, was inspired by the Illyrianist ideals of Ljudevit Gaj; and France Prešeren (1800-49), one of the greatest Slovenian writers of all time.

### The Later Nineteenth Century

The failure of the 1848 revolution had an adverse effect on Slovenian literature.

It was not until 1858, when the literary review *Slovenski Glasnik* (Slovenian Messenger) was founded, that Slovenian literature began to recover its European standing.

The poetry of Simon Jenko (1835-69) and Simon Gregorčič (1844-1906) contains echoes of Romanticism and pessimism. But, at the same time, there was a realistic trend in writing, led by Fran Levstik (1831-87), a poet and writer of short stories, including the classic story *Martin Krpan* (1858).

The work of the following generation was based on realism but, again, shows traces of Romanticism. Some of the more important writers were Janko Kersnik (1852-97), whose satirical prose works are mainly concerned with the life of the provincial bourgeoisie; Anton Aškerc (1856-1912), who began by writing mainly lyric verse but later turned to epic poetry, in which he treated themes from Slovenian history; and Ivan Tavčar (1851-1923), whose novels and short stories have historical and social themes.

#### MODERNISM

A far more vital trend was that of Modernism. The most important representatives of Slovenian Modernism were Dragotin Kette (1876-99), whose posthumously published volume, *Poems* (1900), reflects his spiritual torment, and discusses a wide range of intensely felt philosophical problems; Josip Murn-Aleksandrov (1879-1901), a pessimistic writer; Ivan Cankar (1876-1918), a writer of powerful prose, whose numerous short stories, novels and plays were inspired not only by his love of women and of his mother, but also by the great national and social problems of the time; and Oton Župančić (1878-1949), a vigorous poet whose many works reflect his own experiences.

#### OTHER TRENDS

Even while Modernism was at its height, some writers followed different trends; there are thus also naturalists, Catholic moralists and socialist revolutionaries among the writers of the time. They include Ksaver Meško (1874- ), a subjective lyric poet and a writer of psychological short stories; and Fran Saleski Finžgar (1871- ), whose early poems and short stories were in the peasant idiom, although he later turned to political and social themes, which form the basis of numerous short stories as well as the novel *Pod svobodnim soncem* (Under a Free Sun) 1907.

### Twentieth-Century Literature

Slovenian literature developed after World War I partly along the lines already laid down and partly in a fresh direction, due to the entirely new political situation of the country.

One group of young poets represented a transitional stage between prewar and postwar Modernism. The best of these was Alojz Gradnik (1882- ), a profound and thoughtful writer.

Another school of writers active after World War I was particularly concerned with social matters. Three members of this school were Tone Seliškar (1900- ), the first of the proletarian poets and a writer of incisive prose; Srecko Kosovel (1904-26), whose favorite themes were his native province of Karst, his own personal problems and the social upheaval of the time; and Mile Klopčić (1905- ) who, in his work, moved between the intimate and the revolutionary.

Vladimir Bartol (1903- ), Ivo Grahor (1902-44) and Ludvik Mrzel (1904- ) turned to expressionist experiment.

Yet another group, dominated by the strong personality of Prežihov Voranc (pseudonym of Lovro Kuhar, 1893-1950) and including Miško Kranjec (1908- ), Ciril Kosmač (1910- ), Anton Ingolič (1907- ) and Ivon Potrc (1913- ), is interested in social realism.

The names of two poets have emerged from the period of partisan struggle: Matej Bor, pseudonym of Vladimir Pavšić, (1913- ), and Karel Destovnik-Kajuh (1922-44).

## THE THEATER

ANY SURVEY OF THE DEVELOPMENT of drama in Yugoslavia must cover the country's two main linguistic groups—the Serbo-Croatian and the Slovenian. Until the kingdom of the Serbians, Croatians and Slovenians was formally proclaimed after World War I, cultural activities had separate regional characters.

### Croatian Drama

Croatia, established as a kingdom during the 10th century, was the first to produce significant dramatic works.

Liturgical performances were given in Zagreb Cathedral as early as the 12th century, but the first written collection of plays dates from the 16th century, when the poet and Benedictine friar, Mavro Vetranović (1482-1576), dramatized biblical events in *Posvetilište Avramovo* (Abraham's Sacrifice) and *Od Poroda Jezušova* (The Tribe of Jesus).

### SACRED AND PROFANE

Religious drama quickly began to acquire secular features; two chief exponents of this trend were Hanibal Lucić (1485-1553), from the island of Hvar, who wrote *Robinja* (The Slave Girl) 1520, a drama of courtly love that reveals the influence of the Italian poet Petrarch (1304-74) but also draws on national folk material; and Marin Držić (1508-67), who wrote several pastoral plays and some successful comedies such as *Novela od Stanca* (The Tale of Stanac) and *Dundo Maroje* (Uncle Maroje), containing witty observations on contemporary society in Dubrovnik. Similar social comment was attempted by Nikola Nalješković (1510-87), but with less dramatic impact.

One of Europe's oldest theaters was built in 1612 on the island of Hvar. Works by all the important Dalmatian writers were staged there, including those of Junije Palmotić (1606-57), perhaps the most prominent of 17th-century Dalmatian playwrights. Palmotić wrote comedies and tragicomedies, inspired by mythological themes, and a drama in praise of his native town Dubrovnik entitled *Pavlimir*.

The gradual decline of the nobility of Dubrovnik—since the 13th century the cultural élite among the southern Slavs—coincided with the process of Germanization carried out between 1740 and 1790 by the Austrian rulers Maria Theresa (1717-80) and her son Joseph II (1741-90).

Zagreb began to take over as the focal point of cultural activity, but the emphasis was on German culture.

When the city acquired a permanent German theater during the eighties there came a patriotic reaction which inspired more Croatian drama.

The most outstanding Croatian playwright of this period was Tito Brezovački (1757-1805). His work, written with a didactic purpose, is nevertheless full of vitality. *Sveti Aleksij* (Saint Alexis) and *Grabancijas Dijak* (The Sorcerer's Apprentice) are based on legendary themes, but contain pertinent criticism of the degeneracy and backwardness of Croatian society.

### THE ILLYRIAN MOVEMENT

The early 19th century saw the growth of a movement which resisted Magyar domination and aimed at cultural and political unification. Its leaders were Ljudevit Gaj (1809-72) and Janko Drasković (1770-1856), whose enthusiasm soon roused Serbia as well as Croatia. The Illyrian movement, which took its name from the province created by Napoleon in 1809, stimulated Romantic and nationalist thought and laid a firm basis for modern Yugoslavian literature and drama, by selecting a single Serbo-Croatian dialect as a common language. One of the major works produced by this movement was *The Turks at Sisak* (1840) by Ivan Kukuljevič (1816-89).

In the latter part of the 19th century there was increased activity in the world of the theater.

Split, Rijeka, Dubrovnik and Zagreb all acquired their own theaters and the first professional company of Croatian actors was formed. They performed works by contemporary writers such as Franjo Marković (1845-1914) and the popular Josip Eugen Tomić (1843-1906), both of whom were inspired by historical or current political events. Marković, for example, wrote *Karlo Drački* as a protest against absolutist Austro-Hungarian domination, while Tomić, more realist in his observation, described events in Croatian history in *Zmaj od Bosne* (The Dragon of Bosnia) 1879, and the decline of the Croatian nobility in *Melita* (1899).

The theater established in Zagreb in 1895 gradually asserted itself as

*A scene from the comedy* Novela od Stanca (The Tale of Stanac) *by Marin Držić (1508-67), performed at the summer festival of Dubrovnik. Greatly influenced by the Italian commedia dell'arte, Držić wrote several pastoral plays and popular comedies, which were performed with great success by amateur companies in the Dalmatian capital. Most of Držić's plays, many of which have local settings and contain satirical portraits of his contemporaries, are full of a spirit of youth and gaiety.*

the most important center of dramatic art.

## MODERNISM

It was at this time that Croatian drama began to achieve a reputation in Europe, due partly to the energy and reformatory zeal of the Zagreb theatrical director, Stjepan Miletić (1868-1908), and partly to the playwright Ivo Vojnović (1857-1929). The latter, a contemporary of the Croatian realist writers, led the way to Modernism, being concerned with examining the psychology of his characters rather than their social condition. One of his early works was *Psyche* (1889), but it was not until 1895, with his drama *Ekvinocij* (The Equinox), that Vojnović succeeded in winning the understanding and approval of the Croatian public. His masterpiece is *Dubrovačka Trilogija* (The Dubrovnik Trilogy) 1900, translated into English in 1921. Other successful works include *The Lady with the Sunflower* (1912) and *Masquerade beneath the Roof* (1922).

Croatian drama continued to have a special character of its own after the constitution of the state of Yugoslavia in 1918.

It was, and is, dominated by Miroslav Krleza (1893- ), whose many works—novels, poems and plays—have been widely translated and acclaimed. His first dramatic success was *Golgota* (Golgotha) 1922, followed in 1928 by *U Agonija* (In Agony) and a year later by *Gospode Glembayevi* (The Glembays) describing the disintegration of society in prewar Zagreb.

It is against this background of the declining bourgeoisie that the work of the expressionist Josip Kalundžić (1899- ), author of *Midnight* (1921) and *The Scorpion* (1926), should be considered, as well as that of Miroslav Feldman (1899- ).

### Serbian Drama

The theater in Serbia was late in developing. There was little dramatic work produced until the 19th century, when, in 1815, the actor and writer Joakim Vucić (1772-1847) founded the Theater of the Serbian Princes at Kragujevac, which was the seat, from 1818 to 1839, of the ruler Miloš Obrenović (1780-1860). Among its first writers were Jovan Sterija Popović (1806-56), who founded the Belgrade theater, providing it first with historical plays, then with a series of witty, satirical comedies: *Laza Paralaza* (Liar and Superliar),

*A scene from* The Miraculous Mandarin *(1918-19) by the Hungarian composer Béla Bartok (1881-1945), performed by the ballet company of the National Theater at Belgrade. The founding of this theater in 1862 was a result of the rapid cultural developments that took place in 19th-century Belgrade.*

*Tvrdica* (The Miser) and many others.

The Romantic movement in Serbia, whose first exponent was Laza Kostić (1841-1910), produced few works of any lasting value. Not until the early years of the 20th century did Serbian drama begin to show any further signs of vitality. This was mainly manifested in the popular comedies of Branislav Nušić (pseudonym Ben Abika, 1864-1938).

### Slovenian Drama

Slovenian drama really began to develop only in the 19th century, although some Slovenian interpolations in the texts of scholastic Latin plays date from the 17th century.

At the end of the 18th century, Žigmund Zois (1747-1819), an intellectual of Italian and Slovenian parentage, gathered around him a group of writers and artists with the common aim of improving Slovenia's cultural status. One of the most prominent members was Anton Tomaž Linhart (1756-95), who wrote two plays, *Županova Micka* (Micka the Mayor's Daughter) 1789 and *Matiček se Ženi* (The Marriage of Matiček).

The first semblance of a national theater in Slovenia appeared when the writer Fran Levstik (1831-87) founded a dramatic company, composed entirely of Slovenians, in Ljubljana in 1876. Its most successful period came later with the advent of Slovenia's greatest writer, Ivan Cankar (1876-1918), who raised his country's drama to an international level. Cankar's *Za Narodov Blagor* (For the Good of the People) 1901, *Hlapci* (Servants) 1910, and *Lepa Vida* (The Beautiful Vida) 1912 examine the psychology of ordinary people and the suffering that life imposes on them; they often represent a bitterly satirical view of the cultural and economic situation in Slovenia.

The younger generation of Slovenian dramatists was led by the expressionist writer Ivo Brnić (1912-43), a literary critic and active partisan who, while fighting against Serbian collaborators, wrote *Between Four Walls*; and by Bratko Kreft (1905- ), whose major works are *Creature* and *The Count of Celje*.

### Since World War I

With the union, after World War I, of Serbia, Croatia and Slovenia, a closer relationship began to evolve between the various regions; the increase in cultural cooperation produced a considerable number of dramatic works, based particularly on war and rehabilitation.

They were performed in the three main theatrical centers: Zagreb, where the theater, thanks to the vigorous activity of its director, Julije Benesić, was rehoused in 1923; Belgrade, where the theater was rebuilt in the same year; and in Ljubljana, under the direction, until World War II, of Oton Župančić (1878-1949), the Slovenian poet, who wrote only one verse play, *Veronika Deseniska* (1924). The Slovenian theater is at present directed by the dramatist and poet Matej Bor (the pseudonym of Vladimir Pavšić), born in 1913.

Since the end of World War II, the growth of the theater in a united Yugoslavia has been phenomenal. In 1945 there were only six professional theaters; by 1950 there were at least 50. Almost every large town has an academy of dramatic art, and a repertory company performing an average of five plays a season, often with two casts playing alternately.

## THE MUSIC

THE DEVELOPMENT OF MUSIC IN Yugoslavia is a reflection of the country's history and its constant struggle for survival. Conditions were never ideal for the growth of any artistic form, but a national musical tradition began to assert itself in the 16th century.

Yugoslavia has an extremely rich and varied collection of folk melodies, which have been a constant source of inspiration to most native composers.

### Yugoslavian Composers

A Slovenian, Jacobus Gallus Petelin, known also as Jakob Handl (1550-91), was Yugoslavia's first well-known musician. He composed much religious music in a style that reveals the influence of the Venetian school.

The first Croatian composer of any real importance was Vatroslav Lisinski (1819-54). Lisinski, who lived an obscure and poverty-stricken existence, wrote the first opera with a Croatian libretto, *Love and Malice* (1846).

A contemporary of Lisinski, Ivan Zajc (1832-1914), studied at the Milan conservatoire and subsequently worked in Rijeka and Vienna. Appointed director of the Zagreb Opera House in 1870, he wrote a group of operatic works, of which the most popular was *Nikola Subić Zrinjski* (1876).

Serbia's best-known composer, Davorin Jenko (1835-1914), did much to make Yugoslavian musicians aware of European trends. As conductor of the Belgrade orchestra, Jenko composed many operas, overtures and choral works. His musical comedy *The Fortune Teller* drew extensively on Serbian folk melodies. Three other composers helped further Jenko's efforts to open up Yugoslavian music to modern Western ideas, without abandoning the rich background of folk tradition; they were Stevan Mokranjac (1856-1914), Franjo Serafin-Kalski Vilhar (1852-1928) and Emil Adamič (1877-1936).

Other composers, however, preferred to remain within the bounds of Serbia's own musical heritage. Petar Krstić (1877-1957) revealed some of its richness in his opera *The Highwayman* (1928), while Petar Konjović (1883-    ) and Miloje Milojevic (1884-1946) worked toward expressionist interpretations of folk themes.

Perhaps the most important composer working within this tradition was Josip Slavenski (1896-1955), whose work, orchestral, vocal and chamber, blends folk themes and modern techniques in such a way as to express effectively the passion and mysticism of the people of the Balkans. It has achieved international acclaim.

The Croatian composer Antun Dobranić (1878-1955) taught at the Zagreb Academy of Music from 1922 to 1940, during which time he produced a great variety of works, including 11 operas, five ballets, ten cantatas, seven symphonies, five string quartets and several other chamber compositions.

### CONTEMPORARY COMPOSERS

Some of the most significant recent work in Yugoslavia has been written by Božidor Sirola (1899-1956), Milko Keleman (1924-    ) and the conductor Lovro Matačič (1899-    ), who now lives in Berlin. Other important composers include Boris Papandopulo (1906-    ), who conducts the opera in Sarajevo; two of his operas are *Amphytrion* (1940) and *Sunflower* (1954). Jakov Gotovac (1895-    ) became conductor of the Zagreb opera in 1923; his work, such as the opera *Morana* (1930) and the highly successful *Ero the Joker* (1935), uses many elements of Croatian folk music.

The Yugoslavian people's love of music and the celebration in song of contemporary national heroism continues to inspire modern composers and enrich the development of a native musical tradition in Yugoslavia.

## THE FILM

YUGOSLAVIA HAD NO NATIONAL FILM industry before the end of World War II. The country was poor and weak after the rigors of World War I. There was, in addition, a lack of interest among potential investors in a film industry, because of the necessarily small audience for Yugoslavian films outside Yugoslavia itself.

Before 1946, there was only sporadic production of films in Yugoslavia. Most of the films produced were documentaries made by the cinematographic unit of the army.

Despite the dearth of home-produced films, an interest in the cinema began to awaken in Yugoslavia in the 1920s. Film clubs were formed in the towns. To satisfy the demands of the members of these clubs, foreign films —mostly American and German— were imported.

### The National Film Industry

The organized production of films in Yugoslavia began after the end of World War II. Studios were built in Belgrade (Serbia), Ljubljana (Slovenia), Zagreb (Croatia) and Sarajevo (Bosnia). Macedonia and Montenegro now also have studios, at Skoplje and Budva respectively.

Yugoslavia's film industry is not centralized, as in neighboring Hungary and Rumania. The two main centers for the production of films are Belgrade and Zagreb, and the film companies of these two cities are virtually rivals.

### First Feature Films

The very earliest productions of the newly established national film industry were a few short films and documentaries made in 1946.

The first feature film was *Slavica* (1947), directed by Vjeko Afrić (1906-    ). This initiated a series of many films dealing with the Yugoslavian Resistance in World War II and the effect of the war on the lives of ordinary people.

Another of these early films of the

*A scene from the film* Živeće ovaj narod *(This People Will Live) 1948, directed by Nikola Popović. This was one of the first Yugoslavian feature films. The action takes place in April 1941, when the German Army invaded Yugoslavia. Like many other early postwar films, it deals with the activities of Yugoslavian partisans in the Resistance against Germany in World War II.*

Resistance is *Živeće ovaj narod* (This People Will Live) 1948, directed by Nikola Popović.

### Folk Stories, Peasant Life and Partisans

Because of its tragic immediacy, the Resistance was by far the most popular source of screenplays in the early postwar years.

In the early 1950s, however, a few directors sought inspiration in other spheres. *Čudotvorni mač* (The Magic Sword) 1950, directed by Vojislav Nanovic (1922-    ), was based on popular folk tales and set in a fairytale world of wicked monsters and brave heroes.

In *Sumnjivo lice* (The Suspect) 1953, directed by Predrag Dinulović (1917-    ) and Sofija-Soja Jovanović (1922-    ), the action takes place at the end of the 19th century.

The peasant world and its traditions inspired the excellent work of Fedor Hanžeković (1913-    ), director of *Svoga tela gospodar* (Master of his Own Body) 1957.

#### VLADIMIR POGAČIĆ

One of the leading directors of this period is Vladimir Pogačić (1919-    ), an actor and director with the National Theater of Zagreb. His first successful film was *Veliki i Mali* (Big and Little People) 1952, which is noteworthy for its psychological subtlety.

Pagočić's *Pukotina raja* (Heaven without Love) 1960 is the story of an unhappy marriage ending in the suicide of the wife.

#### TALES OF WAR

World War II and the Resistance have continued to fascinate Yugoslav

directors, dominating their work even into the 1960s. Velicu Bulasić, who has made several good semi-documentary films, was less successful with his more ambitious film *Rat* (War) 1961. Its screenplay was by Cesare Zavattini (1902-    ), a leading Italian scriptwriter.

*Deveti krug* (The Ninth Circle) 1961, directed by France Stiglić (1919-    ), is one of the best recent Yugoslavian films. It concerns a Jewish girl who, to save her life, marries a Christian after the Nazi pogroms.

*Vrtlog* (Whirlpool) 1964, directed by Hajrudin Krvavac and Gojko Šipovac, is a trilogy of three short films dealing with incidents in the war.

### Animated Films

Yugoslavia is particularly outstanding in the field of animated films. The center for the production of these films is Zagreb, where a brilliant team of animators has been making cartoons since 1956.

The Zagreb cartoons are often witty satires. In *Surogat* (The Substitute) by Dušan Vukotić, a plastic, inflatable universe is occupied by plastic, inflatable characters.

Many of the Yugoslavian cartoons nevertheless show great warmth and sympathy with the human condition.

*Piccolo* (1959), by Dušan Vukotić, which portrays the trials of the "little man," won First Prize for animated films in the Cork (Ireland) Film Festival of 1959.

One of the most brilliant films produced by the Zagreb company is *Don Quixote* by Vlado Kristl. In this film, with the introduction of live-action windmills, there is a marriage of cartoon and live-action forms.

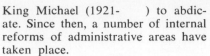

## POSITION AND BOUNDARIES

RUMANIA IS A COUNTRY OF DANUBIAN Europe, roughly circular in shape, situated in the northeast part of the Balkán Peninsula. The country has a total area of 91,678 square miles and a population of around 18,681,000.

Rumania is situated between latitudes 48° 20′ N.—near Lipkany, on the U.S.S.R. side of the frontier—and 43° 70′ N.—near Zimnicea, on the Bulgarian border. Its easternmost point is at 29° 30′ E., at Sfantu-Gheorghe on the Danube Delta, its westernmost point at 20° 20′ E., about 15 miles southwest of Mako (in Hungary).

Rumania is bordered on the south by Bulgaria; on the southwest and west by Yugoslavia; on the northwest by Hungary; on the north and east by the U.S.S.R.; and on the southeast by the Black Sea. Its coastline on the Black Sea extends for about 180 miles in a straight line, from north of Sulina, near the border of the U.S.S.R., in the north, to below Mangalia, near the Bulgarian border, in the south.

## ORGANIZATION OF THE STATE

### Administrative Districts

THE RUMANIAN PEOPLE'S REPUBLIC was proclaimed on Dec. 30, 1947, the date on which the ever-increasing power of the Communist party forced King Michael (1921- ) to abdicate. Since then, a number of internal reforms of administrative areas have taken place.

A measure of stability appears to have been achieved in 1960, when the country was divided into 16 administrative areas, with two additional autonomous administrations for the major cities of Bucharest and Constanta.

In alphabetical order, the administrative areas of Rumania are now: Arges; Bacau; Banat; Brasov; Bucharest; Cluj; Crisana; Dobruja; Galati; Hunedoara; Jassy; Maramures; Mures (also called the Hungarian, or Magyar, Autonomous Region); Oltenia; Ploesti; Suceava; and the city administrations of Bucharest and Constanta.

### The Constitution

The first Constitution of the Rumanian People's Republic was promulgated on April 13, 1948. It was replaced by the Constitution of Sept. 24, 1952, which was amended in 1954 and 1961.

The Constitution defines Rumania as a state of urban and rural workers, who exercise complete power through their elected representatives. Civil liberties, freedom of speech, press and political demonstration, and the rights to work, leisure, social security and religious belief are guaranteed to all citizens. Fascism and "anti-democratic" activities are outlawed.

### The Legislature

The supreme legislative and administrative power is vested in the Grand National Assembly, which is composed of deputies elected for a four-year term, on the basis of one deputy for every 40,000 inhabitants. The Assembly elected in 1961 was composed of 465 deputies. Every citizen over the age of 18 has the right to vote and the right to stand for election after being put forward by one or other of the recognized social or political organizations.

#### THE RUMANIAN WORKERS' PARTY

The Grand National Assembly is dominated, like all Rumanian poli-

*The Danube at Varciorova, a village in southwestern Rumania. Varciorova lies three miles above the Iron Gate, a gorge where the river narrows to pass between the Carpathians and the Balkans. Nearby is Ada-Kaleh, a small island the majority of whose inhabitants are Turkish, and which is noted for tobacco and sugar.*

*Lacul-Rosu (Red Lake), situated in the Eastern Carpathians at an altitude of 3215 feet, is a noted vacation resort. It lies about 15 miles away from the town of Gheorgheni, an important lumbering center. The geological structure of the Carpathians resembles that of the Alpine chain, but the elevation of the Carpathians is less and contours softer.*

tical life, by the Rumanian Workers' Party. Although only 6 per cent of the population are party members (as in Russia, it is difficult to become a party member), at the 1961 election 70 per cent of deputies elected belonged to the party. In fact, this election was conducted with a single list of candidates, described as the Popular Democratic Front, and the remaining 30 per cent of elected deputies, though officially described as "independent," differ very little politically from the general party line.

Voting in elections is regarded as a primary duty of the citizen, and the total poll is usually around 99 per cent of the electorate. In addition to its control of the Grand National Assembly, the Rumanian Workers' Party also elects the powerful organs of the Politburo and Secretariat, which exercise enormous power in determining internal and external policy.

The Grand National Assembly convenes for two short sessions every year. When it is not in session, power is exercised by the State Council, which is elected by the assembly from among its members. The State Council consists of the Head of the State, as chairman; three deputy-chairmen; 12 members; and the secretary.

### PEOPLE'S COUNCILS

On a regional level, executive power is wielded by the People's Councils, under the direction of the Grand National Assembly. These are elected for two-year terms by the electors of the various regions, districts, urban and rural areas. They are responsible for the proper working of local government, the control of economic and cultural activities, the preparation of local budgets and the administration of the higher executive's laws with regard to local conditions.

## The Judiciary

Justice is administered by courts ranging in importance from the Supreme Court, down through the 16 Regional Courts, to the local People's Courts. All courts, however, are under the supervision of the Procurator-General, who is appointed for a five-year term by the Grand National Assembly and the State Council, to whom he is responsible. In addition, People's Assessors, appointed for four-year terms, sit in equal cooperation with judges in all courts.

Since 1956, all private legal practice has been illegal. All advocates are now appointed and supervised by the Ministry of Justice.

## Religion

Freedom of religion is guaranteed to all citizens by the Constitution. In practice, however, religion is by no means encouraged and clergy of all denominations are sometimes subjected to obstructions or restrictions in the exercise of their duties. All religions are subject to the supervision of a special government department —the Department of Cults. Religious education is discouraged and, in some cases, totally banned.

### THE RUMANIAN ORTHODOX CHURCH

The greater part of the population belongs to the Rumanian Orthodox Church, which has an estimated membership of over 13,500,000. Under a law passed on Feb. 23, 1949, the Church is administered by four administrative and legislative bodies, the chief of which is the Holy Synod.

In 1958, the Rumanian Orthodox Church was divided into 12 dioceses,

Sibiu respectively, while the Unitarians have a bishopric at Cluj. Of the other Protestant sects, the Baptists, Adventists, Evangelicals and Pentecostals have formed a federation with about 2000 congregations throughout Rumania.

The Jews (140,000) have three separate congregations, which are now federated under a Chief Rabbi, while the Moslem minority is governed by a Mufti, whose seat is at Constanta.

### Education

Education in Rumania is free and compulsory for all children between the ages of seven and 15 years. The educational system is rigidly supervised by the state, and great emphasis is laid on scientific and technological subjects, as well as on political education.

In recent years, great improvements have been made in the provision of secondary and higher education. In 1963, there were 7615 kindergartens and primary schools; 15,496 general and evening schools; and nine teachers' training colleges. In addition, there were three universities —at Bucharest, Jassy and Cluj—and eight provincial institutes of higher education, offering between them the choice of 165 faculties to 98,810 students.

The highest scientific education is provided by the Rumanian Academy of Sciences, which has its headquarters at Bucharest, branches in Jassy and Cluj and research centers at Timisoara and Targu-Mures.

It administers 32 research institutes and an observatory, and accommodates around 2500 research workers.

Some 3500 schools exist for the various national minorities of Rumania. The medical faculty of Cluj University provides instruction in Hungarian, while the well-organized German minority is estimated to have 264 elementary schools, 11 secondary schools and a theological college at Sibiu.

### Language

The Rumanian language has a Latin basis, which has undergone Slav, Turkish and other Eastern influences.

with 10,165 clergy. There were 5814 members of monastic and conventual orders, two theological colleges and six seminaries.

The Great Catholic, or Uniate, Church became united with the Orthodox community after breaking away from the Vatican (with which it had been associated since 1698), in 1948, when it was estimated to have around 1,300,000 members.

#### THE ROMAN CATHOLIC CHURCH

The Roman Catholic Church in Rumania is in a difficult position, since it has not been approved by statute and is not officially connected with the Vatican. Roman Catholic clergy have been imprisoned for varying periods and the administrative divisions of the church have been limited to the archbishopric of Bucharest-Jassy and the bishopric of Alba Iulia. It is estimated that the Roman Catholic Church in Rumania now has around 820 priests and 254 members of monastic orders.

The Calvinists (780,000 members) and the Lutherans (250,000) have bishoprics at Cluj and Oradea and at

It has four main dialects, of which Daco-Rumanian is the language used by most of the 15 million Rumanian-speaking nationals. The other dialects are Macedo-Rumanian, spoken mainly in Greece, Yugoslavia and Bulgaria; Megleno-Rumanian, spoken in isolated areas of northern Greece; and Istro-Rumanian, spoken mainly in Istria, on the northern Adriatic coast.

A large number of languages are spoken by minorities in Rumania. In order of importance these are: Hungarian (1,653,700); German (395,374); Ukrainian and Ruthenian (68,252); Russian (54,029); Yugoslavian (43,057); Hebrew and Yiddish (34,337); Tatar (30,574); Turkish (14,228); and Bulgarian (13,189).

### Coinage, Weights and Measures

The basic monetary unit of Rumania is the *leu* (plural *leï*), which is divided into 100 *bani*. Since 1954, the value of the *leu* has been tied to that of the Russian *rouble,* with an exchange rate, in 1961, of 6.67 *leï* to 1 *rouble.* The *leu* is valued at 0.148112 grams of gold, giving an exchange rate of around 6 *leï* to the U.S. dollar. However, exchange rates differ according to whether the currency is being used for commercial or non-commercial transactions, and concessions are often made to give more favorable rates to foreign tourists or businessmen, in order to encourage trade with other countries.

The State Bank of the Rumanian People's Republic was founded in 1948, after the dissolution of almost all other banks. It is under the supervision of the Ministry of Finance, and issues notes for 10, 25 and 100 *leï.*

The metric system of weights and measures has been in official use in Rumania since 1876.

---

## PHYSICAL GEOGRAPHY

---

### The Relief

RUMANIA'S SURFACE IS CHARACTERIZED by a wide variety of contours, since the country is divided almost equally into mountains (26 per cent), hills (39 per cent) and plains (35 per cent).

#### THE CARPATHIANS

The most important feature of the country's topography is the great chain of the Carpathian Mountains.

The Carpathian chain extends through Czechoslovakia and the U.S.S.R. into Rumania. The mountains run in a southeasterly direction for some 185 miles, separating Moldavia from Transylvania, and here are often known as the Moldavian Carpathians. The chain then turns to run in a southwesterly direction toward the Yugoslavian border, completing a semicircle which encloses the Transylvanian Basin, separating it from Walachia and the lower Danube plain in the extreme south. This stretch of the Carpathians is generally known as the Transylvanian Alps, and extends for some 150 miles.

Outside the arc of mountains enclosing Transylvania, to the south, lies the great alluvial plain of Walachia, into which the mountains descend in a series of foothills. East of this plain lies the area of Dobruja, on the coast of the Black Sea.

*A panoramic view of the central part of the Moldavian Carpathians (185 miles long and 35 miles wide), the natural boundary between Moldavia in the east and Transylvania in the west. The Moldavian Carpathians reach their highest point in the peaks of Ciucas (6425 feet) and Ceahlau (6245 feet). Like the other Carpathian ranges, the Moldavians are very thinly populated.*

The Carpathians may be loosely considered as a continuation of the Alps, linking them to the Balkans. Their structure is, however, extremely complex. The earliest corrugations of the earth's surface which led to the formation of the Carpathians probably took place in the Paleozoic era, some 45-100 million years ago, while the latest date from the Pliocene period, some 2-11 million years ago.

The Carpathians differ from the Alps in having a lower overall height, more rounded summits and a general lack of sharp outline, caused by intense erosion. Thus the Carpathians, though extensive, have never offered a serious obstacle to communication between one part of Rumania and another.

### THE MOLDAVIAN CARPATHIANS

The Moldavian Carpathians are separated from the southern Carpathian ranges, or Transylvanian Alps, in the region of the Predeal Pass, near Brasov. The Moldavian Carpathians, which are thickly forested, consist of three more or less parallel chains, the center chain consisting of ancient crystalline rocks, while the eastern and western ranges are composed mainly of softer rocks of later periods. Elevations in general decrease from north to south, and the central range is generally higher than the eastern and western ranges, which fall fairly steeply into Transylvania in the west and more gently, in a series of foothills, to Moldavia in the east. The western range is also distinguished by a number of features of volcanic origin, containing rich mineral deposits.

### THE TRANSYLVANIAN ALPS

The Transylvanian Alps lie at right angles to the Moldavian Carpathians, stretching from the Predeal Pass to the Iron Gate gorge on the Yugoslavian border. They are composed of granites, slates and crystalline rock formations and are generally higher than the Moldavian Carpathians, the main peaks being Negoi (8346 feet), Moldoveanu (8344 feet), Retezat (8236 feet) and Godeanu (7278 feet).

The Transylvanian Alps are also characterized by their undulating foothills to the south, utilized by shepherds as summer pastures; a wide distribution of glacial formations giving rise to a number of lakes, natural amphitheaters and areas of plateau; and the many passes caused by the erosive action of rivers flowing either northward into the Banat or southward into the Walachian Plain. One of these rivers, the Olt, completely traverses the range between Avrig and Valcea, a distance of some 50 miles, with a further course through the foothills to the south.

### THE WESTERN CARPATHIANS

In the northwest of Rumania the Western Carpathians, or Apuseni

*The Iron Gate, a narrow, desolate gorge, two miles long, on the Danube. It lies three miles below Varciorova and separates the Balkans and Carpathians. In 1896, the construction of the Sip Canal removed the rocks on the river-bed, which had formerly proved dangerous to navigation.*

Mountains, complete the encirclement of Transylvania and mark the last part of the Carpathian system in Rumania. This range consists of an ancient mass of upthrust and fractured rock, deeply scored by watercourses and characterized, like the Moldavian Carpathians, by the presence of volcanic formations containing mineral deposits and by rounded summits.

Rumania is divided into five historical areas, which roughly correspond to geographical areas: Moldavia, Transylvania, the Banat, Walachia and Dobruja.

### MOLDAVIA

Rumanian Moldavia lies between the foothills of the eastern Moldavian Carpathians and the Prut River, which marks the border of Rumania with the Moldavian Republic, part of the U.S.S.R. The southern part of the area consists mainly of plain and marshland interspersed with patches of loess. Central and western Moldavia consists mainly of hill country, and northern Moldavia is mainly high plateau, these regions having an average elevation of between 1000 and 2000 feet. The areas of hill and plateau are traversed by numerous watercourses, notably the Siret, Barlad and Prut and their tributaries, most of which flow from north to south.

### TRANSYLVANIA

Transylvania, in west-central Rumania, is enclosed, as has been described, by the various ranges of the Carpathian system. It is not so much a plateau as a collection of hills of varying heights separated by valleys. It has an average elevation of around 1500 feet, sloping downward from east to west and from south to north.

Transylvania is watered by a number of rivers flowing between the Moldavian Carpathians and the Bihor Mountains, notably the Tîrnava Mica and Tîrnava Mare, the branches of the Mures River, and the Aries River. It is rich in both vegetation and mineral resources.

### THE BANAT

Only the eastern part of the Banat region, in the extreme west of Rumania, is Rumanian territory, the remainder belonging to Yugoslavia. It is composed of the southern fringe of the Hungarian Plain, which was formerly a great lake and is still subject to subsidence. In appearance, it is a flat plain covered by steppe and

*The wild and picturesque Bicaz Gorge, a popular tourist resort in Bacau province, northeastern Rumania. The nearby village of Bicaz is a base both for excursions to this resort and the neighboring one of the Ceahlau Mountains. At one time, Bicaz was the summer residence of Rumanian royalty.*

marshland, but drainage has made it an extremely fertile area and it is therefore thickly populated.

To the north of the Banat and the northwest of Transylvania lie other small portions of the Hungarian Plain, which form part of the Rumanian territory. These are the regions of Crisana and Maramures, whose geographical characteristics closely resemble those of the Banat.

### WALACHIA

Walachia is situated in southern Rumania between the foothills of the Transylvanian Alps and the Bulgarian border, which is marked by the Danube River. It is separated from Dobruja by the lower Danube, which flows from the Bulgarian border around Silistra to the U.S.S.R. border of Rumania, the easternmost part of which it delineatates, east of Galati.

Walachia slopes gently down from the Transylvanian Alps to the Danube. It is characterized by coniferous forests in the foothills of the extreme north, large tracts of broadleaved forest in the center, and extensive areas of steppe in the south and east. The extensive plains nearest to the Danube are subject to heavy flooding in the spring and there are large areas of marshland.

### DOBRUJA

Dobruja is situated in the extreme east of the country, between the lower Danube and the Black Sea coast. It is mainly flat and low-lying with an area of higher elevation, the Dobrujan massif, in the north near the border of the U.S.S.R.

The greater part of Dobruja consists of arid steppe-land of chalk and sandstone, furrowed by deep valleys

*The headquarters of Rumania's Ministry of Transport and Telecommunications in Bucharest. From this modern building the Communist government controls the telephone system, radio and television. The last two, being state-owned, are widely used to disseminate political propaganda. Rumania has 15 broadcasting stations.*

running from the Black Sea to the Danube. Its western borders and the extreme north, in the area of the Danube Delta, are marshy and its interior poorly watered, so that the greatest areas of settlement are found on the southern borders and the coastline.

### The Coastline

Rumania's Black Sea coastline, which corresponds to the eastern border of Dobruja, extends for around 180 miles. It is characterized in the north by the marshy area of the Danube Delta and in the center by large lakes, or lagoons, formed by relatively recent geological subsidences. The southern stretch is most suitable for the construction of harbors, and it is there that the main ports, such as Constanta and Mangalia, are situated.

### Hydrography

In spite of certain unfavorable tendencies in the climate, the river network of Rumania is well developed. An exception is in Dobruja, where a preponderance of calceous rock restricts the development of surface hydrography. The main Rumanian watercourses rise in the mountainous central part of the country and flow outward into the plains, finally merging with the Danube.

### THE DANUBE

The Danube, with a course of 1750 miles, is the second longest river in Europe. About two-fifths of its course, some 675 miles, is through Rumania, though the greater part of this course defines the borders with Yugoslavia and Bulgaria in the south and, for a short distance, with the U.S.S.R. in the north.

That part of the Danube which divides Yugoslavia from Rumania passes through the impressive gorge known as the Iron Gate, situated on a stretch of about 40 miles between Orsova and Turnu-Severin. The gorge is more than 100 yards across at its narrowest point, and is deep and swiftly flowing.

After emerging from the Iron Gate, the Danube flows southward for a short distance, bending eastward south of Radujevac to mark the Bulgarian border. The Walachian lowland, on the north bank, is low-lying and marshy, in contrast to the higher ground on the southern, Bulgarian bank. This long border stretch, extending as far as Silistra, has a uniform gradient and is on average just over half a mile wide. It is here that the Danube receives most of its important Rumanian tributaries.

At Silistra, the Danube makes a sharp northward turn, leaving the

Bulgarian border and flowing past the foot of the Dobrujan massif. A little to the east of Galati, the river bends sharply eastward, to form the border with the U.S.S.R. It is flanked on the northern, Russian bank by a number of large lakes, and on the Rumanian side it branches out into three main arms which enclose its delta.

### TRIBUTARIES OF THE DANUBE

The first group of the Danube's tributaries reach the river by way of the Tisza River. These are the Sebes Koros, in the extreme north, and the Crisul Negru, further south, which receive their waters from the Bihor Mountains. Further south, the Mures flows between the Bihor and the Transylvanian ranges to join the Tisza slightly to the north of Szeged in Hungary. The Mures, fed by mountain streams, is subject to heavy flooding in spring and summer.

The second group of the Danube's tributaries are the rivers which flow southward or southeastward from the Transylvanian Alps. These are the Jiu, with its tributary the Motrul; the Olt, which rises in the Moldavian Carpathians; the Vedea; and the Arges; all these rivers join the Danube on the Bulgarian border between Orekhovo and Turtucaia.

To the third group of the Danube's tributaries belong those which rise to the east of the Carpathians. The most important of these are the Siret, with its tributaries the Barlad and the Buzau, and the Prut. The Prut rises in Soviet territory and the greater part of its course, before joining the Danube at Reni, marks the eastern border of Rumania with the U.S.S.R.

### LAKES

Rumania has a large number of lakes, but most of them are small and of little importance. The most important as regards area is Lake Razelm, a 25-mile-long stretch of water, rich in fish, which lies on the Black Sea coast in Dobruja. Of the Danubian lakes the most important is Lake Brates, situated on the border of the U.S.S.R. near the confluence of the Prut and Danube.

### Climate

Rumania has a predominantly European continental climate, with mountainous characteristics in the Carpathians and steppe characteristics in the plains. However, the country is subject to great seasonal and regional variations in climate.

*CLIMATIC VARIATIONS*

These variations are partly due to the presence of the mountain masses, which form a barrier to masses of moving air, and partly to the influence of two prevailing winds. These are the winter *crivat*, a northeast wind from the Russian steppes, and the summer *austru*, a southwest wind, which renders summer temperatures more extreme.

The variation in temperature may be illustrated by the average winter and summer temperatures of Bucharest, where there is an average January temperature of 26.6° F., sometimes falling below 10° F., and an average July temparture of 71.6° F., frequently rising to over 100° F. Similarly, Bucharest has around 80 days of frost each year, with a similar number of days of tropical heat.

Broadly speaking, Rumania has only three seasons—winter, summer and fall—since the transition between winter and summer is a very short period. Winters are long and hard, with frequent snow; the Carpathians have a rate of snowfall which is among the highest in Europe. Summer conditions are characterized by extremely high temperatures, while fall is the most temperate season in all parts of the country.

*RAINFALL*

Rainfall reaches a maximum in early summer and falls to a minimum in late summer, when periods of drought often occur. The plains of Moldavia and Walachia have the lowest rainfall, with less than 20 inches annually, while the Carpathians, particularly the western Transylvanian Alps, have the highest rainfall, sometimes approaching 60 inches annually.

## HUMAN GEOGRAPHY

### History of Settlement

RUMANIA IS, GENERALLY SPEAKING, A favorable area for human settlement and has probably been populated since the earliest times. The oldest known remains date back to the Paleolithic age, when the area appears to have been inhabited by a nomadic, cave-dwelling Neanderthal type.

Numerous traces of settlement during the Neolithic age have been discovered, notably around Jassy and Craiova, revealing the existence of a people living by primitive agriculture and stockraising. After about 2000 B.C., Indo-European nomads from the northeast passed through Rumania on their migrations westward, and it is from their fusion with the indigenous inhabitants that the Dacians, the ancestors of the modern Rumanians, sprang.

### THE INFLUENCE OF INVADERS

It is not possible to establish exactly the effect of Roman occupation of Dacia on the modern Rumanian ethnic makeup. Dacia was conquered by the Romans around the end of the 1st century A.D., and finally abandoned by them in 271 A.D.;

*Bucharest from the Balcescu Boulevard, the wide avenue stretching across that part of the city which includes the Institute of Economic Sciences, the Institute of "Lenin" Planning and the Curtea Veche Church. Some of the most important public buildings in the capital face onto this boulevard, such as the University Central Library, the National Theater, the State Bank and the Savings Bank.*

## RUMANIA AREA AND POPULATION

| REGION | AREA (sq. miles) | POPULATION (1962) |
|---|---|---|
| Arges | 6099 | 1,184,000 |
| Bacau | 5172 | 1,089,000 |
| Banat | 8415 | 1,236,000 |
| Brasov | 5825 | 1,052,000 |
| Bucharest | 7905 | 1,677,000 |
| Bucharest (city) | 374 | 1,354,000 |
| Cluj | 6493 | 1,212,000 |
| Constanta (city) | 205 | 151,000 |
| Crisana | 4725 | 874,000 |
| Dobruja | 5968 | 512,000 |
| Galati | 4983 | 1,056,000 |
| Hunedoara | 4246 | 646,000 |
| Jassy | 4285 | 1,041,000 |
| Maramures | 4053 | 774,000 |
| Mures (Magyar Autonomous Region | 4729 | 810,000 |
| Oltenia | 7836 | 1,568,000 |
| Ploesti | 5057 | 1,451,000 |
| Suceava | 5308 | 994,000 |
| TOTAL | 91,678 | 18,681,000 |

a number of modern Rumanian towns have sprung from what were originally Roman settlements.

In later periods, the inhabitants of Rumania were also influenced both ethnically and culturally by settlement or military occupation of large numbers of Slavs, Hungarians, Germans and Turks.

### Development of Population

In 1914, before the territorial gains made as a consequence of World War I, the population of Rumania was estimated at 7,600,000. By 1930, however, this had risen to 18,025,237, and in 1940 to 19,930,000, its highest total to date. World War II, however, saw great loss of life and a further diminution of the population, due to the murder or deportation of a great number of Jews. Territorial losses were accompanied by the emigration of many of the remaining Jews to Israel and the expulsion of a great number of Germans and Hungarians. In 1948 the population had fallen to 15,872,624.

In recent years, however, the population of Rumania has risen rapidly. This increase is due partly to the absence of emigration, partly to a fairly high birthrate (amounting to 17.5 per 1000 population in 1960, with an infant mortality rate of 69 per 1000 live births), and partly to an increasingly low mortality rate (8.7 per 1000 population in 1960).

### Distribution of Population

The average density of the population has risen from around 96 per square mile in 1930, to around 123 per square mile in 1956 and an estimated 126 per square mile in 1963. The average density does not differ very greatly from region to region, since settlement is fairly evenly distributed throughout the country.

The highest population is found in the region of Bucharest, which had a total population of 1,677,000 in 1962. The other most densely populated regions in the same year were, in order, Oltenia (1,568,000); Ploesti (1,451,000); the Banat (1,236,000); and Cluj (1,212,000).

### RACIAL MINORITIES

Of the racial minorities, the Hungarians, the most numerous, live mainly in Mures and in the towns of the northwest, near the Hungarian border. The Germans are mainly concentrated in Brasov and Sibiu, in central Rumania, and in the Banat region. The chief Jewish communities are near the Russian border in the Prut Valley, as are the Ukrainian and Ruthenian minorities. The Yugoslavians and Bulgarians tend to concentrate in the towns nearest to the borders of their respective countries of origin, while the Turks and Tatars are mainly settled in the coastal district around Constanta.

### Cities

BUCHAREST (*pop. 1,354,000*)

Bucharest, the largest city of Rumania, is the capital of the country and of the region to which it gives its name. It is situated in the center of the Walachian Plain on the Dambovita River and covers an area of around 40 square miles. The city is built on the site of the Roman fortress of Cetatea Dambovitei, and its development dates from the 14th century. Bucharest underwent a period of great expansion in the 17th and 18th centuries, when the population included a Greek majority, and became the capital of Walachia and Moldavia in 1859. It suceeded Jassy as capital of Rumania in 1881.

The modern city, surrounding part of the old town, lies on the right bank of the river, while the remainder of the old town is situated on the left bank. A number of ancient buildings, including the 16th-century Curtea Veche Church, the 17th-century Coltea Church and three 18th-century churches, lie on the left bank, while on the right bank are the monastery church of Prince Mihai (1594) and the 18th-century monasteries of Antim and Vacaresti.

Among notable modern buildings are the University, founded in 1864 and rebuilt after damage during air-

*The Boulevard 23rd August in Timisoara, a town situated in the middle of the Banat 250 miles northwest of Bucharest. The center of the town was formerly surrounded by ramparts which have now been converted into boulevards. Among its more interesting buildings are a Roman Catholic church with a leaning tower and a 15th-century castle of the Hunyadis.*

raids in World War II, the Palace of Justice (1895), the Palace of the Council of Ministers (1938), the Opera House (1953), and the Scinteia Printing House, the largest building in the city (built 1950-55).

Modern Bucharest is a cultural center, with various types of colleges, excellent theaters, museums, art galleries and libraries; and a communications center, with a modern airport at Banasea. The rate of its commercial expansion in the present century may be judged by the comparison of its present population with the 1914 figure of 345,628 and the 1939 figure of 648,162. Its main industries include textiles, automobiles, agricultural machinery, grain processing, chemicals and pharmaceuticals, and oil refining.

## ARAD *(pop. 113,730)*

Arad is situated on the Mures River in western Rumania, not far from the Hungarian border. An ancient town, it was fortified as a military stronghold by the Turks in the 17th century and was the headquarters of the Hungarian revolt against the Turks in 1849.

Arad is a center of railroad communications and a rapidly developing commercial and industrial city. It serves as a market for the agricultural produce of the surrounding region and its industries include wine, grain-processing, tobacco, leather goods, textiles and timber.

## BACAU *(pop. 64,130)*

Bacau, the capital of the region of the same name, is situated on the Bistrita River, a tributary of the Siret, in the Carpathian foothills of eastern Rumania. It is an important center of railroad communications and commerce, and its industries include

oil-refining, textiles, paper and timber products.

## BRAILA (pop. 116,364)

Braila is an important river port on the Danube, situated not far from the Russian border some 140 miles northeast of Bucharest. It is the chief center of grain exporting, possessing three-and-a-half miles of modern port installations and a warehousing capacity of 300,000 tons. It is also a center of railroad communications on the main line from Bucharest into the U.S.S.R. Lacu-Sarat, six miles away, is a popular tourist resort.

## BRASOV (pop. 131,172)

Brasov (renamed Orasul Stalin between 1950 and 1960) is the capital of the region of the same name in Transylvania. It is situated in the western foothills of the Transylvanian Alps, not far from the Predeal Pass. The city was founded as a Saxon stronghold in the 13th century and contains a number of ancient buildings, notably the Black Church, a Gothic structure dating from 1385-1425.

Modern Brasov is an important center of road and rail communications, and also a commercial center. Its industries include engineering and metallurgical workshops, chemicals, textiles, cement and petroleum.

## CLUJ (pop. 164,933)

Cluj is the largest city of Transylvania and is the capital of the region to which it gives its name. It lies on the Little Somes River at the eastern foot of the Bihor Mountains. Cluj was founded in the 12th century and from the 16th century onward was a center of Hungarian influence. Its notable buildings include the Gothic church of St. Michael (1396-1432) and the University.

Cluj is now an expanding industrial center, and a center of uranium mining. Its industries include textiles, brewing and paper-making.

## CONSTANTA (pop. 151,000)

Constanta, the capital of the region of Dobruja, is a seaport on the Black Sea some 125 miles east of Bucha-

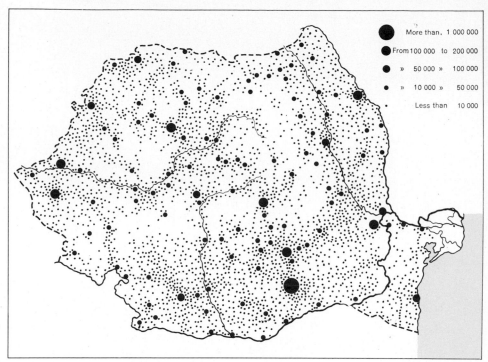

*Map showing the distribution of population in Rumania.*

rest. It is an ancient town, founded by the Roman Emperor Constantine in the 3rd-4th centuries A.D., but it is now mainly of modern construction, having been rebuilt in the 19th century and again after extensive damage in World War I.

Constanta is Rumania's major seaport, with three miles of modern quays capable of accommodating 30 vessels. It is the main center for the export of petroleum and wheat and for the import of fuel, textiles, machinery and manufactured metal goods.

## CRAIOVA (pop. 115,706)

Craiova, the capital of the province of Dolj, is situated on the Jiu River in western Walachia, in a rich agricultural area. The city was founded as a Roman settlement, under the name of Castra Nova, and has a long history as the center of Walachian military and political life.

Modern Craiova is the chief commercial center of western Rumania, providing a market for the produce of the region, mainly cattle and cereals, and for local pottery, textiles and leather goods. Its industries include the manufacture of soap, candles, rope and railroad rolling-stock.

## GALATI (pop. 109,657)

Galati, the capital of the region of the same name, is situated on the

Danube, in Moldavia. It is an important river port, the main center for the export of timber and the center for all imports. The city has a cathedral and a number of fine churches and is an important military base.

## JASSY (pop. 124,853)

Jassy is the capital of the region of Moldavia to which it gives its name.

It became the capital of Moldavia in 1565. Its ancient buildings include two 15th-century churches and the Byzantine church of Trei Ierarhi (1640).

Jassy is a cultural center with the oldest university in Rumania and a number of fine museums and art galleries. Its industries include wine, foodstuffs, textiles and chemicals.

## ORADEA (pop. 109,269)

Oradea is the capital of Bihor province in Crisana and is situated on the Rapide Körös River, near the Hungarian frontier. Oradea has had a stormy history, being occupied between the 13th and 20th centuries, by Rumanians, Tatars, Austrians, Turks and Hungarians, before finally returning to Rumania after World War II.

Among the ancient buildings preserved in Oradea are the 12th-century church of St. Ladislas, the Roman Catholic cathedral (1752-79) and the

*Characteristic of many of the churches scattered throughout Walachia and Moldavia are the frescoes that decorate the exterior walls of this 15th-century church of St. Nicholas in Jassy. The city is notable for its university, many academies and museums and for its outstanding church architecture. It was the capital of Rumania from 1565 to 1861, and during the last century became a leading center of culture.*

Legend (map):
More than 1 000 000
From 100 000 to 200 000
» 50 000 » 100 000
» 10 000 » 50 000
Less than 10 000

*Despite increasing attention to development of industry, Rumania is still a predominantly agricultural country, with about 70 per cent of the working population employed on the land. The government, which has nationalized almost all the land, has embarked on a crash program of mechanization to increase production.*

18th-century Rococo palace of the Roman Catholic bishop. Modern Oradea is a railroad junction and a marketing center for agricultural produce. Industrial development in the present century, mainly in the fields of ceramics, engineering and distilling, has been mainly responsible for the increase in population from 47,018 in 1900 to the present figure.

### PLOESTI (pop. 129,222)

Ploesti the capital of Prahova province in Walachia, is situated in the Carpathian foothills, some 45 miles north of Bucharest. The old quarter of the city contains the Orthodox church of St. Mary (1640).

Modern Ploesti is situated in an area which is rich in deposits of petroleum, and the city is Rumania's main center of the petroleum industry. There are many large oil refineries and plants for the manufacture and maintenance of oil-drilling machinery. In addition, there are industries for the manufacture of cardboard, rope and leather goods.

### SIBIU (pop. 99,318)

Sibiu, the capital of the province of the same name, is situated in central Rumania in the northern foothills of the Transylvanian Alps. The city stands on the site of the Roman settlement of Libinium and was founded as a Saxon stronghold in the 12th century. Today a large proportion of the population is of Germanic extraction.

Sibiu was an important city during the Middle Ages, and a number of ancient buildings still remain, among them a 14th-century church with a 15th-century font and murals, and a 15th-century town hall. The town is a cultural center with an excellent museum.

Industries include brewing, distilling and the manufacture of textiles, leather goods, footwear and soap.

### SUCEAVA (pop. 23,603)

Suceava is situated on the Suceava River, in Bukovina. It is an ancient city which was, until 1564, the capital of Moldavia and the seat of the Moldavian princes. Among its historic buildings are a 14th-century fortress and the 17th-century Byzantine monastery of Dragomirna. The town is a tourist resort and is famed for its leatherwork.

### TIMISOARA (pop. 147,738)

Timisoara is the capital of the province of the same name in the Banat, in western Rumania, and is situated on the Bega canal not far from the Yugoslavian frontier. It was destroyed by the Tatars in the 13th century and later suffered occupation by the Hungarians, Turks and Serbs.

Among the historic monuments preserved in Timisoara are the Roman Catholic church (1735-57), the Greek Orthodox cathedral, and the arsenal, which is composed of the remains of the 15th-century Hunyadi Castle.

Modern Timisoara is an important center of communications and commerce. Industrial expansion, mainly in the fields of petroleum, paper and tobacco, has been rapid.

#### OTHER IMPORTANT TOWNS

Other important towns in Rumania include Baia-Mare (pop. 44,422), the capital of the Maramures region and a mining center on the Somes River; Hunedoara (pop. 51,911), an iron-mining and metallurgical center in Transylvania; Pitesti (46,492), the capital of Arges province, and a manufacturing and fruit-growing center; Resita (pop. 46,475), a center of heavy industry in the northwestern foothills of the Transylvanian Alps; Satu-Mare (pop. 62,642), a pottery and textile center on the Somes River in northwestern Rumania; and Targu-Mures (pop. 72,853), the capital of Mures province in central Rumania, an important manufacturing and cultural center.

---

## ECONOMIC GEOGRAPHY

### Development of Industry

BEFORE WORLD WAR II RUMANIA WAS industrially under-developed. Agriculture was the dominant occupation, and in spite of agrarian reforms carried out from the mid-19th century onward and the development of new ground for agrarian purposes, the large estate, often run on feudal lines and badly administered, was the major type of holding.

Existing industrial development was mainly in the hands of foreign companies, whose main concern was the profitable export of raw materials, rather than the stable development of the Rumanian economy.

At the end of World War II, the country was in an even worse position. Shortage of labor and three years of drought had precipitated an agricultural crisis, while existing industrial plants, in particular the oil fields which represented the main source of the country's wealth, had been almost completely destroyed by military action in the area.

The Communists, who had come to power at the end of the war, were quick to act. Far-reaching agrarian reforms were at once put into action and finally, on June 11, 1948, all natural resources, factories, mining and processing activities, transport and communications were nationalized. The years of depression immediately succeeding the war were combated by two Five-Year Plans and currently by the Six-Year Plan of 1960-65.

In addition, the currency was twice devalued in the immediate postwar years, thus halting inflation, and was tied to the Russian *rouble,* thus achieving stability. Economic and technical aid from the U.S.S.R. was readily forthcoming, so that natural resources might be properly exploited.

A number of joint Rumanian-Soviet companies were formed. These were nominally joint stockholdings but were, in fact, under the complete control of Russian experts. In recent years a number of these great industrial combines have come under Rumanian control but it is difficult to assess the respective profit derived from them by the two countries.

In spite of increased industrialization, Rumania was still basically an agricultural country in 1960, at least in terms of employment. In that year it was estimated that of the total labor force of 9,360,000 some 6,300,000 people were employed in agriculture and forestry, compared to 2,900,000 in the public sectors of industry and services and 91,000 in the remainder of private industry.

## Agriculture

The agrarian reforms which took place between 1864 and the end of World War II aimed at a more equable distribution of land—the breakup of large estates and the establishment of peasant farmers.

The Communist government, however, preferred to encourage collectivization and state farms on the Soviet model.

### DISTRIBUTION OF LAND

In 1954 it was estimated that 83 per cent of arable land was still held by individual peasant farmers, but by 1962 the government was able to announce the completion of the collectivization program. In that year there were 5398 collective farms, occupying 77.4 per cent of all arable land, and 597 state farms, occupying a further 3,410,000 acres of arable land, together giving a total of 92.8 per cent of all available land. These farms were served by 250 agricultural machinery stations, with 57,500 tractors and large numbers of seeding machines and combine harvesters.

The distribution of land in 1962 was estimated at 24,515,000 acres of plowed land, 15,807,000 acres of forested land, 10,198,000 acres of pasture, and 1,473,000 acres of vineyards and orchards.

### INCREASE IN PRODUCTION

In recent years, agricultural production in Rumania has increased both in quantity and quality. This is due to improved drainage and irrigation, to the widespread use of chemical fertilizers and to intensified mechanization of methods of farming. Although production decreased as a result of the loss of the rich agricultural districts of Bukovina and Bessarabia to the U.S.S.R., the figures now stand considerably above the prewar level.

### MAIN CROPS

The cultivation of grain plays a leading part in Rumanian agriculture, since it provides a basic foodstuff, supplies fodder for the livestock-raising which is an increasingly important element in the economy, and is also a profitable export.

The chief crop is corn, which is grown mainly in Transylvania and in the Moldavian and Walachian plains in the Danube area. Production in 1963-64 amounted to 5,964,000 metric tons. Wheat, grown in the same areas, takes second place, with production of 3,791,000 metric tons. Barley, oats, and rye are also grown, although in considerably smaller quantities.

Vegetables, including potatoes, green beans and green vegetables in general, are grown mainly in the Carpathian foothills of Moldavia and Walachia. The same area is also the main center for fruit-growing and vineyards.

The greatest increase in production in industrial crops is sugar-beet, grown mainly in Moldavia, of which about 2,500,000 metric tons were produced in 1963-64. Other important industrial crops include sunflowers, from which edible oil is extracted, soya, tobacco, cotton and hemp. Some rice is grown in the parts of the Danube plain subject to flooding.

*The breeding of livestock in Rumania, though curtailed by the ceding of Bessarabian territory to the Soviet Union after World War II, is still a prominent feature of the country's agriculture. Agricultural products, such as beef, cereals and vegetables, form a very substantial part of Rumania's exports.*

### LIVESTOCK-RAISING

Stockraising plays an essential part in the Rumanian economy, supplying both foodstuffs and hides. Sheep-farming is most important; in 1963 there were an estimated 12,200,000 sheep.

Cattle, like sheep, are raised mainly in Transylvania, and were estimated at 4,700,000 head in 1963.

Pigs (4,600,000 in 1963) are raised mainly in the Banat and Crisana regions, which are also the chief centers of fodder-production.

About 709,000 horses are still in use for transport, communications and farm work in mountainous regions.

Poultry-keeping is common throughout the country; in 1963 there were an estimated 44,600,000 fowl.

### FORESTRY

Around 15,807,000 acres of land in Rumania are forested. It was estimated in 1962 that 4,300,000 cubic meters of timber were cut, of which 2,800,000 cubic meters were coniferous. In the same year, 185,300 acres were replanted with trees.

The main forested areas are found in the Carpathian Mountains and in the high plateaus of Transylvania.

## Natural Resources

The most important natural resources of Rumania are the deposits of petroleum, found mainly in southern Moldavia, the Prahova Valley and Oltenia. These deposits were first exploited in the later part of the 19th century and, until they were nationalized after World War II, were mainly worked by foreign companies. Production fell sharply in the immediate post-World War II years, but has since risen to well above the prewar level, with an estimated total of 12,233,000 metric tons of crude oil produced in 1963.

Many refineries have been constructed in the oil-producing areas, and pipelines carry the product to the Danube ports and to Constanta on the Black Sea for export. The oil-producing areas are also rich in deposits of natural gas, which is also found in Transylvania. This gas is used for lighting and heating; 14,661,000,000 cubic meters were produced in 1963.

Coal and lignite, of not very high quality, are mined mainly around Petrosani in the upper Jiu river valley in the southern Transylvanian Alps. Production in 1963 amounted to 10,268 metric tons. Further deposits are found in the Banat, in southern Transylvania, around Filipestii-de-Padure and at Comanesti, in the Moldavian Carpathians.

Iron ore is found mainly in the Banat and in Transylvania, with the main foundries at Resita and Hunedoara. In 1963, 2,287,000 metric tons were mined.

### OTHER MINERALS

Other important minerals include bauxite, mined in the mountains, of

*A tractor parking lot in a large engineering works at Brasov, 75 miles northwest of Bucharest. The production of tractors and other agricultural machiney, which is continually increasing, is one of the most active branches of the country's engineering industry, which also manufactures drilling rigs, railroad equipment, and electrical, textile and other kinds of machinery.*

which 88,392 metric tons were produced in 1960; manganese ore (198,000 metric tons in 1962); copper ore; and chromium. Lead (12,400 metric tons in 1962) is mined in northern Transylvania and the Bihor Mountains, as are silver (643,000 fine oz. in 1962) and gold (71,728 fine oz. in 1947).

Salt is mined in the lower Carpathians over an area of about 250 square miles between Bukovina and Oltenia; 1,480,000 metric tons were produced in 1962, of which about one-fifth was exported.

### ELECTRICITY

Under the Ten-Year Plan for electric power (implemented 1951-60), installed power in Rumania was increased from 740,000 kw. to 1,863,000 kw., giving a total output of 11,655,000,000 kwh. in 1963.

A joint Rumanian-Hungarian plan for the construction between 1964 and 1971 of a hydroelectric power station on the Danube at the Iron Gate gorge is expected to produce a further 10,000,000,000 kwh. annually.

### Industry

The engineering and metal-working industry centers on the foundries of Resita and Hunedoara and the factories of Brasov, Galati, Constanta and Cluj, besides the rapidly expanding industrial quarter of Bucharest. Production figures for 1962 included: 1,511,000 metric tons of pig iron; 2,451,000 metric tons of steel; 456,000 metric tons of steel tubing; and 1,667,000 metric tons of rolled steel. In addition, manufactured goods included 267,000 bicycles, 251,000 radios, 41,400 television sets and 16,400 sewing machines.

The cement and chemical industries, situated mainly in the Bucharest and Brasov areas, provide important exports. In 1962 production figures amounted to 3,489,000 metric tons of cement, 288,000 metric tons of washing soda, 160,000 metric tons of caustic soda, and 131,000 metric tons of chemical fertilizers, the last of great importance to agriculture.

The growth of the textile industries, centered on Bucharest, Timisoara, Arad and Brasov, is now relieving Rumania of the necessity of importing manufactured clothing. In 1963, production amounted to 301 million square meters of cotton materials, 38 million square meters of woolens, and 30 million square meters of silk.

### FOOD PRODUCTION

Industrial food production is dominated, as might be expected by the high production of cereals, by the milling industry. In addition, 342,000 metric tons of sugar, 162,000 metric tons of edible oils, and 14,600 metric tons of butter were produced in 1962. The distilling of wines is sufficient to meet national needs.

The hide and leather industry, one of the oldest in the country, is centered on Cluj, Bucharest, Oradea and Timisoara. It is in a state of expansion and government factories produced 34,366,000 pairs of boots and shoes in 1963.

*The 175-mile-long Bistrita River is used to float logs downstream from the wooded heights of the Eastern Carpathians. They are processed in the numerous mills placed at intervals along the lower course of the river.*

## Trade

By a law passed on May 6, 1948, the majority of trade, both internal and external, came under state control and is now strictly supervised by the Ministry of Commerce. As might be expected, the bulk of Rumania's trade is done with other countries of the Communist bloc.

### EXPORTS

In 1963 the total value of Rumania's exports was 5,491,000,000 *leï*. It is difficult to express this figure in terms of American or British currency, since, as has already been noted, favorable rates of exchange are often granted to both importers and exporters in order to encourage trade.

The main exports are crude oil, oil products and oil-refining equipment; cement and cement-milling equipment; timber and timber products, including paper; agricultural produce and machinery; chemical workshop equipment; shipbuilding products; and railroad rolling stock.

In 1962, the main countries to which goods were exported, together with the value of exports, were, in order of importance: the U.S.S.R. (2,061,000,000 *leï*); Czechoslovakia (350 million *leï*); West Germany (310 million *leï*); East Germany (280 million *leï*); Hungary (230 million *leï*); and Italy (185 million *leï*).

### IMPORTS AND EXPORTS

The total value of Rumania's imports in 1963 was 6,136,000,000 *leï*, showing a figure of 645 million *leï* in excess of exports. Imports consisted mainly of iron ore, coke, processed metals, electrical cables and equipment, diesel engines and industrial equipment of various kinds.

The main countries from which goods were imported in 1962, together with the value of imports, were, in order of importance: the U.S.S.R. (2,224,000,000 *leï*); Czechoslovakia (532 million *leï*); West Germany (480 million *leï*); East Germany (334 million *leï*); the U.K. (264 million *leï*); Hungary (219 million *leï*); France (124 million *leï*); and the People's Republic of China (63 million).

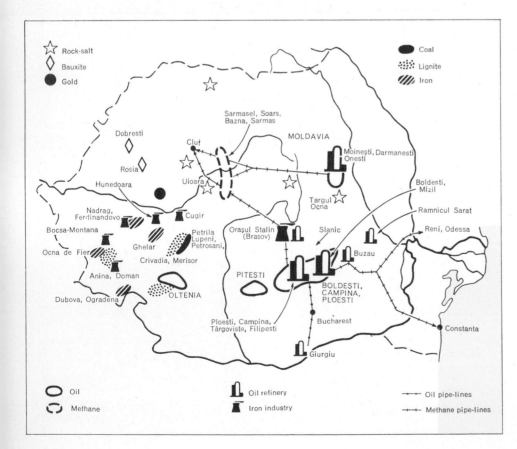

*Map showing Rumania's power centers and mineral resources.*

*Map showing the location of major industries in Rumania.*

## Communications

### RAILROADS

Rumania's internal and external trade is rendered difficult by the lack of adequate rail communications. In addition, the railroad network is unevenly distributed over the country, since the Banat region is well served, while Dobruja, the area of the main ports, is under-developed.

The first railroads in Rumania were constructed in 1854. In 1962 Rumania had around 6798 miles of railroad, of which 6417 miles were single-track lines and only 381 miles double-track.

### HIGHWAYS

The road system is at its best in Transylvania and mediocre elsewhere, though great improvements are now being made. In 1962, Rumania's road network amounted to a total of around 7124 miles, of which 3805 miles had modern surfacing.

### WATERWAYS

Rumania's main inland waterway is the Danube, which provides an internal trade route, subject, however, to delays due to freezing and flooding and to the caution needed to navigate such stretches as the Iron Gate gorge. The main Danubian ports, not far from the Black Sea, are Braila and Galati, and the river is navigable for ships of up to 3000 tons as far as Braila. The only commercial port on the Black Sea is Constanta.

The Rumanian merchant marine (NAVROM) consisted, in 1962, of 24 vessels of 70,557 gross tonnage.

### AIRLINES

The state airline, Transporturi Aeriene Romine (TAROM), operates all internal and some international flights. The main airport is at Baneasa, Bucharest. In 1962 the airline carried 217,000 passengers. International flights are also provided by Belgian, Russian, Czechoslovakian, East German, Austrian and Hungarian airlines.

*Building a ship on the stocks in the yards of Galati on the Danube Delta, 120 miles northeast of Bucharest. The ship building industry has its biggest yards at Constanta, the only major Rumanian city with a frontage on the Black Sea.*

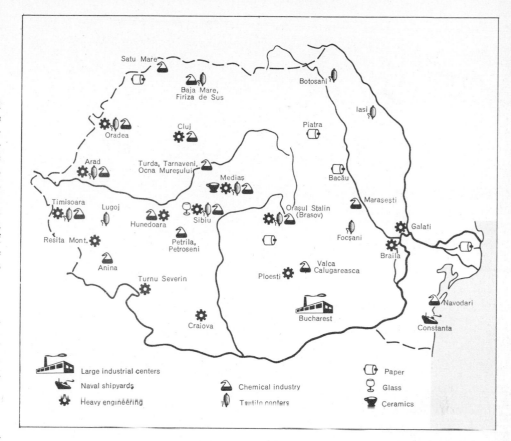

Large industrial centers

Naval shipyards

Heavy engineering

Chemical industry

Textile centers

Paper

Glass

Ceramics

## THE RUMANIAN CHARACTER

THE RUMANIAN POPULATION IS ETHnically mixed. The largest single group consists of true Rumanians but there are Magyar, German, Slav and some less numerous minorities. The minority groups tend to live separate lives, often maintaining strong relations with their mother countries.

### The Rumanians

Physically and temperamentally the Rumanians are a Latin people, but their customs and folklore often show the influence of their Slav neighbors.

#### ORIGINS

It is generally accepted that the modern Rumanians are partly descended from Roman merchants and war veterans who settled in Dacia, a Roman province, in the 2nd and 3rd centuries A.D. Dacia covered roughly the area of the Rumanian Carpathians and present-day Transylvania.

The other strain in the Rumanian blood is that of the native Daci, an ancient Thracian people with whom the Roman settlers intermarried.

#### THE PEASANT NATURE

The Rumanians are predominantly peasants and have all the toughness usually associated with peasants. Despite centuries of oppression they still maintain a firm optimism and a belief in their ability to achieve progress.

The Rumanian peasant has a keen intelligence and a clear sense of beauty. His aesthetic sense is reflected in the perfect harmonies of color and design in his traditional clothing and carpets. It is also apparent in Rumanian folk songs and dances.

The peasant's sense of beauty seems, however, to be limited to his own traditions. On a visit to a town he may buy some commercial massproduced "luxury article," which he will display as proudly as he does the beautiful products of his own hands.

#### PHYSICAL APPEARANCE

The Rumanians are typically Latin in appearance. They tend to be short

*A girl from the village of Praid in Transylvania wearing her festive costume. The white blouse forms an item of the national dress in all parts of Rumania. The girl's elaborately embroidered apron, with its clear, soft reds and blues, shows the harmony of color which typifies Rumanian folk art.*

in stature and dark-haired. Their small features and delicate hands and feet are in strong contrast to the more usual physical coarseness expected of a peasant people.

### The Magyars

The Magyars form the second largest unit of the Rumanian population. Most of them are town-dwellers, mainly concentrated in Transylvania (central Rumania).

Although they are an industrious section of the community, the Magyars generally work for themselves and have never become integrated with the rest of the population. They have been constantly encouraged, by the Magyars of Hungary, to oppose the rule under which they live. For this reason the Magyars have always been considered politically unreliable by their Rumanian countrymen.

### The Germans

The Germans are the third largest ethnic group in Rumania. They have immigrated into Rumania since the 12th century and in 1224 their independence was recognized. They are mostly Alsatians, Rhinelanders and Saxons.

Like the Magyars, the Germans are hard-working both as farmers and town-dwellers. They maintain strong links with the mother country but, unlike the Magyars, have always been loyal to the Rumanian national regime.

## DWELLINGS AND EVERYDAY LIFE

A RUMANIAN PEASANT HOME IS SIMple. In poorer regions primitive one-room huts may still be found. These are constructed with four beams and walls of timber and clay.

### The Three-Room House

The most usual type of Rumanian house is rectangular and has three rooms. It is built of wood or of mud bricks with a tiled or thatched roof.

Where houses are built of wood, in the forest regions, the walls are made from tree trunks shaped to fit together at the corners. The doors and window frames are also made of wood.

The roof, made high and steep to allow snow to slide off easily, projects beyond the walls to protect them from rain, which is frequently torrential.

At each end of the house is a high gable decorated with carved patterns. The ends of rafters and beams are

*A Moldavian peasant woman wearing the costume of her region. On her head she wears a maramă, the commonest type of headdress worn by Rumanian women. The maramă is a simple, silk or soft linen scarf which is worn in a variety of ways in different parts of the country. In this case, the woman wears it draped loosely over her head and shoulders. Elsewhere, it is wound around the head as a turban-like headdress.*

also carved, as are the gateposts and balustrades of the house.

A wooden loggia runs along the front of the house, which is usually whitewashed or painted blue or yellow.

A Rumanian farmhouse is surrounded by smaller buildings, and the whole complex is enclosed in a wooden stockade.

### Collectivization

The pattern of peasant life has naturally suffered some changes since the Communist regime came to power in 1948. The agricultural policy of the Communists is aimed toward collectivization, but the peasants, as all peasants throughout Europe have done, constantly oppose this. On collective farms peasants must pool all land, equipment and livestock, losing all property rights. The Rumanian peasants fought total collectivization so relentlessly that the government was forced to allow the compromise of agricultural associations in which property rights may be maintained.

## NATIONAL DRESS

RUMANIAN PEASANT CLOTHING IS FAIRly standard throughout the country, although each region has its own variations.

### Men's Dress

The basic costume of the rural man is a white linen shirt, or tunic, worn over white trousers with a wide belt. A jerkin or short jacket is worn over the shirt.

The shirt varies in style from region to region. In the Transylvanian mountains of central Rumania and in Walachia, southern Rumania, it is short and loose. There the shirt is worn with a broad, woolen belt in red or green, or with a decorated leather belt. The belt contains pockets for the man's pipe, tobacco and knife.

In the plains of the west the shirt is worn wide and long.

Trousers are made of wool or linen. These also vary in form from

region to region. In Moldavia in the east and in Walachia the trousers cling tightly to the legs, recalling the costume of the Dacians represented on Trajan's column.

The trousers of the peasants of eastern Transylvania are wide. They are drawn in at the ankles in the Hungarian style.

In the Danubian regions of the south and east, peasants wear baggy trousers which they fasten, below the knee, with the long laces of their sandals.

The woolen jacket worn as an outer garment again differs in form in the various regions of Rumania. In Walachia the jacket is usually white with traditional designs embroidered in black. Another type of jacket worn in this region is made of dark-colored cloth, richly embroidered with red, blue and yellow flowers.

The Moldavian peasant of eastern Rumania wears a *suman,* a type of cloak made of coarse brown wool and undecorated. It is buttoned down the front with large, black, cloth buttons.

A gayer type of jacket, also worn in Moldavia, is the *cojoc,* which is made of white leather gaily embroidered in geometric designs.

In south Bukovina, northeastern Rumania, jackets are often longer. They have long sleeves and collars which can be turned up if desired.

The most common footwear is a type of sandal called *opinci,* consisting of a piece of leather attached to the foot by means of laces which

Above left: *Two young Rumanian women working at the traditional tasks of spinning and embroidery. The wool and linen for the family's clothes are spun and woven at home, and women take pleasure in embroidering beautiful traditional motifs and patterns on the blouses, aprons and jackets of their national costumes.*
Above right: *Three young women enjoying a break from work. Even within a single community there is variation in traditional clothing styles. The plain dress and stiff headdress of the girl on the right are in contrast to the embroidered costumes and the soft headscarves worn by the other two girls.*

are tied crosswise up the leg. Archaeological finds from Turda in Transylvania testify to the existence of similar sandals in the Neolithic period.

In more prosperous parts of Moldavia the peasants wear high boots which sometimes reach above the knees.

The usual headgear for men is a fur or leather cap. In Moldavia the hat is tall, whereas, in some regions, the top is flattened.

In parts of western Transylvania, in Bukovina (northeastern Rumania) and in Moldavia, hats are often provided with a ribbon and decorated with a peacock's feather or with a pattern of beads.

### Women's Dress

The costume of the Rumanian peasant woman consists of a blouse worn inside a long skirt or tight apron. The usual footwear is sandals of the same type as are worn by men.

The blouse is similar to the man's but it is very long and worn inside the skirt. Made of white linen, it is embroidered in colored wool, along the sleeve and around the wrist. The sleeves are wide and gathered in at the wrist. In Moldavia the front and

sleeves of the blouse are decorated with embroidered stripes of various colors.

In many regions of Rumania the skirt worn over the blouse is actually a type of double apron. In Walachia this is made from two separate pieces of material joined only at the waist.

In Bukovina and in the mountains of northern Moldavia a married woman's costume is distinguished by a slit in the sides of her apron. A section of her blouse, folded in a particular way, protrudes through the slit.

The apron-skirt is always richly embroidered. The front section is the most elaborately decorated. The color combinations, although vivid, are always harmonious. Often the background is black with designs in pale green, pink or dull yellow. The whole is frequently interwoven with gold or silver thread.

In the Banat, in western Rumania, where Turkish influence is stronger, skirts are worn very short and have a long, red fringe which covers the white undergarment. The whole is decorated with gold and silver thread. This heavily ornate garment is sometimes worn only at the front and at one side. In this case an ordinary

apron is worn at the other side.

The most common type of Rumanian head-covering worn by women is a scarf of silk or soft linen, called a *maramă*. There are many ways in which it can be folded or twisted, so that headdresses differ greatly from region to region.

A most ancient variant of the scarf headdress is found in the districts around the Olt River in south-central Rumania. Here the *maramă* is worn over a frame of wood or wire, a fashion of Dacian origin.

In the mountains of Walachia and among the Hungarians in Moldavia the *maramă* is so long that it often reaches the ground.

The women of Fagaras, a town in Transylvania, wind the *maramă* around their heads several times, forming a type of turban.

In the Banat the veil is replaced by a bonnet embroidered with gold and silver threads. It has an additional ornamentation of rows of gold coins.

### SONG, DANCE AND SOCIAL LIFE

AFTER A DAY'S WORK IN THE FIELDS and the house the Rumanian peasants like to relax and enjoy traditional pleasures. Their favorite pastimes are dancing and singing. Since the coming of the Communist regime, with its attempts to control all aspects of life, traditional activities have been somewhat curtailed. But music and dance are too vital a part of Rumanian life ever to die out completely.

## The Dance

Each region of Rumania has its local dances, so that there must be some 3000 dances in the country.

Dancing has an important function in the life of the community, because it is the primary means of social contact within the group.

The *hora*, the most celebrated Rumanian dance, is danced every feastday. All the inhabitants of the village either take part or watch. For a girl who is taking part for the first time the dance is something like an initiation into the social life of the village. A girl often meets her future husband in the dance.

### RITUAL DANCES

On certain occasions special dances are performed by particular members of the community. Ritual dances, now disappearing, were danced at certain seasons to bring rain or ensure fertility.

At a wedding the bride performs a special bride's dance, called the *hora miresii*.

The *bărbuncun* is a special dance performed by the young men of a community before military conscription.

### GROUP DANCES

The most popular Rumanian dances are group dances, which are danced either in a circle or in long lines.

The *hora* is danced in a closed circle. It begins slowly. As the pace increases the dancers hold each other by the waist, forming a chain of bodies bending and writhing in time to the music. There is a strong note of eroticism in the dance.

The *brîul* is a dynamic group dance in which the dancers form lines or semi-circles, their hands over their partners' shoulders. The steps of this dance are very intricate.

A similar group dance, very quick and lively, is the *sírba*.

### CHARACTER OF THE DANCE

In spite of the great variety of dances, certain characteristic traits recur in dances from every part of Rumania. Free, individual improvisation is, for instance, a typical element of Rumanian dance.

There is frequently a lack of concord between the steps of the dance and the accompanying tune. This produces a certain polyrhythm with such elements as syncopation.

Rumanian dancing has great dynamism but it is not wild. The movement is always disciplined. There are no exaggerated gestures with the arms and the steps are quick but measured.

The leader of the dance is also the caller. He shouts commands for the rest of the dancers to follow. His calls are not, however, always restricted to simple commands. *Strigătun* are satirical verses, mocking certain habits or situations, and with which the caller sometimes intersperses his commands.

## Folk Song

Songs also play an important part in the life of a Rumanian peasant

Below left: *Two women in festive costumes. Their skirts and jackets are made from white woolen material. Here the* maramă *(headscarf) is worn over a stiff, bonnet-like headdress. On their feet the women are wearing* opinci, *sheepskin sandals attached to the feet by leather thongs tied crosswise up the leg. Below right: A girl from Oltenia, in the western part of Walachia, where some of the most beautiful Rumanian costumes are found. The embroidery here is in the best possible taste. The apron and the sleeves and fronts of the blouse are discreetly embroidered in bands with geometric motifs.*

community. They are sung to accompany dances, at weddings, at funerals and on every other possible occasion.

### THE EPIC TRADITION

As elsewhere in the Balkans, the epic tradition is still alive in Rumania. Rumanian verse ballads are known as *cântece bătrânesti*. They have a wide variety of themes and styles. The subject matter ranges from the fantastic world of legend to everyday pastoral life.

Some Rumanian ballads date from the time of the Turkish invasion (in the early 15th century). These are songs of rebellion against the oppressor and they express the Rumanian people's aspirations in their struggle for freedom.

### LYRIC SONGS

The spirit of the Rumanian people is best expressed in lyric song. There are three main types: *doine, bocete* and *colinde*.

*Doine* are songs which express an undefined longing. They are frequently love songs. The mood is always melancholy and the melody is slow and drawn-out. *Doine* are sung in every part of Rumania.

*Bocete,* or dirges, are sung during funeral rites. In the earlier part of the rites the *bocete* take the form of laments for the dead, in which an inconsolable sorrow is expressed. Later, however, on the way to the cemetery, the songs are less sad. At this stage they consist of greetings to be sent to dead loved ones or advice for the new life.

Christmas songs are called *colinde*. They take the form of hymns recounting the main events of the life of Christ and beseeching heaven's blessing. The tunes are closely akin to some dance tunes. They are sung by girls between the ages of seven and 12, who form groups called *colindători*.

### THE 'PLUGUSOR'

A special song is sung on New Year's Day. This is the *plugusor*, the song of the plow. A plow, decorated with fir branches and paper flowers, is drawn by a team of oxen and followed by a group of young people, who sing the song of the plow.

The *plugusor* is a glorification of farming and nature. More a recitation than a song, it has its own particular rhythm and cadence. The accompaniment takes the form of tinkling bells and cracking whips.

The hopes, adversities and labors of the farmer are described together with the succession of the seasons. The *plugusor* ends with wishes for wealth and prosperity.

### The 'Sazatoare'

A group of men and women—or occasionally just women—will sometimes meet and hold a *sazatoare*. This is simply a social gathering at which people work together for a while and then later, their work put away, play at riddles and other word games. They also sing and retell old tales.

### Markets and Fairs

The main activity in both fairs and markets is the buying and selling of

*This slope, in the Transylvanian Alps (central Rumania), with its dense covering of trees, is crowned by the castle of Bran. This 13th-century castle of the Teutonic Knights was restored in the 17th century. The gay costumes of the two women in the foreground probably differ little from those of their predecessors who were alive when the castle was built.*

goods made by village craftsmen.

But a fair is also a place of pleasure. There are merry-go-rounds and food stalls, where the food can be seen cooking on a charcoal grill. Fairs are the haunts of gypsies who are traditionally horse dealers and musicians. Gypsy musicians also provide music for the merry-go-rounds or for impromptu dances in the evening.

Markets are places where marriageable girls meet the young men of neighboring districts. They are therefore important in providing for both an exchange of goods and for marriage between the people of different villages.

## SPORT

SINCE THE RUMANIAN PEOPLE'S Republic came into existence in 1948 sporting activity has been greatly encouraged.

### Clubs and Competitions

Sports clubs have been established in both urban and rural centers, and these attract a large number of young people. In 1958 there were 6900 such clubs with a total membership of 1,400,000.

In 1950 a sports badge was instituted by the Rumanian government. Anybody is free to compete for the G.M.A. badge, as it is known. To win one it is necessary to pass standard tests in several branches of sport.

In the spring and autumn, cross-country races are held, in which hundreds of thousands of boys and girls participate.

For the young people of the villages special sports competitions are held, for which the number of entrants is very large. The most successful village wins the Village Cup.

### Hunting and Fishing

Hunting and fishing are very popular pastimes in Rumania, a land rich in game. At vacation time men and women leave the towns and set off for the mountains and lakes.

Many of the mountains in the Baia-Mare province of Crisana-Maramures, in northwestern Rumania, are volcanic in origin and are covered by vast forests of pine, oak and beech. Among the animals still living in these forests are stags, wild boars, bears, lynxes, wolves, badgers and martens.

There is also good hunting in the southern part of the country. The oak forests of Slobozia, in southeastern

*A Rumanian ballet, in national costume, staged in Bucharest. The dance continues to be a popular form of entertainment in Rumania. In rural areas the villagers still perform the traditional folk dances, of which Rumania has some 3000. Contact with other countries and recent social changes have naturally had their effect on the dance, as on other aspects of life, so that only the efforts of folklore societies are keeping some dances alive.*

Rumania, teem with pheasant and hare.

The Danube Delta is a paradise for both hunters and ornithologists: it is a gathering-place for the migrating birds of the entire continent. Among the birds found there in the autumn are white and black storks, cranes, pelicans, singing swans and rare species of ducks and geese.

Rumania is as rich in fishing as in hunting-grounds. Most of the mountain streams contain trout, and salmon are caught in the Bistrita River of eastern Rumania.

The best lake fishing is in the Danube Delta, in the marshes and salt lakes.

## FOLK CUSTOMS AND RELIGION

ALTHOUGH MOST RUMANIAN PEASANTS are Christians, despite the Communist government's efforts to weaken the churches, remnants of the ancient Rumanian mythology survive in peasant superstitions. Rumanian folklore has been very much influenced by that of the neighboring Slav peoples.

### Malignant Spirits

Like other Balkan peasants, the Rumanians fear certain malignant beings who live in the fields and woods and endanger the lives and well-being of men.

The *naluce* are spirits of the air.

They interfere in human affairs and often actually influence the fate of men.

It is believed that there is danger of swallowing *naluce* with wine or water. To avoid this a Rumanian would, before drinking, pour a little of the liquid onto the ground and blow on it.

Some Rumanians still believe in vampires, souls of the dead who suck the blood of the living. Vampires are thought to roam abroad on St. Andrew's Eve. The most effective method of keeping vampires away from a house is to tie a bunch of garlic to the front door.

For three days, at the feast of the Holy Trinity, *the rusalule*, the most terrifying of all spirits, bring havoc to the world. The *rusalule* were believed to be the three spinster daughters of a mythical emperor. Never having married, they grew resentful and bitter. They therefore took pleasure in tormenting men and causing the disastrous summer storms.

Their activity was greatly dreaded by country people. Twigs of wormwood worn around the waist and placed under the bolster were thought to give protection against the wrath of the *rusalule*.

During the three days of their activity no work was done and nobody laughed. Children were warned that, if they made faces, they would retain distorted expressions.

The kitchen of a Rumanian house. In most homes this is the smallest room and is used solely for cooking. The cooking is done in a brickwork oven or on an open fireplace. Rumanian peasants have a relatively unvaried diet. Their basic food is mămăliga, a type of cornmeal porridge.

I will choke you with incense/ I will catch you in my hand/ I will hurl you beyond the seas."

At one time the curing of illnesses was entrusted to the *Calusaries*, a group of young dancers who met in May after an initiation ceremony. Their dances were thought to prevent and cure illness.

The three most important events of human life—birth, marriage and death—are surrounded by numerous customs and rituals.

### Birth and Baptism

When a woman is in labor the Saxons of Transylvania untie all the knots in her clothing. They believe that, by sympathetic magic, the birth will thus be made easier. Similarly all the locks, on doors and furniture, are unfastened.

Birth is felt to be a great mystery. The Rumanians believe in three Fates who determine the course of a man's life. On the third night after birth the Fates meet at the foot of the child's cradle and there decide on his future.

Great efforts are made, on the part of the child's family, to gain the goodwill of the Fates. A table, laden with good things, is left in the room where the newborn baby is sleeping, the room is kept closed and nobody is allowed to go in, for the baby must meet the Fates alone.

The whole family retires early to bed, the watchdogs having been taken to the neighbor's for the night so that their barking will not disturb the Fates.

January 6 (Epiphany) is called *Bobotează*, the baptismal feast. This is the traditional day for baptisms. A child may be several months old when he is baptized, for parents often prefer to wait until *Bobotează*, when many children are baptized. All children baptized in the *Bobotează* ceremony are known as the "brothers of the cross." The name derives from the part of the ceremony in which the priest throwns a valuable crucifix into the river. The cross is immediately retrieved by one of the men who stand ready to dive after it.

Special rites are performed on the day after baptism. The child is washed in consecrated oil poured into a font in which have been placed a coin and a piece of bread, to ensure the child's safety and happiness. Some basil, thought to make a child docile and obedient, is also placed in the font.

In the west of Maramures province, in northwestern Rumania, children are given a small knife and a wallet after baptism. These they keep

### The Soul

In Transylvania there is a belief that the soul leaves the body during sleep. One of the outlets through which the soul escapes is the mouth. Since there is a danger that, once it has escaped, the soul will forget to return to the body, children are warned not to sleep with their mouths open.

As elsewhere in the Balkans, there is a traditional Rumanian belief that a building will stand only if a human soul is buried under the foundation stone or built into the walls.

In former times a human being, often a child, was actually sacrificed. The sacrifice was later replaced by a ritual in which the soul is represented by a person's shadow. The builder would secretly measure a shadow with a piece of string which was then buried under a wall or corner stone. It was feared that anyone so losing his shadow would die within 40 days.

### Illness and Cures

Illness in Rumania is traditionally thought to be caused by a spirit possessing the body. It was thought that it could be frightened away by threats, and certain charms used to be recited to achieve this. In one such spell the speaker threatens the illnesses as follows: "I will cut you with an axe/

An outbuilding to a rural Rumanian family home. The building is used as a cellar and a larder for provisions. The steep roof, a typical feature of Rumanian peasant buildings, is so made to allow snow to slide off quickly. The roofs of Rumanian houses also often project beyond the walls to protect them from the torrential rains.

with them all their life and after death are buried with them. The knife is believed to have power to protect them from illness and all other harm. This belief is based on a very ancient idea that iron has the power of repelling evil spirits.

### Courtship and Marriage

Young people are given opportunities to meet at communal dances and at fairs.

Marriageable girls often visit fairs to meet the young men of neighboring districts. At their waist they wear the *naframa*, an embroidered handkerchief which they present to the young man of their choice.

As a pledge of his affection the young man gives the girl the *furca*, or distaff, which he has painstakingly and lovingly carved. The distaff forms part of a girl's dowry and is a symbol of authority in her new home.

At the village of Gaina, in western Rumania, a fair is held every year on July 20 (St. Elia's Day). Here marriageable girls offer themselves for bids to prospective husbands.

Young girls and married women, dressed in their festive costumes, arrive at Gaina from the surrounding countryside.

The feast begins at dawn. It is announced by the bray of sprucewood trumpets, some of which are seven or eight feet long. Throughout the day gypsy musicians play and the people divide into groups to dance.

Finally all the unmarried girls form a line ready to be inspected by the young men, who are resplendent in their best clothes and their hats decked with peacock feathers or flowers.

When a young man finds a girl he would like as his wife he asks her if she will marry him. If she agrees the parents will arrange the dowry and although the contract is by word of mouth only, it has the force of law.

The religious and civil ceremonies take place at a later date but a wedding feast is immediately improvised, continuing far into the night until there is no more food and drink.

#### WEDDINGS

Marriage ceremonies generally take place on a Sunday, but the festivities begin three days earlier and on Friday the wedding presents are carried through the streets to be admired by everyone.

Saturday is a day for visits. The bridegroom, with a small escort of friends, goes to visit the bride. At

*A house in the region of Hunedoara in Transylvania. This single-story house, built over spacious cellars, is grander than the usual Rumanian peasant home. Most houses are built of wood or of clay bricks and have only three rooms—a kitchen, a guest room and a general room for living and sleeping.*

her house the best man steps forward and recites a few lines dedicated to the bride. Then the young lady brings a jug of water with which she sprinkles the whole company, who then run away.

Later the bridegroom brings the bride his personal presents. These always include the wedding dress, some loops of gold lace and the veils and flowers.

On the Sunday the bride is dressed by her attendants, who comb her hair, decorate her gown with orange blossoms and hang a silver coin around her neck for good luck.

Before she leaves home her mother and friends throw down a belt, over which she must walk. Bride and bridegroom then leave for the church in a carriage. A tree, which is later hoisted on to the chimney coping of the bridegroom's house, is also carried on the carriage.

At the church two crowns, made of flowers or metal, are placed on the heads of the bridal couple. At the appropriate moment they exchange these crowns and the priest joins their hands. To round off the ceremony the whole company walks three times round the altar.

After the ceremony all go to the house of the newly-married couple. Little girls, holding pails filled with clear water, wait for the procession to pass. The full pail signifies the wealth of happiness which is to fill the lives of the young couple, and the clarity of the water symbolizes the purity of their love.

On the threshold of the house the young bride is welcomed by her sister-in-law with bread and salt.

### Funeral Customs

A death is accompanied by elaborate rituals of mourning.

After a death in a Rumanian village it is the custom for all the women of the village to gather around the bereaved family's house to lament the departed. It is believed that, if no tears are shed when a person dies, the soul will not enjoy eternal peace in the other world.

*Bocete* (dirges) are sung from dawn until late in the night. In some places *bocitoare* (professional female mourners) are employed to sing laments. The *bocitoare* are seldom paid in money. Instead they are invited to dinner or given presents.

The deceased is dressed in fine garments and adorned with flowers and icons (religious pictures). In the evening the mourners gather around the body carrying lighted candles, which they place around the pillow to the accompaniment of a special dirge.

Throughout the night the mourners tell old tales and play games to dispel the tension of mourning.

The journey to the cemetery and the actual burial are less sad than the earlier mourning. It is felt that the deceased is starting on a long journey at the end of which he will meet former friends and relatives already dead. These sentiments are echoed in the *bocete* now sung, which contain greetings to be passed on and good advice for the journey.

Two funeral banquets are held. The first takes place immediately after the burial. The guests are usually so numerous that they are forced to eat in two or three sittings. A second feast is held on the third day of mourning, when more lamentations are chanted at the graveside. This second feast marks the end of the funeral rites.

## Religious Festivals

In the customs associated with specifically Christian festivals, such as Christmas and Easter, Christian and pagan elements sometimes intermingle.

Christmas is the most important festival of the year in Rumania. Its approach is accompanied by great activity. Houses are cleaned; cakes and tarts are baked ready for Christmas Eve.

In Bukovina province, in northeastern Rumania, at this season a cake is baked in the shape of a figure eight. This is kept until the spring, when the men take it into the fields to eat before the first plowing.

At midnight on Christmas Eve Rumanian women break several cakes into pieces. They coat the pieces with syrup, putting them in layers in a stone jar with spices between the layers. The priest who comes to bless

*A group of Tatar women banqueting during a festival. The population of Rumania, although predominantly Rumanian, includes several minority groups. One of these is formed by the Tatars, a Turkic people of Moslem religion, which they rigorously and devotedly practice. Most of their settlements are in the province of Dobruja in southeastern Rumania.*

the house is the first to taste this conserve.

On Christmas Eve all borrowed objects must be returned to their owners. A failure to do this will, it is believed, be followed by sorrow.

Various rituals, connected with animals, land and everyday household objects, are intended to ensure prosperity in the coming year.

A horseshoe is placed in the family water-jug and the domestic animals are given some of the water to drink on Christmas Eve: it is believed that, in drinking this, they will become as hard as iron.

Chimneys are swept and the soot is sprinkled about the orchard to make fruit trees and vines bear good fruit. In another ritual connected with fruit trees the men threaten to cut down barren trees. Their wives, however, beg them to spare the trees. The threat is repeated three times. The men finally agree to spare the trees in the hope that they have been frightened into bearing fruit.

Every tool and utensil in the house is touched, so that it will continue to serve its owners during the coming year. Dishes are carried three times round the house. It is thought that after this rite they may always be filled with good things.

### MOTHER CHRISTMAS

Many Christmas Eve customs appear to bear little relation to the Christian festival of Christmas. Others, however, reflect traditional legends connected with the Christmas story.

It is believed that, on "Holy Night," the cattle whisper among themselves of the mysteries of the Nativity and nobody may therefore intrude upon them or sleep in the stables on Christmas Eve.

In Transylvania a cake, in the shape of a hand, is traditionally baked. This custom commemorates the local story of Mother Christmas, whose hands were cut off by Father Christmas when she went to help the Virgin Mary at the birth of Christ. But the Virgin breathed on the severed hands and made them whole. The coating of sugar and egg-white on the cake is intended to represent the new smoothness and beauty given to Mother Christmas's hand by the Virgin.

### CAROL SINGING AND CHRISTMAS PLAYS

*Colinde* (Christmas carols) are sung by groups of young girls, who dress

up as Magi and shepherds and walk through the streets singing. They carry a large paper star at the end of a long stick. At the center of the star is a lighted candle and the star itself is painted with the scene of the Adoration of the Magi.

The singers often stop and sing under the windows of a house, and a particular song is addressed to each member of the household.

Folk plays are performed from Christmas to Epiphany. They deal with the Nativity and the Adoration of the Magi. The characters portrayed are the Magi, Herod, angels, shepherds, soldiers and servants. The players are dressed in Oriental-looking costumes and wear masks.

### EASTER CUSTOMS

On Palm Sunday the men of a Rumanian village gather at the inn, where each buys a round of beer. This round signifies mutual forgiveness of past wrongs and is a preparation for that peace of the soul which has come from the long Lenten fast and for the sacramental Confession, which takes place before Easter.

The Thursday before Easter is the day of the dead, and cakes and wine are brought to the church as offerings in memory of the dead. These are later distributed by the priests to widows and the poor.

On Good Friday a table, high enough to allow a man to pass underneath, is placed before the crucifix in the church and a cloth, bearing a picture of Christ, is spread over the table. People bring flowers and pass three times under the table.

In the evening all the people of the village gather and sing a special Easter song, the *prohod*. In procession they walk all round the church and then proceed to the cemetery. There candles are lit on every grave and carried back into the church, where the procession again passes under the high table.

Each person takes his lighted candle home. With it he traces the sign of the cross on all four walls of his house to keep away evil. Sacred icons are then decorated with flowers.

On the morning of Easter Saturday women and children go to Holy Communion. The men wait until Midnight Mass, to which they bring a white hen and painted eggs. At the end of the service lighted candles are carried around the church. Finally Easter

eggs—symbols of the rebirth of nature coinciding with the Resurrection of Christ—are exchanged, accompanied by the greeting "Christ is risen" and the response "He is indeed risen."

## Seasonal Rites

Certain rituals, carried out especially at springtime and harvest-time, are undeniably pagan in origin and intent.

In peasant communities spring, the season of new growth, is the most important time of the year. There are, in Rumania, traditional festivals in which the death of winter and the return of spring are celebrated.

The figure of Green George is recurrent in Eastern Europe. In Rumania the feast of Green George is particularly associated with the gypsies, who celebrate it on Easter Monday or St. George's day, April 23.

Green George is a personification of the reawakening of the vegetable world after its long winter sleep, and he is represented by a boy dressed from head to foot in green leaves.

The feast of Green George is closely associated with the willow, which, in Rumania, is connected with the power of facilitating childbirth, rejuvenating the old and curing the sick.

On the eve of Green George's day a young willow tree is uprooted and decorated with flowers and garlands. Then it is replanted. Expectant mothers leave a garment under the tree overnight. If they find a leaf on the garment next morning they are assured of an easy birth. The old and the sick spit on the willow saying, "You die quickly, but make us live."

Green George, in his aspect of spirit of the willow, has the function of providing fodder for the cattle and of propitiation to the water spirits. His first act is to throw a handful of greens to the cattle. This ensures that they will have fodder throughout the coming year.

In a special ritual Green George propitiates the spirits of water. Taking nails which have lain soaking in water for three days, he hammers them into the tree. He then extracts them and throws them into the nearest stream. Green George himself, in the form of a puppet made from leafy branches, is finally thrown into the water.

### THE FUNERAL OF CARNIVAL

Carnival, like Green George, symbolizes the spirit of fertility. Carnival must be killed and buried, so that he may rise again.

In Transylvania, Carnival was traditionally hanged. On Shrove Tuesday or Ash Wednesday a sled, carrying a straw dummy and drawn by two white and two chestnut horses, was followed by two lamenting boys dressed as old men. The procession was followed by the rest of the village boys riding on horseback and by two girls wearing wreaths of green leaves and riding in a cart.

The procession would halt at the village inn where Carnival was sentenced to hang. His followers would try in vain to save him but he would be snatched from them and hanged from a tree.

### THE EXPULSION OF DEATH

In some parts of Rumania a traditional ritual is the expulsion of death from the village. In a village near the town of Sibiu in Transylvania the ritual is carried out by children.

Death, in the shape of a dummy made from straw, is made by school children after they have been to Mass on Ascension day. The dummy is dressed in a red cloak with silver buckles and many ribbons along the sleeves and on the front.

As the bells for Vespers ring, the dummy is placed on an open window for all to see. After the service two girls, holding Death by the arms, walk at the head of a procession of other girls.

The girls finally strip Death of his finery and throw him to the boys. They catch the dummy, run out of the village and throw it into the nearest pond.

As this is happening one of the girls puts on the clothes and ornaments that Death has discarded. The procession forms once more and marches singing along the streets.

### Harvest Sacrifices

Harvest-time rituals are generally aimed at obtaining abundant crops in the following year. The chicken, still sacrificed today in parts of Rumania, may be a distant echo of former human sacrifices.

The Hungarians of Transylvania tie a white chicken to the last sheaf of wheat in the harvest and stab it with a spit. The skin and feathers are kept until the next spring, when, at seed-time, the grain of the last sheaf of the previous year's harvest is mixed with the chicken's feathers and scattered over the field. The chicken represents the spirit of fecundity and is killed so that it can be resurrected in the following year.

Near the city of Cluj, in west-central Rumania, a hen is buried in the harvested field with only its head left above the surface. A boy must strike off the head with a single stroke of a sickle. If he fails he is given the nickname of Red Rooster, which he keeps throughout the year. When this happens it is feared that the next harvest will be poor.

Sufficient rain is vital to an agricultural community and Rumanian peasants have various rituals to combat drought. In a rainmaking ritual in Walachia a girl is crowned with a wreath made from the last sheaves of the harvest. Wearing this wreath she walks toward the village and everyone she meets splashes her with water.

The gypsies combat drought by the action of the *paparude*, who are young gypsies dressed in leaves and decked with ribbons. The *paparude* dance from house to house while the oldest child chants an invocation to the rain.

In some places, when there is drought, the farmers throw a clay doll into a stream.

---

## CRAFTS

RUMANIAN PEASANTS, BOTH MEN AND women, are skilled at many handicrafts and take pride in the beauty of their work. Most products of their skill are used to decorate their homes.

### Wood Carving

The almost severe simplicity in the lines of domestic architecture in Rumanian villages is relieved by profuse carving on the exteriors. Gateposts, balustrades and the ends of rafters and beams are carved. In this architectural carving the designs are mainly geometric with such motifs as circles, crosses and stars.

The high gables of the houses are carved with the most complex and individualistic designs and these are different on every house. Many motifs are taken from the plant world and include patterns of tulips and lilies in full flower or in bud.

Many household objects, such as

*A village church set in a wooded landscape. Churches, like houses, are frequently built of wood, since this is the most abundantly available building material. Despite the Communist regime's efforts to suppress religious activities in Rumania, the faith of the peasants and the devotion of the rural clergy have ensured the continuation of religious customs and churchgoing.*

*A group of Moldavian women and children hearing Mass outdoors. In Rumania, women and children frequently worship separately from the men. Most Rumanians belong to the Orthodox Church, which is recognized by the government. Other churches, such as the Roman Catholic and Uniate, have been completely suppressed so that their members are unable to practice their rites.*

*A family of Moldavian peasants riding in a farm cart. Family life still forms the basis of Rumanian peasant society. The peasants have resisted the government's attempts to enforce collectivization on the land, so that relatively few have lost the independent way of life by which each family owns its own holding.*

wooden bowls or spoon handles, are also carefully carved. The designs used are often abstract and include rosettes, crosses, circles and dotted patterns. Occasionally, motifs are taken from the animal world and include strangely stylized cocks and other birds.

In accordance with the general passion for carving, a shepherd will carve his staff with complex, traditional designs. The fishermen of the Danube Delta also carve the handles of their fishing rods.

The object which typifies Rumanian peasant carving is the distaff, given by a young man to the girl of his choice. A man applies all his skill in carving to the decoration of the distaff, since it symbolizes his love for his lady.

The patterns carved on the distaff may be either abstract or realistic. Common abstract motifs are stars, rhombs and wheels. Motifs taken from everyday life include flowers, ox-horns and even human figures.

## Carpets

The Rumanian housewife spins and weaves the cloth for all the family's clothes. This alone takes up much of her time. But she also spends many hours making rugs to decorate the walls of her house. Carpets are never laid on the floors of a Rumanian house, but are hung on the walls of the rooms or laid over beds and benches.

Rug-making is a very old craft in Rumania. The traditional designs show a definite influence from the East and are magnificent in both composition and color.

The carpets made in Oltenia, in western Walachia, are justly famous for design and color. The basic colors are a blue and red of a unique softness and clarity. The designs are floral with patterns of scattered flowers, single or in bunches of two and three. The borders comprise small bunches of flowers symmetrically arranged. Sometimes, instead of a pattern of flowers, a rug may have a design consisting of a great tree with twisting branches.

The second most celebrated rug-making area of Rumania is Moldavia. Moldavian carpets are also characterized by floral designs, but the flowers in these designs tend to be more conventionalized than those in Oltenian carpets. The colors are less vivid, with a prevalence of grays, browns and blacks.

The women of Crisana-Maramures, in northwestern Rumania, are skillful weavers and dyers. Their carpets generally have geometric designs, but there is also some use made of the human form. A carpet design from this region may depict, for example, a group of women dancing the *hora*.

The colors are very varied and are obtained from certain vegetable dyes. These dyes are resistant to sun and water. Black dye is made from the bark of the alder tree; yellow and red are obtained from local plants.

## Pottery

Whereas Rumanian carpets show Oriental influence, the pottery of Rumania appears to have been influenced by that of Mediterranean countries.

Black pottery has been made in Rumania since Neolithic times and can still be found today. This type of pottery is crude and simple. The black surface is obtained by firing the pots in a carbonizing atmosphere produced by smoke. After firing, the surface is burnished with a stone.

One of the main decorative motifs on this pottery is the spiral, which has been found on pottery from the Danube regions since Neolithic times.

In some parts of Rumania glazed pottery of a high quality is produced. The potters of eight villages in the region of the town of Oradea, in Crisana province, are noted for their glazed ware. The pots have a unique simplicity of line and subtlety of design.

Some of the best Rumanian pottery is made near the town of Bistrita in Transylvania. Here modern ceramics and pots in the old traditional designs are produced side by side. The glaze on this ware has a characteristic iridescent pink quality.

## Painted Easter Eggs

Athough their making is confined to the season of Easter, decorated eggs are a characteristic form of Rumanian folk art.

The traditional process for decorating the eggs is an elaborate one. The eggs are washed in sour milk and warmed beside a fire. The decoration is applied in wax, which is squeezed onto the surface from a narrow tube. The egg is dipped in dye and then into boiling water to remove the wax. Where other colors are required, the process is repeated as often as necessary. The most frequent colors are red, blue, green, mauve and yellow.

The designs are of an immense

*A Rumanian gypsy with the proud expression and the long, tangled hair typical of his people. The gypsies form one of the larger minority groups of the Rumanian population. Traditionally musicians and horse-dealers, they provide much of the music and color at local fairs. Gypsy orchestras were, at one time, popular entertainers in the cafés of Bucharest.*

*School children at work in a Bucharest school. The children, both boys and girls, are making model airplanes, which they will later enter in flying competitions. The teaching in Rumanian schools emphasizes vocational training, so that young people will enter life trained in a skilled trade.*

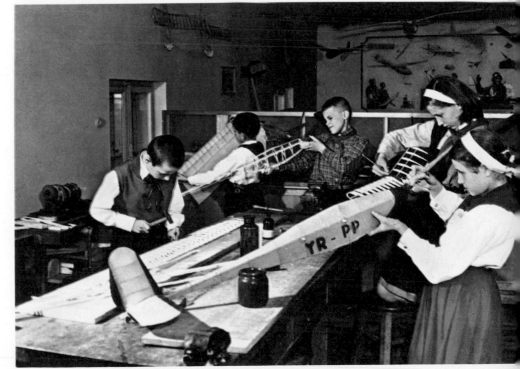

*A young man and woman from the Banat, in western Rumania. Dressed in beautifully embroidered regional costumes, the couple embody the attractive qualities of the Rumanian people. The gaiety and charm in their faces is reflected in the beautiful songs and dances of the Rumanians.*

variety. They include abstract, linear motifs and also naturalistic patterns such as sleds, fishing hooks, plowshares, birds' feet, snails, frogs and dragon-flies.

## FOOD AND DRINK

RUMANIAN FOOD TENDS TO BE HEAVY and rich, but it is appetizing and well-flavored. Certain dishes show the influence of Russian, Hungarian and Turkish cuisine, but there is a distinct national Rumanian cuisine with its own individual characteristics.

### 'Mămăliga'

Rumania is a cereal-growing country. This circumstance has determined the staple diet of the Rumanian, which is a type of cornmeal porridge called *mămăliga*.

*Mămăliga* is made by stirring cornmeal into boiling water until the mixture thickens. It is sometimes eaten with milk and sugar but more frequently as part of a savory dish, being served with fried onions, cheese, salt fish or eggs. It is eaten either hot or cold.

When cold, *mămăliga* is sometimes cut into slices and fried over a fire. The mixture is also sometimes baked in the oven to produce a pudding.

For the peasant, *mămăliga* is the basis of a meal, but it is also eaten as an accompaniment to more sophisticated dishes.

### Soups

Most Rumanian soups are flavored with sour cream and this shows Russian influence.

*Ciorba* is a soup, usually of fish or chicken, flavored with sour cream. It is enriched with butter and mixed vegetables.

*Ciorba de perisoare* is a variant of this soup with added meat balls. A marrow bone is simmered for two hours with carrots, parsnips and onions. Sliced tomatoes are then added. The meat balls, about the size of walnuts, are made with minced beef, rice and bread crumbs. They are cooked in the soup for a further hour. A beaten egg is finally added. The soup is served with sour cream and chopped parsley.

### Hors d'Oeuvres

A great variety of hors d'oeuvres are eaten in Rumanian. One of the most popular is caviar (from sturgeon), which is usually eaten fresh or pressed in a salad.

Other hors d'œuvres are pickled mushrooms, small spiced sausages and hot goose liver on toast. *Pastramă*, which is cured beef, pork or goat's meat, is eaten as an appetizer or as a snack with wine.

A popular cold dish, eaten as an hors d'œuvre, is egg plant salad. The egg plants are baked on an open fire until their skins are almost charred. They are then removed from the fire and cooled with cold water, after which they can easily be peeled. The peeled vegetables are crushed to a pulp, to which olive oil is added drop by drop. The mixture is flavored with lemon juice and finely chopped onion. It is finally garnished with sliced red peppers.

### Meat Dishes

Rumanian meat dishes are most often highly flavored. *Mititei* are sausages made from minced beef flavored with mixed spices, black pepper, crushed garlic and cloves. The mixture is rolled into thin sausages, which are brushed with olive oil and grilled over a hot flame.

Another typical Rumanian dish is *sărmala*. These consist of balls of rice and chopped meat wrapped in a cabbage leaf. In a summer variant of this dish the meat balls are wrapped in a young vine leaf. The *sărmala* are cooked very slowly and finally topped with fresh cream. They are often eaten with *mămăliga*.

*Tuxlama* is a dish made from tripe with calf's foot. The tripe and calf's foot are simmered together with pepper corns, salt, onion, parsley and celery. While they are simmering a sauce of carrots with egg yolk and lemon juice is prepared. After two hours the stock is drained from the tripe and calf's foot and the meat removed from the latter. The carrot sauce is poured over the tripe and meat and the dish is cooked for a further half hour.

*Tocană* is a ragout of veal in tomato sauce. It is usually eaten with *mămăliga*. Another ragout is *ghivecin*. This is composed of a variety of vegetables finely chopped and cooked with pieces of pork.

A dish of Turkish origin is *mousaka*. It consists of layers of minced meat, egg plants and tomatoes, topped with a sauce of beaten eggs and sour cream and baked in the oven.

Rumania abounds in game of all kinds, but there are no specific national dishes based on game. Woodcock or duck is marinated for 24 hours before it is roasted. It is usually served with olives.

### Fish Dishes

The most popular fish in Rumania is the carp, which is cooked in a variety of ways. It can be spit-roasted, cooked in tomato and oil or made into a sour soup.

*Umplut* (stuffed carp) is one of the tastiest of Rumanian fish dishes. The fish is cleaned, then stuffed with a mixture of chopped olives, garlic, chives, cayenne and olive oil. It is coated with bread crumbs and baked for about an hour. Other stuffings are made with nuts, eggs and aromatic herbs.

Fresh-water crabs are a favorite delicacy. They are boiled in vinegar with aromatic herbs which include chervil. Garnished with a sauce made from groundnuts, oil and garlic, they are served with rice.

The fish soup made by the fishermen of Lake Suhaia, on the Rumanian-Bulgarian border, is famous throughout the country.

The soup is cooked as soon as the fishermen return from the day's fishing. The preparation is a very old tradition. The method of cooking is extremely simple: a great variety of fish are thrown alive into a cauldron of boiling water, together with herbs and tomatoes. The tender flesh of the fish is very quickly cooked. The herbs, bitter tomatoes and fresh fish combine to give an excellent flavor.

### Cheeses

One of the best Rumanian cheeses is *brănza de burduf*. This is a cheese of sheep's milk preserved in the bark of a fir tree, which gives it a special flavor.

Two other cheeses are *cascaval* and *urda*. *Urda* is a soft cream cheese made from the whey of sheep's milk.

### Sweet Dishes

Rumanian cuisine is not distinguished for its cakes and dessert dishes. *Mămăliga* is sometimes eaten with sugar or with sweet conserves. *Cumere* is a type of batter cake, eaten either with apples or soft cheese.

A sweet dish of Turkish origin is *cataif*. It is made from noodles with almonds and sugar. A caramel sauce is poured over the noodles, and the sweet is served cold.

There are many types of Rumanian jam. Some are flavored with rose petals, chocolate or coffee. *Dulceată* is a sweet preserve made from many different fruits. It is the symbol of Rumanian hospitality and any guest, even a complete stranger, is always offered a spoonful on his first entering a house.

The traditional Christmas food which a guest is offered is *cozonac*, a type of sandwich filled with poppy seeds and nuts.

### Beverages

#### TEA AND COFFEE

The most popular non-alcoholic drink in Rumania is tea. This is an example of Russian influence. In some parts of the country, as in Russia, a samovar, a type of urn in which the water is heated by charcoal placed in a pipe passing through the urn, is used. Tea is drunk at all times of the day.

Coffee is less popular than tea and always is of the Turkish variety, which is very strong and sweet, and made by boiling finely ground coffee two or three times.

#### 'TUIKA'

*Tuika*, the national drink of Rumania, is a spirit distilled from plums, which are the most widely-grown fruit. It is drunk in all parts of the country both in the towns and in rural areas.

#### WINES

There is a long tradition of wine-making in Rumania and, although not exciting, the wines are of a consistently good quality.

The best wines are grown in the province of Jassy in Moldavia. The name of *babeasca*, one of the wines of Jassy, is explained by a legend. Stephen the Great of Moldavia (1433?-1504) is said to have visited Jassy on one occasion. On meeting an old peasant who lived alone, he asked him how he was able to bear his solitude. The man replied, pointing to his wine-bottle, that he was not alone, as he always had his old *baba* (woman) to keep him company.

Cotnari, a village of Jassy, is especially renowned for its wines. One of these, the *Grasă*, is a golden-yellow, aromatic wine, which is both sweet and acidic.

Elsewhere in Rumania the wines of Dragasani, Walachia, of Segargea, in southern Rumania, and of Odobesti, in eastern Rumania, are excellent.

*School children on a Sunday outing. The Rumanians take a great interest in their children and their education. In Rumania, education is free at all levels and is compulsory for all children between the ages of seven and 15 years. There is a bias toward technological, scientific and political education in schools, but children are also taught to enjoy nature and the open air.*

## EARLY HISTORY

THROUGHOUT ITS HISTORY, RUMANIA has acted as a kind of buffer state between greater powers. In classical times it became an outpost of the Roman Empire, held against the Germanic tribes to the north; but from the late Middle Ages until modern times it owed what measure of independent existence it enjoyed mainly to a precarious balance of power between the Ottoman Empire to the south, the Habsburg Empire to the west, and the Russian Empire to the north.

The Roman imperial policy during the 1st century A.D. had been the maintenance of the Danube as the northern frontier. The boundaries of the empire were usually flanked by "client kingdoms" as an extra protection. One exception was the kingdom of Dacia beyond the Danube, occupying the same area as the modern Rumanian Republic.

Dacia was hostile to Rome and in 107 A.D. the Emperor Trajan (53-117) invaded the country and established Roman rule. Its king, Decebalus, committed suicide.

The province of Dacia remained a bulwark against the pressure of the Gothic tribes in the northeast until the Emperor Aurelian (c. 212-275) decided to evacuate all military personnel in 271. His intention was to withdraw the Roman frontier to the Danube, as the most easily defensible line. The northern tribes, however, eventually overran the whole empire, and Dacia was swallowed up in a series of invasions by migrating tribes.

The Goths, the Huns, and the Avars were followed in the 6th century by the Slavs. None of these tribes remained long, but moved further westward; only the Bulgars, in the 7th century, set up a system of permanent government, but this was swept aside by the Magyar invasion at the end of the 9th century. The main group of Magyars settled further west in what is now Hungary, but retained a loose control over the remnants of Dacia. The Hungarian King Stephen I (c. 975-1038) annexed that part of Dacia known as Transylvania completely, but the Mongol invasion of 1241 erased all traces of Hungarian rule in the rest of the country.

By the end of the 13th century local chieftains had established two separate states. These states, Walachia and Moldavia, were at first partly subject to the Hungarian crown, but in 1330 Walachia won complete independence, and Moldavia did so shortly afterward.

## MOLDAVIA AND WALACHIA

THEIR DIVISION FROM CATHOLIC HUNgary was the more complete since their inhabitants, the Vlachs, belonged to the Orthodox Eastern Church. This branch of the Church had been introduced in the 9th century, while they were under the rule of the Bulgars. Attempts to re-establish Hungarian rule were met with resistance by the Vlachs. Eventually, however, the greater threat of Turkish invasion forced Mircea the Old, king of Walachia from 1386 to 1418, to make an alliance with Hungary in 1395 for mutual protection. But in 1417 he was forced to recognize the sultan as his overlord.

Throughout the 15th century Walachia was a theater of war between Turkey, Hungary and Moldavia. Under the Hungarian hero János Hunyadi (1387-1456), who was of Vlach descent, and the Vlach King Vlad IV, who acknowledged Hungarian overlordship in 1456, the Turks were resisted for some years; but on Vlad's death resistance crumbled, and Walachia fell more and more under Turkish domination.

Meanwhile, Moldavia was reaching the height of its power, under Steph-

*The University Square, Bucharest. The equestrian statue in the foreground commemorates the Rumanian national hero, Michael the Brave (ruled 1593-1601). Michael rallied Walachia and Moldavia against the Turks and succeeded in unifying both principalities and Transylvania for a brief period. This was the last union of all Rumania until 1918. Michael was murdered in 1601, and the country was split up again under Turkish domination.*

*The medieval castle at Bran, which was built in the 13th century as a stronghold for the Teutonic Knights, who were invited by the Hungarian King Andrew II to help defend Transylvania against the Cumans and the Mongols. The castle decayed during the Turkish domination, but was restored in the 17th century and later served as a summer residence for the kings of Rumania.*

en the Great (ruled 1457-1504). Culture and the Church flourished in his time; while the Turks were defeated again and again. After his death, however, his son, Bogdan III (ruled 1504-17), was forced to pay tribute to the Turks.

Until the crown was seized by the Prince of Walachia, Michael the Brave, in 1600, most of Moldavia's rulers were puppets. Michael owed his Walachian home to the Turks, but threw off their yoke and for a brief time ruled Walachia, Moldavia and Transylvania. This was the last union of all Rumania until 1918. Political rivalry led to the assassination of Michael in 1601, and Rumania was once more divided into vassal states. Walachia and Moldavia were dominated by the Turks while Transylvania was disputed between the Turks and the Habsburgs until the defeat of the Turks before Vienna in 1683. Afterward it fell under Habsburg rule, and eventually, after the creation of the dual monarchy of Austria and Hungary in 1867, under Magyar domination.

In Walachia and Moldavia the Turks turned increasingly to families of Greek origin to supply their puppet rulers, though at first these rulers were related to the Bessarabia dynasty that had ruled Walachia since 1330.

Eventually, however, tired of the constant intrigues of these rulers with Austria and Russia, the Turks imposed on the principalities the Phanariot regime, so named because its members came from Phanar, the principal Greek district of Constantinople. The Phanariots were, in effect, tax-collectors appointed by the Turkish authorities. Their rule was so oppressive that thousands of peasants emigrated.

## The Danubian Principalities

In the latter half of the 18th century the expansion of the Russian and Habsburg empires and the slow disintegration of Turkish power in Europe affected the vassal states.

Russia invaded them in 1769, and by the Treaty of Kuchuk Kainarji, signed in 1774, she established the right to intervene in them. From this date Moldavia and Walachia were ruled virtually as one unit and they are usually called the Danubian principalities. Austria exacted payment for her neutrality in the form of some northern territories of Moldavia that linked Transylvania to her newly acquired territory in Galicia.

Turkey continued to change the *hospodars* (rulers) of Moldavia and Walachia frequently, despite assurances to the contrary. The effect of this policy was to increase taxes, as each new *hospodar* was set higher amounts to collect for Turkey. Russia opened hostilities in defense of her treaty rights in 1787, but in 1792, under the Treaty of Jassy, she withdrew from the principalities. The Dniester River was established as the Russian frontier.

In spite of renewed promises to change their policy, the Turkish authorities kept up their practice of appointing new *hospodars* almost every year until 1802, when Russia obtained a treaty stipulating that *hospodars* could not be removed without Russian assent and must hold office for a minimum of seven years.

But in 1806, under the influence of the French, the Turkish government dethroned the *hospodars* without consulting Russia. Russia responded by invading the principalities. She ruled them so harshly, milking them of their produce and deporting dissidents to Siberia, that her six-year occupation became a new spur to Rumanian nationalism. Moreover, under the Treaty of Bucharest (1812), which ended hostilities with Turkey, Russia obtained the Moldavian territory of Bessarabia.

### AN ABORTIVE REVOLT

In 1821 Alexander Ypsilanti (1792-1828), son of a former *hospodar* of Moldavia who had been deposed in 1805, placed himself at the head of a revolt in Moldavia. The year before, this Greek officer in the service of the Russians had been elected president of the Greek revolutionary society, *Philiké Hetairia*. While Ypsilanti was organizing his Moldavian expedition, Tudor Vladimirescu, a Rumanian member of *Philiké Hetairia*, raised the standard of revolt in Walachia. But the rebels were soon seen to be at odds with one another. Vladimirescu's followers were largely impelled by social grievances against the *boyars* (nobles); Vladimirescu himself was mainly concerned with ousting the Phanariots; while the Greeks wanted nothing less than complete independence. Ypsilanti, regarding Vladimirescu as a traitor, had him assassinated.

By promoting revolution in Rumania the Greeks had hoped to secure Russian intervention; but the

be appointed for seven years only.

The Russian troops did not withdraw until 1851, and they reoccupied the principalities during the Crimean War (1854-56), when Russia was at war with Turkey, France and Britain. The Paris treaty which ended the war dissolved the Russian protectorate but left the principalities under Turkish rule. Russia was forced to return southern Bessarabia to Moldavia.

The possibility of uniting the principalities was brought up at this time by the French emperor, Napoleon III. In 1857 the *ad hoc* committees of the principalities met a European commission at Bucharest to consider the constitutions. The decision of the committees was unanimous: the principalities required a unified Rumanian state, free from Turkish rule and with a guarantee of neutrality.

Turkish opposition to this led to the compromise of the Paris convention in 1858. Walachia and Moldavia were to remain under separate princes but to be united by a permanent alliance. A central commission was set up to advise on matters of common interest. This partial union became complete on Jan. 17, 1859, when the assemblies of both principalities elected the same prince, Alexandru Ion Cuza (1820-73), to rule both principalities.

## RUMANIAN UNION

THIS DE FACTO UNION HAD THE SUPport of France and Russia, but was opposed by Austria. However, Austria was prevented from intervening by her war in Italy against France and Piedmont. Turkey was forced to accept the dual election but refused to view it as a unification of the two principalities.

Under Cuza the franchise was greatly extended and in 1864 the peasants were freed from serfdom, but these and other reforms were bitterly opposed by the *boyars,* while the seizure of monastic estates alien-

Russians gave them no aid and Ypsilanti was forced to seek asylum with the Austrians, who promptly threw him into prison, where he remained until his death seven years later.

The Turks took good care to divide the Greeks and Rumanians still further by making concessions to Rumanian nationalists, including the appointment of native princes as *hospodars.* But the first native *hospodars* appointed aroused the antagonism of the Russians by their anti-Greek policy; for Russia felt a certain identity of interest with the Greeks, who also belonged to the Orthodox Eastern Church, and had ambitions of bringing the whole of the Balkans under her influence.

The convention of Akkerman (1826) restored Russia's right of intervention in the election of *hospodars,* which had lapsed during the hostilities. Russian forces, however, occupied the principalities when war with Turkey broke out again in 1828.

The following year, 1829, peace was concluded at Adrianople. This time the principalities, while remaining formally under Turkish rule, be-

came virtually Russian protectorates, and Russian troops occupied them until 1834. Furthermore, a Russian official, Count Pavel Kiselev, supervised the reorganization of their government. It was made less autocratic in character, assemblies of *boyars* and the higher clergy being set up to collaborate with the two *hospodars,* who were elected for life.

### A NEW RUMANIAN NATIONALISM

However, the new constitutions were not nearly democratic enough for those Rumanian nationalists who looked to the West for inspiration and they were swept aside by the uprising of 1848. The *hospodar* of Walachia fled, but the new provisional government led by Ion Brătianu (1821-91) lasted only a few months. Russia and Turkey combined to crush these dangerous liberal tendencies and to restore the constitution that had been drawn up under Kiselev.

In the following year at the Balta-Liman conference, the two powers replaced the elected assemblies with *ad hoc* committees and reverted to the agreement that *hospodars* should

ated the Church, and Cuza's autocratic ways offended the liberals. In 1866 Cuza was deposed by a military conspiracy. His successor was Prince Karl Eitel Friedrich of Hohenzollern-Sigmaringen (1839-1914), who ruled as Prince Carol. He was the candidate of Ion Brătianu, who persuaded Napoleon III to support him.

Carol was forced to accept an agreement with Turkey that defined Rumania as a Turkish province. Meanwhile, frequent changes of government made the country's internal condition unstable. However, in 1876 Brătianu became premier, and for 12 years he headed a Liberal administration.

During the Franco-German War (1870-71) Carol became alarmed lest Russia should invade Rumania while the other powers were preoccupied. He therefore made overtures to Austria. They resulted in the trade agreement of 1875, which subordinated Rumania's economy to that of Austria.

The Treaty of San Stefano, signed in March 1878, recognized Rumania's independence. Russia obtained Dobruja under the treaty and handed over the northern part of it to Rumania, as compensation for annexing southern Bessarabia once more.

In 1877 war broke out again between Russia and Turkey. Rumania had signed a secret agreement allowing Russian troops to cross her territory and a Rumanian contingent led by Carol himself took part in the capture of Plevna, a decisive victory in the war.

The Congress of Berlin, which met in June 1878 to revise the San Stefano treaty, ratified Rumania's independence on condition that equality of rights was granted to its Jewish population. Under the constitution of 1866, only Christians could be citizens. On the insistence of the powers this article was repealed. In March 1881 Rumania was proclaimed a

*An equestrian statue commemorating Gheorghe Doja, who led a peasant revolt against the boyars (wealthy landowners) in 1514. After his defeat he was captured and buried alive. The peasantry of Rumania were not emancipated until 1864. Even then little notice was taken of their wretched condition until the revolt of 1907. The land redistribution begun after World War I was only partially successful due to inadequate financial backing, and there were still left nearly 600,000 landless peasants in 1928. The Communists passed two further land distribution measures in 1945 and 1949.*

kingdom. This move by the Liberal government, which had held strongly republican policies, was part of the reaction to the assassination of the Russian tsar, Alexander II, in 1881, which sparked off a fear of revolution in European countries.

### Internal Developments

After Ion Brătianu's Liberal administration, a Conservative government was formed in 1888. This was replaced by another Liberal regime under Dimitrie Sturdza (1833-1914) in 1895. Except for quite brief periods of Conservative government, the Liberals were in power almost continuously until the rise of peasant and other working-class parties after World War I.

Neither of the old parties, which in effect represented only the bourgeoisie and the *boyars*, took the agrarian problem sufficiently seriously. About 80 per cent of Rumania's population were peasants. Most of them owned very little land, and their poverty had forced them into debt. In 1907 there was a serious peasant

rising in which both Jews and large landowners were attacked. The Conservatives, who had come to power the year before, failed to check the rising and gave way to a Liberal administration. It restored order but did little to remove the causes of unrest.

The main preoccupation of Rumanian statesmen in this period was foreign affairs. The frontiers of Central Europe and the Balkans had been determined by the varying fortunes of the great powers in their struggle for supremacy. Except when it had suited them, they had paid little respect to the principle of national self-determination. Consequently the smaller states were at odds with one another, as well as with the great powers, over the territory they controlled. Rumanians were in a majority in Transylvania and the Banat (controlled by Hungary), southern Bukovina (controlled by Austria) and Bessarabia (controlled by Russia). They formed a majority in the Rumanian territory of northern Dobruja and a large minority in the Bulgarian territory of southern Dobruja; Ru-

*Map showing Rumania from after the Congress of Berlin (1878) to the Treaty of Trianon (1920).*

mania also claimed recognition as protector of the Vlachs of Macedonia and Rumanian minorities throughout the Balkans.

### The Balkan Wars

These causes of friction, plus the declining power of the Ottoman Empire, whose frontiers still enclosed millions of southern Slavs, Vlachs and Albanians, formed the backdrop to the Balkan Wars of 1912-13.

When the Serbians, the Greeks and the Bulgarians opened hostilities against Turkey in 1912, Rumania proclaimed her neutrality; but when the victorious allies fell out over the division of the spoils, Rumania took her chance and seized southern Dobruja. After Bulgaria had been defeated by all her enemies this area was formally ceded to Rumania by the Treaty of Bucharest, which was signed in August 1913.

The treaty brought a pause to open hostilities in the Balkans, but tension was increasing over Austria-Hungary's support of Bulgaria on the one hand and her suppression of the Rumanians in Transylvania on the other. Rumania turned more and more toward Russia. Tsar Nicholas II (1868-1918) and Carol I met at Constanta on the Black Sea in June

1914 and at the same time conversations were held between the Russian minister for foreign affairs, Sergei Sazonov (1866-1927), and Rumania's premier, Ion Brătianu (1864-1927), eldest son of the founder of the Liberal party.

Nevertheless, when World War I broke out in August 1914, leading Rumanians were still wavering among siding with the Central Powers, siding with the Allies, and neutrality. Rumania had been secretly allied with Germany and Austria-Hungary since 1883, and they promised her Bessarabia as a reward for standing by the treaty. Russia, France and Britain, on the other hand, offered her Transylvania if she joined them.

Eventually, after much hard bargaining, the Allies undertook to restore to Rumania virtually all her historic domains except Bessarabia. From Austria she was to receive Bukovina up to the Prut River; from Hungary, not only Transylvania, but the Banat and a large slice of the Hungarian Plain, up to the Tisza River. These inducements brought Rumania to war on Aug. 22, 1916.

### World War I

Rumania's first campaign was disastrous. As her forces crossed the

Carpathians and advanced into Transylvania, the German general in command of Balkan operations, Field Marshal August von Mackensen, launched the Bulgarians against her southern flank. After desperate fighting Bucharest was captured on December 6.

The Rumanian government had already been evacuated to Jassy in Moldavia and the remnants of the army also withdrew north to cover it. When Mackensen launched a new major offensive in August 1917, the Rumanians met it with fierce resistance ; but the decision of the Russian government to withdraw from the war, following the Bolshevik coup in November, forced Rumania to sue for peace.

An armistice was signed on December 6 and humiliating terms were imposed on Rumania by the peace treaty signed on May 7, 1918; but the treaty was never ratified, and on November 9, two days before the armistice was concluded on the western front, Rumania declared war again.

Besides entering the territories promised them by the Allies, Rumania took advantage of the anarchy in Russia to occupy Bessarabia, whose council had voted for union with Rumania on Dec. 9, 1918. But there was trouble in Hungary, where on July 22, 1919, Béla Kun's Communist government launched an offensive against the troops occupying the country east of the Tisza River. The Rumanians counter-attacked and pushed on to Budapest, which they entered on August 3. They remained there, in defiance of the Allies, until November 14.

By the treaties of St. Germain (Sept. 10, 1919) and Trianon (June 4, 1920) Rumania was more than doubled in size, but she did not get all the territory she had been promised. Part of the Banat with a mainly Serbian population was given to the new kingdom of Serbians, Croatians and Slovenians and a small section was retained by Hungary. Rumania acquired Transylvania and the old Rumanian province of Crisana-Maramures to its west, but not the Hungarian Plain beyond it.

### GREATER RUMANIA

NEVERTHELESS, GREATER RUMANIA came into being with a large proportion of resident aliens, whose rights were protected by the treaty. Their presence added to the uneasiness of the internal situation in Rumania after World War I.

Political parties were in a state of flux. The old Conservative party, whose pro-German policy was now discredited, soon disappeared. Many of its members turned to the military hero, Alexandru Averescu (1859-1938), for leadership. Averescu's party was named the People's Party and offered an alternative to the more radical National Popular party led by Iuliu Maniu (1873-1951) and Alexandru Vaida-Voevod (1871-1950). The peasant cause was represented by the party of Ion Mihalache (b. 1882).

The only group to survive in its old form was the Liberal party. Its leader, Ion Brătianu, had been premier when the peace treaties were being negotiated, but had resigned in protest at the minorities clause and at Yugoslavian occupation of half the Banat.

Two fundamental reforms had been accepted as necessary by the main political parties during the war. The first of these was the expropriation of land in favor of the peasants, which had been agreed to in July 1917 by the parliament sitting at Jassy. But stiff opposition remained, and Vaida-Voevod's coalition government of radicals and Peasant party leaders which followed the Liberals into power resigned in 1920.

Averescu formed a government, and his minister of agriculture, Constantin Garoflid, put the agrarian bill though parliament. The effect of the bill was small, for the redistribution of land was not backed by adequate provision for technical and financial assistance to the new owners.

## The New Constitution

The other fundamental reform was the decree of Nov. 8, 1918, announcing universal manhood suffrage. This was put into effect by the adoption of a new constitution in March 1923 under Brătianu, who had returned to power at the beginning of the previous year.

The extension of citizenship to the Jewish population provoked sharp criticism from the nationalist elements. The problem was, however, overshadowed by the opposition to the centralization of government re-

*Peles Castle, near Sinaia, stands at the foot of the Transylvanian Alps. Built by order of King Carol I between 1873 and 1883 in the German Renaissance style, it houses one of the richest art collections in Rumania.*

sulting from the implementation of the constitution. Transylvania was particularly hostile to this move, because the province had expected some degree of self-government.

The minority problem remained a constant threat to internal stability and successive governments failed to find a solution. The Liberal government weathered a series of crises and remained in power until 1926.

Its last years in office were particularly strained by the scandal caused by the liaison between the heir apparent, Carol (1893-1953), and Magda Lupescu (b. 1904?), a divorced Jew. Carol was obliged to renounce his right of succession, and on the death of Ferdinand I in 1927, Carol's son Michael (1921-    ), a boy of six, succeeded to the throne under a regency.

The amalgamation in 1926 of the National Popular party led by Iuliu Maniu and Vaida-Voevod and of the peasant group led by Ion Mihalache created a strong alternative to the Liberal party. Widespread support for the new National Peasant party, which supported decentralization, was not reflected in the rigged elections of 1927, which returned Brătianu to power in succession to Averescu. However, an economic crisis, peasant demonstrations and the death of Brătianu brought about the fall of the Liberal government, and Michael's regents turned to Maniu to form a government. The new government suppressed the censorship and lifted the state of emergency. Together with the introduction of administrative reforms and the easing of the economic situation, these measures produced a calmer atmosphere.

There was general dissatisfaction with the regency, and all the major parties agreed to Carol's return in 1930. However, Carol, who had promised to seek reconciliation with his wife, Princess Helen, insisted that Magda Lupescu be allowed to return to Rumania, and Maniu resigned in protest, handing over the government to his party colleague, Gheorghe Mironescu (b. 1874).

## FOREIGN AFFAIRS

Instability continued to be a prevailing feature of internal politics and the international field was equally uneasy. A series of alliances was established to protect Rumania's position. The very able Liberal minister, Take Ionescu, concluded the first of these with Poland in 1921, and others with Czechoslovakia and Yugoslavia quickly followed; but Ionescu died in the following year, before his project for a Balkan bloc could be realized. Nicolae Titulescu (1883-1941) set about bringing it to fruition when he became foreign minister in 1927, and in 1934 he succeeded in getting the Balkan Pact signed by Rumania, Yugoslavia, Turkey and Greece. Meanwhile, during Averescu's ministry (1926-27) pacts had been signed in 1926 with France and Italy.

The associated problems of Bessarabia and Rumanian recognition of the U.S.S.R. still remained unsettled. The U.S.S.R. had protested against the Allied decision in 1920 to leave Bessarabia under Rumanian control. When the two countries signed a non-aggression pact in 1933 they side-stepped the issue of Bessarabia. In 1934 the U.S.S.R. was admitted to the League of Nations. Rumania, always a staunch supporter of the

Below left: *Tudor Vladimirescu, who in 1821 led a revolt of the Walachians against the Phanariot regime (Greeks appointed by Turkey and named collectively from the Phanar district of Constantinople). Vladimirescu's revolt was timed to coincide with a revolt in Moldavia led by Alexander Ypsilanti, but the aims of the two leaders were so different that they quarreled, and Ypsilanti had Vladimirescu assassinated.* Below right: *Ion Voda, called the Terrible, a prince of Moldavia in the 16th century. From the 15th to the 19th centuries Moldavia's history was one of ceaseless struggle to retain some independence from the Turks. Their rulers, called* hospodars, *were vassals of the sultan, and most of them were puppets.*

*Ana Ipatescu, a heroine of the rising of 1848. This movement, partly nationalist and partly social in character, and one of a series of risings throughout Europe, was suppressed by Russia and Turkey after a brief period under Rumania's first Liberal government, headed by Ion Brătianu.*

League, then established diplomatic relations with her. The rapprochement was largely the personal achievement of Titulescu, who supported the collective security policy of the League of Nations. The question of Bessarabia was raised again when Titulescu was replaced as foreign minister in 1936.

In internal politics Carol II quickly showed his ambitions for absolute power. Opposition to him grew stronger and was aggravated by the world-wide economic crisis, but at the same time his intrigues were splitting the political parties. Between Maniu's resignation in October 1930 and the return to power of the Liberals under Ion Duca in 1933, four different ministries were formed.

### The Iron Guard

Hitler's rise to power in Germany was paralleled by the growth in Rumania of the anti-semitic movement called the Iron Guard, led by Corneliu Zelea-Codreanu (1899-1938).

The Guard was responsible for several outrages, including the assassination of two prime ministers, Ion Duca in 1933 and Armand Calinescu in 1939. Proscribed by Duca's successor, George Tatarescu, it simply changed its name, and the shooting of Zela-Codreanu and 13 of his followers in 1938, allegedly while they were trying to escape after they had been sentenced to ten years' imprisonment, failed to break it.

Carol had secretly supported the Iron Guard, but began to see it as a rival to his own power and in 1937 instituted a personal dictatorship. On Feb. 20, 1938 a new constitution of a corporative type (based on the representation of groups rather than of individuals) was proclaimed. Under this constitution, which bore some resemblance to that of Fascist Italy, the electorate was reduced from 4,500,000 to 2,000,000, and some politicians, including the leaders of the National Peasant party, refused to accept it.

In April 1939, seeing the mounting danger of German expansion, Rumania secured a guarantee of territorial integrity from France and Britain. However, under the pact of August 1939 between Germany and the U.S.S.R., Germany agreed to allow the Russians to reannex Bessarabia, and after the collapse of France in 1940 Rumania had no choice but to obey Russia's demand that Bessarabia and northern Bukovina be ceded to her. This was followed by the enforced cession of northern Transylvania to Hungary and of southern Dobruja to Bulgaria.

These territorial losses increased Carol's unpopularity and on Sept. 6, 1940, he abdicated in favor of his son Michael. General Ion Antonescu (1882-1946) then formed a government whose vice-premier was the new leader of the Iron Guard, Horia Sima. A reign of terror ensued, in which the Iron Guard assassinated 64 leading political opponents. But the Germans, who had been playing off one group against another, now supported the military in putting down the Iron Guard in January 1941.

The military dictatorship shared the Iron Guard's policy of persecuting democrats and Jews. Massacre and flight eventually reduced the Jewish population of around a million to about 140,000.

### WORLD WAR II

Rumania had joined the Tripartite Pact, whose original members were Germany, Italy and Japan, on Nov. 23, 1940, and by now there were some 500,000 German troops in the country. Rumania refused to take part in the German assault on her ally Yugoslavia in April 1941, but she became a base for the offensive, and on June 22 she joined Germany in the invasion of Russia.

Rumania quickly reoccupied Bessarabia, and military success at first strengthened Antonescu's position; but by the beginning of 1943, with the great Russian victory at Stalingrad, the eventual defeat of the Axis began to seem certain.

Approaches were made in the spring of 1944 to the Allies and later to Russia alone. As a result, immediately after the Soviet troops had crossed the Rumanian frontier in August 1944, an armistice was signed, restoring the Soviet-Rumanian boundaries of 1940.

The Russian invasion was very swift, since not only did the Rumanians not offer resistance, but a section of their forces joined up with the Russians against the Germans and Hungarians.

In 1947 the Paris treaty restored northern Transylvania to Rumania, but confirmed the cession of southern Dobruja to Bulgaria and of Bessarabia and northern Bukovina to the U.S.S.R. Under the terms of the treaty the U.S.S.R. was given the right to station troops in Rumania until the signing of a peace treaty with Austria so that she could maintain lines of communication with her occupation forces there. The Inter-Allied Control Commission that was set up was also to be dissolved when peace was concluded with Austria.

## THE COMMUNIST REGIME

THE FIRST POSTWAR GOVERNMENTS were coalitions based on the national bloc formed by the National Peasants, the Liberals, the Social Democrats and the Communists in the spring of 1944. However, in March 1945, under Russian pressure Petru Groza, leader of the pro-Communist peasant party known as the Ploughmen's Front, was made premier and the National Peasants and the Liberals were excluded from office. The United States and Great Britain withheld recognition on the grounds that the government was unrepresentative.

Following the elections of Nov. 19, 1946, the Communists secured all the key posts but that of foreign affairs, which was given to the Liberal leader Tatarescu. Soon afterward the Communists began to arrest their political opponents. The most prominent of the victims was Maniu, who was condemned to life imprisonment on November 11, and died in prison in 1952. Evidence given at his trial was used to oust Tatarescu from office.

Maniu's party, the National Peasants, the only Rumanian party with a mass following, was outlawed in August 1947. The Social Democrats had been split by Communist tactics. The main section, which had refused to join the Communist-dominated government, was suppressed. The minority section merged with the Communists in February 1948 to form the Rumanian Workers' party. With the Ploughmen's Front and the Hungarian Popular Union, a Popular Democratic Front was set up.

With effective opposition already suppressed, the elections of March 28 were virtually uncontested.

Michael had been forced to abdicate on Dec. 30, 1947 and the republican constitution adopted in April 1948 was modeled on that of the U.S.S.R.

The ruling party had already begun to purge itself. The leading wartime Communist, Lucretiu Patrascanu, was imprisoned in February 1948 and eventually, in 1954, executed. In 1949 nearly one-fifth of the total party membership was expelled, and in May 1952 three Communist ministers, including the foreign minister, Ana Pauker, were purged.

Gheorghe Gheorghiu-Dej (1901-65) party secretary since 1945, maintained his position, however. He replaced Groza as premier in 1952, but gave up the post to become first secretary again in 1955. He was elected president in March 1961, once more replacing Groza, but this time he retained his party post as well. Chivu Stoica succeeded Gheorghiu-Dej as premier in 1955, and was himself succeeded in 1961 by Ion Gheorghe Maurer. On Gheorghiu-Dej's death in March 1965, his former party deputy, Nicolae Ceausescu, became first secretary and Stoica became president.

### Rift with Russia

While Stalin ruled in Soviet Russia, Rumania had been a model satellite. Those who dissented from this policy of subservience were purged. After Stalin's death a few slight indications began to appear that Rumania might not be prepared to follow Russia's new leaders so unquestioningly. Then suddenly, in 1962, the two countries were seen to be in open disagreement over the question of economic co-operation.

Rumania's Five-Year Plan had put heavy emphasis on industrialization and her leaders were determined to achieve the maximum possible self-sufficiency in this sphere. They therefore resisted Khrushchev's proposals for enforcing a kind of international division of labor tasks through Comecon (the Council for Mutual Economic Assistance), which had been set up in January 1949 to co-ordinate the economic plans of the Communist states. Gheorghiu-Dej and his colleagues refused to yield to Russian pressure, and in July 1963 Comecon acknowledged Rumania's right to turn down proposals that were considered to be against her national interests.

---

## FUNDAMENTAL DATES

**A.D. 107-271**  Rumania a province of the Roman Empire.

**9th century**  Orthodox Eastern Church established under Bulgar rule.

**13th century**  The principalities of Walachia and Moldavia emerge.

**1600-01**  Walachia, Moldavia and Transylvania united under Michael the Brave.

**1774**  Turkey recognizes Russia's right to intervene in the Danubian principalities of Walachia and Moldavia.

**1812**  Russia acquires the Moldavian territory of Bessarabia.

**1859**  *De facto* union of Walachia and Moldavia.

**1913**  Rumania seizes southern Dobruja from Bulgaria in the second Balkan War.

**1916**  Rumania joins the Allies in World War I; under the treaties which end it, she regains her historical territories.

**1933**  Assassination of the Liberal prime minister, Ion Duca, by the Iron Guard.

**1937-40**  Carol's dictatorship.

**1940**  Russia reannexes Bessarabia.

**1941**  Rumania joins Germany in the attack on Russia.

**1945-47**  The Communist party seizes power and suppresses all opposition; Michael is forced to abdicate and Rumania becomes a republic.

**1963**  Comecon recognizes Rumania's right to reject proposals for economic co-operation with other Communist states felt to be against her interests.

*The Patriarchal Church was built in Bucharest during the 17th century. It is a superb example of the decorative style which developed in Walachia during the feudal period. The structure, based on an Orthodox central type of plan, includes a Greek cross inscribed within a square. Cupolas have been placed above the east and west façades, as in Russian and Greek Orthodox churches. The flamboyant decoration derives from both Moorish and Byzantine styles. A mixture of the two is evident in the designs on the columns.*

## PREHISTORIC TO FEUDAL ART

PRESENT-DAY RUMANIA CONSISTS mainly of the historical principalities of Transylvania, Walachia and Moldavia. The art of Transylvania is closely related to Western and Central European styles, while the art of the other two areas is akin to Middle Eastern traditions.

### Protohistoric Art

During the late Stone Age (4000-2000 B.C.), there were a number of settlements in the area which is now Rumania, consisting of Indo-Europeans, the ancestors of the Dacian people. They are distinguished by their painted pottery with a high quality of design (similar to that on page 126), which is related to contemporary Oriental pottery.

During the Bronze Age (2000-750 B.C.) in the territory which is now Rumania, refined bronze and gold objects were made, including some of the best examples of vessels and decoration produced in Europe and the Near East at the time.

In about 750 B.C. the Iron Age began in the area with the invasion of the Scythians, migrants from the East and southern Russia. The Scythians produced highly refined pottery and metal objects, which they decorated with sophisticated geometric patterns (see page 126). Like the art of the indigenous people, these pieces were related to Far Eastern art styles.

Due to their similar origins, Scythian art was easily absorbed by the ancestors of the Dacian people.

### Greek Settlements

During the 7th century B.C., Greeks settled near the Black Sea in today's Constanta province, where they remained until the 1st century A.D. The Greeks left behind much evidence of their settlement. Most important is the city near Mamaia which includes ruins of Doric temples and residential quarters which were comparable to those at Pompeii.

### The Dacian Empire

During the 3rd century B.C., the powerful Dacian Empire was established with one of its centers in Valcea. Still remaining are the ruins of a fortified town, which is similar to the ruins of a Mycenaean citadel, with ten-foot-thick stone walls and sparse living quarters.

### The Romans

Dacia became a Roman province during the 2nd century A.D. The Roman occupation, which lasted until 271-73 A.D., is important, as it gave Rumania that Latin character, maintained to the present, which is clearly reflected in the arts.

Important Roman ruins in Rumania include the Tropaeum Trajani (Trajan's Trophy, 109 A.D.), a monument at Adam-Clisi in Constanta. Only the huge, circular stone and mortar core remains of this monument, which was once decorated with marble freestanding and bas-relief (low relief) sculpture. These included *Statue of a Roman Judge* and metopes representing *A Barbarian Prisoner* and *Roman Legionaries* (now in the Bucharest National Museum of Antiquaries). These and other remains, including the carvings found at Roman centers near Alba-Iulia and at Saramisegetuza, are late Roman in style. Many of the sculptures found on Roman tombstones are naturalistic descriptions of famous heroes.

### Barbarian Invasions

From the 3rd to the 12th century, and later, in some areas, barbarians invaded the territory of present-day Rumania. First were the Goths, who succeeded the Romans; they were

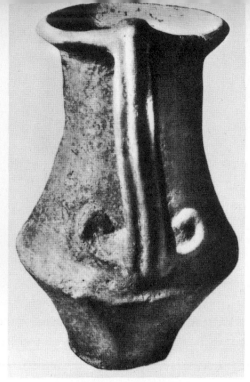

Above: *This glazed vase, found in the province of Galatia, was made some time shortly before 1100 B.C. It was created by the Indo-Europeans, who were among the earliest settlers of the territory which is now Rumania and the ancestors of the Dacian people. The design and the shape of the vessel are closely related to the form of similar objects which were made at the same time in the Orient.* Below: *This Iron Age pot, found at Zimnicea near the Danube, was made by Scythians who had migrated to the area from the East in about 750 B.C.*

followed by the Huns, the Avars and the Bulgars, who introduced Eastern Orthodox Christianity to the area. At the end of the 9th century the Magyars arrived, and after them came the Turks.

With two important exceptions, very little of artistic merit was left behind by the migrants who arrived before the 10th century.

### BARBARIAN TREASURES IN RUMANIA

The first exceptional find is the *Gold Treasure of Petrossa* (Bucharest, National Museum), which was produced by Hunnish settlers during the 4th century. It includes chalices, ewers and jewelry decorated in the polychrome style (where gold surfaces are inlayed with colored stones).

The second is the *Nagy-Szent-Miklós* (now Seica-Mare) *Treasure*, which was created during the 9th century (Vienna, Natural History Museum). The 23 objects in the collection were made by the Avars, who introduced filigree into the area. Filigree, used on all the pieces in the treasure, is metalwork decoration consisting of fine wires joined together to create intricate, open, decorative patterns. Filigree came to be widely used in Transylvania during the 15th century.

## The Magyars

Toward the end of the 10th century, the Avars were succeeded by the Magyars or Hungarians, migrants from the Ural Mountains. The Magyars brought to the area which is now Transylvania their skill at engraving metal with designs based on abstract plant and animal forms. Magyar design motifs became important in 12th- and 13th-century Romanesque stone carvings in the regions where the Magyars settled.

In 1003, Transylvania was taken over by the Hungarian King Stephen I (ruled 997-1038). From the 11th to the 16th century, Transylvanian art is closely related to Hungarian styles and is therefore distinguished from the remaining areas of present-day Rumania.

### FEUDAL ART IN TRANSYLVANIA

## The Romanesque Period

THE ROMANESQUE STYLE, WHICH ORiginated in Western Europe, first appeared in Transylvania during the 11th century and dominated the architectural and art forms through the first half of the 13th century. Central Europe, especially Hungary, and Lombardy, were the main direct sources for the Transylvanian style.

### CHURCH ARCHITECTURE

The earliest Transylvanian churches, built before the region came under Hungarian rule, were made of wood. They were based on the basilican plan, which includes a central nave or hall culminating in an apse at the eastern end. The nave is flanked by two aisles, which have roofs that are lower than the roof over the nave. Most of the churches built in Transylvania through the feudal period were based on this plan.

### HALL CHURCHES

However, some were made more elaborate by the addition of apses on the eastern ends of the aisles, and by the addition of transepts, arms projecting from the nave near its eastern end, forming a Latin Cross plan. During the 15th century, the "hall church" type (where the nave and aisles are built under the same roof), which originated in Germany, was used in Transylvania. Occasionally, the central type of plan, derived from Orthodox Russia and Greece and ultimately from the Byzantine Middle East, was employed.

During the 11th century, stone replaced wood as the major building material in Transylvania, a practice taken from Hungary and Lombardy, and used up to the end of the 19th century. However, small churches and several large 13th-century structures were made of wood.

The Romanesque churches in Transylvania are characterized by heavy, rectangular proportions and a massive quality derived from Lombard architecture.

### CATHEDRAL OF ALBA-IULIA

One of the earliest extant Transylvanian Romanesque churches is the Roman Catholic cathedral of Alba-Iulia, originally built for the Hungarian King Stephen I in about 1020. Only the original foundations, based on a basilica, remain with the 13th-century late Romanesque reconstruction and the Gothic and Renaissance additions.

The basic 13th-century structure is similar to the Hungarian cathedral of Esztergom constructed during the 12th century by Lombard architect-builders.

Other examples of Romanesque churches in Transylvania include Sebes Cathedral (late 12th to early 13th century) located near Alba-Iulia, the Cistercian abbey church near Sibiu (late 12th century) and a small cathedral near Bistrita (early 13th century). All of these churches include narrow western façades flanked by two massive towers. Basically Romanesque, they also include some minor Gothic features, such as the pointed arches which form windows and doorways.

### SECULAR ARCHITECTURE

Several fortresses were built during the 10th century in Transylvania. They consisted of heavy stone walls, large towers, necessary for defense purposes, and living quarters within the central courtyard.

Examples of Romanesque fortress-castles can be seen at Deva and Bran, both built during the first half of the 13th century. Bran Castle (see page 117), now a museum of medieval art, was built by Teutonic Knights who, along with Saxons, settled in Transylvania during the 12th and 13th centuries. Many additions have been made since its original construction

and reconstruction during the 14th century.

The earliest decorative sculpture in Transylvania derives from the art styles that developed before the 11th century. Sculpture on 11th- and 12th-century churches and monastic buildings is basically geometric and includes twisted and flat abstract forms. The 12th-century carvings on the west façade of Alba-Iulia Cathedral are the best examples of the Transylvanian Romanesque decorative style.

Transylvanian Romanesque painting was similar to Hungarian painting; both were based on Lombard styles. Fresco painting was the most important mode at this time. However, only fragments have survived in Transylvania.

## The Gothic Period

The Gothic style, although introduced into Transylvania around 1150, did not become important until about 1300. Transylvanian Gothic ultimately comes from France, especially from Burgundy. The French Gothic style was first brought to Hungary by the Cistercians, a Benedictine order of friars, who built monasteries in Hungary as well as the late-12th-century abbey near Sibiu in Transylvania.

### CHURCH ARCHITECTURE

In Transylvania, 13th-century wooden churches, although not of Gothic construction, have a strong Gothic atmosphere. Stone churches which were built at the same time include Gothic vaulting systems, but retain a heaviness which is more characteristic of Romanesque architecture.

St. Michael's Cathedral (c. 1380-1432), at Cluj, a "hall church," is the first completely Gothic church

Below left: *This fragment of a fresco painting is in St. Nicolae Domnesc Church at Curtea-de-Arges. Painted during the 14th century, when Walachia was under Turkish rule, the fresco is Byzantine in style.* Below right: *The tombstone of Gerog Apaffi (1638) was carved by Elias Nicolai (active 1635-60). Working in Transylvania, which was part of Hungary at the time, Nicolai was influenced by Western and Central European sculptural styles.*

in Transylvania. The nave, built during the 14th century, is early Gothic; the aisles and façade are late Gothic, distinguished by the more elaborate flamboyant vaulting and decoration.

*Biserica Neagra* (Black Church, 1385-1477) at Brasov, another example of a "hall church," has features similar to St. Michael's. There are also elements derived from German and Polish architecture. Most notable of these is the asymmetrical western façade, with the single tower placed slightly to the right of the entrance.

The Hungarian Reformed Church, originally the Church of the Franciscan Monastery at Cluj (late 15th century), is an example of the fully developed Gothic style in Transylvania.

### SECULAR ARCHITECTURE

The most outstanding example of secular Gothic architecture in Transylvania is Hunedoara or Hunyadi Castle (1267 and c. 1450-90), now an art museum. The existing structure consists of a reconstruction of the Romanesque fortress-castle, as well as a chapel and Knight's Hall, which were added in 1452 by János Hunyadi (c. 1387-1456). The basic plan, like the original structure, is rectangular and includes a central courtyard. Based on the French Gothic style, the castle includes elaborate roofs over the corner towers and over the main entrance of the exterior walls.

Other examples include the 15th-century French Gothic town hall and market hall at Sibiu.

### SCULPTURE

Of the few remaining pieces of monumental Gothic sculpture in Transylvania, the most outstanding is the tomb of János Hunyadi, carved in about 1456 for the cathedral of Alba-Iulia. It consists of a sarcophagus covered with bas-relief sculpture representing scenes from Hunyadis' major battles. On the top is a gigantic piece of portrait sculpture in a late Gothic style.

The form of decorative Gothic sculpture on churches and secular buildings is derived from France and reached Transylvania through Hungary. The most important Hungarian models were the sculpture on the abbey church of Jak and on St. Elizabeth's Cathedral at Kassa (now Kosice, Czechoslovakia).

Examples of decorative Transylvanian Gothic sculpture are found on the cathedral of Alba-Iulia and on St. Michael's Cathedral at Cluj. The latter also has some wood sculpture, including the carved panels on the sacristy door. The style of these and other wood carvings is often related to German works of art.

### PAINTING

Fresco painting continued to develop in Transylvania during the Gothic period. It did not reach the importance it achieved in Hungary until the 15th century. In addition to the Western and Central European styles which Transylvanian artists adopted, they occasionally used a style based on the Near and Middle Eastern Byzantine traditions.

Left: *The monastic Church of the Three Hierarchs at Jassy, which was built in about 1639. The architect-builders and the craftsmen who decorated the exterior were influenced by the Walachian Byzantine style, as well as by Moorish and Russian architecture and decoration. The surfaces of the building are completely covered with low-relief carvings, which form beautiful abstract patterns of design. The basic, central plan of the church, like most of those built during the feudal period in Moldavia and Walachia, is based on central plans which originated in Constantinople.*

Outstanding are the fresco paintings in the fortress-church at Sacueni (1419), near Oradea. The paintings are dominantly French Gothic in style; a few details, however, reveal Byzantine influences as well. The frescoes depict the life of St. Ladislas, who brought Catholicism to Oradea during the 11th century.

Dated slightly later are the frescoes in Hunyadi Castle, painted in about 1450.

The names of a few Transylvanian Gothic panel painters have been preserved. They include Thomas de Kolozsvar (c. 1377-1450) one of the greatest Central European panel painters of the 15th century.

Thomas de Kolozsvar's only definitely known work is the three-part altarpiece painted in about 1427 for a northern Hungarian church (Esztergom, Christian Museum). The central panel depicts *The Crucifixion;* the side panels show scenes from the lives of Christ and various saints. His style is a combination of late-Gothic and early Italian Renaissance painting. The latter style had begun to influence Hungarian and northern Transylvanian artists during the end of the 15th century.

John of Roznava (now in Czechoslovakia), active during the first half of the 15th century, painted the *Crucifixion* (1455) for the parish church at Sibiu. His late-Gothic style resembles contemporary southern German paintings.

Above left: *These extremely ornate decorations enhance the interior of the 16th-century Episcopal church at Curtea-de-Arges, which is in the historical principality of Walachia. Various styles may be distinguished, including the Byzantine, which is the most outstanding, and the Moorish and Orthodox Russian modes. The early-16th-century fresco paintings, visible in the background, are similar to those in the 14th-century St. Nicolae Domnesc Church, also in Curtea-de-Arges.* Above right: *The cathedral at Cluj, in Transylvania, was built in 1890.*

## MINOR ARTS

One of the greatest artistic achievements during the Transylvanian Gothic period was in the field of metalwork. The art of filigree, first brought to the area by the Avars, was perfected during the 15th century by goldsmiths at Cluj, Mures, Sibiu and Brasov. Craftsmen in the same areas also produced so-called Transylvanian enamel, which was often incorporated with relief sculpture and filigree.

## Renaissance and Baroque Styles

Toward the end of the 15th century, the Italian Renaissance style penetrated Hungary. Several Italian architects, sculptors and painters worked in Hungary during the reign of Matthias Corvinus (ruled 1458-90). As a direct result, Transylvania was affected, especially from the beginning of the 16th century.

The Italian Renaissance style which reached Transylvania at this time includes classical architectural motifs revived from ancient Greece and Rome.

The earliest completely Italian Renaissance structure in Transylvania is Lazay Chapel (c. 1500), which was added to the cathedral of Alba-Iulia in 1512. Built by an unknown Lombard architect, the chapel is a rectangular block decorated with classical columns and pilasters.

Zapolya Castle, near Oradea, was built during the first quarter of the 16th century by an unknown architect from Bologna. Its most Renaissance feature is the classical arcade set on Doric columns.

After the middle of the 16th century, building was secular rather than ecclesiastical. The Renaissance style continued through the 16th and well into the 17th century; this is exemplified by the Vintul-de-Jos Castle (1450), Banffy Castle (c. 1550), near Cluj, and Bethlen Castle (1559-98) at Chinyadevo (now in the Ukrainian S.S.R.).

## BAROQUE ARCHITECTURE

The Baroque style was first introduced into Transylvania in about 1686, when Austria took over the region. The Hungarian Baroque style became an important influence during the 18th century.

The influence of the great Austrian architect Johann Lukas von Hildebrant (1668-1745) is evident in 18th-century Transylvanian buildings;

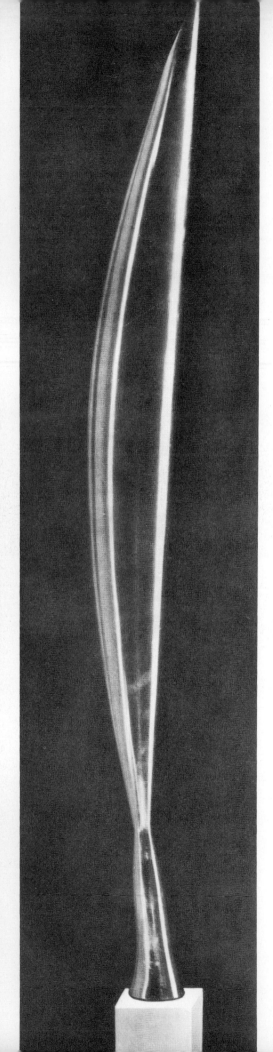

however, Transylvanian architects tended toward soberness and simplicity, and, therefore, modified the Austrian and other elaborate national variants of the Baroque and Rococo styles.

The most outstanding Baroque structures in Transylvania include the early-18th-century Jesuit church at Cluj and the Uniate Church (1792-96), also at Cluj. Both are Austrian Baroque in style. Secular works include Bruknethal Palace in Sibiu, now a museum, and another castle of the Bethlen family at Deva, both of which were built during the 18th century.

During the 16th and 17th centuries, the Italian Renaissance style dominated monumental sculpture in Transylvania.

The names of two important sculptors from this period have been preserved: Elias Nicolai (active 1635-60) whose mortuary monument to Gerog Apaffi (1638) is in the National Museum at Budapest (see page 127); and Peter Dioszegi, active during the first half of the 17th century; who carved the monument to Gerog Süküsk in 1632 (Cluj Museum).

From 1690 to the end of the 18th century, a modified Baroque sculptural style prevailed in Transylvania.

It is evident in the late works of the outstanding sculptor and goldsmith Sebastian Hann (1644-1713). Hann's most important work is the *Epitaph of Valentin Franck* (1697, Sibiu, Bruckenthal Museum). The epitaph includes a portrait bust of Franck and relief sculpture on the base representing Old Testament stories.

During the 16th century, very little painting was executed in Transylvania. Toward the latter part of the 17th century, the art of fresco painting was revived. It was used to decorate the interiors of palaces and elaborate private dwellings. The major inspiration for the style came from Austria and Hungary and ultimately from Italy.

## FEUDAL ART IN WALACHIA AND MOLDAVIA

### The Middle Ages

WALACHIA WAS UNDER TURKISH RULE, almost without relief, from the be-

*Bird in Flight was sculpted in 1940 by Constantin Brancusi (1876-1957), Rumania's greatest modern artist.*

ginning of the 14th to the 19th century. Turkish domination began in Moldavia in 1504 and continued up to 1828-29. The Eastern influence brought by the Turks to these historical principalities is important in the development of their art.

Ruins of Walachian churches built before Turkish rule was established reveal Western and Central European influences. For example, the foundations of a 12th-century church in Campulung, built by Teutonic Knights, was based on the basilican plan. However, from the 14th century, the Byzantine influence was almost absolute.

The original construction of St. Nicolae Domnesc Church at Curtea-de-Arges (c. 1350) is the earliest Byzantine structure in Walachia. It is based on a central type of plan with a Greek Cross (where four arms of equal length project from a central sanctuary) inscribed within a square. Over the crossing is a cupola. This type of plan, which became common in Walachia during the feudal period, derived from Instanbul (Constantinople), either directly or through Orthodox Russia and Greece. Especially influential was the monastic district of Mt. Athos in Greece, an area under direct Byzantine rule.

During the 14th century, a minor but important architectural trend was introduced into Walachia by Serbian monks. Churches built in the Serbian mode include the monastic church at Tismana (1393) and the convent church of Cozia near Calimanesti, which is one of the best-preserved 14th-century churches in Rumania. Based on a Greek Cross plan, the church of Cozia has three apses at the end of each arm, except for the west façade, which is decorated with a portico.

By the end of the 15th century and throughout the 16th and 17th centuries, Walachian architecture acquired its own character. Churches were built by local master-builders who incorporated Byzantine, Serbian and other Slavic styles. The most outstanding Walachian structure from this period is the Episcopal church at Curtea-de-Arges (1512-21). Based on a Greek Cross plan, like the St. Nicolae Domnesc Church, it has a cupola over the crossing, a tower above the eastern façade and two turrets above the western end.

### ARCHITECTURE IN MOLDAVIA

The oldest preserved architecture in Moldavia dates from the 14th century. The same influences that created Walachian styles were present in Moldavia. In addition, some Moldavian builders were inspired by the Polish and Transylvanian Gothic styles.

Churches from the 15th century in Moldavia are characterized by their unusual height, which is emphasized by a tall, narrow tower over the western façade. The exteriors of these churches are often decorated by glazed, colored ceramic tiles arranged in geometric patterns. The most interesting are the church at Voronet (now Gura-Humorului, 1488) and St. Nicholas' Church, located near Jassy (see page 92).

Several Moldavian churches built during the 16th century are distinguished by an open porch added to the western façade and by fresco paintings which cover the entire exterior surface. Architecturally, these churches are similar to small Italian Byzantine churches. They were usually built as fortress-churches, set within a fortified wall, or as part of a monastic setting.

### SCULPTURE

Ornamental sculpture in Walachia and Moldavia developed out of the art of the people of the region before the 14th century. The Byzantine style was added to the indigenous modes.

Decorative sculpture in Walachia is exemplified by the exterior and interior carvings at the Episcopal church at Curtea-de-Arges (see page 129). Oriental and Russian Georgian elements based on Byzantine art are combined with motifs inspired by local traditions and styles brought to the area by the Avars.

From the 14th to the 16th century, decorative sculpture in both historical principalities was made of flat, abstract geometric patterns.

Monumental sculpture, including tombstone carvings and portraiture, is represented by 14th- and 15th-century gravestones at St. Nicolae Domnesc Church at Curtea-de-Arges.

Occasionally, Central European Romanesque and Gothic styles influenced stone-carvers, especially those in Moldavia. For example, the early Gothic style is evident in the 15th-century carvings which decorate the monastery at Snagov.

### PAINTING

The earliest existing paintings in Walachia and Moldavia are found in St. Nicolae Domnesc Church at Curtea-de-Arges (see page 127). Exe-

cuted during the 14th century, they are Byzantine in both style and in the presentation and interpretation of the subjects. The frescoes include a narrative of Christ's life, portrayals of the Prophets and the *Madonna in Glory*, which adorns the inside of the cupola.

Most of the medieval churches in both Walachia and Moldavia are decorated with fresco paintings similar to those in St. Nicolae Domnesc Church. Examples include the paintings in the Episcopal church at Curtea-de-Arges produced during the first quarter of the 16th century.

Moldavian 15th- and 16th-century painting surpassed the painting in Walachia. Some of the churches in the northern area of Moldavia, in the present-day province of Suceava, were decorated with frescoes on the exteriors as well as within. The subject and style of the paintings, which do not differ considerably from church to church, were the result of a combination of Eastern Orthodox and Western European traditions.

Of the 12 surviving churches which bear exterior frescoes, the most impressive are: St. George's Church (1522-35) at Marginea; the monastic church of Humor, built in 1530 and painted in 1535, located near Gura-

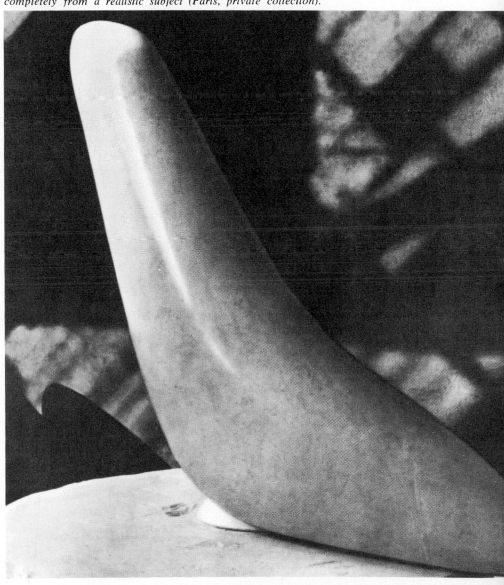

The Miracle *(1940) by Constantin Brancusi (1876-1957) is made of highly polished marble. The form and subject derive from his earlier works including* Newborn *(1915) and* Beginning of the World *(1924). After studying in Walachia, Brancusi sculpted in Paris, where he was influenced by Auguste Rodin (1840-1917). Even in his seemingly abstract works such as* The Miracle, *Brancusi never broke away completely from a realistic subject (Paris, private collection).*

Humorului; and the monastic church of Voronet (now Gura-Humorului), built in 1488 and painted in about 1547.

### The Late Feudal Period

During the 17th and 18th centuries, architecture and decorative sculpture in Walachia and Moldavia became more elaborate. The same elements which determined the styles during the Middle Ages in these areas persisted. In addition, Moorish art from the Near East was an important influence.

#### WALACHIAN ARCHITECTURE AND DECORATION

The best examples of the flamboyant style in Walachia are: Horezu Convent (1693), the church of Mogosoaia Palace (c. 1650) near Bucharest, and the 17th-century Patriarchal Church in Bucharest (see page 125).

#### MOLDAVIAN ARCHITECTURE AND DECORATION

Moldavia was influenced by Walachian architecture, especially during the 17th century, as well as by Moorish and Russian styles. The most important Moldavian churches of the period are the Dragomiresti Monastic Church (1609) and the monastic Church of the Three Hierarchs at Jassy (c. 1639, see page 128). The façade of the church at Jassy, like the façades of churches in Walachia, is entirely decorated with exquisite, flat Byzantine and Moorish patterns carved in low relief, which create an impression of embroidery in stone.

## THE NINETEENTH CENTURY

ALTHOUGH TRANSYLVANIA WAS UNDER Austrian rule and Walachia and Moldavia under Russian and Turkish power during most of the 19th century, the distinctive artistic characteristics of the historical principalities began to diminish and by the end of the century, an art style common to all three areas arose. In most places, secular architecture and art dominated over religious works.

Architects and artists in the area which is now Rumania became more aware of Western European styles; by 1850 many were studying in Western Europe, especially at Paris. Also, many were artistically recognized beyond their country. In addition, foreign architects and artists, including Austrians, Hungarians and Italians, worked in the principalities.

### Architecture

During the last quarter of the 18th century, Walachian and Moldavian styles were closely related. The Neoclassical style, introduced during the 19th century by Russia, was intensified by additional Western European influences. The neo-Baroque style, also brought from Western Europe, became equally common during the period.

There was a period of intense building during the 19th century, which included the construction of new towns, reconstruction of old towns and the creation of public buildings in Bucharest. Among the Neoclassical and neo-Baroque structures in Bucharest are the Palace of Justice (c. 1860), built by Albert Ballu (active 1849-89), the Rumanian Athenaeum (see opposite) and the University, designed by Alexander Orascu (1817 94) during the last quarter of the 19th century (see page 116).

#### THE NATIONAL STYLES

During the second half of the 19th century, there was a Gothic revival in Rumania, which brought about a renewed interest in the national and local styles. This resulted in a revival of the Rumanian medieval house, seen in the Ghikas vault in Bellu cemetery at Bucharest and the Nicolescu-Dorobantzu mansion in Bucharest. Both were built in about 1875.

The interest in national styles also led to the Rumanian eclectic style (a form of architecture made up of several distinguishable older styles). The Rumanian eclectic style differed from other national variants of the style, as architects drew on Byzantine as well as Western European modes. The cathedral at Cluj (c. 1890) is an example of the eclectic taste in Rumania (see page 129).

Toward the end of the 19th century, there was a reaction against national and eclectic styles. This was led by architects who had studied at Paris. At first, the reactionaries revived the Renaissance style, which in turn laid the foundations for modern architecture in Rumania; however, the modern methods and designs in building were not used in Rumania until the 1940s.

### Sculpture

Most 19th-century Rumanian sculpture is Neoclassical. Sculpture was used to adorn contemporary buildings, filling classical pediments and decorating tops of columns. This is exemplified by the décor on the Princes' Palace at Jassy (1806).

Several important sculptors emerged in Rumania during the second half of the 19th century, many of whom studied abroad, especially at Paris. The most important was Karl Storck (1826-87), who, after extensive training in Western Europe, worked in Rumania in a Neoclassical style. He produced a number of portrait-busts and images of historical figures. His work includes the pediment sculpture (1862) which adorns the University of Bucharest.

Storck taught the important 19th-century sculptors who succeeded him. They included his son Carol (1854-1924), Paul Focseneanu (1840-67), Ion Georgescu (1856-98) and Stefan Ionescu (1856-1918). These sculptors are well represented in the National Museum of Art at Bucharest.

### Painting

Secular painting, including portraiture, miniature and historical painting, replaced religious works of art during the 19th century. During the 1848 revolution artists were commissioned to paint works which would exalt the cause of the masses. The basis for the new styles, required for these and similar subjects, was acquired abroad, especially in Paris.

Theodor Aman (1831-91), inspired by the revolution, was the first Rumanian painter to achieve Western European fame. After studying in France, he painted several works based on the history of Walachia and Moldavia, as well as a number of portraits. Aman was the founder of the art school of Bucharest and the art galleries at Jassy and Bucharest.

Rumania's most outstanding 19th-century painters were Ion Andreescu (1850-82) and Nicolae Grigorescu (1838-1907).

Andreescu studied at Paris, where he was influenced by the pre-Impressionists. When he returned to Rumania, he painted a number of landscapes in a 19th-century French style. Many of his works are in the Bucharest Picture Gallery.

*The Athenaeum, built in Bucharest during the last quarter of the 19th century, is an example of the European neo-Baroque style as it developed in Rumania. European architectural styles, used in Transylvania during the feudal period, penetrated into the historical principalities of Walachia and Moldavia during the 19th century. The Rumanian Athenaeum is used as a museum of art.*

*The wash drawing illustrated above was produced by Samuel Mutzner, a contemporary graphic artist and painter. It is typical of the works which the Rumanian government commissions to bring art closer to the working people. This drawing exemplifies the propagandist demands made upon artists by the Communist government; in practice, these demands have led to the stultification of art in many countries behind the Iron Curtain.*

Nicolae Grigorescu, born in Walachia, studied in Bucharest. His earliest paintings were icons and murals. During a visit to Paris in 1861, Grigorescu studied a number of paintings in the Louvre and was influenced by Jean Corot (1796-1875). After his return to Rumania in 1869, Grigorescu painted a great number of portraits and peasant scenes, several now in the Rumanian Art Museum at Bucharest. His style is characterized by the use of soft colors and delicate brushwork, which he acquired in France.

Outstanding late-19th-century Rumanian painters include: Gabriel Popescu (1868-1948), a landscape painter influenced by French art; Stefan Luchian (1868-1916), whose style is like contemporary Italian paintings; and Octav Bancila (1872-1944), who, with his expressionistic portrayal of the Rumanian peasants' courage and suffering, did much toward enlisting support for their uprising.

## MODERN ART

### Architecture

DURING THE FIRST 40 YEARS OF THE 20th century, the revival styles continued in Rumania. These included the neo-Renaissance, neo-Baroque and Neoclassical, as well as a new interest in Moorish style.

#### ARCHITECTURE AFTER WORLD WAR II

After 1944, Rumania began to build in a modern style, using new methods and materials, such as reinforced concrete, glass, and steel. Rumanian buildings also eliminated added ornamentation from their structure. Suburbs surrounding Bucharest and several cities in Rumania have been built or rebuilt in the modern postwar style. Projects include housing areas, industrial plants, factories and schools.

Examples of modern buildings in Bucharest are Broadcasting House, the Ministry of Transport and Telecommunications (see page 88) and the palace of the president of the Council of Ministers (see page 91).

### Sculpture

Karl Storck and his followers determined the style of sculpture executed during the early part of the 20th century in Rumania.

In about 1910 there was a reaction against the academic Neoclassical style. Sculptors began to study the modern sculpture of Western Europe, as well as archaic African and Oceanic carvings, all of which formed the basis for the modern Rumanian movement in sculpture.

Since 1944, however, there has been a return to the old 19th-century styles, in an attempt to exalt the peasant uprisings, the revolutions, and the working class. Post-1944 sculpture in the Socialist-Realist style includes portrayals of peasants and working-class people performing their tasks. Most of these were and are being commissioned by the government.

#### CONSTANTIN BRANCUSI

Constantin Brancusi (1876-1957) is Rumania's most distinguished artist. Born in Walachia, he studied at the Academy of Art in Bucharest. After studying at the École des Beaux-Arts in Paris, Brancusi settled in France, where, with the exception of a short period during the 1930s, he remained until his death.

Brancusi's earliest works, mostly portraits, are similar to the late sculpture of Auguste Rodin (1840-1917). In about 1915, Brancusi's sculptured forms became abstract and the surfaces very smooth. This development is apparent in *Newborn* (1915) and *Beginning of the World* (1924), both in the Museum of Art at Philadelphia.

From 1919, Brancusi began to work on the theme of a bird in space. One of the first in this category is *Bird in Flight* (1919, Philadelphia, Museum of Art). He also continued to execute portraits, exemplified by *Head of Mme. Pogany* (1913, New York, Museum of Modern Art).

In 1937, Brancusi created a large-scale project for a park in Turgi-Jiu near his birthplace in Walachia. It includes *Gate, Table and Stools*, and *Endless Column*.

From 1940 to his death, Brancusi continued to work on themes he had begun in the early part of his career, exemplified by *Miracle*, (see page 131, Paris, private collection) and another *Bird in Flight* (see page 130, Venice, Peggy Guggenheim Collection), both made in 1940. During this period, Brancusi also worked in wood.

Constantine Baraschi (1902-     )

is the most important sculptor to have remained in Rumania. Born in Walachia, he suited at the Academy of Fine Arts, in Bucharest and at the Julien Academy in Paris. Before 1944, Baraschi's style was related to that of modern sculpture, as seen in *Ecstasy* (c. 1938), an abstract, smooth-surfaced marble figure. Since 1944, he has carved several large portrait-busts and monuments in the Soviet Socialist-Realist style, as is evident in *Monument to Eminescu* (1961, Bucharest).

Two contemporary and internationally recognized Rumanian sculptors are Etinne Hajdu (1907-    ), who works near Paris, and Zoltan Kemeny (1907-    ), who lives in Zurich. While Hajdu's works are often like Brancusi's, Kemeny uses modern sculptural materials, such as leather and copper.

### Painting

The same tendencies that are present in 20th-century Rumanian sculpture are evident in the development of modern painting. In about 1910, painters broke away from the academic styles that dominated the 19th century. Since 1944, however, some painters have returned to the style of the previous century because of the government's attempt to bring art closer to the people and to create a link between art and everyday life. A great number of contemporary paintings portray peasants in a realistic 19th-century style.

One of the outstanding Rumanian painters is Victor Brauner (1903-    ), who moved to Paris in 1925. Brauner spent 19 years working in a Surrealist style, after which his paintings became more decorative.

Among the 20th-century Rumanian painters who have remained in their homeland are Gheorghe Petrascu (1872-1949), Jean Steriadi (1880-1956), Iosif Iser (1881-1958) and Camil Ressu (1880-    ).

In 1965, official state censorship of the arts in Rumania came to an end and the resultant liberation in choice of subject and style has led to a new lease on life for the artist in Rumania.

*A wooden madonna of the 14th-15th centuries. In the Middle Ages, religion was the main inspiration for literature no less than for sculpture.*

## BACKGROUND TO RUMANIAN LITERATURE

### Linguistic Origins

CONSIDERING THE COMPLEX MOVEments, in early times, of the peoples whose descendants inhabit modern Rumania, the Rumanian language has, not suprisingly, several unusual characteristics. It is a Romance language, deriving from Latin, but with a strong admixture of Slavonic and Oriental elements.

### Language of the Roman Soldiers

The earliest origins of the neo-Latin tongue, which came into use in Rumania around the 13th century A.D., are found in the provincial Latin spoken by the Roman soldiers and colonists who occupied the region of Dacia in the 2nd and 3rd centuries A.D. Some Rumanian scholars insist that modern Rumanian is directly derived from Latin, and many distinguished schools of writing have flourished in this belief.

### Four Main Dialects

Whatever may be the case, modern Rumanian has emerged as an important literary language. The spoken language has four main dialects, and of these the most important, the Daco-Rumanian dialect spoken by nearly 15 million people, is the major literary and only official language. The three remaining dialects are the Arumenian, or Macedo-Rumanian, spoken in the Balkan Peninsula, in parts of Greece, Yugoslavia, Albania and Bulgaria, which has a small body of popular literature of its own; the Meglenitic, or Megleno-Rumanian, spoken mainly in northern Salonika; and Istro-Rumanian, spoken in and around the Istrian Peninsula.

### Folk Literature

In addition to external cultural and linguistic influences, Rumanian literature draws an added richness from its wealth of traditional material. Rumanian traditional literature presents an important link between Western and Eastern folklore, since it has been both influenced by and has in turn influenced Western Balkan and Russian Ukrainian folk literature.

#### *LOVE LYRICS, CAROLS AND DIRGES*

The most important field is that of lyric poetry. In this group the largest body of work falls into the class of *doine,* or love lyrics, simple, sentimental and nostalgic songs, with a tendency toward gentle melancholy.

As in other literatures, there are a number of narrative ballads with historical or legendary subjects, the *cantece batranesti,* as well as traditional plays, the *Vicleim* or *Irozi,* for performance at great religious festivals. Finally, there is a considerable body of prose, including traditional tales, proverbs and sayings

## EARLY RUMANIAN LITERATURE

THE EARLIEST PRINTED WORKS TO appear in Rumania, from 1508 onward, were mainly Protestant tracts and other religious works. The earliest are printed in Slavonic, but the use of Rumanian soon spread. Cyrillic characters were most often used, but Latin characters appear to have been used for the first time as early as 1570.

### Religious Literature

Early religious literature consists chiefly of tracts, gospels and psalters translated from Slavonic. These were produced in a number of centers, notably in Brasov, where one Deacon Coresi is known to have printed works in Rumanian between 1560 and 1581. The most interesting original work of the time is the *Teachings of Neagoe Basarab,* a dissertation on morals and behavior addressed by the prince of that name to his son. This was written in the 16th century, but was not printed in Rumanian until around 1654.

#### *THE PRESS AT SNAGOV MONASTERY*

The Moldavian Metropolitan Varlaam published a collection of ser-

*A view of Bucharest, capital of Rumania since 1862. The city became a center of the Rumanian national movement in the early 19th century. It was here that Ian Heliade Radulescu (1802-72) founded, in 1828, the first Rumanian daily newspaper,* Curierul Romanesc, *and, in 1836,* Curierul de ambe sexe.

mons in Rumanian in 1643, while the Metropolitan Dosoftei (1624-94) compiled the *Lives of the Saints* and was also responsible for the earliest example of Rumanian poetry in his *Rhymed Psalter* (1673), published while he was exiled in Poland.

A center of printing for the Orthodox writers was the press at the Snagov monastery, near Bucharest, run by Antim Ivireanu.

### THE BIBLE AND THE LAWS

The first complete translation of the Bible, made by Radu and Serban Greceanu, appeared in Bucharest in 1688, and marked an important step in the establishment of Rumanian as a literary language. In addition, a number of important codifications of ecclesiastical and civil law were made by Moldavian princes, among them the *Laws of Vasile Lupu* (1646) and the *Laws of Matei Basarab* (1652).

## Chronicle Writers

During the 16th and 17th centuries a school of chronicle writers flourished in the monasteries of Moldavia. Many of their histories were fiercely nationalistic in character, as is evident in one of the earliest, the *Letopisitul Tarii Moldovei* (Lives of the Princes of Moldavia), written by Grigore Ureche (1590-1647). This work, which covers the period between 1359 and 1595, is written in a careful yet vivid style in a Rumanian which is almost completely Latinistic and free from Slavonic forms.

The history of Moldavia was carried up to 1661 in the *Annals of the Moldavian Land* by Miron Costin (1633-91), who also wrote in Latin, Polish and Hungarian and translated his own work into Polish. His work was expanded by his son Niculae Costin, and the history of Moldavia was brought up to 1743 by the nobleman Ion Neculce (1672-1745), who also made the first collections of folk literature. An outstanding historical narrative in the medieval style is the *History of the Rumanians* (1698), by the Moldavian Prince Dimitrius Cantemir (1675-1723), which was translated from the writer's Latin in 1710.

## Founding the Literature

The first period of Rumanian literature, described above, may be said to have ended in the mid-18th century. Altough this establishes Rumanian literature as one of recent development compared to other European countries, the state of modern Rumanian writing proves that the early religious writers and chroniclers laid

*A view of Timisoara, a city in the Banat of western Rumania. It was formerly the seat of Roman Catholic and Orthodox bishops and, with its universities and libraries, is now the main cultural center of western Rumania. Throughout its history, Rumanian literature has been influenced by the Christian churches, and churchmen, bishop and monks were among Rumania's more important writers.*

a sure foundation for the development of a lively and original tradition. In addition, further variety was added in the early period by the translation of many secular works in Greek, Slavonic, Byzantine and Oriental languages into Rumanian.

## THE EIGHTEENTH CENTURY

### A Contrast of Influences

DURING THE 18TH CENTURY, THE cultural propaganda of the Phanariots, the Greek princes and officials appointed by the Turks, had some influence in literary circles, both through the spread of Hellenistic sympathies among members of the upper classes and in the substitution of Greek for ecclesiastical Slavonic as the liturgical language. The greater part of the Rumanian people, however, looked on the Greeks as oppressors, and their powers provoked a nationalistic reaction in literature in a number of centers.

### THE LATINISTS

This was particularly the case around Blaj, where a group of writers known as the Latinists came into being. These writers were mainly Italian-educated; nationalistic in sym-

pathy, they pursued the ideal, a common one in Rumanian literature, of a completely Latinized language free of Greek or Slav elements.

The leaders of the group were Samuil Micu-Clain (1774-1806), Gheorghe Sincai (1753-1816) and Petru Maior (1755-1821). These three writers collaborated on a Rumanian-Latin dictionary, finally published in 1825. Nicu-Clain was also responsible for the first full Rumanian grammar, the *Elementa linguae dacoromanae sive valachicae*, published in 1780, and for a revised version of the Rumanian Bible of 1688, published in 1795.

### The Early Poets

The later 18th and early 19th centuries saw the appearance of the first important Rumanian poets. The most important of these was the lyric poet Ieanache Vacarescu (c. 1740-1800), a member of a noble family who had written a Rumanian grammar and a *History of the Ottoman Empire* (1788). He drew his inspiration mainly from Rumanian folk literature, though Hellenistic, Roman and Oriental influences may also be perceived in his works, which are mainly simple, deeply emotional lyrics.

A fluent versifier was Ion Budai-

Above: *Mihail Eminescu (1850-89), Rumania's greatest lyric poet. His poems, many of which are meditations on love or death, are deeply pessimistic and reflect the tragedy of the poet's life, which ended in insanity. The* Poezii *(Poems), 1884, were influential in the development of modern Rumanian poetry.*

Deleanu (c. 1760-c.1820), whose major work was the mock-heroic epic of gypsy life *Tiganiada* (1812). Other notable lyric poets of the period were the Moldavian Matei Milo (c. 1750-c. 1802), Nicolae Vacarescu (died c. 1828) and the nationalistic writers Naum Ramniceanu Protosinghelul (1764-1839) and Vasil Fabian Bob (1795-1836).

Vasile Aaron (1770-1822) was a deeply religious poet who was influenced both by the English poet John Milton, as in his long poem on the *Passion of Christ* (1805), and by classical literature. French influence was also strong, as it remained into the 20th century, and is reflected particulary in the lyrics of Barbu Paris Momuleanu (1794-1837) and Alecu Beldiman (1760-1826), who translated the works of Voltaire.

## Journalism

A number of educationalists pioneered the publication of journals and newspapers. The first Rumanian daily newspaper was the *Curierul Romanesc*, launched by the Walachian Ian Heliade Radulescu (1802-72) in 1828. Radulescu was much influenced by Italian literature, which influence he spread in his literary magazine *Curierul de ambe sexe*, founded in 1836, and also made

translations of the works of Byron and Lamartine. He pioneered the foundation of the Bucharest National Theater with the foundation of his *Societatea Filarmonică* in 1833.

Gheorghe Lazar (1779-1823) and Gheorghe Baritz were educationalists who encouraged the spread of journalism in Transylvania, while in Moldavia the Italian-influenced Gheorghe Asachi (1788-1869) founded two periodicals and set up a school for the training of actors.

## THE NINETEENTH CENTURY

### The Romantic Movement

THE ROMANTIC MOVEMENT WHICH spread all over Europe in the early 19th century received its main impetus in Rumania from the interest in the work of the great French writers Chateaubriand, Lamartine, De Musset and Victor Hugo.

One of the foremost of French-influenced writers was Grigore Alexandrescu (1812-85), whose earliest works, such as the *Poems* (1832), showed the influence of Lamartine, as did his *Meditations*, published in 1863. He also produced a number of elegant and witty fables based on traditional folklore, in the manner of La Fontaine.

### TREND TOWARD NATIONALISM

Constantin Negruzzi (1809-69) was responsible, through his translations from French and Russian, for a growing interest in historical fiction and, indirectly, for a trend toward nationalism in literature, which was to lead to a revolt against foreign models and a return to traditional material.

This trend toward nationalism was also furthered by the work of Alecu Russo (1819-59), who compiled collections of nationalistic songs, wrote a lyrical prose work in biblical style entitled *The Canticle of Rumania*, and also left a number of interesting biographical fragments.

### MIHAI KOGALNICEANU

One of the leaders of the nationalistic school of writers was the his-

torian and politician Mihai Kogalniceanu (1817-91), who became an important political figure in the late 1850s. As well as editing literary and historical periodicals, he was responsible for the first modern edition of the Moldavian chronicles, the *Letopisetele Moldovei*, in 1845-52.

### The Later Nineteenth Century

One of the foremost figures in later-19th-century Rumanian literature was the versatile Vasile Alecsandri (1821-90), a man of wide culture who had traveled in Europe and the Middle East and also achieved political eminence. In his lyrical poetry, such as the *Doine si lacrimioare* (1853), and other collections, he comes close to the fresh simplicity of the traditional songs which he brought to the popular notice with his anthologies of 1852-53 and 1866. Alecsandri was also a prolific playwright and an accomplished writer of prose.

Two other important writers were Alexandru Odobescu (1834-95) and Bogdan Hasdeu (1836-1907).

Odobescu was an archaeologist, philologist and art critic, and was responsible for casting the historical novel in its modern form in such works as *Doamna Chiajna* (1860) and for laying the foundations of modern art criticism in his *Pseudokinegetikos* (1874).

Hasdeu was a more conventionally romantic writer who wrote historical epics in both prose and poetry, such as the verse drama *Razvan si Vidra* (1867), in a style much influenced by Victor Hugo.

### MIHAIL EMINESCU

It was at about this time, when the Romantic movement was beginning to give way to the new realistic spirit, that Rumania's best-known poet made his appearance. This was Mihail Eminescu (1850-89), a follower of the German philosopher Schopenhauer, whose mood of Rom-

Right: *Ioan Luca Caragiale (1853-1912), one of Rumania's best-known playwrights and also a writer of satirical short stories and sketches. In his writings Caragiale boldly attacked injustice and authoritarianism. His views brought him so much adverse criticism that he felt enforced to spend the last part of his life in voluntary exile in Berlin.*

*Mihail Sadoveanu (1880-1961), one of the most important Rumanian novelists and short-story writers of the inter-war years. Although his works include successful historical novels such as* Fratii Jderi *(The Brothers Jderi) 1935, his chief talent lay in descriptions of landscape and peasant life.*

antic pessimism was heightened by his unhappy life which terminated in insanity. In spite of the influence of Germanic and Oriental philosophy upon his work, Eminescu's moving lyric poetry is mainly written in a style of expressive simplicity, which puts it close to traditional songs and ballads, especially in his lyrics inspired by the Moldavian countryside.

Into his simple compositions Eminescu introduced a note of fantasy and allegory, specializing in meditations upon the themes of unhappy love and death. In addition, a number of his works display a spirit of deep patriotism and an advanced social consciousness. His *Poezii* (Poems), 1884, were probably the most important single influence on the development of Rumanian poetry in the 20th century. Eminescu also produced prose works on philosophical and political themes.

## The Realistic Movement

In Rumania, as in the rest of Europe, the later years of the 19th century were marked by a growing trend toward realism in literature. In Rumania, an important part in establishing this new trend was played by the philosopher, politician and literary critic Titu Maiorescu (1840-1917). Maiorescu founded the *Junimea*, or Youth, movement, to propagate the new ideals, in 1863 in Jassy, and four years later this group gave rise to the periodical *Convorbiri Literare* (Literary Conversations), which was to exert an important influence over writers for years.

Among the many contributors to *Converbiri Literare* was Ion Creangă (1837-89), a writer of peasant stock whose tales of rustic life are set in an idealistic, patriarchal world and are rooted deep in the native idiom of the Moldavian people. Among his works are the nostalgic and moving *Childhood Reminiscences*.

### WRITER ABROAD

A writer of a rather different kind was Ioan Luca Caragiale (1853-1912), whose Bohemian life and forthright opinions did little to endear him to the literary establishment.

Caragiale was a militant Socialist

and an upholder of the rights of the Jewish minority, who have suffered persecution in Rumania up to very recent times; eventually his extremist views led ·to his leaving the country to settle in Berlin. His melodramatic tragedies, such as *False Accusation* (1889), has some effect on modern Rumanian theater, but he is at his best in his short stories and sketches, which are distinguished by their disturbing realism and penetrating satire. The best known of these is *An Easter Candle* (1890), a tale of fear and madness with a Jewish setting. Late in his career, Caragiale turned to witty and extravagant fantasy, as in *Kir Ianulea* (1909), which is set in Rumania during the last years of Greco-Turkish rule.

### POLITICIAN AND WRITER

A more typically Rumanian note was struck by Barbu Stefanescu (1858-1918), who is usually known as Delavrancea. A politician and writer on political subjects, he is best known for his patriotic and nationalistic trilogy of dramas, *Sunset, The Hurricane* and *Evening Star* (1909-10). He is at his best, however, in his short stories, in which realism is blended with satire and sentiment, as in *Sultanica* (1885) and *The Parasites* (1893).

Perhaps the most flourishing prose form during the later 19th century was the short story, a form adopted by many notable writers. Among the most distinguished of these were Ion Brătescu-Voinești (1868-1946?), whose moving and tragic tales include the collections *In The World of Justice* (1906) and *Light and Darkness* (1912), and the writers Calistrat Hogas (1847-

1916), Emile Garleanu (d. 1914), C. Sandu Aldea (d. 1927) and Ion Dragoslav (d. 1928).

## Late-Nineteenth-Century Poetry

The more traditional approach to literature is exemplified in the work of the poet and prose writer Alexandru Vlahutza (1858-1919), a deeply religious writer whose subjects were drawn from peasant life. Vlahutza's novels and tales, marred by over-sentimentality and rather shallow patriotism, are now little read, but he was capable of producing love lyrics with deep and genuine feeling, as may be seen in his *Complete Poems* (1915). His religious preoccupations are expressed in *At the Threshold* (1887).

### JOYFUL AFFIRMATION

The work of George Cosbuc (1866-1918) owes much to the earlier Romantics. A nationalistic writer on rural life, his prose is akin to that of Slavici, but his lyrical poems, published as *Ballads and Idylls* (1893), have an air of joyful affirmation of the value of Rumanian rural life. Cosbuc was also important as a translator, producing excellent versions of Homer, Virgil, Byron, Schiller and Dante's *Divine Comedy*.

### VERSATILE WRITER

Perhaps the most important poet to emerge in Rumania during the late 19th century was Alexander Macedonski (1854-1920), a versatile writer long resident in France and a precursor of the Symbolist movement in Rumania. Macedonski wrote essays, literary criticism, verse plays and exotic novels and tales, among them

the novel *Calvary of Fire* (1906). Macedonski's poetry betrays the pre-dominant influence of the new French movements, and includes *Prima Verba* (1872), *Excelsior* (1895) and the strange and powerful *Poem of the Rondels,* which was not published until 1927.

### SATIRICAL AND ELEGANT

Among other notable poets of this period were the neo-Romantic Ste-phen Iosif (1875-1913), who wrote nationalistic poems and dramas on historical themes and translated Sha-kespeare, Corneille, Goethe, Heine, Verlaine and Ibsen; Panait Cerna (1881-1913), who was much influen-ced by German philosophy; the satir-ical and elegant versifier Demeter Anghel (1872-1914), whose works such as *In the Garden* (1903) have affinities with the *fin-de-siècle* writers of France and England; and D. Iaco-bescu (1893-1913).

## THE TWENTIETH CENTURY

### Divergent Trends

BY THE END OF THE 19TH CENTURY, the comparative unity imposed on Rumanian literature by the *Junimea* movement had considerably weak-ened. Political developments and a general spirit of social unrest had brought to the foreground a popular literature rooted in social realism and dedicated to improving the rights of the people, a praiseworthy aim but one which has not always been pro-ductive of memorable literature. On the other hand, an increase in the influence of modern movements in other countries, particularly France, saw the growth of a number of wide-ly divergent styles.

### LITERARY REVIEWS

During the first years of the 20th century, many highly influential liter-ary reviews made their appearance in Rumania. The most important among these were *Viata Romaneasca, Sămănătorul* and *Viata Noua,* the first two expressive of the more traditional trends in Rumanian liter-ature and the last-named the chief organ for the dissemination of the new movements.

*Viata Romaneasca* was founded in Jassy in 1906, as the organ of a social reform group. It represented a view-point based on Russian social theory, called *poporanism,* which was bas-ically a popular rural movement. After World War II this journal reap-peared under the same name but with a much more obvious Marxist bias. The contributors to *Viata Romane-asca* were critics and political theo-rists rather than creative writers, but their ideas appear to have been in-fluential on one of the most important Rumanian novelists, Mihail Sadove-anu (1880-1961).

### MIHAIL SADOVEANU

Sadoveanu's prolific output of no-vels and tales has a definite bias toward the naturalistic treatment of peasant and lower class urban life, which explains its current popularity in the Communist state.

Sadoveanu came from a prosper-ous, middle-class background and achieved political eminence, but his unpopularity with the Antonescu dic-tatorship brought him still closer to the extreme left, in both politics and writing. He is equally well known for his short stories, such as *Father Precu's Tavern* (1905) and *Battleaxe* (1930), and for his historical novels, such as the colorful *The Brothers Jderi* (1935) and *Mitrea Cocor* (1950).

### TRADITIONAL VIEWPOINT

The second important journal, *Să-mănătorul* (The Sower), was founded in 1901, and represented a much more traditional viewpoint both po-litically and socially than did *Viata Romaneasca.* Its most important con-tributors were the critic and historian Nicolae Iorga (1871-1940), and the poets Iosif, Cerna and Anghel, men-tioned above. The most important poet of this group, however, was the fiercely nationalistic Octavian Goga (1881-1938), the Transylvanian au-thor of *The Earth is Calling Us* (1909).

### VIOLENT REALIST

Among the prose writers associated with *Sămănătorul* was the violently realistic Livius Rebreanu (1885-1944), who committed suicide after the fall of the right-wing government in World War II. Rebreanu is best remembered for his war novels, which include *Ion* (1920) and *The Forest of the Hanged* (1922), the latter a deeply felt ex-ploration of the physical and mental ordeal of a Rumanian deserter from the Austro-Hungarian army. He also wrote novels and tales of peasant life, such as *Ragamuffins* (1916), and tragedies, including *Ciuleandră* (1927) and *Embers* (1934).

### RURAL AND DOCUMENTARY

Ion Agârbicieanu (1882-    ), who also founded a periodical of his own called *Luceafărul* in 1902, was a prolific writer of tales of rural life in realistic settings. His works, such as *In the Country* (1906) and the novel *Archangels* (1914), are more noted for their documentary qualities than for their imaginative merit, though they are sometimes permeated by exotic or erotic undertones.

### WESTERN TRENDS

The third important journal was *Viata Noua* (New Life), founded in 1905 by the philologist and critic Ovid Densusianu (1873-1938). This was an almost exclusively literary periodical, with no political leanings, and was devoted to the dissemina-tion of modern Western trends in literature, in particular the theories of the French Symbolist movement.

Two of the most important writers to be connected with the Symbolist movement, the poetic movement in-spired mainly by the works of the French poets Baudelaire, Laforgue and Verlaine, were Ion Minulescu (1881-1944) and Gheorghe Bacovia (1881-    ). Minulescu was a master of free verse, who also wrote novels and plays, while Bacovia was much influenced, in such works as *Plumb* (1916), by the fantastic qualities and romantic gloom of Edgar Alan Poe.

### After World War I

One trend in literature after World War I was exemplified in the editorial policy of the periodical *Gandirea* (Thought), founded in 1920, which aimed at the reconciliation of the nationalistic Rumanian tradition with the Greco-Turkish tradition, an attitude which led to a political bias toward the right wing.

#### A RELIGIOUS TREND

The traditionalism of this group often had a religious tendency, as may be seen in the work of Nichifor Crainic, a poet and essayist of peasant stock and a theological student, who wrote religious lyrics such as *Darurile pământului* (1920) and translated the work of Rainer Maria Rilke, the Austrian poet. A similar religious trend appears in the work of the literary critic and anthologist Ion Pillat (1891-1945), also influenced by Rilke, who wrote pleasantly of rural subjects in *My Village* (1925) and *The Church of Once Upon a Time* (1926).

#### PROGRESSIVES AND A MYSTIC

Many writers, however, remained more influenced by European progressive movements. Notable among these were Adrian Maniu (1891-     ), Aron Cotrus (1891-     ), Lucian Blaga (1895-     ), Ion Barbu (1895-     ) and Ilarie Voronca (1903-     ).

Maniu, a dramatist and lyric poet, was close to the traditionalists in feeling, with an almost mystical approach to the subject of Rumanian nationalism, evident in *Toward the Stars* (1930) and *The Book of the Fatherland*. He is also notable as having translated Henrik Ibsen's *Peer Gynt* in 1925. The free verse of Cotrus is mainly preoccupied with social and political themes, but much greater imaginative qualities are displayed in the verse and dramas of Blaga, such as *At the Courts of Desire* (1938).

#### SURREALISM AND SCIENCE

The poems of Ilarie Voronca, like those of Cotrus, are often concerned with social themes, but in the work of Voronca, such as *Patmos* (1934), there are surrealistic qualities. Since he lived for a long time in France and often wrote in French, these suggest the influence of Tristan Tzara, who also influenced Ion Vinea (1896-     ), the founder of the periodical *Contemporary*. The work of Ion Barbu, such as *Second Play* (1930), has a scientific basis which also derives from French models.

#### MONK AND ANARCHIST

Perhaps the most interesting modern poet to appear in Rumania has been Tudor Arghezi (1880-     ), whose obscure symbolism cannot disguise his great gifts. Arghezi is a former monk who turned to political satire after losing his faith, becoming a political prisoner for a time in the 1920s. His attitude is that of the anti-authoritarian anarchist and his language, in both poetry and prose works, rich and imaginative, forceful and colorful. His poems, which include *Assorted Words* (1927) and *Little Evening Book* (1935), were published in a complete edition in Bucharest in 1956.

#### TRANSLATORS AND TRADITIONALISTS

Of those poets most influenced by the Symbolist movement, Al Stamatiad (1885-     ), the author of *Black Pearls* (1920) and the translator of the French poet Baudelaire and Oscar Wilde, the Irish dramatist, poet and novelist, and Helen Farago (1878-     ), who has translated the Belgian author, Maeterlinck, are most notable.

*Painting (executed after 1944) by Camil Ressu (1880-     ). Since 1944 both painters and sculptors have reverted to a 19th-century pictorial style in an attempt to exalt the peasant and his condition. There has also been an effort in present-day Rumania to bring the arts closer to the masses, as is evident in this painting, which hangs in the National Museum at Bucharest.*

Other poets associated with this movement are Claudia Millian (1889- ), I. Rascu (1890- ) and Camil Balthazar (1902- ).

The more traditional school of poetry is headed by Nicholas Davidescu (1888- ), a translator and critic of French literature and a novelist of some distinction. He is a fine lyric poet, whose works include *Inscriptions* (1916) and *The Middle Ages* (1937). The poet and dramatist V. Voiculescu (1884- ) is a notable figure of the introspective and religious school of traditional poetry. Other notable figures of the more conventional schools of poetry are George Gregorian (1886- ), George Topirceanu (1890-1937), D. Ciurezu (1901- ), N. Crevedia (1904- ), R. Gyr (1905- ) and Dan Botta (1907- ).

### EXPERIMENTALISTS

Among the experimental poets, names of importance include Demosthenes Botex (1893- ), whose pessimistic free verse compositions include *Life's Days* (1927) and *Words from Beyond* (1934); Alexander Philippide (1900- ), whose imaginative and colorful language is displayed in *Rocks by Lightning Struck* (1930); Virgil Gheorghiu (1905- ), whose verse resembles that of Voronca and Vinea; and Horia Stamatu (1912- ).

## Prose

A number of interesting prose writers stand aside from those that have already been discussed in connection with the various literary movements of the earlier 20th century.

Gala Glaction (1879- ), an orthodox priest and mystic, is the author of novels and tales which unite the practical religion of a social reformer with realistic settings, as in *At the Crossroads of the Centuries* (1935). He produced an excellent translation of the Bible in 1938 and has written biblical novels, such as *Roxana* (1930).

### JOURNALIST AND NOVELIST

One of the most important realistic novelists of this century is Caesar Petrescu (1892- ), whose prolific output includes a fine biography of the poet Eminescu. Petrescu began his career as a journalist, and a great eye for detail is reflected in such starkly realistic works as *The Dream Man* (1925) and *The Fantastic Symphony* (1929). His later novels are concerned with the social and industrial life of urban Rumania, as in *Black Gold* (1934), set in the oil fields.

### FOLLOWERS OF PROUST

Some modern Rumanian writers have been influenced by the school of psychological novelists which may be said to stem from the work of Marcel Proust, the great French novelist. Foremost among these are Hortensia Papadat-Bengescu, who displays a mood of bitter irony in *The Fiancé* (1935), and Anton Holban (d. 1936), whose major novel is *Ioana* (1935). Considerable psychological tendencies are also displayed in the work of Victor Ion Popa, in his novels of rural life such as *Velerim* (1933), and the stream of conciousness technique of Mircea Eliade's *Return of Paradise* (1934).

### PROBLEMS OF IDENTITY

Two of the most important writers of the immediate prewar period are Camil Petrescu (1894-1957) and Ionel Teodoreanu (1897-1954). Petrescu was a poet, essayist and dramatist, as well as a powerful novelist. His best-known novel is *The Last Night of Life and the First Night of War* (1930), while his plays, including *Strong Souls* (1925) and *Danton* (1931), are still popular in the Rumanian theater. Teodoreanu made a deep and moving examination of the problems of personal identity in his trilogy of novels *Medeleni* (1926-27), *Noah's Ark* (1936) and *Masked Ball* (1939).

*Alexandru Tomar, poet of the struggles of the people since 1894. He was not able to publish his collection of poems* The Song of Life *until 1950.*

### AN ELEGANT STYLIST AND OTHERS

Other notable writers of the prewar period include the elegant stylist Matei Caragiale (d. 1936); the painstakingly naturalistic novelist Emanoil Bucutza (1887- ), who wrote *Sefki's Fugue* (1926) and *Our Lady of the Sea* (1930); the versatile Gib Mihăescu (1894-1935), who wrote short stories, plays, such as *Pavilion of Shadows* (1928), and novels, including *Donna Alba* (1935); and the novelists Constantine Ardeleanu, Ion Peltz, George Zamfirescu, George Vladescu and Mihail Sebastian.

## After World War II

The end of World War II, into which Rumania had been forced on the side of Germany, ended in the collapse of the monarchy and dictatorship of the right and the establishment of a Communist government dominated by the U.S.S.R.

As in many other countries in the same situation, a number of prominent writers left Rumania to seek intellectual freedom in the West. The dominant, indeed almost the only literary activity permitted by the new regime was the style known in the arts as "Socialist Realism," the glorification of peasants and artisans and of the achievements of Marxist society.

### CENSORSHIP AND THE WRITERS

However, there was, as has already been seen, a tradition of social realism already firmly established in Rumanian literature, and many prominent writers were thus able to continue working or at any rate to escape suppression. Thus the political revolution was less dramatic in its effect on literature in Rumania than in many other centers.

In recent years, there has been a relaxation of literary censorship on political groups in the U.S.S.R. and its satellite countries. This relaxation has been particularly apparent in Rumania, where, in March 1965, a conference of writers was able to affirm its right to produce the literature of its choice without interference from the state.

The works of the younger generation of Rumanian writers are only now beginning to appear in translation in the Western world, but already it is evident that the Rumanian tradition is still strong, and that new and individualistic writers are once again producing work in the high traditions of their literary forebears.

# THE THEATER

## Earliest Traces

TRACES OF EARLY THEATRICAL ACTIVITY have been found in the area of present-day Rumania. As early as the 7th century B.C. the Greeks founded colonies along the Black Sea coast of Rumania. These cities—Histria, Callatis and Tomis (present-day Constanta)—contain evidence of the worship of Dionysus with its accompanying dramatic performances. The cities founded by the Greeks have also yielded terra-cotta figurines representing masked actors of comedy.

The land which is now Rumania later came into the sphere of Rome. The Roman colony of Dacia (107-271 A.D.), like other provinces of Rome, took over some of the more spectacular aspects of Roman culture. These included the gladiatorial combats in which armed men were pitted against wild animals for the entertainment of bloodthirsty spectators. These spectacles are attested by the remains of Roman amphitheaters and by funerary steles (small monumental columns) commemorating gladiators killed in combat.

## Folk Plays

Although a theater, in the sense of dramatic performances on the stage, has existed in Rumania for only a short time, there is a long tradition of folk drama.

The most characteristic of the Rumanian folk plays are religious performances related to the French *mystères* and the English miracle plays. The best known of such plays are the *Irozii* (plays about Herod) and the *Vicleimul* (plays about Bethlehem).

The popular comic plays of Rumanian folk culture are known as *Jocul păpuşilor*. These plays are adaptations of popular Turkish farces caled *Karagöz*. The characters are peasant types and the humor is broad.

Another type of non-religious performance is the *oratsi de nuntă* (wedding oration), which accompanies a marriage ceremony. This dialogue takes the form of primitive dramatic verse which, with the accompanying action, underlines the main phases of the ceremony. The elaborate ritual of the marriage ceremony is, in itself, similar to the development of a dramatic action.

Before the 19th century there was little theatrical activity in Rumania

*A scene from* Apus de soare *(Sunset), 1909, by Barbu Delavrancea (1858-1918), presented at the National Theater, Bucharest, in 1956. The play deals with the last actions and heroic death of Stephen the Great (1457-1504) of Moldavia.*

and no national theatrical tradition.

Foreign artists—mainly Italians and Germans—were invited to perform at the courts of the Turkish princes who ruled in Moldavia and Walachia in the 17th and 18th centuries.

Toward the end of the 18th century a few Rumanian intellectuals turned their attention to dramatic literature. Their first excursions into the theater were dominated by Italian influences. The most admired writer was Metastasio (Domenico Bonaventura Tropasi, 1698-1782), the Italian poet and dramatist.

## Early Nineteenth Century

The first Rumanian theater was founded in Jassy, the cultural center of Moldavia, in 1817.

The most important individual in the early history of the Rumanian theater is Ian Eliade Radulescu (1802-72), a man of wide culture and extensive literary activity. In 1833 he founded the *Societatea Filarmonică* (Philharmonic Society), which later gave rise to the National Theater in Bucharest. The society's aims were

those of liberal reform and the creation of a Rumanian theater.

In 1834 a school of dramatic art was opened under the literary direction of Radulescu. Its main function was the teaching of elocution. At the end of the school's first course, the students performed, with great success, Radulescu's translations of the French classics, Voltaire's *Mahomet* and Molière's *Amphitryon*. There were, as yet, no original plays in the Rumanian language.

### NATIONAL THEATER AT JASSY

In 1840 the two theaters at Jassy, one of which performed plays in the French language and the other in Rumanian, came under the joint directorship of Constantin Negruzzi (1808-68), Vasile Alecsandri (1821-90) and Mihai Kogalniceanu (1817-.91).

When the theater at Jassy was first established, the repertory consisted primarily of vaudeville (comic musical sketches) and adaptations of the works of popular European dramatists such as Molière (1622-73) and Au-

for the development of the theater in his country.

Between 1840 and 1845 Alecsandri devoted much of his attention to the organization of the Moldavian theater, for which he wrote many of his plays. He traveled in Western Europe and, on his return, resolved to reform the Rumanian theater, improving productions and educating the taste of the public.

Since Rumania had no literary theatrical tradition Alecsandri based his work on the style of the French theater. The characters and problems he depicts are, however, typically Rumanian.

### FARCE AND VERSE

Some of Alecsandri's comedies are built around the character of *Cucoana Chirița* (Mistress Chirița), a woman of the provinces. *Chirița în Iasi* (Chirița at Jassy), 1850, gives a portrait of the vain and ambitious, but credulous woman of the provinces on a visit to the city. The type of comedy here is French, as is the elegant style, but the character of Chirița is wholly Rumanian.

*Iasi în Carnaval* (Jassy at Carnival Time), 1845, is a political farce. Opposed by the authorities, it was well received by its audiences. In style this play is closely related to the folk theater.

Alecsandri's more serious plays include *Ovidiu* (Ovid), 1885, and *Despot Voda* (Prince Despot), 1879. The first—a verse drama in five acts —portrays Ovid as a soldier defending Tomis against the assault of the Getae (the ancient Thracian tribe). *Despot Voda* is a verse drama inspired by the national history as told by the chronicle writers of the 16th and 17th centuries. The many long monologues slow down the action of this play, and the main character, a Greek adventurer aspiring to the Moldavian throne, is not clearly defined.

## Late Nineteenth Century

The treatment of themes based on local situations and national history,

gust Friedrich Ferdinand von Kotzebue (1761-1819), a German writer of comedies and farces.

### FRENCH INFLUENCE

Toward the middle of the 19th century Italian influence on the Rumanian theater gave way to French. The culture of France was already known in Rumania since Parisian intellectuals had been welcomed at

the courts of the Phanariot princes of Moldavia and Walachia from 1711-1821. Now, however, French influences began to be more widely felt.

### VASILE ALECSANDRI

The new trend in the Rumanian theater is seen at its best in the work of Vasile Alecsandri (1821-90). Alecsandri was not only a poet and dramatist, but also a keen worker

already apparent in the work of Alecsandri, continued to be the main tendency in Rumanian drama—in fact in Rumanian literature in general—in the second half of the 19th century. The so-called traditionalist movement, exemplified by the literary review *Dacia Literară*, was a national impulse toward cultural independence.

### IOAN LUCA CARAGIALE

One of the most outstanding figures in the history of the Rumanian theater is Ioan Luca Caragiale (1853-1912). Caragiale was born into a theatrical family—his grandfather and two uncles had been actors—and he developed an early passion for the theater. After studying elocution for one year (1868-69) he joined a touring company of actors as prompter, copyist and translator. He later wrote plays of his own, which achieved immediate success and which still form part of the standard repertory in Rumanian theaters.

### SATIRIZING PARLIAMENT

In 1888 Caragiale was appointed director of the National Theater at Bucharest, where he produced some of his own plays, mainly comedies. *O scrisoare pierdută* (The Lost Letter), 1884, is a fierce satire on the parliamentary system of the time. *D'ale Carnavalului* (Carnival Adventures), 1885, is a three-act farce in the style of a masked play. The characters are traditional types.

Caragiale's comedies are set in a semi-Oriental environment and his characters are people of limited intelligence, culture and ability. There is neither a "hero" nor a central action since all characters are on the same low level.

Caragiale's only serious drama, *Năpasta* (False Accusation) 1890, is less successful than the comedies, since the motives and psychology of the characters are unconvincing.

### TRADITIONALISTS

Another typical representative of the traditionalist trend is Barbu Delavrancea, the pseudonym of Barbu Stefanescu (1858-1918). He made a strong impact on the theater with his historical trilogy *Apus de soare* (Sunset), 1909, *Viforul* (The Hurricane), 1910 and *Luceafărul* (Evening Star), 1910. Set in the Rumania of the 15th and 16th centuries, the plays are patriotic and nationalistic.

The movement toward autonomy in the theater was promoted still more when the review *Sămănătorul* (The Sower), founded in 1901, raised its standard in support. The traditionalist trend of this review was due mainly to its editor, Nicolae Iorga (1871-1940). He based his policy on the principle that cultural union was a preparation for political union.

Iorga, a man of broad culture and knowledge, fought for a theater freed from the exclusive pressure of any foreign literature. His own plays, which include *Cleopatra* (1928) and *Sfântul Francisc* (St. Francis) (1930), show little creative or technical ability. The main characters symbolize a basic idea, to which minor characters and action are sacrificed. In general, Iorga's plays are better suited to reading than to performance.

## The Early Twentieth Century

### CONFLICTING CURRENTS

In the first few decades of the 20th century two conflicting trends become apparent in the Rumanian theater. The first of these is a continuation of traditionalism, making itself felt in a spirit of revolution. The second trend takes the form of a pessimistic awareness of the theater's weakness, so that writers felt obliged to look to foreign literature for models.

Representatives of the first trend are Alexandru Davila (1862-1929) and Victor Eftimiu (1886?- ). Davila's *Vlaicu Voda* (Prince Vlaicu), 1912, is acknowledged as a masterpiece and is considered the best Rumanian historical drama. It deals with the conflict, in the 14th century, between the Orthodox Walachians and the Catholic Hungarians.

Eftimiu's plays often have fantastic or fairy-tale themes. Two of the most popular are *Inșira-te, mărgărite* (Story without End) 1911 and *Cocoșul negru* (The Black Cock) 1913.

Another popular Rumanian playwright whose works betray no foreign influence is Victor Ion Popa (1895- ). His works are simple and realistic. In *Mușcata din fereastră* (The Geranium in the Window), 1929, Popa presents the modest reality of provincial bourgeoisie. The humor is sad but not bitter.

A writer whose plays are influenced by foreign drama is Ioan Marin Sadoveanu (1893- ). *Molima* (Contagion) 1930 depicts a woman who is driven to distraction by boredom in the quiet of her Dobruja environment. This play, like some of the works of George Mihail Zamfirescu (1898-1939), shows Russian influence. Zamfirescu gives surrealistic treatment to the ordinary environment and behavior of the lower middle classes.

## Contemporary Theater

Contemporary Rumanian theater is flourishing. The country has 42 legitimate theaters of which 15 are in

*The opera house and ballet theater in Bucharest. Built in 1953, the theater is one of Bucharest's outstanding modern buildings. Bucharest, the capital and by far the largest city in Rumania, is also the theatrical and musical center of the country. Of Rumania's 42 drama theaters 15 are located here.*

Bucharest and the rest scattered throughout the provinces. There are, in addition, five opera houses, 13 music halls and 22 puppet theaters.

The Rumanian theaters are producing increasing numbers of plays by native writers and while the quality is extremely variable, a few gifted playwrights have emerged in the last 20 years.

Two dramatists of the older generation who entered the cultural climate of the Rumanian People's Republic are Victor Eftimiu and Camil Petrescu (1894-1957).

One of the younger playwrights is Maria Banuş (1916-    ), whose social play, *Ziua cea mare* (Day Draws Near) 1949, is one of the most popular in recent repertory.

Another successful contemporary dramatist whose works are frequently presented is Aurel Baranga (1913-    ). Some of his plays deal with recent phases of Rumanian history. *Annii negri* (Black Years), 1951, evokes the period 1937-38, a time of violence and unrest in Rumania after the defeat of the Liberal government.

Throughout its short history the Rumanian theater has never been in the hands of private enterprise. Today it is subsidized by the state and controlled by the Theater Council, the central administrative body of the Rumanian theater.

Entry into the theatrical profession in Rumania requires years of study. The 21 drama schools select only one out of ten applicants; selection is based on academic as well as theatrical achievement.

## THE MUSIC

### The Beginnings

THE EARLIEST WRITTEN EVIDENCE FOR the existence of Rumanian music dates from the 14th century. Some of these early documents describe specific types of folk music.

#### FOLK MUSIC

The roots of Rumanian folk music probably lie in the music of the ancient Thracians, a people noted in antiquity for their musicality.

Vocal music is particularly archaic. Instrumental music, on the other hand, betrays Western influence.

Special songs are sung on various occasions. *Colinde* are Christmas carols, *bocete* are funeral songs and *doine* are songs of love and regret. Always in a minor key, the melodies of the latter are full of trills, turns and other decorations.

#### CHURCH MUSIC

Although the style of Rumanian church music is quite different from that of folk music, its modal basis is similar.

Because the Rumanian Christians adopted the Slavonic rite of the Eastern church, their music remained outside the current of Roman Catholic church music.

The Rumanians early adopted the Byzantine system of notation, by which glissandos and microtones—very characteristic of Oriental music—could be represented. This Byzan-

tine music of the Eastern church was purely vocal.

### Musical Instruments

The Rumanians, having a long musical tradition, can make music by the simplest means. They can play a tune on a leaf or a piece of birchbark held against the lips.

Village orchestras often accompany the dance. The instruments in these orchestras range from the simplest to complicated modern instruments such as the clarinet or the accordion.

Certain instruments are characteristically Rumanian. The *cobza* is a cross between a guitar and a mandolin; the *bucium* is an alphorn, of which there are five varieties. Other typical instruments are the *taragot*, a type of bass clarinet, and various types of flute and pipes. The simplest flute is the *tilinca* which has neither stopper, holes nor mouthpiece. The Rumanians are perhaps the world's most brilliant exponents of the pan-pipes.

One of the most interesting Rumanian folk instruments is the *buhaiu* (bullock). This consists of a small barrel, one end of which is covered with a skin. Strands of horsehair project through the skin and a deep, lowing sound is produced by sliding the fingers over these.

### The Seventeenth and Eighteenth Centuries

The first scholar to collect popular Rumanian melodies was a 17th-century Transylvanian churchman, Johannes Cajoni. His collection was followed, later in the century, by the *Codex Victoris* (now in the Hungarian Academy of Sciences, Budapest), which contains Walachian dances.

Rumania's first musicologist was Prince Dimitrie Cantemir (1673-1723), ruler of Moldavia (1710-11). He wrote a treatise on music in Turkish, and an *Introduction to Turkish Music* in Rumanian.

During the Turkish occupation of Moldavia and Walachia the only music at court was provided by the Turkish military bands (*meterhanea*).

Western music, however, began to infiltrate into Transylvania in the

*Some typical Rumanian folk instruments: flageolets, pan-pipes and a* cobza *(a stringed instrument similar to a mandolin). Every Rumanian village has its own band, which accompanies dances with traditional tunes. Some of the instrumentalists are brilliant; Rumanian exponents of the pan-pipes have a worldwide reputation.*

18th century, when foreign musicians were invited to perform in the houses of the nobility.

### The Nineteenth Century

Rumania's modern musical development is very recent. No original composers emerged until the 19th century, when the country was at last freed from its Turkish rulers.

Much 19th-century Rumanian music was written for the theater. The Viennese violonist Ludwig Anthony Wiest (1819-59) was one of the first composers to write for the Rumanian theater. Another composer of Austrian origin was Adolf Flechtenmacher (1820-98), whose opera *Baba Hirca* (1848) is based on Rumanian folk tunes.

The first opera companies to perform in Rumania were German. These were followed by Italian companies and finally, after the founding of the National Theater at Bucharest in the mid-19th century, by the first entirely Rumanian company.

Rumanian opera composers of this period include Edward Caudella (1841-1924) and Gheorghe Stephanoou (1843-1925). Caudella composed *Olteanca* (The Girl from Oltenia) 1880, and *Petru Rares* (1900); Stephanescu was the founder of a permanent opera company in 1885. His operetta *Pepelea* is one of his best-known works.

#### NATIONAL MUSIC

In the 19th century, philharmonic societies and conservatories were founded at Bucharest and Jassy (Moldavia).

With these foundations Rumanian national music began to develop. The main source of ideas and themes was the country's rich tradition of folk music.

The first composer to adopt popular melodies for choral music was Gavril Muzicescu (1847-1903). Another important composer of this generation was Constantin Dimitrescu (1847-1928).

### The Twentieth Century

Rumanian music suffered a decline in the years just before World War I, but revived again afterward.

The first Rumanian musician of international standing was Georges Enesco (1881-1955), a gifted composer and virtuoso violonist. Influenced at first by Brahms and Wagner, he soon developed his own style in his compositions.

Such works as his *Rumanian Rhap-*

*Georges Enesco (1881-1955), Rumania's greatest composer. His career as a composer began very early; he was able to give a concert of his own works in Paris at the age of 16. Enesco is also celebrated as a virtuoso violinist and as the teacher of the well-known American-born violinist Yehudi Menuhin (1916-    ).*

*sodies* show the strong influence of folk music. Other works include an opera, *Oedipus* (1936), and three symphonies.

The study of folk music has been intensified in this century, mainly due to the foundation of a vast phonographic library at the National Museum, Bucharest. The Hungarian composer Béla Bartok (1881-1945) used this library when he transcribed and published his collection of Rumanian songs.

With the revival of Rumania's musical life after World War I, more Rumanian musicians began to enter the European musical scene. Nonna Otescu (1888-1940) composed comic operas, ballets and symphonic poems. Stan Golestan (1872-1956) was the composer of a well-known *Rumanian Rhapsody* as well as other orchestral and chamber works.

One of the best-known Rumanian solo performers was the short-lived but brilliant concert pianist Dinu Lipatti (1917-50).

In recent years many schools and musical institutes have been opened. Instrumental and vocal groups of various kinds have also been established.

The composers of the latest period include Paul Constantinescu (1909-    ), whose works include a *Concerto for Stringed Instruments,* and Gheorghe Dumitrescu (1914-    ), composer of an oratorio, *Tudor Vladimirescu.*

---

### THE FILM

BEFORE THE BALKAN WARS (1913) THE history of the Rumanian film industry is extremely vague. The only film of significance was *The Independence War* (1912), produced by the actor Grigore Brezeaunu.

#### Nationalization

The film industry in Rumania did not really begin to gather strength until 1945, when it was nationalized. The first properly equipped film center was founded in Buftea, near Bucharest. Hitherto producers had been obliged to improvise in makeshift studios, and this development marked an important step forward in

the growth of the cinematic art. The Buftea studios, under the auspices of *The State Enterprise of Film Production,* now produce an annual total of between 14 and 20 movies.

Since World War II, Rumanian films have been widely represented in international film festivals, and many (including short subjects, documentary and educational features as well as full-length films) have won important awards.

Despite these successes, however, Romfilm—the sole organization responsible for exporting the country's cinematic products—seldom achieves showings in foreign movie houses.

An exception is the work of Ion Popescu-Gopo, who has won a considerable reputation with his series of short animated cartoons, notably *Short History* (1957), which deals with costume through the ages, *The Seven Arts* (1958) and *Homo Sapiens* (1960). These three feature "the little man," whose progress through the various stages of evolution is depicted with a delicate wit and compact philosophical observation.

# BULGARIA

## POSITION AND BOUNDARIES

BULGARIA LIES IN THE NORTHEAST OF the Balkan Peninsula, between 41° 14' and 44° 12' N. latitude and between 22° 21' and 28° 37 E. longitude.

Except for the short strip between the city of Silistra and the Black Sea, the border between Bulgaria and Rumania in the north is defined by the Danube. The western border is with Yugoslavia; the southwestern with Greece, approaching to within 20 miles of the Aegean Sea; and the southeastern with European Turkey. The eastern border is formed by the Black Sea.

## ORGANIZATION OF THE STATE

### Administrative Divisions

In 1949, 14 *okrag* (provinces) were set up, but two were later abolished. These provinces were subdivided into 95 *okolya* (districts). In 1959 the 12 remaining provinces were abolished and replaced with 30 new provinces with a greater share in the management of the economy at local level.

### The Constitution

As a result of a referendum, the Bulgarian People's Republic came into being on Sept. 15, 1946.

At the general election held on Oct. 27, 1946, the Fatherland Front—composed of the Communist, Agrarian, Socialist and Zveno parties and Independents—won 364 seats, the Communists taking 277, and the opposition won 101.

In 1948, the Fatherland Front was changed into a mass organization whose members were affiliated as individuals rather than through their organizations.

By the constitution of Dec. 4, 1947, a one-house National Assembly came into being.

This is elected every four years by direct universal suffrage operating by secret ballot. Everyone over 18 years is entitled to vote, and there is one deputy for every 30,000 voters. In 1962 there were 321 deputies.

In addition to electing the Presidium (the highest organ of the state), the National Assembly has powers to amend the constitution, vote the National Economic Plan, grant amnesties, proclaim referendums, declare war and make peace.

The Presidium consists of a chairman, two deputy-chairmen, a secretary and 15 members; among its important functions are choosing the dates of elections and summoning the National Assembly.

### THE COUNCIL OF MINISTERS

The highest executive body is the Council of Ministers, which is elected by the National Assembly and is responsible to it. Its duties are to control administration of the state, maintain public order and direct foreign and defense policy.

In effect, this Council of Ministers always consists almost exclusively of the Politburo of the Bulgarian Communist party, for, in the elections for the National Assembly, the overwhelming majority of candidates belong

*Sofia, founded by the Roman emperor Trajan, is the capital of Bulgaria and is situated in a wide basin surrounded by hills. Tourists, who help the national economy by bringing foreign currency into the country, often enjoy a trip by cable car up the mountain slopes, in order to admire the scenery.*

*A wooded landscape in the mountain group of Rhodope in southern Bulgaria. The conifers on the mountain slopes are an indication of the altitude.*

to the Fatherland Front, whose members are Communist or Communist-affiliated.

### The Judiciary

There is no division between civil and criminal jurisdiction.

"Comrades' courts," which may be explained as neighborhood courts, try offenders on minor charges. The "officials" at these courts do not necessarily have any legal qualifications, but they must be members of the Fatherland Front.

Above these are 100 people's courts, three municipal courts in the city provinces, 27 provincial courts and a supreme court.

A prosecutor general is appointed for five years by the National Assembly and is answerable to it alone. He controls observance of the law by all government bodies, officials and citizens. He also appoints and discharges the prosecutors for all courts.

All judges are elected: those of district courts by the people every three years; those of regional courts by regional councils every five years; and those of the supreme court by the National Assembly every five years.

### Religion

Freedom of conscience is constitutionally guaranteed; but no religion may express disagreement with the government.

The "Law of the Churches" of 1949 disestablished the National Orthodox Church, which, however, is still described as the "traditional church of the Bulgarian people."

Although the majority of the people (about 8 million in 1964) are members of the National Orthodox Church, there are also small Roman Catholic, Protestant, Jewish, and Moslem minorities.

### Education

The organization of education is undergoing some change. While the old division into primary, secondary and higher education still exists, the comprehensive school, which groups all types of pupil, has been introduced.

Education is free and is compulsory for children between seven and 15 years.

In 1961 there were 6570 kindergartens with 298,790 children; 2408 elementary schools with 620,971 pupils; 316 secondary schools with 158,004 pupils; and 227 vocational schools with 91,981 students.

At universities and other places of higher education, there were 71,500 students and 4000 faculty members in 1962.

Churches are no longer allowed to control schools and youth movements. They may, however, organize theological seminaries.

### Language

Almost everyone speaks Bulgarian, a south Slav language which has been subject to Turkish, Greek, Albanian and Rumanian influences. Macedonian is the most widespread of the dialects.

### Currency and Measurements

In 1947 all banks were nationalized.

The Investment Banks grant long-

*Winter view of Vikhren Peak (9558 feet), the highest point of the Pirin Mountains of southwest Bulgaria. The relief is clearly Alpine in character, as can be seen from the abrupt slopes of the highest region. The people of this high-lying region live chiefly by pastoral farming and forestry.*

*Dominating the valleys of the Iskar, Struma and Mesta rivers, which flow from their slopes, are the Rila Mountains. Musala Peak (9592 feet) is the highest point in Bulgaria and in the Balkan Peninsula. The lower slopes are covered in thick coniferous forests, whose timber is commercially exploited.*

term credits to cooperative farms, and convert or postpone the repayment of loans by distressed farms.

The unit of currency is the *lev,* which, at current rates, is valued at about $0.855.

The metric system for weights and measures is in general use.

## PHYSICAL GEOGRAPHY

### The Coastline

THE RELATIVELY SHORT COASTLINE (192 miles) formed by the Black Sea is generally uniform is appearance.

To the north, in southern Dobruja, are the Balkan Hills, the high cliffs that run down to the sea in broad terraces. Further south, in the Varna region, the coast is fissured in many places as a result of the encroachment by the sea dating from the Quaternary era.

The low-lying valley of the Provadiya River ends in Varna harbor, which is closed to the sea by a sandy isthmus.

### The Relief

The total area of Bulgaria is 42,830 square miles.

The most prominent division of the country is formed by the Balkan Mountains, which, running across Bulgaria from west to east, cut it into two distinct agricultural areas: the northern plateau, and the valleys and basins of the Maritsa River in the south.

From north to south, the country can be further divided into the Danubian Platform, the Balkans, the sub-Balkan depressions, the anti-Balkans, the Upper Thracian Plain, the Western Highlands and the Rhodope massif.

#### THE DANUBIAN PLATFORM

This plateau opens to the north of the Balkans from the low-lying escarpment, the Rumanian Plain, which ranges in altitude from about 500 to about 650 feet. It is preceded by a wide band of hills which slope down to the Danube in shallow undulations scarcely disturbing the broad, steppe-like surface of this vast, natural terrace facing. The thick layer of loess (a deposit of fine silt or dust transported into its present position by wind) and the Tertiary deposits that cover the platform rest on a bed of cretaceous limestone.

In the west, the platform goes on rising gently to the southeast, where the wooded slopes of the Deliorman Hills merge into central Dobruja and the wild broken region between the Provadiya Planina (Highlands) and the Kamchiya River.

The valleys of the Iskar, Vit, Osam and Yantra rivers, which have a typically broad, dug-out section shut between high limestone bastions, divide the tableland into monotonously similar units.

Human settlements are found only in wooded, sheltered corners of the valleys.

The Deliorman, formerly covered with large oak forests, is in the northeast of the platform. This fertile and potentially rich agricultural area was, at one time, allowed to lie fallow but is again being exploited.

### THE BALKAN MOUNTAINS

The Balkans are an extension of the Alpine-Carpathian folds and stretch across Bulgaria in an arc about 375 miles long which runs almost parallel to the Danube. They start at the Timok River on the Yugoslavian frontier and end abruptly at Cape Yemine (200 feet high), on the Black Sea. They range in width from 12 to 30 miles.

The Balkans are not the insuperable barrier they appear to be in maps; in fact, they are crossed by about 20 highways, three railroad passes and the Iskar River. They are also the northern limit of the Mediterranean influence on climate.

To the ancients they were known as Mount Haemus and to the Bulgars as Stara Planina (Old Mountain).

The entire system may be divided into three geologically and morphologically distinct sections.

The Western Balkans extend for about 125 miles between the Timok River and the Botevgrad Pass. This section is crossed by the Iskar and rises to 7113 feet at Midzhur Peak.

The Central Balkans, which stretch for about 125 miles between the Botevgrad and Vratnik passes, are the narrowest section, and nowhere do they exceed 18 miles in width. Botev Peak (7783 feet) is the highest point of both this section and the system as a whole. The sandstone which has been sculpted by rainwater gives the landscape a picturesque blood-red appearance.

The Eastern Balkans, which stretch for about 90 miles between Vratnik Pass and Cape Yemine, reach their highest point at Balgarka Peak (3785 feet).

Southward, the Stara Planina drops to a low-lying, narrow zone divided into further sections or minor basins, such as those of Sofia, Zlatitsa, Karlovo, Kazanlik, Karnobat and Sliven. They are almost hemmed in by high mountains and are linked by gorges that are sometimes 125 feet deep.

The zone is dominated by the Sredna Gora (Medium-Sized Mountain), and the Sirnena Gora (Wedge-Shaped Mountain), a range which rises to 5061 feet at the peak of Bogdan.

### THE RHODOPE MOUNTAINS

The Rhodope range of northeastern Greece and southern Bulgaria is the major mountain system of the Balkan Peninsula. It runs in a generally northwest to southeast direction for about 180 miles from Struma River to the lower Maritsa River on the Turkish frontier between the Thracian Plain and the Aegean. East of the Struma are the Rila Mountains (9592 feet at Musala Peak) in the northwest and the Pirin Mountains (9558 feet at Vikhren Peak) which are separated by the Mesta River from the Rhodope proper. The Rhodope proper is higher in the west (rising to 7576 feet at Slov Peak) than in the east, where it slopes down to the Thracian Plain.

Green pastures alternate with tree belts on the slopes to a considerable height, a feature that makes this region not typical of high mountain country. Eastward, the valleys open out into progressively wider basins, such as Devin and Pavelsko, which are cultivated and possess rich meadowland.

Along the lower hill slopes cluster villages of small wooden houses, where predominantly Moslem owners prefer the high ground to the valley floors, which, while fertile, are often boggy and unhealthy.

### THE WESTERN HIGHLANDS

Joined to the western side of the Stara Planina are the highlands from which rise the Nisava, Struma and Iskar rivers. Isolated groups of volcanic rock rising to elevations of 1650 to 2600 feet frame sunken basins, such as those of Kyustendil, Radomir, Trin, and Sofia. These are overlooked by the Vitosha group, which rises to 7056 feet at Chernivrakh.

Here the winters are very severe, summers scorching hot, and rainfall low. From the Yugoslavian border the mountains appear to be arid and

*The "Rocks of Belogradchik" (28 miles south of Vidin) in northwest Bulgaria are a product of intense erosive action on the sandstone of the hills that surround the town. The rocks with their bizarre shapes—and also caves with prehistoric relics and ruins of an ancient fortress—attract many tourists to Belogradchik.*

parched, and it is only along watercourses that occasional trees may be seen.

### THE MARITSA DEPRESSION

Between the anti-Balkans in the north and the Rhodope in the south lies the Thracian Plain, the country's largest plainland. This is a broad basin with a height of between 300 and 650 feet.

In prehistoric times this was an extensive lake system but is now drained by the Maritsa, which crosses it.

To the northwest is a saddle which, crossed by the 2696-foot Vakarel Pass, separates the plain from the Sofia Basin. To the south the Thracian Plain is confined by the defile of Kharmanlii. Upstream opens out the 72-mile-long and 30-mile-wide plain of Plovdiv, which is dominated by the hills on which Plovdiv stands.

Downstream from Plovdiv the plain narrows; its flanks rise up between the foothills of Rhodope in the south and wide undulations of the Stara Zagora Basin in the northeast.

Still further east, the hills flanking the lower course of the Tundzha River meet the Yambol Basin. Because of the dry climate, the soil of this region was originally covered by steppe vegetation, which the Turks used as pasture. Since 1878, through industrious irrigation by people from Macedonia, the steppe landscape has been transformed into one of the richest and most verdant areas of Bulgaria.

To the east, the crystalline bedrock between Yambol and the plain of Burgas forms outcrops in the flattened relief of the Strandzha Mountains, which lie mostly in Turkey. The Strandzhas, which are broken into precipitous faults, form long stretches of desolate cliffs on the Black Sea coast.

### THE COASTAL REGION

Eastward, the anti-Balkan region is joined to the Varna region, but here the land configuration is much younger. Sedimentary layers, deposited in a vast sunken area, have been fashioned by encroachments and withdrawals of the sea. North of the Everenska Planina, erosion has uncovered rare varieties of quartz.

The rivers flow sluggishly into wide flat valleys, while the whole coast seems pushed back by a recent rise in the level of the Black Sea.

Toward the coast, the sub-Balkan depression forms the territory of Burgas. Here, the action of the sea has been more moderate than around Varna. It has formed low cliffs which are fringed with sand and sand bars.

## Climate

Bulgaria's climate is affected less by its latitude than by the configuration and elevation of its land-surface, whereby the country is exposed to the climatic influences of the Black Sea and that of the steppes of southwestern Russia.

For morphological reasons, it is obvious that the Bulgarian climate cannot be homogeneous; the Stara Planina, while not very high, acts as a climatic curtain which causes slight differences between the northern and southern watersheds.

### THE DANUBIAN REGION

The Danubian Basin, which resembles an immense corridor, is exposed to the influence of the Black Sea as well as to the more pronounced influence of the Russian steppes. This low-lying area is in the grip of icy air currents which, for a large part of the year, cause the temperature to swing between -5° F. and -13° F. After a brief spring comes the blazing hot summer, and the bone-dry earth often becomes fissured to a depth of three feet.

Summer is also the season of short-lived rains from violent cloudbursts which end the frequent and long droughts. In the fall, the winds from the steppes are made warmer by the Black Sea, thus prolonging the season. Winter is harsh.

The range between the warmest and coldest months is wide—that between absolute maximum and minimum wider still.

The mean annual temperature of the Danubian region, however, stays between 48° and 54° F.

The annual rainfall (heaviest in summer), varies between 24 and 30 inches.

### WESTERN BULGARIA

Western Bulgaria has a pronounced continental climate, altitude notwithstanding. Sofia (1820 feet) has an average temperature of 22° F. in January and 69° F. in July—a difference of 47°. But its extremes range from -17° F. to 100° F.

Precipitation rarely exceeds 24 inches per annum and rain is more frequent in the summer. A substantial part of the precipitation is contributed by snow.

The curtain formed by the Balkans retards the southward spread of continental conditions, while accentuating, in high-lying areas, the rigors of winter and tempering the summer heat with increased precipitation on hillsides.

### THE ANTI-BALKANS

South of the Balkans, the character of the climate changes. In the anti-Balkan valleys and hollows, which are protected form the cold northerly and northeasterly winds, the thermometer in January does not fall below zero and the summer is not unbearably hot. Rain, which is abundant, falls mainly in the spring, thus revealing the influence of the not-too-distant Mediterranean. At Kazanlik (1270 feet), the average temperature in January is about 32° F. and in July 80° F.

Annual rainfall increases to 28 inches as one gradually goes south.

### THE MARITSA BASIN

The Maritsa Basin and the less elevated regions of the East Rhodope Mountains, though having substantial summer rains, tend to get heavier falls in the winter and spring months; this distribution marks the change to the climatic conditions of the Thraco-Macedonian coast. The middle valley of the Maritsa, as far as Plovdiv, has the better climate, though its temperature range is still wide. The summers, however, are hot enough for subtropical cultivation, especially if it is done under irrigation. At Plovdiv, (500 feet) the average temperature in January is 42° F. and in July 64° F. Annual rainfall is 11 inches.

### THE COASTAL REGION

The coastal area enjoys the influence of the Black Sea. It is reflected in the high winter temperature, a warm fall, that is wetter than the spring, and a fairly hot summer. At Burgas the average temperatures are 36° F. in January and 73° F. in July.

### SOUTHWESTERN BULGARIA

In the whole southwest of Bulgaria, the more rugged conformation of the Rhodope area—though a short distance from the warm Aegean— makes for a truly Alpine climate. In the western section the mean annual rainfall is about 32 inches, occurring chiefly in summer. The eastern section is wetter (35 inches), with rain mainly in winter.

The snow, which permanently covers the highest peaks and can be seen

*Sofia has several buildings of architectural and historical interest. Shown above is one of its famous landmarks, the mineral baths, which lie in the western suburb of Krasno-Selo. The nearby mosque of Banya Bashi (not shown), which is still used for worship by Moslems, is another famous building.*

*Lovech, on the furthest slopes of the central Balkans, 19 miles south of Pleven, is situated on both banks of the Osam River. It is an ancient Roman town, which under Turkish rule (1396-1878) became an important stronghold. Today it has a leathercraft school and is the center of a large tanning industry.*

in Sofia 30 miles away, falls for 140 days a year between September and May. The high altitude influences the temperature. At Musala Peak, (9592 feet) the annual mean is 26° F. with an absolute minimum of -24° F.

## Hydrography

### THE DANUBE

This river, called the Dunav by the Bulgars, is about 1750 miles long and is Europe's second longest (next to the Volga).

Between its confluence with the Timok (northwest of Vidin) and the Silistra it forms the frontier between Bulgaria and Rumania. The Rumanian bank is low and fringed with marshland while the Bulgarian is high and steep. The river is slow-flowing and often splits into winding rivulets and arms divided by sandy spits and islets, of which about a hundred belong to Bulgaria.

Before the Danube reaches this section it is already navigable and the major Bulgarian towns on it are Vidin, Nikopol, Svishtov, Ruse and Silistra in that order.

### THE ISKAR

The Iskar (or Isker) is the major Bulgarian affluent of the Danube. It is formed by the confluence of three headstreams in the north Rila Mountains. It flows north past Sofia and through the west Balkans and then northeast to join the Danube at Boril 250 miles from its source.

The river is used to generate electricity for large power stations, such as those of Passarel and Kokoljane.

### THE YANTRA

This river, 168 miles long, is another important tributary of the Danube. It is formed by the confluence of three streams just south of Gabrovo in the Shipka Mountains, where it drains a large area. It then flows north past Gabrovo, northeast past Tirnovo and then northwest to join the Danube 12 miles east of Svishtov. Farming and some industry is carried out in the valley of the Yantra.

These rivers, with the short Timok, Vit, Ozam, Lom and others, are of great importance from the point of view of communications, since, in a country where natural routes are rare, they provide access to the high shut-in mountain valleys.

### THE MARITSA

Bulgaria is also crossed by rivers that flow into the northern Aegean.

The Maritsa River rises on Musala Peak in the Rila Mountains southeast of Sofia. For 170 of its 300 miles it flows in Bulgaria, first east, and then southeast to Svilengrad, where it enters Greece.

The Tundzha (206 miles), which rises in the Central Balkans, and the Arda (180 miles), which rises in the Rhodope, both join the Maritsa at Adrianople, in European Turkey. The valley of the Maritsa, which lies between the Sredna Gora Mountains and the Rhodope massif, is a major highway between Europe and the Bosphorus.

### THE MESTA

This river (150 miles) rises on Kolarov Peak in the Rila Mountains and flows between the Pirin and Rhodope mountains in a southeasterly direction, through wide valleys and deep ravines, to enter Greece, where it is called the Nestos, beyond the broad Delchev Basin.

### THE STRUMA

The Struma, (215 miles—166 in Bulgaria) rises in the Vitosha Mountains at the south foot of Chernivrakh Peak, and flows through Blagoyevgrad to cut the Greek border east of Petrich. Its valley, which was formerly one vast lake, is now silted up and forms the direct route between Sofia and the Aegean.

## BULGARIA AREA AND POPULATION

| PROVINCES | AREA (Sq. miles) | POPULATION (1960) |
|---|---|---|
| Blagoyevgrad | 2503 | 295,100 |
| Burgas | 2917 | 366,500 |
| Dimitrovo | 921 | 187,600 |
| Gabrovo | 794 | 156,400 |
| Khaskovo | 1569 | 293,300 |
| Kolarovgrad | 1286 | 234,300 |
| Kurdzhali | 1560 | 264,500 |
| Kyustendil | 1173 | 195,800 |
| Lovech | 1598 | 213,900 |
| Mikhailovgrad | 1386 | 243,600 |
| Pazardzhik | 1677 | 293,800 |
| Pleven | 1596 | 352,100 |
| Plovdiv | 1763 | 308,000 |
| Plovdiv (city) | 374 | 287,200 |
| Razgrad | 1015 | 191,700 |
| Ruse | 1025 | 255,300 |
| Silistra | 1108 | 167,800 |
| Sliven | 1388 | 207,800 |
| Smolyan | 1373 | 148,400 |
| Sofia | 2812 | 326,500 |
| Sofia (city) | 434 | 766,400 |
| Stara Zagora | 1895 | 330,300 |
| Tolbukhin | 1818 | 236,400 |
| Turgovishte | 1050 | 171,400 |
| Turnovo | 1808 | 344,500 |
| Varna | 1433 | 189,500 |
| Varna (city) | 72 | 148,600 |
| Vidin | 1197 | 188,000 |
| Vratsa | 1604 | 310,700 |
| Yambol | 1681 | 230,100 |
| **TOTAL** | **42,830** | **7,905,500** |

### THE BLACK SEA

Because of highland features so near the coast, the rivers that flow into the Black Sea, like the Provadiya (45 miles), Mandra (50 miles) and Kamchiya (23 miles), have short, irregular courses and in many places flow through marshy areas.

Their lower reaches, because of a recent rise in sea level, have been submerged and transformed into long gulfs or bays or lakes.

### LAKES

Bulgaria has a variety of lakes, both in the mountain area, where glaciers are more common, and along the seaboard.

In the northeast is Lake Varna (7 square miles), which is fed by Provadiya River and opens into the Black Sea through a gulf four miles long by three miles wide.

## Flora and Fauna

Vegetation mostly resembles that of Central Europe but in the south there is some *maquis* (Mediterranean scrub).

In the northeast, where the climate is drier, halophytes (thick-leaved plants) begin to appear. This is an early sign of the Black Sea steppe vegetation, such as the rhododendron, which is found east of the Rhodope and Strandzha mountains at heights of between 2300 and 4300 feet.

### AFFORESTATION

The changes by which man has replaced wild with cultivated plants have profoundly altered the face of the land, largely at the expense of forested areas. About 80 per cent of afforestation is in the mountains, but its economic value is low, since the more important varieties of trees are found in the higher lying areas and are therefore difficult to exploit. According to altitude, the following distribution of trees can be observed: ash, maple, poplar, lime, willow, in valleys and up to 2500 feet; oak forests, up to 2800 feet, beech, up to 5000 feet, the fir, above 6500 feet, and at higher altitudes still, only the pine.

### ANIMAL LIFE

The fauna of Bulgaria is of great interest because of the presence of animals which have vanished from most, if not all, of Western Europe. Jackals are numerous; there are many wolves and lynxes, and *Spalax typhlus*, a kind of Asiatic rodent, exclusive to the Balkan Peninsula, is also found in large numbers. In more inaccessible regions the small gray bear is easily encountered, and in the Burgas and Strandzha regions are found jackals, foxes, badgers, hares, wildcats, martens, polecats and wild boars. Large numbers of stags and

*A large open square in Sofia. Very few people drive automobiles in Bulgaria; hence the relatively quiet appearance of the streets. The two nearest buildings are, on the left, a modern store, and, on the right, the Hotel Balkan. The façade of the building in the center background includes Neoclassical as well as neo-Baroque elements.*

chamois are to be found in the woods —the chamois preferring the lonely Rila and Rhodope mountains.

Bird life is plentiful, with specimens of birds of prey, such as *aquila orientalis* (an eastern eagle) and *occipiter brevipes* (a short-clawed hawk).

There are also several varieties of snakes and tortoises.

## HUMAN GEOGRAPHY

### History of Settlement

IT IS CERTAIN THAT BULGARIA HAS been populated since the Neolithic Age. But the first inhabitants of whom there is historical knowledge were the Thracians, a people of Indo-European origin, who later came under Roman cultural influence. This ancient Romanized indigenous population, known as Vlachs, was still numerous in the Middle Ages.

In the 7th century A.D. peaceful tribes of Slav peasants crossed the Danube and soon imposed their language and culture on the inhabitants. In 671 A.D. a Bulgarian horde, estimated to be 25,000 strong, crossed the Danube and they, in their turn, imposed their powerful military and political organization upon both the Slavs and the natives.

But this warlike race was soon to fuse with the Slavs, whose religion, language and culture it adopted. Later waves of Tatar, Avar, Kuman and Pecheneg immigrants or invaders underwent a similar process.

#### THE TURKISH CONQUEST

The Turkish conquest (1396-1878), through the stationing of large groups of colonists in Bulgaria and through the spread of Islam and cultural influences, had a fundamental effect on the Bulgarian people.

### Nationality

About two million Bulgars live abroad—in Rumania, the Ukraine, Greece and Asia Minor. Another 170,000 have emigrated to the United States and Australia.

National minorities include Macedonians, Turks, Gypsies, Jews, Ar-

*Rila monastery (founded in the 10th century), in the village of Rila, near Sofia, is the most famous in Bulgaria. It is a typical example of a fortified holy place—the battlement tower looks a little incongruous next to the domes of the church. Although the monastery is Christian, the architecture shows unmistakable signs of Oriental influence.*

menians and Rumanians. The Turks were the largest minority (656,000 in 1950) until 1951, when they began to leave the country in large numbers.

Along the Danube, in the Rhodope area, and in the neighborhood of Vratsa there was once a Rumanian minority of about 69,000, but most of them have left Bulgaria for northern Dobruja, in exchange for the Bulgars who were repatriated from there.

### Population

The 1964 census estimate shows that Bulgaria had 8,100,000 people on its 42,830 square miles, giving an average density of 189 per square mile. This comparatively low density is due not so much to the rugged configuration of the land or to the mainly agricultural economy, as to the tragic wars that have ravaged the country in the past.

There is a considerable variation of population density from area to area: it is higher in the north than in the south and southwest. The highest density is in the strip of foothills lying north and south of the Balkans, where the Bulgarians took refuge from the invading Turks.

The lowest recorded density (64 per square mile) is in some districts of the Rhodope and Strandzha mountains, while the highest (nearly 300 per square mile) is in the Danubian area. There are other high density pockets in the middle basin of the Maritsa and especially in the district of Sofia, the capital and only large city in the country.

#### GROWTH OF POPULATION

Over the years the population has grown considerably, but the continual political and boundary changes to which Bulgaria has been subjected do not allow us to have accurate comparative figures. Although, as in many European countries, there has been a fall in the birth rate, this still remains fairly high—19.5 per 1000 in 1956. However, the death rate has also decreased—from 12.6 per 1000 in 1948 to 8.1 per 1000 in 1960.

The population is chiefly rural and lives in small country towns and compact villages or hamlets.

Urbanization has been fairly slow: town dwellers formed 27 per cent of the population in 1883 and in 1959 only 34 per cent.

### Cities and Towns

One indication of the poor urban development in Bulgaria is the very small number of large towns. According to the 1959 census only three towns had more than 100,000 inhabitants and only six had between 50,000 and 100,000.

### SOFIA (*pop. 766,400*)

Sofia, the country's largest city, became the capital of Bulgaria in 1878. It is situated at an altitude of 1820 feet in western Bulgaria in the Sofia basin of the Iskar, north of the Vitosha Mountains.

Sofia is an important transportation center connected by railroad to Istanbul (300 miles away), Salonika, Burgas, Varna, Ruse, Bucharest, Belgrade (206 miles away), Vidin, Kyustendil and Petrich, and by air to several cities, such as Belgrade, Budapest, Bucharest, Prague, Moscow, Amsterdam and Damascus.

Armaments, electrical equipment, textiles, furniture, processed foods, cigarettes, carpets and cosmetics are among the chief manufactures.

It is an important commercial center and is the chief market for the agricultural produce of the Sofia Basin.

Sofia is the most important cultural center in the country, with a large university (1880), modern schools, colleges and other teaching establishments, museums, art galleries and academies of science.

Sofia is an ancient Thracian city. Under the Romans it was known as Serdica, and under the Byzantines as Triadica. It was not named after its saint until the 14th century. It has been destroyed and rebuilt several times, but has never lost its importance as an administrative and economic center.

### BURGAS (*pop. 91,700*)

Burgas, on the Gulf of Burgas, 215 miles east of Sofia, to which it is connected by two railroads, is the country's major port.

Though standing on the site of the Byzantine town of Pyrgos it is a relatively new town which, in 1887, was a small fishing village with only 7000 inhabitants.

Industries include fishing and fish canning, manufacture of agricultural machinery, food processing and liquor distillation. Copper is mined in nearby Meden Rudnik and there are salt pans round Lake Atanasovo in the north.

### DIMITROVGRAD (*pop. 34,162*)

Dimitrovgrad, founded in 1949 on the Maritsa nine miles north of Khaskovo, is an important railroad junc-

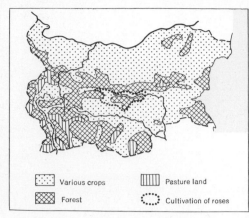

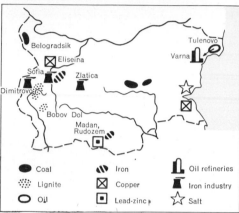

Large industrial centers

Naval shipyards

Heavy engineering

Glass

Ceramics

Chemical industry

Textile centers

Left: *Maps showing,* top, *Bulgaria's utilization of soil;* middle, *the country's industrial and power centers; and* bottom, *the location of the major industries.*

tion and the country's major center of the chemical industry.

### GABROVO (pop. 45,000)

Gabrovo, on the Yantra River, 50 miles southeast of Pleven on the northern slopes of the Central Balkans, is an important railroad terminal linked with Kazanlik in the south through the Shipka Pass. Textiles and gunpowder are the chief manufactures.

### KOLAROVGRAD (pop. 49,153)

Kolarovgrad, called Shumen till 1950, is a railroad junction in the southern part of the Deliorman, 50 miles west of Varna. It is a handicraft center with leather and woodworking industries and was founded in the 10th century by Tsar Simeon the Great.

### PERNIK (pop. 60,800)

Pernik, called Dimitrovo from 1949 to 1962, is on the Struma River 15 miles southwest of Sofia. It is a major industrial center with metallurgical and heavy engineering plants and coal mines.

### PLOVDIV (pop. 287,200)

Plovdiv, standing on both banks of the Maritsa River 80 miles southeast of Sofia, is the country's second largest city.

It is a major transportation center with six railroad lines. There are a large cotton mill, tobacco factories, a sugar refinery and several breweries.

Plovdiv has a university, several teacher-training colleges, theaters, museums and a national library.

Originally a Greek settlement, it became a fortified town under Philip II of Macedon and subsequently capital of the Roman province of Mesia. In its long history, the town has been known by several names, the most famous being Philippopolis.

### RUSE (pop. 111,983)

Ruse, 150 miles northeast of Sofia, is the most important port on the Bulgarian side of the Danube and is connected with Giurgiu, in Rumania, by ferry and by a bridge.

Though an ancient town, it owes its growth to the recent development of industries such as metallurgy, textiles, food processing and petroleum refining.

### VARNA (pop. 148 600)

Varna stands 230 miles northeast of Sofia on a sandy isthmus between the Gulf of Varna and the eastern shore of Lake Varna. It is the country's second seaport and is an important railroad terminal. From 1949 to 1956 it was known as Stalin.

Grain and canned fish are exported through Varna, which is also an important seaside resort.

The town has a university, a naval academy, several ancient churches, mosques, and ruins of 6th-century fortifications.

### ECONOMIC GEOGRAPHY

LIKE OTHER COMMUNIST COUNTRIES, Bulgaria is transforming its economy on the Soviet pattern.

State economic planning was begun in 1947 under Soviet direction. Private property was abolished; the land and means of production were collectivized; industrial production was rapidly expanded and the exploitation of mineral resources was made more efficient. By 1952 private enterprise had almost completely disappeared.

In spite of rapid industrialization (industry now accounts for two-thirds of the economy), agriculture is still important and gives employment to 76 per cent of the working population.

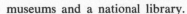

*Inside a tobacco-processing plant. Bulgarian agriculture is becoming increasingly dependent on industrial crops like tobacco. Cultivation has substantially increased since Bulgaria annexed the tobacco-growing parts of southern Macedonia and Thrace. Factories are rapidly being developed to process the tobacco, which, as cigars and cigarettes, is one the country's major exports.*

## Agriculture

The Danubian plateau, with its steppe-like climate and vegetation and its Aeolian deposits (soils like *loess* that have been transported by wind from one place to another), provides an ideal environment for cereals such as wheat, corn and barley.

South of this region stretches the Balkan strip with its two open ends to the south and the north. It is rugged in configuration and has valleys running lengthwise and crosswise.

This area has been settled since ancient times and lends itself well to agriculture, stock-raising and afforestation.

### CENTRAL BULGARIA

Between the Balkan zone and the Rhodope massif stretches Central Bulgaria, which has greater morphological variation and therefore a more diversified kind of agriculture.

Grain cultivation is less important than cultivation of plants that give rise to industry—like roses, tobacco, cotton, oil-bearing seeds and timber-yielding trees. Market gardening and viticulture are also important.

### THE SOUTH

The south is completely mountainous. It consists of the Eastern and Western Rhodope Mountains, joined to the western side of the Macedonian heights and on the east to the Strandzha Mountains.

The alternation of high, level surfaces with deep gorges or ravines and of fertile valley bottoms with fault bottom valleys or depressions is reflected in the alternating pattern of pastoral life, forestry and agriculture proper.

### COOPERATIVE FARMS

Before the People's Republic was declared, Bulgaria was a land of peasants and small landowners. About 85 per cent of private estates were less than 25 acres in area and only 0.6 per cent exceeded 75 acres. After 1945, private property was limited to a maximum of 50 acres per person; about 410,000 acres were taken from monasteries and other land-owners for distribution among landless or dispossessed peasants and cooperative farms.

Even in 1946, 23 per cent of small farms and holdings still had no draft animals and 19 per cent did not even have plows. Bulgarian agriculture was retarded by lack of capital, technical equipment, and by continued use of outmoded methods, coupled with

*Threshing at Parvomai on the Maritsa River in the Plovdiv district. Although the development of industrial crops is receiving more attention, the growing of cereals still plays a vital part in the national agricultural production. Only recently has mechanization been introduced into Bulgarian farming.*

the effects of World War II.

The new direction in economics and politics sought to remedy this by the creation of cooperative farms (which in 1958 numbered about 3351), modeled on the Soviet *sovkhos*, and by the introduction of tractor and agricultural machine stations (225 in 1961) with 44,200 tractors, 6000 combines and 5000 threshers. At the end of 1958 cooperatives were thoroughly reorganized and reduced to 640 large units of 17,300 acres each. Dobruja was converted into one vast collective farm in accordance with a special Six-Year Plan. The third Five-Year Economic Plan (1958-62) aimed at a 30 per cent growth in agricultural production.

### CEREALS

Cultivation of cereals has always dominated Bulgarian agriculture, even if nowadays cultivation of industrial crops tends to prevail. Grain production rose from an average of 362,000 tons in 1948-52 to well over 4,400,000 in 1962 to 1963. Wheat and corn are the basic cereal crops and together form about 83 per cent of all grain production. Rye, barley, oats and rice are less important; yields have hardly increased and have

*The Iskar dam on the Iskar River, 20 miles southeast of Sofia. Construction of this project was begun in 1951 and includes three hydroelectric power stations at Pasarel (on the dam site), Kokalyane and Sofia. The reservoir is also used to irrigate the semi-arid plain of Sofia. To meet increased industrial needs, Bulgaria is stepping up output of electricity.*

*The end of a street in the busiest part of Sofia's city center showing the Hotel Balkan and a large department store. The city was severely damaged during air raids in World War II. It has since grown again and now has a completely modern aspect. Sofia is the largest city of Bulgaria and is a manufacturing center.*

sometimes even dropped.

The production of wheat is one of the highest in the Mediterranean world and supports a thriving flour-milling industry and export trade.

A crop which is well adapted to mountainous country, where cereals are excluded because their yield would be too low, is the potato, whose production in 1962 to 1963 was 361,000 tons.

### TOBACCO CULTIVATION

Bulgarian agriculture has now become more dependent on industrial crops, especially tobacco and oil-bearing plants.

Cultivation of tobacco has increased considerably since Bulgaria annexed parts of southern Macedonia and Thrace where tobacco is widely grown. Other areas where tobacco is cultivated are the valley of the Maritsa, the Rhodope and, especially, the valley of the Arda. Production and areas of cultivation have shown a remarkable increase since World War I, yielding 120,000 tons in 1963.

Tobacco is not only a major export but also supports a flourishing domestic cigarette industry.

### OTHER CROPS

Cultivation of the sunflower, which was introduced from Rumania in 1921, is becoming of great importance. Other oil-producing seeds are the sesame and the colza. From these three the country is able to meet all its requirements for edible oils.

Cultivation of sugar beet and sugar refining are also gaining in importance.

Roses, which are grown in the Tundzha valley and near Karlovo and Kazanlik, support a rose oil industry which, in 1958, produced 2400 lbs of rose oil (nearly 80 per cent of the world's total).

### FRUIT AND WINE

Parts of the Plovdiv area specialize in the cultivation of strawberries. Most of the crop is processed and only small quantities of fresh strawberries are exported.

Cotton is grown in the Struma valley and in the Maritsa basin. Production is being steadily increased.

Apples, plums and dessert grapes are exported.

Wine-making is an important industry and Bulgarian wines are exported to other countries.

### Raising of Livestock

Another mainstay of the national economy is the raising of livestock. Almost all parts of Bulgaria are favorable for this. The north is more suitable for cattle and pigs; the south for sheep and goats.

But, as in all Mediterranean lands, the raising of sheep and goats takes first place. In 1960 there were 8,700,000 sheep and 272,400 goats, as against 1,600,000 cattle. Sheep and goats are the mainstay of the peasant, supplying him with wool, milk, cheese, meat and skins.

The standard of animal husbandry has not risen appreciably above the pre-World War II level. In large measure this is due to the losses suffered during the war.

Pig-breeding (2,330,000 animals in 1960) is also quite important and poultry-breeding (21,600,000 birds in 1960) even more so, as there is a large export trade in eggs.

Bee-keeping and the breeding of silkworms are also of some importance and are carried out all over the country.

### Mining and Industry

Steps have been taken to increase industrial output at a quicker pace than agricultural output. In 1962 a planning program, taking 1960 as a base year, envisaged a growth, by 1980, of 250 per cent in agriculture, 700 per cent in industry, 500 per cent in the manufacture of consumer goods, 450 per cent in steel and iron, 2700 per cent in chemicals and an increase in production of motor vehicles from nil in 1960 to 120,000.

The Tulenovo Deposit in Dobruja, which is connected by a 93-mile-long pipeline to the Varna refineries, produced 248,640 tons of petroleum in 1958 and 224,000 in 1962 but is expected to increase production in 1965.

### ELECTRICITY

Production of electricity rose from 266 million kwh. in 1938 to 7182 million in 1963 and is planned to reach 11,250 million in 1965. Electricity is chiefly produced by thermal stations, but hydroelectric stations (mainly in the Rhodope and Maritsa Basin and the Iskar valley) have increased both in number and output.

Extraction of minerals, though modest as yet, is steadily increasing. In many cases, exploitation of minerals was begun only after World War II. Iron, zinc, copper and magnesite are already being mined. Important deposits of bauxite have been discovered near the Yugoslavian border and uranium exists in Bulkovada. The output of steel and iron is increasing. Lead and zinc foundries are in operation at Krdjati and Pirdop.

### TEXTILES

The textile industry is rapidly expanding. Silk is manufactured at Ruse, Plovdiv, Kazanlik and Karlovo. There is also a considerable increase in the manufacture of synthetic fibers.

## Communications

The highway and railway system is not yet sufficient for the country's economic potential.

### RAILROADS

There were 3577 miles of railroad (including 270 miles of narrow gauge) in 1963. This network density is one of the lowest in Europe.

The main line is that over which the Simplon-Orient Express runs. It serves Sofia and Plovdiv and is part of the international route from Calais to Istanbul. In 1963 the Sofia-Plovdiv line (97 miles) and the Ruse-

Gorna - Oryakhovitsa line (71 miles) were electrified. The railroads, while carrying the bulk of freight (about 60 per cent), are beginning to lose passengers to road transport.

In 1961 the railroads carried 34,500,000 passengers and 2,396,800 tons of freight, consisting mainly of coal, minerals, building timber and sugar beet.

### HIGHWAYS

In 1961 there were 17,200 miles of roads, including 1410 miles of highway. In the same year there were 9300 automobiles, 20,000 trucks and 2300 buses. In 1962 the buses carried 441 million passengers and 67,200,000 tons of freight.

### SHIPPING

In 1962 the merchant navy based on Varna, had 37 vessels totaling over 110,000 gross tons.

At the Varna shipyards, production is mainly for export to other European Communist countries.

### AIRLINES

TABSO (Bulgarian Airline) connects the main centers of Bulgaria

and, in cooperation with Hungarian and Czech airlines, links Sofia with Budapest, Prague and Belgrade. AEROFLOT, the Soviet airline, connects Moscow with Sofia via Kiev and Bucharest, while K.L.M. (Royal Dutch Airlines) has a weekly service to Sofia on the Amsterdam-Athens-Beirut-Damascus flight.

## Trade

Imports exceed exports. Whereas at the beginning of this century cereals and livestock accounted for 80 per cent of exports, these products have been joined, more recently, by tobacco, fruit and minerals. The chief imports are machinery, metals and petroleum.

### DIRECTION OF TRADE

Before World War II Bulgaria traded chiefly with the Western European countries but since the war the direction of trade has drastically changed: nearly all trade is now with Communist countries, the Soviet Union accounting for more than half.

However, official Bulgarian statements stress the need for increasing trade with non-Communist countries

*The Danube River at Nikopol. The banks of the river on its lower course present a strange contrast to one another; the Rumanian side (seen in the distance) is low-lying and fringed with marshes; the Bulgarian bank is rugged and steep. Nikopol was founded by Heraclius, the Byzantine emperor, in 629 A.D., and became an important fortification during Turkish rule. It is now a busy river port.*

## SLAVONIC CHECKER-BOARD

SITUATED IN THE SOUTHEASTERN corner of Europe, at the gateway to Asia, Bulgaria has special features that distinguish it from its neighboring countries. Bulgaria is not entirely European, but neither can it be said that it is Asiatic. Bulgaria is a kind of Slavonic checker-board, on which five centuries of Turkish occupation left a deep impression.

Bulgarians are quite different from other Slav peoples. The latter more commonly have qualities of sentiment, impulsive generosity and fiery imagination, but in the extremely rational Bulgarians calculation and tolerance predominate.

The first known inhabitants of Bulgaria were the Thracians. In the first half of the 7th century the land was settled by Slavs, who almost absorbed the existing population and determined the essential ethnic features of the modern nation. Of less importance were the subsequent immigrations of the Turko-Tatar tribe of Bulgars, who, though giving their name to the country, did not influence its Slavonic language and culture. But Turkish rule, beginning in the 14th century, made a very deep impression.

### FIVE CENTURIES OF ISOLATION

For five centuries Bulgaria was isolated from the West and exposed to Islam and Turkish culture. The Turks drove the Slavs into the mountains and there the peasant population found a good environment, where they kept intact their traditions and beliefs. Thus, while in character, food and folk art, there are clear Asiatic influences in Bulgaria, in customs relating to work on the land and to religious observance, the original Slav features have been preserved.

## BIRTH, MARRIAGE AND DEATH

DEVOTION TO THE LAND, PROPER TO a peasant folk, is reflected in the old legends and rituals that attend the various important occasions of human life.

On the third day following a birth, the child is visited by the *oristnici*, beings similar to the ancient Fates, who station themselves at the head of the bed and decide the future of the newborn baby.

### Women and Schools

Equal rights with men, obtained by Bulgarian women in 1944, have caused far-reaching changes in the methods of bringing up and educating children. They have given marriage in Bulgaria a more secure social foundation. In the past a woman enjoyed very limited civil rights. A widow, for example, had to entrust to others the care of her sons. Today women take part in community life in all its forms, and most of them go out to work during the day.

### SCHOOLS AND MARRIAGE

Education has always had a very important place in the nation's life. Even in the past, when living conditions were harder and more wretched for the peasant, the percentage of illiterates was low, always less than among other Balkan peoples.

Today all villages vie with one

*A dance step executed by the ballet company of Plovdiv. The Bulgarian national dance is the* horò, *a round dance performed to the sound of the* gerdulka *(a kind of mandolin), the* kavàl *(similar to a flute) and drums. The dancers of the* horò *move into a circle, in the center of which other young people dance in mime, representing courting couples meeting and falling in love.*

another for the school building to be the finest in the area. Many a young person leaves the primary school and continues his or her studies at an institute of higher education or at the university. Women enjoy these social advances and their new dignity is reflected in family life.

### FLOWERS AND SERENADES

But Bulgarians marry young and despite their pragmatism they are a romantic people. During courtship the young men, with clusters of flowers at their ears, stand beneath their fair ladies' windows and improvise serenades, accompanying themselves on the *kavàl* (flute).

The women's songs are sad: they evoke bitter times, when marriages were arranged between parents and marriage for a woman was a thankless and painful experience.

### The Well

Bulgarian wedding customs are similar to the traditional practices of all Slav countries. The bride-to-be remains shut up in her home for a whole week before the marriage without receiving anyone. When this period is passed, the bride's girl friends bring her to the village well or spring and together they walk round it three times. This is a propitiatory rite to ensure fertility; it is associated with the ancient water-rite.

### Funeral Rites

In funerals, too, are found usages similar to those of other Slavs. The Bulgarians are accustomed to prepare wine and napkins for those taking part in the last rites. The wine and napkins are placed on the coffin. Songs are intermingled with thoughts of dying.

Wailing women intone laments around the corpse. The funeral procession is headed by boys, who bear a consecrated cross and church vessels, followed by the elders with baskets loaded with food. Then come the priests walking before the coffin, which is often open so that people may see the dead person. Behind the remains come members of the family, friends and acquaintances.

---

## DANCE AND SONG

IN COMMON WITH OTHER BALKAN peoples, Bulgarians love dancing and singing.

The national dance is the *horò*, similar to the Rumanian *hora* and

*A dance step performed by a group of professional dancers. In Bulgaria, the dance is often accompanied by songs which bring to mind, by their melodic sound, the Portuguese* fados. *Bulgaria preserves, almost intact, a rich heritage of folk songs, many of which are linked with the country's turbulent history of invasion and others with marriage, family life and death. Many are interlinked with the folk dances to which they act as an accompaniment.*

the Yugoslavian *kolo*. It is a round dance performed by long chains of dancers. In the center of the ring, some youngsters improvise a dance depicting love scenes, full of rustic coquetry.

### Wild yet Mellow Songs

The songs have the same nostalgic tone as Rumanian gypsy songs, but with a more Western accent. They resemble the Portuguese *fados*, and are impetuous and sweet at the same time.

The heritage of folk song is vast indeed. More than 30,000 songs have been collected and divided into four main branches according to subject: lyric songs, ritual songs, ballads, epic songs.

Love is the principal theme of the lyric songs, and it is an idealized love, full of tenderness and soft images.

### Range of the Ballads

The subjects of the ballads cover practically all the events of human life. They include comic (sometimes even ribald) episodes from married life, village chronicles and the highly-colored and fanciful adventures of supernatural beings dwelling in the woods and streams.

### Minstrels and Epics

Epic song still survives in western and southwestern Bulgaria, where the old *gustaro* (minstrel) goes from village to village, singing and playing his homemade single-stringed violin.

*A wandering bagpipes player in Bistrica, a village near Sofia. There is no musical folklore which does not count among its traditional instruments this primitive goat-skin wind instrument.*

The hero of Bulgarian epic is Marko Kraljević, a semi-legendary figure, whose words and deeds also fill the melancholy verses of the Serbian wandering singers. Marko Kraljević lives in a magic world. He has a magic horse that speaks and an invincible fiery sword; he also has an old mother, and a mistress. In an unknown cave, guarded by two dragons, he sleeps and awaits the great day of Bulgarian nationalism for his awakening. When that moment comes, the golden bells in the sunken Church of the Assumption at Tirnovo will be rung anew by the angels.

### THE BRAVE BULGARIAN BRIGANDS

Many of the songs are dedicated to the *haiduks*, who were generous brigands, patriotic and brave. The *haiduks* were inspired to live outside the law by Turkish persecution.

In popular songs the *haiduks* appear as defenders of the oppressed. Unable to bear tyranny, they take to the wilds where they live in the forests and mountains ever ready to rush to the help of their brothers in time of danger. These men inspired legends which served to rouse and sustain the Bulgarian people in their times of trial. Their songs became patriotic hymns.

## RELIGION

BULGARIANS ARE FOR THE MOST PART Orthodox by religion. But there is a large Moslem minority and a small Roman Catholic minority. The spread of Marxist materialism has accentuated Bulgarian agnosticism and the abandonment of religious observances. But this attitude, widespread in urban centers, becomes less evident in the countryside and in the mountains.

### The Sun, a Handsome Bachelor

In the Bulgarian legends arising from folk religion the Sun lives by night in a palace under the sea. He lives with his many brothers and sisters and one of the latter, Dawn, has the task of awakening him early each morning so that he may continue his journey round the earth. This is an arduous and tiring journey and when he returns at night, anxiously awaited by his mother, the Sun evinces an unusually large appetite and devours his supper to recuperate his lost strength. The Sun is handsome and perfect, good and full of grace; he is a bachelor and will never marry.

In popular Bulgarian beliefs many traces of pagan sun-worship survive. When the sun comes up and appears through the clouds, peasants doff their caps and cross themselves. The most propitious time of the month is the period of the new moon: it is the best time for sowing, for planting and watering trees, for marrying and doing business.

There are as many stars as men, for it is believed that at the birth of a child, a star lights up in the sky, but none can recognize his own star save with the help of astrologers. Knowledge of the stars enable the latter to foretell the future, a profitable business in Bulgaria.

### Devils and Goblins

According to Bulgarian legend, Earth was much more spacious at the moment of creation; but in order to form the mountains God was compelled to fold back its edges.

Earth, too, abounds in benign and malevolent beings but more especially the latter.

First and foremost is the Devil, who

takes many forms and shapes. There is a small devil that has one foot shorter than the other and walks with a limp, and a one-legged devil who, despite his single limb, still manages to cause all sorts of mischief and crime. The black devil has the power to put the evil eye on people. Finally there is Anti-Christ, who will appear on earth to announce the end of the world and will assist in his own destruction.

There are also *brodnici*, goblins that haunt rivers, streams and mill-races, and are always in direct contact with evil spirits.

## Lovely Females on Winged Stags

The *samvili* are female creatures, lovely beings that dwell on the banks of lakes and in the shade of pine-trees. They feed on white bread and honey, drink fruit-juices, ride winged stags and love to bathe in the waters of mountain streams. They can be seen only by shepherds when leading their flocks to summer pasture, and sometimes by huntsmen.

### Ritual of Fire

In Bulgaria fire rituals take two forms: the fire of life that is lit according to need, and the festal fire that is kindled at fixed times in the year.

The fire of life is lit in times of epidemics. On a moonlit night a place is chosen where the waters of two rivers meet, or where two trees form a kind of arch with interlacing branches. Two lime-twigs are then rubbed together until a flame is kindled, and a great bonfire soon lights up the darkness. Men and beasts walk in procession to the fire and pass over it. From that moment on, it is believed, they will be preserved from plague, small-pox and hoof-and-mouth disease.

#### FIRES FOR LOVE

The most typical festal fire is lit on the eve of Lent. Much preparation is made. Young people go into the woods and prepare ten thin maple-wood arrows. On the night before the beginning of Lent, everyone goes to a hill, where bonfires are lit. Girls then appear at the windows of their homes and the young men break

*A peasant couple from the western region. The white embroidery on the man's jacket adds to the elegance of the costume, as does the pattern on the knees of his close-fitting trousers. The woman's costume has almost a Renaissance beauty: the stylization of the embroidery on the dark skirt is perfect.*

loose. They leap through the flames, light the arrows and fling them at their sweethearts. Since the more arrows directed at a girl, the more passionately she is loved, the girls run after the flaming arrows, counting and re-counting. When they have thrown all their arrows, the young men light torches and walk in procession through the valley, dancing and twirling the torches above their heads.

## The Lord of the House

The cult of the "Lord of the House" survives in some mountain districts. It is believed that the spirit of an ancestor, who was particularly worthy of respect during his lifetime, hovers over each house and protects it. The whole family venerates this spirit, because due to him members of the family may reach an advanced age, flocks increase and fields yield a good harvest.

The "Lord," for his part, is not very demanding. He comes to life only when hungry. At such times, he knocks on doors, windows or ceilings or appears to someone in a dream. Then the "Lord's pittance" must be prepared. But first the house must be cleaned from top to bottom and the whole family must put on its best clothes. A black cockerel is killed and its blood drained into a hole in the ground. The cockerel is hung beneath the arch of the family doorway and on the table are placed a pie and the *banitza*, a cake made with puff-pastry. The eldest woman pours a half glass of wine on the fire-place and half on the fire itself, saying: "Be of good cheer, sir, and you, O my family, rejoice." One of the family takes pieces of chicken, pie and *banitza*, and three glasses of wine and sets them down at three different points in a barn for the "Lord." Finally, everyone sits at the table and before the meal begins the old woman addresses the protector of

the house: "O you who pass, come and bring us the dew, you who are come from the fields, bring us the grape..." During the meal, she raises her glass from time to time and continues to entreat the "Lord" to grant long life to all, easy childbirth and fecund livestock.

### Spring Festivals

The traditional Bulgarian festivals are connected with the seasons and the soil. Spring is celebrated in Thrace with a ceremony which has its origins in ancient Greek culture, the *kukkeri*. On the Sunday before Lent, the young men form themselves into groups of ten or 15 and put on masks. The costume of the *kukkeri* is made from a kind of goat-skin jacket, caught in tightly at the waist with a belt of little bells.

All wear high, conical hats, and their faces are covered with grease-paint or by goat-skin masks.

In one hand the *kukkero* holds a saber, in the other a wooden shield, painted red. A procession is formed, in which the *kukkeritza* also takes part; this individual is a man dressed as a woman, according to the custom of the ancient Greek theater. Each young man plays a particular part in the procession.

The group passes through the village, calling at house after house, improvising lighthearted, satirical and sometimes scurrilous scenes.

### PRAYING AND SHOOTING

The ceremony continues in the evening in the village square. The people elect a "king," a youth disguised as an old man with a long white beard, a papier-mâché crown on his mouth, and a majestic linen cloak enveloping him from head to foot. After a lavish meal the "king" is dragged into the fields on a wooden wheat-tub by the *kukkeri*, where he sows the wheat-grain into furrows.

As the "king" sows, he drinks and prays: "May the Lord give us abundance! May our children be born in great numbers!"

Meanwhile the *kukkeri* fire volleys of shots, pretend to kill the "king," and he throws himself to the ground as if dead.

The *kukkeritza* then arrives and wails over his corpse with the ancient laments of pagan funerals.

### Christmas in Bulgaria

The Christmas festivities in Bulgaria are in some respects related to the ancient Roman festival of the birth of the sun. At sunset, women place a broom outside the family courtyard or at a crossroads; this, they believe, will keep off flies in summer. Then they cook ritual cakes. All over Bulgaria, baking on the days before Christmas takes on the nature of a rite. Different types of cakes or pastries are made for various purposes: the *veciernik*, the *oftciarnik*, the *pogacia*, the *kraveta*. The ingredients of *pogacia* include small fragments of plow-handle wood and small coins. The finder of one of these will have security and good fortune throughout the year. If he does not find one, on the other hand, he may suffer indigestion.

The Bulgarian Christmas table is decorated with loaves which have magic powers. The younger daughter saves the first mouthful and puts it under her pillow when she sleeps. Later she may give it to the domestic animals, in order that they may thrive and grow.

On Christmas Eve, groups of boys go from house to house carrying a stick called *koledarka*, at the ends of which hang two rings. They stop in front of every door and striking the ground with the stick, cry: "God is born; it is Christmas!"

The housewives appear at their windows, greet the children and give them the ceremonial cakes.

On Christmas Day the great yule-log is kindled on the hearth and the table is set, a place always being reserved for the unknown guest.

### CHRISTMAS CAROLS AND CATS

Groups numbering ten or more go through the villages singing the *kolede*, Christmas carols telling of the birth of Christ, the renewal of

*A kindergarten in Sofia. A great many Bulgarian children grow up in children's homes built by the state; they then move on to primary schools, which are compulsory and where they must stay for seven years. Education has made great advancement in Bulgaria in recent years, but it always was valued by the people, who at all times were the most literate in the Balkans.*

*An old house in Koprivshtitsa. The Oriental influence in this secular building is visible ·in the motif used in the fretwork balustrade, in the open trelliswork beneath, and in the use of wood as the predominant material. This "weaving" of strips, thick and thin, and wood carving has affinities with Asiatic building and probably derives from Bulgaria's position on the Asiatic trade routes.*

the earth and ending with expressions of good omen. Each group consists of an old man and an old woman, known as the *starets* and the *baba,* of a piper, a collector of gifts, four singers and some others called cats, who imitate feline "miaows."

Festivities continue on New Year's Day, when livestock, houses and hearth are blessed, great logs of new wood are kindled and farming implements are carried into the room where the family has its meals.

These rituals are relics of pre-Christian ceremonies that some believe retain their propitiatory force. After the inaugural chants others are intoned, realistically describing family life and work on the land. These also end with prayers for prosperity, a good harvest and many sons.

## HOMES AND CRAFTS

A CHARACTERISTIC OF BULGARIAN settlement is the way houses appear to be jumbled together without a plan; yet they end by forming compact villages. The open country abounds with straw huts, forming winter quarters for cattle and other livestock.

On the Danubian plains semi-underground dwellings are frequently found. These are dug out of the clay soil, leaving only a low, sloping roof visible; the roof is often covered with earth. Such dwellings are warm in winter and cool in summer.

Two other types of home are also found in Bulgarian rural regions. One is Mediterranean-type, with the walls and roof built of curved tiles or slates. The other is of Turkish or Oriental origin; it is wholly or partly built of wood, and set on wood piles with an upper story overhanging the street. The interior is sparsely furnished.

### Wood Carving

Bulgarian craftsmanship dates back to very distant times and bears traces of a succession of different cultural influences.

The most ancient expression of Bulgarian craftsmanship is wood carving, which had reached a high stage of development even before the creation of the ancient Bulgar kingdom. Indeed, wooden houses were decorated with intaglio carvings as early as the 5th century A.D., as also were articles of domestic use.

### Ceramics

Side by side with wood carving is a flourishing industry producing the ceramic articles widely used by Bulgarians in daily life. The traditional and characteristic forms of these ceramics are represented by plates, cooking-pots, jars for preserving fruit and vegetables, soup-tureens and porringers. They are distinguished by austerity and purity of line. The commonest ornamentation consists of straight or wavy lines or circles and

spirals that closely follow the shape of the piece.

## Metalwork, Ancient and Modern

Other flourishing crafts, also of ancient origin, include that of the goldsmith. Work in gold reached its highest development in the 13th and 14th centuries and magnificent, massively-fashioned specimens of this period have survived. Nowadays craftsmen follow the two classic types that have always distinguished the work of Bulgarian metalsmiths: filigree work and beaten gold and silver. The styles are based on traditional models or are ornamented toward modern forms, corresponding more to the demands and the fashion of today.

## Embroidery

Embroidery is one of the Bulgarian folk arts still very commonly seen today. It is used mainly to decorate clothes and its ornamental character transforms the simplest dress into festive garb. The decoration is multicolored, worked directly onto the material.

## NATIONAL DRESS

BULGARIAN FOLK COSTUME IS THE richest and most varied among the Balkan peoples. But in recent times it has undergone many changes to adapt itself to the demands of modern life. Oriental influences flavored its essentially Slav character, helping to give it a boldness and diversity of form not found elsewhere.

### Black, White and Embroidered

Of the men's costumes, the oldest, the so-called "white costume," has now disappeared. This was completely white and comprised a pair of long, narrow breeches, a shirt or blouse and a waistcoat. The embroidery, differing from region to region, struck the traveler's eye because it stood out magnificently against the white background.

On the other hand, the black costume, worn in eastern Bulgaria, still survives, adapted to suit present-day conditions.

### Aprons for Ladies

The women's costume was of three basic types: the double-apron type, the *sukman* type and the *saya* type.

The first, and oldest, has now disappeared. Worn in the Danube region, it consisted of two pleated aprons, one hanging down in front, the other behind, over an embroidered tunic.

The *sukman* and *saya* costumes are still extant, undergoing constant variations according to the influences of mass production, fashion, individual taste, and also day-to-day needs. The *sukman* type is worn especially in mountain districts and in southeastern Thrace. It is distinguished by the upper garment, a tunic—the *sukman* itself—woven in black or dark blue richly embroidered cloth, falling to the knees.

The *saya* costume is especially common in the southern part of the country; its main feature is a tunic worn over the blouse; this tunic is called the *saya*. The *saya* comes to the knees and may have either long or short sleeves. The material has stripes, white, black, blue, more rarely green.

### Headdresses

Female attire is completed by a headdress which is simple: it is a kerchief, the *marahama*, bordered with red and falling freely to the shoulders. Sometimes the picturesquely knotted handkerchief forms a kind of point or protuberance in the middle of the head.

There are other more elaborate headdresses still in use: in some districts, the women put on high coifs bent forward in a kind of platform, wrapped round in ample white kerchiefs or wimples, giving an imposing look.

## FOOD AND DRINK

BULGARIAN COOKING HAS TWO BASIC features. These are the vegetables that the fertile soil of the country produces in large quantities, and various kinds of spices that season the meager fare and make it especially appetizing.

Throughout every season the fruits of the earth cover Bulgarian tables. Fresh vegetables are regarded by Bulgarians as the best foods to purify and fortify the blood in springtime. Spices and herbs are used in abundance and give the food an unmistakable flavor.

Bulgarians are particularly fond of hot and cold side dishes or snacks: *banitza*, puff-pastry with cheese, meat and spinach; *fassul*, string beans with salad; of *pasteoma*, dried beef; *tarator*, yoghurt and water, cucumbers, nuts and flavoring; *turchiya*, various vegetables pickled in brine and eaten during the winter.

### The National Dish

Bulgaria's national dish is *ciorba* (soup).

The most typical forms of this soup are the *sc'kembe ciorba*, with tripe, garlic and red peppers; the *narodna ciorba sas messo*, with meat; the *pilec'ka ciorba*, with chicken and the *ciorba ot kisselo zele*, with sauerkraut.

### Bulgarian Ragout

Ragout is a special dish in Bulgarian cuisine. It is prepared in the following way: small pieces of meat are browned, then cooled: onions are separately browned; the meat is returned to the heat, seasoned with salt and pepper; when the meat is half-cooked the vegetables are added: all are then cooked slowly until ready.

Rabbit or mutton roast is cooked in Bulgaria by putting the meat, flavoring and spices into a casserole and sealing the lid with pastry.

The *macédoine à la viande* is particularly tasty. This dish is prepared from pieces of mutton or pork browned with dripping and onions; during cooking, egg plants, peppers, peas, potatoes, tomatoes, ground pepper and parsley are added. Another national dish is *kebab*, a kind of ragout, cooked in a sheet of greased paper in a very little sauce and flavored with salt, pepper, paprika, parsley, thyme and mint.

### MOUSAKA AND VINE LEAVES

Minced meat is one of the great stand-bys of the Bulgarian kitchen. It is used to prepare many dishes, such as *mousaka,* forcemeat balls, stuffed peppers and tomatoes, stuffed cabbage and vine-leaves.

### Sweets and Drinks

The commonest sweets are *halva,* made from bran-flour and fruit, and flaky pastry stuffed with cheese, jam or fruit. Yoghurt, which was invented by the Bulgarians, is widely consumed.

The most common drink is the local brandy or *rakia*. The most highly regarded is *slivovitza* (plum brandy). Bulgaria produces excellent red wines. The best of these go well with roasts. White wines are served with boiled meat and stews.

*The making of carpets is a traditional craft practiced by Bulgarian women. Bulgarian handwoven carpets are prized by connoisseurs throughout the world.*

# THE HISTORY

## The Bulgarian Empire

THE BULGARS WERE ORIGINALLY A Turkic-speaking people who migrated westward from Central Asia. In 679, led by Khan (chief) Asparukh, they crossed the Danube into the Byzantine province of Moesia (in the region now known as Dobruja), defeating the forces of the Emperor Constantine IV. There they settled as overlords, but gradually assimilated the language and customs of their Slav subjects.

## The Two Great Decisions

The Bulgar assault on the Byzantine or Eastern Roman Empire did not end there. Under Khan Krum the Terrible they captured Sofia in 809. Two years later they destroyed an avenging imperial army in a great battle, in which Emperor Nicephorus I lost his life. Part of Macedonia and all Thrace fell under Bulgarian sway, and in 813-814 Constantinople itself was besieged by Krum's forces.

Two decisions of great moment to the consolidation of the Bulgarian nation were made by Boris I (d. 907), who came to the throne in 852. He made Slavonic the state language and, following his own conversion in 865, forced his subjects to adopt the Christian faith.

For some time he wavered between the rival claims to spiritual supremacy of Rome and Constantinople, but finally decided in favor of the latter. And so the Bulgarian Church became a member of the Orthodox Eastern Church. Boris welcomed to his kingdom the followers of the brother apostles Methodius and Cyril, who had translated the scriptures into Slavonic and given the Slav peoples the Cyrillic script, based on the Greek alphabet.

## Simeon I

Under Boris's son Simeon I (reigned 893-927) the first Bulgarian Empire reached its greatest extent. Simeon's sway extended to the Adriatic, and he repeatedly waged war against the Byzantine Empire. The Bulgarians captured Adrianople (Edirne) and several times threatened Constantinople during his reign. His capital, Preslav, was even said to rival Constantinople as a center of culture.

### THE BOGOMILS

After the death of Simeon, however, the Bulgarian Empire, disrupted from within by a rising of the Serbians, by social unrest among the peasantry, and by the Church reformation movement of the heretical sect of the Bogomils (who denied the validity of the Incarnation and the Christian sacraments, and went so far as to ban marriage and procreation), rapidly crumbled away under renewed attacks from without. By 1018 the Bulgarians were once more subject to the Byzantine emperor, and it was not until 1185 that a Bulgarian national state rose again.

### MOUNTAIN HERDSMEN

The most widely scattered of all the races inhabiting the Balkans were the Vlachs or Rumans, a people whose language is of Latin derivation and who now form the core of the Rumanian nation. Goaded by the imposition of heavy taxes, these mountain herdsmen revolted against the emperor in 1185. They were joined by Bulgars, and under the leadership of two nobles, the brothers Asen (d. 1196) and Peter (d. 1197), they established a new Bulgarian Empire, under the Asenid dynasty.

## The Asenid Dynasty

The first four rulers of the Asenid dynasty all died at the hands of rivals, and not till the reign (1218-41) of Asen's son, Ivan Asen II, did Bulgaria enjoy anything like her former glory. Under the rule of Ivan Asen II, not only was the empire enlarged, but literature, the arts, religious and secular architecture, and trade all flourished.

After his death, however, Bulgaria was plunged into anarchy again. The last of the Asenids, Ivan Asen III, was overthrown by a peasant rising in 1280.

## The Turkish Conquest

The Bulgarian dominions were gradually chipped away by the assaults of Mongols, Greeks and Serbs, and by the time the Ottoman Turks began to fall on the Balkans in force, in 1345, only the newly-founded Serbian empire was capable of effective resistance. Plovdiv (Philippopolis) fell to the Turks in 1363 and Sofia in 1382.

## Last of the Tsars

The last of the Bulgarian tsars, Ivan Shisman, had recognized the Ottoman sultan, Murad I, as his overlord in 1371, but after the rout of the Serbians and their allies at Kosovo in 1389 the Bulgarian state was doomed. Its capital, Tirnovo, was taken and sacked by the Turks in 1393, after a three-month siege. With the fall of Vidin in 1396, Bulgarian independence was extinguished.

### THE DESPOTIC SULTANS

For nearly 500 years the Bulgarians were subjected to the temporal despotism of the sultan and the spiritual despotism of the Greek Patriarch of Constantinople, who was recognized by the Turks as representing all the Christian communities of their Balkan domains. The Bulgarian patriarchate of Tirnovo was abolished, the Slavonic liturgy was banned and Church posts were filled by Greeks. Education, too, was in the hands of Greek priests, who taught Greek exclusively.

The Turks imposed on the people a new feudal structure, based on discrimination between Moslems and Christians. Non-Moslems were heavily taxed and forced to do many services for their overlords. Military service was not among these services, but many Christian boys were carried off, taught the Moslem faith and trained as Janissaries, members of a corps constituting the main fighting force of the Ottoman Empire.

### GREEK MONOPOLISTS

In most respects the peasants were no worse off economically under the Turks than they had previously been under the *boyars* (nobles), but in the towns, manufacture and trade were for many centuries monopolized by Greeks.

Many of the *boyars* retained some of their privileges by embracing Islam, but conversions among the common people were rare. Nor did the Turkish efforts to destroy the people's sense of their nationality succeed. It lived on in their folk songs

Right: *Tsar Kaloyan with his wife, Princess Dessilava, in a fresco in a church at Boyana. Kaloyan, third of the Asenid rulers, succeeded his elder brother Peter in 1197. Under his leadership the Bulgarian Empire was enlarged, but in 1207 this cunning, ruthless ruler was slain by one of his own followers.*

and stories, occasionally bursting into flame in popular risings and fed constantly by the exploits of the *haiduks*, bands of outlaws who waged guerrilla warfare from their mountain strongholds.

### Period of National Revival

Not till the 19th century, however, did Bulgarian culture revive. Between 1835 and 1845 some 50 Bulgarian schools were founded, and they did much to heighten the national consciousness that led to the great rising of 1876; so did the movement for an autonomous Church based on the Bulgarian language, which received much support from the Russian Church. To quiet the unrest which this issue caused, the Porte (the Turkish Government) eventually, in 1870, imposed a solution to the dispute between the Bulgarians and the Patriarchate of Constantinople. It gave the Bulgarians jurisdiction over 15 dioceses; but the dispute continued and in 1872 the Exarch (head of the Bulgarian Church) and his flock were excommunicated by the Patriarch of Constantinople. Though remaining in close communion with other Orthodox Churches, the Bulgarian Church was not reunited with them until 1945.

Meanwhile, the apostles of an underground movement were preaching insurrection. The Bulgarian Central Revolutionary Committee, linked with hundreds of groups all over the country, set May 13, 1876 as the date for a general uprising. However, the revolutionaries were betrayed and the Turks took terrible vengeance, massacring indiscriminately more than 30,000 men, women and children.

### Russia Intervenes

The severity of the Turks was their undoing. Not only did it arouse the wrath of the civilized world, but it led to the armed intervention of Russia, when Turkey refused to carry out the reforms agreed on by an international conference in London. Russia declared war on April 24, 1877, and, after suffering a number of setbacks her forces, together with those of her ally, Rumania, and the Bulgarian volunteers, were victorious.

#### CONGRESS OF BERLIN

By the Treaty of San Stefano (March 3, 1878) Turkey recognized the existence of an autonomous Bulgarian principality under her sovereignty. The new Bulgaria covered three-fifths of the Balkan Peninsula and had some 4 million inhabitants. But the great powers of Western Europe were not prepared to see a "Great Bulgaria" under Russia's wing, and at the Congress of Berlin they drastically revised the country's frontiers and installed Prince Alexander of Battenberg (1857-93) as ruler. To avoid the formation of an alliance against her, Russia accepted the revision.

#### ALEXANDER ABDICATES

The settlement did not last long, however. The Congress had made the southern part of Bulgaria a separate self-governing province under the name of Eastern Rumelia. In 1885,

*A 19th-century icon of the Archangel Michael in a church at Arbanasi. The Bulgarians were converted to Christianity under Boris I (d. 901) in 865 and their Church became a member of the Orthodox Eastern Church. Ever since, the Bulgarian Church has been a rallying point for Bulgarian nationalism.*

and in the second Balkan War which followed she was defeated by Greece and Serbia and lost southern Dobruja to Rumania, which had joined them.

## War and a Peace Treaty

Bulgaria entered World War I on the side of the Central Powers, Germany and Austria-Hungary, in the hope of reconquering the Macedonian territories and obtaining a larger opening onto the Aegean. In the autumn of 1918, however, prostrated by the long campaigns and bloody battles and trusting in the clemency of the Allied Powers, she signed an armistice at Salonika, on September 29. Four days later Ferdinand abdicated in favor of his son Boris. Under the peace treaty, signed at Neuilly on November 27, 1919, Bulgaria lost Aegean Thrace, her most important gain from the Balkan Wars.

### Postwar Politics

Bulgaria's first postwar premier, Aleksandr Stamboliski (1879-1923), leader of the Agrarian party, ruled as an autocrat. His government began to repress left-wing movements, but at the same time instituted a policy of expropriating land from large estates to give to landless peasants. This alienated wealthy sections of the community, while his conciliatory foreign policy alienated the extreme nationalists. Bulgaria's unsuccessful wars had left hundreds of thousands of Bulgarians outside her frontiers and turned many more into destitute refugees. In 1923 a revolutionary organization aiming to make Macedonia autonomous joined with other nationalists and right-wingers to overthrow the Agrarian government.

The coup d'état ushered in a period of virtual civil war. Armed uprisings and terrorist attacks on the part of Agrarians, Communists and other left-wing groups were answered with mass executions and imprisonment by the new government of Aleksandr Tsankov (1879-1959). His government resigned on Jan. 2, 1926, and an amnesty was declared.

at the instigation of the Rumanian Liberal party, Bulgaria annexed the province. Serbia, which opposed the annexation as upsetting the balance of power in the Balkans, was defeated in a brief war, and no other country moved against Bulgaria. But its ruler, Prince Alexander of Battenberg, had acted against the wishes of Russia, and in the following year (1886) he was forced to abdicate.

### An Independent Kingdom

Under Alexander's successor, Prince Ferdinand of Saxe-Coburg-Gotha (1861-1948), Bulgaria eventually became reconciled with Russia. In 1908 Ferdinand proclaimed Bulgaria an independent kingdom, and in the following year, after an indemnity had been agreed on with Turkey, the great powers recognized her independence.

#### A SWIFT CAMPAIGN

In 1912 Bulgaria joined Greece, Serbia and Montenegro in a Balkan League against Turkey. They defeated her in a swift campaign opened in October; but, cheated out of her expected share of liberated Macedonia, Bulgaria turned on her allies,

### Fascist Government

Eight years of relative peace followed. Then, on May 19, 1934, another coup d'état brought in a Fascist government headed by Kimon Georgiev, which suppressed all political parties, exercised a strict censorship and closed a large number of schools to limit the growth of the intelligentsia. In the following year King Boris III took over the reins, ruling autocratically until his mysterious death in 1943.

### World War II

In 1941 Bulgaria joined the Axis powers. She refused to join Germany in her attack on Russia, but she did allow German troops to use her territory in their attack on Greece and Yugoslavia, and her own forces later occupied Greek Thrace, Yugoslav Macedonia and part of Serbia.

### Communist Bulgaria

An underground movement had sprung up in Bulgaria during World War I, the first partisan band being formed within a few months of her entry into the war. By 1944 the movement was so strong that it could plan a general uprising for September 2. A few days later Russian troops crossed the frontier; a "Fatherland Front" government was formed by resistance leaders representing the Agrarians, the Communists, the Social Democrats, and the Zveno party, whose leader, Kimon Georgiev, became prime minister. Under Soviet command, Bulgarian forces took part in the liberation of Yugoslavia, Hungary and Austria.

#### WAR TRIALS

Trials of war criminals and of prominent figures under previous regimes were held, 2680 death sentences and 6870 prison sentences being passed, and the civil service and armed forces were purged. But the Fatherland Front also repressed other left-wing groups and then began to break up itself over the issue of whether independent lists of candidates should be allowed in the forthcoming elections. Six cabinet ministers resigned and for a time the U.S. and Britain withheld recognition.

#### THE COMMUNIST REPUBLIC

In September 1946, after an overwhelming vote in favor of a referendum, Bulgaria was proclaimed a republic. In the elections of October 1946 the Communists gained an absolute majority. The new Fatherland government was headed by the veteran Communist leader Georgi Dimitrov (1882–1949), who had returned from exile in Russia.

#### THE TERROR

In 1947 the Agrarian party was suppressed, its leader, Nikola Petkov, being executed on a charge of treason, and in the following year the Social Democrats were suppressed or ab-

*Painting by A. S. Popov of one of the battles for the Shipka Pass during the Russo-Turkish War of 1877-78, which gave the Bulgarians their independence. The scene of great heroism on the part of Bulgarian volunteers, Shipka became a symbol of the liberation and a monument was erected there to commemorate it.*

*Georgi Dimitrov (1882-1949), first Communist prime minister of Bulgaria. He played a leading part in the early struggles of the trade union movement, but fled abroad after taking part in an abortive rising in 1923. His name became world-famous through his successful defense against the Nazi accusation that he had started the Reichstag fire of 1933.*

## FUNDAMENTAL DATES

**679 A.D.** The Bulgars, migrating from Central Asia, cross the Danube into Byzantine territory and begin to establish themselves in the Balkans.

**865** Under Boris I the Bulgarians are converted to Christianity and adopt Slavonic as their state language.

**1018** After a revolt against the Byzantine emperor, a second Bulgarian Empire is founded.

**1396** Bulgarian independence is extinguished by the Ottoman Turks.

**1878** Bulgaria obtains self-government under the Treaty of San Stefano.

**1908** Bulgaria is proclaimed an independent kingdom.

**1913** Greece, Serbia, and Rumania defeat Bulgaria in the second Balkan War.

**1918** Bulgaria's defeat in World War I shatters her dream of becoming the dominant Balkan power.

**1941** Bulgaria joins the Axis powers.

**1944** General uprising in Bulgaria; Russian troops enter the country; she declares war on Germany.

**1946** After a referendum, Bulgaria is proclaimed a republic; the Communists come to power under Georgi Dimitrov.

**1947-48** Suppression of all opposition parties; Communist party purges begin.

sorbed into the Communist party. A number of Roman Catholic and Protestant clergy were also tried and sentenced for alleged treason. Simultaneously purges of the Communist party itself were begun, and they were continued under Dimitrov's successors. In 1950 the United States broke off diplomatic relations with Bulgaria and they were not restored until 1959.

Vulko Chervenkov, who had become premier in 1950 and whose policy of subservience to Russia, particularly during Stalin's time, had made him widely unpopular, was forced out of office in 1956 and was succeeded by Anton Yugov, who had been disgraced in 1950. (Yugov remained premier until 1962, when Todor Zhivkov, who had replaced Chervenkov as party secretary, also became the leader of the government.) Another victim of the purges,. Traicho Kostov, who had been convicted on false evidence and executed, was posthumously rehabilitated.

### SOCIAL REFORMS

A number of fundamental social reforms had been made by the first Fatherland Front government, including the limitation of individual land holdings to just under five acres and the granting of equality to national minorities and to women. Widespread nationalization of private industry began in 1947 and, under the new one-party state, the first Five-Year Plan was instituted in 1949.

### DISCONTENT UNDER COMMUNISM

When the Communists came to power Bulgaria had a predominantly peasant economy. Two of their policies provoked strong opposition. Rapid industrialization was pushed through, despite the dearth of raw materials and of technically trained manpower, and the collectivization of farmland was enforced. These policies have produced severe shortages of staple foods and of consumer goods, since development was concentrated on heavy industry, though the economic situation has improved in recent years.

In the spring of 1965 news of the arrest of several prominent figures said to have plotted a coup against the government indicated that dissatisfaction with official policies was still rampant.

## INTRODUCTION

THE CULTURAL DEVELOPMENT OF THE region which is now Bulgaria varied in ancient times according to the geographic divisions of the territory. This may be seen from the division of the region under Roman rule, when it consisted of the provinces of Moesia, in the northern Danubian area, which were separated by the Balkan chain of mountains from the province of Thrace. The whole area extended beyond the present boundaries of Bulgaria, to include parts of what is now Yugoslavia, Rumania and Greece.

In the Middle Ages, the Bulgar empire covered a wide expanse of territory, at one time with its center in Macedonia. Historically, however, it may be considered a natural bridge between Europe and Asia, or between the Danubian and Mediterranean cultures. The Danubian-Balkan culture of the region's earliest period gave way to a Thraco-Illyrian Hellenistic culture, which was in turn engulfed by Roman culture around the beginning of the Christian era. The Bulgar state was founded in the 7th century A.D., nourished by both Iranian and Byzantine traditions, and passed through a period of considerable artistic development before the Turkish conquest in the 14th century, completed in 1396.

In 1878, with the eradication of the last outposts of Turkish rule, Bulgaria emerged in what is approximately its present form.

## PREHISTORIC AND HELLENIC ART

### Early Remains

THE REMAINS OF THE HIGHEST EXpression of the early Danubian-Balkan culture in Bulgaria date from the late Neolithic period (20,000-2000 B.C.) and the Bronze Age (2000-750 B.C.), and have been found in cave dwellings and in *tell* (low mound dwellings). Artifacts include coneshaped vases; vases and vessels shaped in animal forms; clay models; drinking vessels of clay, terra cotta and wood; religious figures of clay, terra cotta and marble; gold ornaments; and primitive copper utensils.

#### THE BRONZE AND IRON AGE

The Bronze Age, with its more advanced techniques, marked the end of the Danubian-Balkan culture and the growth of influence from the south. A valuable example of this period, dating from the later Bronze Age, was discovered at Valchi-tran in the Pleven region in 1924 and is now in the National Museum, Sofia (see this page). This consists of a large vessel, four drinking cups with handles, seven plates with center bosses and a vessel consisting of three half-oval shapes joined together. They are mainly of gold, trimmed with amber and bronze and with inlaid spiral decorations of silver, and were probably for use at religious rites.

Thracian culture is apparent from

*Treasure of Valchi-tran, found in the Pleven district of Bulgaria in 1924. The relics in the 8th-century-B.C. treasure reveal the high quality of craftsmanship achieved during the Bronze Age (c. 2000-c. 750 B.C.) in the Pleven region, part of the Danube area, of present-day Bulgaria. The vessels, cups and plates—made of gold, bronze and silver—are decorated with spiral designs and inlays of semi-precious stones. It is most likely that the exquisite objects were used for religious rites and ceremonial purposes (Sofia, National Museum).*

the Iron Age (which began about 750 B.C.) onward, and many artifacts have been discovered in burial-mounds of the period. Besides objects of imported Greek manufacture, many artifacts of purely Thracian inspiration have been found in tombs such as those at Mezek and Kazanlik, dating from between the 5th and 3rd centuries B.C.

### Hellenization

The Thracian culture was, however, quickly permeated by Hellenic influences, stemming from the earliest Greek colonies founded in the 6th and 5th centuries B.C. Among the most important of these colonies

Funerary Stele of Anaxandros, *made during the 6th century B.C. The stele (or tombstone) was found at Sozopol, the site of the ancient Greek city of Apollonia in the Burgas region of Bulgaria near the Black Sea. The relief sculpture was made by a Hellenic stone carver who had settled at Apollonia. The naturalistic representation includes the depiction of a man and his dog—a scene taken from everyday life. Similar works of art were produced in Greece as early as the 8th century B.C. (Sofia, National Museum).*

were Mesembria (modern Nesebar), Odessos (Varna), and Apollonia (Sozopol). The last was the site of a magnificent stele, or funerary monument, dating from the end of the 6th century B.C. and now in the National Museum, Sofia (see page 176).

Although only a few ruined traces still remain of these Greek cities, many objects of Greek workmanship have been preserved.

#### HERCULES AND OTHER HEROES

Among the precious objects of Hellenic origin now preserved in Bulgarian museums are silver medallions bearing busts of Hercules and other heroes; an amphora, or wine jar, with handles shaped like centaurs and decorated with scenes from the Trojan War; an open dish decorated with a row of acorn moldings, three rows of moldings of slaves' heads, three cameos of female heads and a handle in the shape of a sphinx (Sofia, Archaeological Museum, see opposite); and drinking horns terminating in representations of animal heads, decorated with scenes from Greek mythology.

---

## ROMAN ART IN BULGARIA

### Roman Urbanization

BY THE LATE 2ND CENTURY B.C., THE Roman Empire, expanding to the east and north, had begun the military occupation of the Bulgarian region, aided by the internecine warfare between the Macedonians, Syrians, Thracians and invading barbarian tribes, which had followed the death of Alexander the Great in 323 B.C. The occupation was firmly established under the emperors Tiberius (ruled 14-37 A.D.) and Claudius (ruled 41-54 A.D.) around the beginning of the Christian era, and urbanization proceeded rapidly thereafter.

#### ROMAN CITIES AND CAMPS

The Roman cities began as military centers; but with increased pacification, with the building of efficient road networks, with increased immigration from Asia, Greece and Italy, and with the Roman policy of making land grants to military veterans in conquered areas, they developed into prosperous commercial and cultural centers.

At Nikyup, founded by Trajan (ruled 98-117 A.D.), an arcaded forum and other remains show the influence of Hellenic architecture, probably due to the influence of Trajan's chief architect, Apollodorus of Damascus, who is known to have drawn up the plans of many of the emperor's foundations.

### Funerary Monuments

By the 3rd century A.D. classical art flourished in Bulgaria. The works of the Greek sculptors Praxiteles and Lysippus were particularly popular, as is evidenced by the numerous copies of their works extant, such as the bronze of Praxiteles' *Eros*, and by the reproduction of their statues on coins issued by a number of cities.

The best examples of Roman art are, however, to be found in funerary monuments. Many funerary steles follow the Greek pattern, with representations of the deceased surrounded by his wife and servants and votive tripods, and dressed in Greek-inspired filleted costume. Portrait medallions, sometimes with full-length representations are also found, with figures set in relief in a decorative frame.

---

## BEFORE THE MIDDLE AGES

EARLY CHRISTIAN ART APPEARS TO have flourished in Bulgaria, in spite of the long period of conflict attendant upon the separation of Western and Eastern empires and the influx of barbarian invaders: the Goths, the Slavs and, finally, the Bulgars. Tombs, inscriptions and the remains of church buildings show that the region remained a center of culture during this period, the main influence being that of the Byzantine capital at Constantinople (Istanbul) fused with that of Roman-Hellenic art.

A number of basilicas built between the 5th and 7th centuries are still in part preserved, among them the 6th-century church of St. Sophia, at So-

*Treasure of Panagyurishte, made during the 4th or 3rd century B.C. Found in 1949 in the Plovdiv region of present-day Bulgaria—an area to which Greek works of art were commonly imported in prehistoric times—the plate is probably of Hellenic origin. The richly decorated object, with its sophisticated symbolic design, is an indication of the advanced civilization in the area during the Iron Age, which began about 750 B.C. (Sofia, Archaeological Museum).*

fia, a domed basilican structure with a lofty central nave and a gallery over the vestibule.

### Early Bulgar Art

Byzantine domination was overthrown by the Slav tribes. These were, in their turn, subdued by the Bulgars, who set up the first Bulgarian kingdom in the late 7th century. The main centers of the early Bulgarian state were Pliskov and Preslav, where there are remains of the monumental stone-built structures typical of the period.

#### HORSEMAN IN A ROCK FACE

These structures include the small palace at Pliskov, consisting of two large chambers surrounded by a corridor, and the fortifications at Preslav, where the palace is still in the course of excavation. This architecture is closer to the Hellenic-Roman tradition than to the Byzantine and, in addition, the Bulgarians introduced Iranian and Oriental characteristics. These characteristics are evident in the magnificent relief known as the *Horseman of Madara*, which is cut into a rock face at Madara, in the Kolarovgrad district.

### Development of Religious Architecture

The conversion of the Bulgarians to Christianity in the latter half of the 9th century had important effects on the development of architecture, since the influence of Byzantine art was much strengthened. However, the Bulgarian church achieved a considerable degree of autonomy and the interior decoration of churches, in particular, reveals characteristics distinct from Byzantine models.

The main basilica at Pliskov was Hellenic in plan, but with the vestibule, archivaults, three apses and external elevation in the Byzantine tradition. The so-called Golden Church, Preslav, excavated in the early years of the present century, was a synthesis of Roman and Byzantine elements.

More ancient traditions were also discernible in interior decoration and in the applied arts.

Up to the 12th century Preslav

Bronze Head of Emperor Gordian III *(c. 224-244 A.D.) The sculpture was found at Nikyup, the site of the ancient Roman town of Nicopolis ad Istrum, which existed from the time of Trajan (52 or 53-117 A.D.) to 600 A.D. The head, cast in bronze, is a realistic funerary portrait of the young Roman emperor; it is stylistically typical of 3rd-century Roman art (Sofia, National Museum).*

tions of Byzantine works had been introduced, probably by refugee Greek artists, and in the 13th century the mural painters of the Tirnovo school produced their finest work.

The most important murals of the period are those in the church at Boyana (see pages 180 and 182). The Byzantine tradition is predominant, but echoes of Western art can also be discerned in certain scenes. The pictures are executed in rich, warm tempera colors, and are striking for their realism of detail and their overall effect of individualistic humanity allied to intense spirituality.

Later 13th-century works fall into three groups. The first comprises works mainly in the Byzantine tradition, which, however, became exaggerated and florid. They are often marred by a straining after effect, as expressed in the fantastic landscapes and architectural details found in the murals at some churches.

In the second group are works mainly inspired by the archaic pre-iconoclastic Byzantine tradition, with an emphasis on decorative motifs, which thus achieved a richer, more popular art form. The main work of this group is found in the church of the Monastery of Zemen, where narrative scenes are painted in reds, yellows and browns. Clumsy but expressive figures are emphasized by heavy contours, and drapery and landscape details are simplified. The compositions are crowded, with little regard for balance and symmetry, and a tendency toward the anecdotal reflects the influence of popular art.

The third group represents a fusion of the first and second into a mediocre and expressionless tradition, relieved by occasional harmony in composition and a general effect of restraint. Such are the heavily stylized murals in the church of St. Peter and St. Paul at Tirnovo, many of which date from the 14th and 15th centuries.

### Miniature Painting

Popular art in the 13th century, and indeed until the 19th century, was mainly limited to icons. These

was the main center of Bulgarian art, and the Byzantine influence was predominant. Two types of churches were common—the one with a single nave and a vaulted roof, with or without a cupola; and the other cruciform in shape and surmounted by a central cupola. Other interesting buildings of the period are the fortifications at important military strongholds, a number of which still remain.

## THE THIRTEENTH TO FIFTEENTH CENTURIES

### Mural Painting

DURING THE 12TH CENTURY TIRNOVO became the artistic center of Bulgaria, after the waning of Byzantine influence. Mural painting had made considerable progress after reproduc-

were mainly influenced by Byzantine models and were often heavily stylized, while Turkish motifs, such as arabesques, often made their appearance in decorative elements during the long period of Ottoman rule.

### ILLUMINATED MANUSCRIPTS

Illuminated manuscripts are known to have been produced in early Christian times in Bulgaria, but the oldest extant examples date from the 14th century. They are based on Byzantine models but have a colorful realism which marks them as a branch of popular art. The most important examples are the *Chronicle of Mannasses,* now in the Vatican Museum, and the *Bible of Ivan Alexander,* now in the British Museum, London.

### Architecture

Bulgarian architecture before the 19th century has suffered greatly, due to the destruction of most large and important buildings during the Turkish occupation, from the later 14th century onward. The main trends in Bulgarian architecture have already been mentioned, and those churches and monasteries built between the 14th and 19th centuries were deliberately designed to attract the minimum of attention, being mainly small timber or brick structures of undistinguished appearance.

Similarly, the greater part of the buildings erected by the Turks were also small, being mainly simple mosques without domes or belfries, often adapted from Christian churches or military fortification works. Among the larger, more notable, examples of Turkish architecture in Bulgaria are the Bouyuk Mosque (1474), Sofia, the Ibrahim Mosque (1614), Razgrad, and the Toumboul Mosque (1747), Kolarovgrad. All of these are in a good state of preservation.

## THE BULGARIAN RENAISSANCE

### Architecture

THE REVIVAL OF THE ARTS IN BULgaria, after a period of stagnation under Turkish occupation, may be said to have occurred in the latter part of the 18th century. The Byzantine influence, hitherto predominant, had declined and Western influence was beginning to make itself felt by way of the Mt. Athos school (founded around 1750), the artists and architects of which were combining archaic Italian and Hellenic forms with the more dramatic tendencies of the Western Baroque.

### THE DRAMATIC BAROQUE

In architecture, Byzantine elements were still apparent in church exteriors with an admixture, for political reasons, of Turkish elements, but interiors began to take on the exuberance of the Italian-inspired dramatic Baroque style. The last decades of the 18th century saw both the stirrings of the nationalistic spirit which was to lead to independence in the 19th century and a new pe-

*Fresco paintings in a Roman tomb chamber at Silistra (4th century A.D.). Silistra, in the Ruse district of Bulgaria, was settled by Romans in 29 A.D. During the 3rd and 4th centuries, it became an important center of Christianity (exemplified by these paintings). Executed in a late Roman style, the frescoes represent a deceased couple and their servants performing tasks of everyday life. Above are two peacocks and a wine vat, pagan motifs related to the after-life which have become Christian symbols identified with the death and resurrection of Christ.*

riod of activity in the building of churches and monasteries.

### TIMBER AND STONE

The first manifestations of this revival took place at the Rila monastery, which was restored in 1780, and had chapels added in 1795, 1799 and 1805. The church of St. Nicholas at Pleven was also restored in 1796.

Restorations were soon followed by the construction of new churches. These mainly took the form of triple-aisled basilican structures, which were often constructed on sunken foundations as a form of camouflage and lacked cupolas for the same reason. Walls were usually constructed of stone, but timber was used for columns, ceilings, galleries and arches.

### NINETEENTH-CENTURY ARCHITECTURE

As the 19th century progressed and Turkish power declined, the scale

of Bulgarian architecture became more ambitious. The forms of the late-Baroque, Rococo and Neoclassical styles, which had affected Europe during the previous century, became established in Bulgaria.

There they were modified both by the use of traditional decorative motifs, by the introduction of Turkish and Oriental elements in exteriors, and by the continued use of timber as an important item in construction. The three-aisled basilica form took on new dimensions, often with lofty timber-vaulted ceilings, and cupolas were added to monasteries and churches in the more remote areas.

### CHURCHES AND ARCHITECTS

The south wing of the Rila monastery, with a basilica surmounted by five cupolas, was built by Pavel Ivanovich in 1847, while Ustabashi Milenko was mainly responsible for

the design of the church at Boboshevo in the same period. The decline of Turkish power saw the increase of Russian influence, again with elements of modification due to the use of timber.

Among the more important architects of the later 19th century were Nikolo Fichev, who designed a number of churches in northern Bulgaria, and Usta Gencho, who built churches in Stara Zagora, Kazanlik, Karlovo and Kalofer. After the liberation from the Turks a number of important buildings were erected in Sofia, notably the National Assembly (1885).

## Painting and Sculpture

The revival of painting and sculpture, like that of architecture, began in the latter part of the 18th century. In wood carving the main influences were those of the Western Baroque, combined with traditional elements and motifs taken from Oriental art. This is apparent in the important works of the period, such as the carved iconostases at the Bishop's Church, Samokov; the Church of the Holy Virgin, Pazardzhik; the church of St. Marina, Plovdiv; and the Church of the Archangel Michael, Tryavna. Western influence is particularly noticeable in the work of Hadji Georgi (active 1814-21), who carved the iconostases in the Church of the Virgin at Koprivshtitsa and in the church of St. John the Forerunner, Gabrovo.

### FOUR CENTERS

The revival of painting was mainly concentrated on four centers, those of Tryavna, Samokov, Bansko and Debur. The most important master working at Bansko was Thomas Vishanov, who studied in Vienna but was mainly influenced by French Rococo painting and by the new German naturalism, as may be seen in the mystical yet realistic frescoes in

*Tsar Kaloyan and Princess Dessilava (detail), a fresco painting in the church of St. Panteleimon at Boyana. This village church in the Sofia district of Bulgaria was constructed during the 11th century. It was decorated with frescoes in about 1259 during the period of the second Bulgarian kingdom (1186-1393). Stylistically, the painting of Princess Dessislava's head, illustrated at the left, represents the popular almost national art style which developed during the 13th century in Bulgaria. The paintings which are part of this current are almost crude when compared to their models, works of art executed in the refined Byzantine style.*

*Saint George and the Dragon, an icon in the church at Arbanasi in the Gorna Oryakhovitsa district of Bulgaria. Because of the Turkish domination and iconoclasm (1393-1878) in Bulgaria, monasteries and small churches such as the 7th-century village church of Arbanasi were constructed in isolated areas of the north. Interiors were decorated with icons—conventionally accepted images of religious subjects— executed in a Byzantine style. Saint George and the Dragon, painted during the late 17th or early 18th century, is a typical example of the iconic style as it developed in Bulgaria.*

the church of Bansko, the Church of the Virgin, Kyustenil, the monastery of Kurilo, and the Chapel of the Virgin in St. Luke's Hermitage, near the Rila monastery.

### THREE BROTHERS

The main masters of the Trevna school were the three brothers Vitan, Simeon and Koyo, all of whom were active before 1800 and who executed icons in the church of St. Sophia at Sliven. Their work displays a great delicacy in the handling of light and color, and it was probably one of these three who executed the portrait of *Bishop Sophronius Bogoridi* (1812), now in the National Museum, Sofia. Their style was perpetuated in the work of their descendants, who included Papa Vitan (died 1840), Ionaki Papa Vitanov (died 1850), Georgi Dimitrov and Simeon Koyov.

### PAINTER OF ICONS

Another important painter of the period was Zahari Monah (active c. 1800), who painted icons and frescoes in the Rila monastery. His work shows Western influences, though, as he was a monk, it is doubtful if he ever traveled abroad.

### NINETEENTH-CENTURY PAINTING

Icon painting declined in quality during the 19th century, when a great amount of work was produced in a style almost completely reliant on the work of Western masters. These influences were combined with the still strong Byzantine tradition and resulted in the production of brightly colored works lacking in the refinements of composition or perspective.

The best works of the period were the icons and frescoes executed at the Rila monastery during the years 1842 to 1846 by artists including Dimiter Dimitrov (1796-1860), Zahari Zograf (1810-53), Dimiter Vishanov (1790-1860), Simeon Molerov (1826-1911) and Ivan Obrazopisov (1795-1854). Also of considerable importance was

Hrista Dimitrov (d. 1835), who studied in Vienna and combined the colorful and sentimental style of the Italian Guido Reni (1575-1642) with Byzantine compositional elements.

### WESTERN INFLUENCE

As the 19th century progressed, the influence of Western academicism became increasingly strong. The first Bulgarian artist to produce works in a purely Westernized form was the portraitist and genre painter Dimiter Dobrovich (1816-1905), who spent much of his life in Rome and whose

portrait of *Cecoli Raffaeli* (1841, National Museum, Sofia), shows the influence of the German Anselm Feuerbach (1829-80). Russian, German and Austrian influences were also apparent, particularly in the works of Stanislav Dospevski (1826-77), Hristo Tsokev (1847-83), Georgi Danchov (1846-1908) and Nikolai Pavlovich (1835-94), all of them portraitists and history painters who had studied abroad.

Academicism in Bulgaria reached its highest point in 1896, with the foundation of the Sofia School of

The Crucifixion (c. 1259) in St. Panteleimon's Church at Boyana. The fresco painting
illustrated here is part of a cycle representing the Passion of Christ. It was executed
in a combination of the Byzantine and early Italian Renaissance styles. Byzantine
features include the formalized facial features of all those portrayed, except for the
figure on the extreme right, and the position of the figures; Italian characteristics
are noticeable in the solidity of the bodies and the slight tendency toward naturalism,
especially in the depiction of the mourner at the right. Also Italian in origin is the
medallion with the profile of the person who commissioned the fresco cycle.

Art, by the painters Anton Mitov (1862-1930), Ivan Angelov (1864-1924), Ivan Murkvichka (1856-1938), Yaroslav Vesin (1859-1915) and Boris Schatz, the last three of whom were Czechoslovakian painters who had settled in Bulgaria. Murkvichka was later instrumental in introducing the influence of French Impressionism into Bulgaria, while Mitov was also influenced by Impressionism and by the color theories of Seurat, as can be seen in his *The Sea near the Palace of Euxinograd* (National Museum, Sofia).

## THE TWENTIETH CENTURY

### Architecture

DURING THE 20TH CENTURY, BULGARian architecture has been mainly influenced by Russian forms. This is apparent in such early buildings in the capital, Sofia, as the St. Alexander Nevsky Memorial Church (1906-12), by A.N. Pomarantsev, and the Palace of the Holy Synod (1908), by P. Momchilov.

Since World War II, a great building program under State supervision has taken place, resulting in the development of the new town of Dimitrovgrad and the erection of many public buildings in the monumental Russian official style, such as the Bulgarian Communist Party House, Sofia. The recent buildings added to the State University complex at Sofia, however, including the Universiade Hall, show an improvement in design and a break from oppressive functionalism.

### Painting and Sculpture

It is impossible in a limited space to give more than the names of the most distinguished practitioners in the main artistic trends in Bulgaria during the present century. It should be noted that in recent years the

*At the Father's Grave, a bronze sculpture by the contemporary sculptor Ilia Vasev. Produced in about 1950, this bronze image of two children is a typical example of the so-called Socialist-Realist style, a mode which developed during this century in Bulgaria and in other countries belonging to the Soviet bloc. Many paintings and pieces of sculpture similar to the one illustrated at the left have been commissioned by the government in an attempt to bring the arts closer to the masses.*

style known as Socialist Realism, prevalent in countries of the Soviet bloc, has forced something of an artistic straitjacket on Bulgarian artists, although there are now indications that the strict party line on the arts is being relaxed.

In the early years of the century the most important painters were the academics, including Nikola Mihailov (1876-1960), Stefan Ivanov (1875-1951), Nikola Marinov (1879-1949), and Atanas Mihov (1880- ), and the Impressionists, including Nikola Petrov (1881-1916) and Elena Karamihailova (1875- ). A nationalistic school of sentimentalized historical painters included Ivan Milev (1900-26) and Pencho Georgiev (1898-1938), while the Post-Impressionists included Boris Denev (1883- ) and Sirak Skitnik (1884-1943).

Since 1930, the main painters of the more progressive schools, including Cubism and Constructivism, have been Kiril Tsonev (1896- ), Ivan Nenov (1904- ), Eliezar Alsheh (1908- ) and Vera Nedkova (1908- ), while more conventional painters have included the landscape painters Ivan Hristov (1906- ) and Ivan Tabahov (1900- ), and the portraitist Dechko Uzunov (1899- ),

In modern sculpture the most important names are those of Ivan Lazarov, Lyubomir Dalchev, Zheko Spiridonov, Vaska Emanouilova, Ivan Founev and Marko Markov.

## THE LITERATURE

### The Early Background

MODERN BULGARIAN, A SOUTHERN Slavonic language spoken by more than 7 million people in the eastern Balkan region, is of recent origin as a literary language. Although Bulgaria is one of the oldest centers of cultural activity in the Balkans, the country's literary traditions, with very few exceptions, date only from the first half of the 19th century.

#### EARLY RELIGIOUS LITERATURE

The earliest works in the development of Bulgarian letters, dating from the 10th century, are ecclesiastical documents in the ancient church Slavonic. Greek elements permeated the ancient ecclesiastical language between the 12th and 15th centuries, and under Turkish domination this mixture was enriched by the addition of Russian, Serbian, Turkish and original Bulgarian elements. It was not until a growing spirit of nationalism in the latter part of the 18th century created the need for a properly established Bulgarian language that attempts were made to codify the grammar and syntax; important works in this field appeared in 1824, 1835 and 1844.

The names of a few of the ecclesiastical writers of the first Bulgarian empire have been preserved. Among these are the 10th-century Bishop Constantine, the author of a didactic gospel prefaced by a metrical prayer; and Simeon, king of Bulgaria from 893 to 927, a patron of the arts and the compiler of a collection of religious texts.

As in many other countries, the monasteries were the main sources of early literature and, indeed, during the long period of Turkish domination it only was in the more remote religious communities that the elements of the Bulgarian literary tradition were preserved.

Among the major figures of the period preceding the Turkish invasion, around the end of the 14th century, were the Patriarch Euthymius (died c. 1393), who founded a philosophical group at Turnova in about 1375, and his pupil Grigorie Camblak (1364-c. 1450), who wrote his master's biography.

### Folk Literature

Folk literature, particularly the folk songs connected with various festivals or customs, played a considerable role in the preservation and development of the Bulgarian language during the Turkish occupation. In folk literature, not only was the language progressively liberated from the old ecclesiastical tongue but also its themes, often heroic and nationalistic, provided an important source of inspiration to the writers of the national revival.

### The National Revival

The emergence of the modern Bulgarian literary language came about with the growing movement toward independence of Turkish rule in the later part of the 18th century. The Turkish rulers had completely neglected the cultural needs of their Bulgarian subjects, who had, as a result, become divided into two main groups: the nobility and merchant classes, who had become almost completely denationalized, and the peasants and artisans, whose idiomatic speech remained static and archaic.

There was thus a great need for the stabilization of the Bulgarian language as an essential part of the struggle for political and cultural freedom. The lead came from the monasteries, where the most important figure was the monk Paisij (1722-98), from the monastery of Hilendar, on Mt. Athos.

His *Slavo-Bulgarian History* appeared in 1762, and, although his

*The monk Paisij (1722-98) writing his* Istoriya Slavyano Bulgarskaya *(Slavo-Bulgarian History), which appeared in 1762. This was the first history in the Bulgarian language and, as a romantic glorification of Bulgaria's past, it appealed to the patriotism of its readers. It had a decisive influence on future writers.*

prose was still strongly archaic and permeated with Russian elements, it appealed strongly to the patriotic and nationalistic emotions of its readers and thus had a great effect on the writers of the national revival.

### Grammarians and Poets

The early years of the 19th century saw the emergence of a number of important grammarians and educators. Notable among these were Peter Beron (1795-1871), whose *Primer* of 1824 laid the basis of elementary education, Neofyt Rylski (1793-1881), who published the first Bulgarian grammar in 1835, and Vasil Aprilov (1789-1847), who founded a model school in the same year.

### THE STRUGGLE FOR INDEPENDENCE

During the period of the struggle for independence, prose and poetry were directed almost exclusively to the rehearsal of past glories and the exhortation to the people to emulate them, and to indirect satire against the foreign rulers and denunciations of Bulgarian inertia. This literature was inspired mainly by folk traditions and by the realistic tendencies of the contemporary Russian literature. Periods of intense nationalism are rarely productive of truly balanced literature, but a number of writers of this period managed to attain a genuine individual standard.

Among these was Georgi Sava Rakovski (1821-67), a historian and journalist as well as an accomplished poet. The basis of the realistic novel was laid by Lyuben Karavelov (1837-79), who is remembered mainly for his short stories of urban life, and by the novelist and dramatist Vasil Drumev (1841-1902). The greatest poet of this early period was Khristo Botev (1848-76), the writer of passionately patriotic lyrics, who fell in battle against the Turks only two years before the final achievement of independence.

Another important poet, though lacking the romantic panache of Botev, was Petko Rachev Slaveykov (1827-95). Slaveykov's work, which includes both nationalistic and satirical verse, was firmly based upon traditional forms, and he did much to display to the Bulgarian people the true value of their popular literature.

### The Later Nineteenth Century

The outstanding literary figure of the later part of the 19th century

*Ivan Vazov (1850-1921), one of Bulgaria's greatest writers. His output was very large and varied. It included lyric and epic poetry, short stories, novels and plays. His patriotism reflects that of the whole of his nation, but it is combined with an insight into general human problems. Originally a Romantic, Vazov later wrote, as a Realist, of the Bulgarians' struggle for liberation from the Turks.*

was Ivan Vazov (1850-1921), one of the greatest of Bulgarian writers. Vazov was a prolific and versatile writer, who succeeded in uniting the fervent patriotism of the older generation with deeply human, emotional qualities which transcended mere nationalism. Vazov's best known work is the novel *Under the Yoke* (1893), a wide-ranging survey of Bulgarian life during the struggle for independence, a theme which was continued in his later novels, *New Land* (1894) and *The Empress of Kazalar* (1903). The Bulgarian revolution also inspired his great cycle of epic poems entitled *Epic to the Forgotten* (1881-1884).

### REALISM AND SENTIMENT

Realism was the dominant element in the work of Vazov's contemporaries, though new influences were introduced by the translations, notably of Italian poetry, of Konstantin Velichkov (1855-1907), an otherwise undistinguished writer of sentimental prose and dramatic works.

Stoyan Mikhailovski (1856-1927) was much influenced by French rationalist philosophy. His earlier works are moralistic satires, while his later books took on a more definitive theological aspect. One of the most popular writers of the period was Aleko Konstantinov (1863-97), whose humorous sketches, collected under the title of *Bai Ganyu* (1895), narrate the experiences of a Bulgarian peasant wandering in Europe.

### TURNING WESTWARD

Around the turn of the century, Bulgarian writers had already begun to turn away from the patriotic realism with which, as has been explained, even Vazov's work was imbued, toward the development of a literature more in key with the neo-Romantic and Modernistic movements which pervaded the Western European countries.

One of the foremost poets of the younger generation was Petko Slaveykov's son, Pencho Slaveykov (1866-1912) who, while retaining the emotional power of the nationalistic movement, introduced wide-reaching

Above left: *Khristo Botev (1848-76), the greatest poet of the earlier 19th century. Both his art and his life were devoted to the ideals of liberty and the fatherland. Botev sacrificed his life to these ideals when he led an armed band against the Turks and was killed in the unequal battle.* Above right: *Aleko Konstantinov (1863-97), a 19th-century Realist, is best known as the author of* Bai Ganyu *(1895). This is a series of humorous sketches in which Konstantinov satirizes the snobbish Bulgarian peasant.*

Western elements into his work.

He was much influenced by the philosophy of Nietzsche, by the masters of the Italian Renaissance and by the English Romantic poets. The delicacy and refinements of his lyric verses are surpassed by the dramatic force of his epics, the most famous of which is the uncompleted *A Song of Blood* (1911-12), dealing with the Bulgarian revolutionary movement of 1876 and the cruelty with which it was suppressed.

### The Twentieth Century

As has been seen, Bulgarian writers at the turn of the century continued to be much influenced by the spirit of the national revival. However, they had begun to pay more attention to form and to expand their choice of subject matter beyond simple patriotic or nationalistic subjects, and to address themselves to the wider field of social problems and a new universality of approach. They did not disregard the achievements of earlier writers, but rather attempted to expand and revise them into a style more suited to the modern world.

The more conventional writers, those closer to the tradition of Vazov, included Anton Strashimirov (1872-1937), a dramatist and novelist, who dealt with the life of people working in town and country, in such works as *Autumn Days* and *Mother-in-law*. In the same tradition was Dimitar Ivanov (1876-1949), who wrote under the pseudonym of Elin-Pelin.

Other important writers in the realist tradition were Georgi Stamatov (1869-1942), whose work is much concerned with sexual morality, and Yordon Yovkov (1880-1937), whose novels, plays and short stories have a depth of psychological perception which transcends their local settings.

A second group of writers comprises those who were more affected by contemporary European developments, in particular the poetry of the French Symbolist movement. Prominent among these were Kyril Christov (1875-1944), whose graceful lyrics extol the delights of a carefree, Bohemian life, in such collections as *Vibrations* and *Songs and Sighs,* and Peju Kračolov Javorov (1878-1914), an introspective and individualistic poet whose lyrics express the dramatic contrast between idealism and reality.

### AFTER WORLD WAR I

The poet Dimcho Debelyanov (1887-1916) was mainly responsible for the link between the Symbolists and the later avant-garde poetic movements. The stress laid on form in his work is reflected in the poems of his progressive contemporaries, such as Nikolai Liliyev (1885-1960), Todor Trayanov (1882-1944) and Lyudmil Stoyanov (1888- ). At the same time, another group of writers, the chief of whom was Nikola Vaptsarov (1909-42), wrote in realistic terms of the working folk in a manner influenced by the Russian poet and dramatist Vladimir Vladimirovich Mayakovsky (1893-1930).

### TRADITION PERSISTS

The more traditional elements of Bulgarian literature were not neglected, though many of the writers who emerged between the two world wars were influenced, to a greater or lesser degree, by modern Western movements. Among the more important of the traditionalists were Elisaveta Bagryana (1893- ), called Belcheva, whose lyrics are both simple and direct, the poets Dimiter Pantaleyev (1901- ) and Nikola Furnadjiev (1903- ), and the novelists Angel Karaliychev (1902- ) and Dimitar Polianov (1876- ).

### COMMUNIST SCHOOL

Since World War II, the advent of the Communist regime in Bulgaria has led to the dominance of the school of writing known as Socialist Realism, with its emphasis on simple tales of proletarian achievement in accordance with Marxist ideology. Among the most prominent writers in this style in modern Bulgaria are Pavel Vezhinov (1914- ), Stoyan Daskalov (1909- ) and Bozhidar Bozhilov (1912- ).

## THE THEATER

FROM THE 9TH TO THE 14TH CEN-turies, the deeply religious character of Bulgarian culture delayed the development of secular drama. During the five centuries of Turkish domination, however, songs, stories and dances played an increasingly important part in popular entertainment.

### Didactic Origins

The true beginning of drama in Bulgaria can be traced back to the middle of the 19th century. In 1840 a Macedonian, Jordon Džinot, presented at Titov Veles some *Dramatic Dialogues* which were basically patriotic propaganda, and which, with their pre-Romantic fervor, sowed the seeds for the development of more systematic theatrical performances. Didacticism was the keynote during these early days of Bulgarian drama.

With the revolutionary movement of 1848-49, drama began to gain a hold as an independent art. Refugees from Poland and Hungary settled in Bulgaria and brought with them, especially to the ancient town of Kalarovgrad (formerly Shumen), a lively theatrical tradition of their own. Their activity stimulated a desire for original Bulgarian drama. The first example was presented in 1856 in a Turkish coffee-house in Kalarovgrad. The play, *Mihail Miškoed,* by a local schoolmaster, Sava Iliev Dobroplodnij (1820-94), was a comedy in the manner of the French playwright Molière (1622-73).

Amateur companies produced translations of works by Molière, by the Italian dramatist Goldoni (1707-93) and by the German Schiller (1759-1805), but the success of Dobroplodnij's work prompted the creation of many more works in the native tongue.

One of the most prominent nationalist playwrights was Dobri Vijnikov (1833-78), the creator of Bulgarian historical drama. His plays *Voivoda Stojan* (1886), *The Christianization of the Count of Preslav* (1868) and *Velislava* (1870) did much to awaken patriotic feeling.

#### PRAISE OF HEROISM

The theater of the pre-liberation period was deeply affected by the political and social struggles and was therefore confronted by a range of problems, from the relations between the Bulgarians and the Greeks, as in *The Bishop of Loveč* (1857) by Teodosij Ikonomov (1836-71), to the revolutionary problems of *The Mountain Insurgents* by Ljuben Karavelov.

### Independent Bulgaria

After the constitution of the principality of Bulgaria, in 1878, the theater's growth in strength was rapid.

In Sofia, the new capital since the liberation, efforts culminated in the creation of a company which took the name of *Osnova* (foundation). As no government help was then forthcoming, the actors built a wooden theater themselves, on the site where the National Theater now stands. In 1888 they put on their first performance and two years later the state decided to grant a subsidy and to incorporate opera into the theater's repertory.

It was not until 1892, however, that a really active professional group was formed. The company, which took the name of The Tears and Laughter Theater, became The Bulgarian National Theater in 1904.

#### IVAN VAZOV

The Bulgarian theater was dominated at the end of the 19th century by the personality of Ivan Vazov (1850-1921), journalist, man of letters and politician. His plays, which include social satire as well as historical and patriotic drama, created a vivid picture of his age. Among the best-known are the comedies *The Journalists* (1900) and *The Job Hunters* (1903), and the historical plays *Borislav* and *Toward the Abyss* (both 1910) and *Yvailo* (1913).

### Modern Trends

The prevalence of heroic and nationalist themes had begun to diminish after the realization of patriotic aims by the liberation of 1878.

It was succeeded by a tendency toward bourgeois drama, which concerned itself with psychological analysis, proclaiming the importance of the individual. The avant-garde move-ment, spreading throughout Europe, was causing writers to re-appraise their attitudes to a drama which had to face the complex problems of man in modern society.

One of the writers who best represents early-20th-century trends was Peju Kračolov Javorov (1877-1914), Bulgaria's first symbolist poet. His feeling for language and his rich imagination found more scope in the field of lyrical poetry, but his drama *At the Foot of Mount Vitosha* (1911) compares favorably with any other European work of the time.

Between the two world wars accepted cultural values depended on the ideas of the extreme right-wing politicians who carried out the coup d'état of 1923. By reaction this created a Marxist-inspired theater of opposition which championed experimental activity and absorbed the first lessons of post-revolutionary Russia.

This transitional phase ended with the proclamation of the Bulgarian People's Republic in 1946. From that time the theater was strongly influenced by the theories of Socialist Realism advanced by Soviet cultural arbiters. The consequent uniformity of style and matter makes it difficult to assess individual talent. Eminent playwrights, whose work is performed both in repertory and at functions such as the annual festival of Bulgarian dramatic art at Sofia, include Orlin Vassilev and Kamen Zidarov.

*Nikola Vaptsarov (1909-42), one of Bulgaria's best-loved poets, is numbered among the martyrs of European anti-Nazi resistance. He was inspired by a deep and unshaken belief in the social progress of humanity. While working in a paper mill, Vaptsarov organized a flourishing dramatic society that aroused great interest among his fellow employees by its productions of socially thoughtful and provoking plays.*

## THE MUSIC

### Folk Music

DURING FIVE CENTURIES OF TURKISH domination in Bulgaria (1396-1878), folk song became a symbol of national self-assertion.

Bulgarian folk songs are essentially functional. They form an accompaniment to work, dancing and many traditional customs.

In general, the versification of Bulgarian folk songs is based on a set number of syllables in each line. The melodic construction corresponds to the line of the text. Rhythms are extremely varied.

The Bulgarians distinguish three types of melody: *dulgi glassovè* (long melodies) are slow and monotonous; *vlacheni glassovè* (drawn-out melodies) are moderately quick; and *secheni glassovè* (broken melodies) are strict recitative tunes in moderate or quick tempo.

The most characteristic Bulgarian folk instruments are the *kàval*, a long flute with a range of two octaves, and the *gusla*, a three-stringed, bowed instrument. Other common instruments are bagpipes, lute-like stringed instruments and various drums.

### Classical Music

Bulgarian classical music began to evolve in the 19th century, when the country was freed from Turkish domination.

Polyphony was introduced into Bulgaria, in the late 19th century, by choirs of Russian soldiers. At about the same time Czech musicians were helping the Bulgarians to form military bands.

The first original Bulgarian composer was Emmanuil Manolov (1860-1902), whose works include songs and an unfinished opera.

Bulgaria's first opera company was an Italian one which appeared in Sofia between 1890 and 1894. In 1908 a permanent opera house was built, and in 1922 the National Opera was formed.

The School of Music in Sofia (established in 1904) was nationalized in 1908. A State Academy of Music was built in 1922.

In the early part of the 20th century Bulgarian composers followed the trends of contemporary European music.

Two composers of this period were Dobri Christov (1875-1941) and Panayot Pipkov (1871-1942), both of whom wrote mainly vocal music.

#### AFTER WORLD WAR II

Since the establishment of the People's Republic of Bulgaria in 1946, Bulgarian music has become strictly national, with the aim of propagating the ideals of socialism and the state. Even composers whose earlier works show musical originality now produce works in the accepted pattern. One such composer is Lyubomir Pipkov (1904-    ), who has written choral, symphonic and chamber music as well as operas and film music.

One of the foremost figures in contemporary Bulgarian musical life is Pancho Vladigherov (1899-    ), pianist, conductor and composer.

## THE FILM

BULGARIA'S FIRST MOVIE HOUSE OPENed in Sofia in 1910. It was about this time that the pioneer of the Bulgarian film industry, Vassil Ghendov, began his work. In many of his early films, including *A Bulgarian is Gallant* (1915), he was director, cameraman and chief actor.

Bulgarian films produced between the wars were generally of a poor standard, with a preponderance of cheap melodramas.

The best film produced before World War II was *Strahil the Chieftain* (1938). Directed and shot by Yosip Novak, it portrays the Bulgarians' struggle for liberation against the Turks.

### After Nationalization

Since its nationalization in 1944 the Bulgarian film industry has been largely based on Soviet artistic and technical aid.

One of the earliest postwar feature films was *Kalin the Eagle* (1949), directed by Boris Borazanov. It deals with the birth of Bulgarian Socialism in the 1890s.

Several younger Bulgarian directors are producing films whose high quality has surprised Western critics. *We Were Young* (1961), by the woman director Binka Zhelyazkova (1923-    ) has been much praised. Ranghel Vulchanov's *Trip Toward Freedom* (1963) gives a moving portrayal of a child's experiences in war.

*The Ivan Vazov National Theater in Sofia is the chief center of drama in Bulgaria. The building, completed in 1906, seats only about 1200 people, and in order to accommodate an ever increasing and enthusiastic audience, an annex has been built nearby. The annex is named after an illustrious Bulgarian actor, Vassil Kirkov. For some years this annex has been the home of the State Satirical Theater.*

# ALBANIA

## BOUNDARIES

ALBANIA, THE SMALLEST OF THE Balkan states, is bounded by Yugoslavia on the northwest, north and east and by Greece on the southeast. It is separated from Italy by the Strait of Otranto.

The Albanians call their country "the country of the Eagles"—an apt description of this mountainous land.

Albania lies between 39°38′ and 42°41′ N. latitude and between 19°16′ and 21°03′ E. longitude. It has a maximum length of about 215 miles from northwest to southeast, and a width ranging from 90 miles, between Lake Prespa and the Adriatic, to less than 50 miles in the north. The total area of the country is 11,024 square miles.

## ORGANIZATION OF THE STATE

DURING WORLD WAR II ALBANIA WAS occupied by the Italian and German armies, and her administrative system was destroyed by the invaders. The Albanian resistance was led by Communists, who, in 1944, when the occupying forces retreated, proclaimed liberation.

Under General Enver Hoxha, the Communists set up a provisional government on Nov. 10, 1945. This government was recognized by the United States, Britain and the Soviet Union, with the stipulation that free elections must be held. Elections were held in December 1945 and a republic proclaimed. But they were not "free elections," and in 1946 the United States and Britain withdrew recognition from Albania and vetoed the country's application for membership in the United Nations. However, in 1955, Albania again applied for membership in the U. N. and was admitted, although the United States abstained from voting.

At the 22nd Congress of the Communist party of the U.S.S.R. (Moscow, Oct. 17-31, 1961) the Albanian representatives were severely criticized for rigidly adhering to the Stalinist interpretation of Marxism. As a result, Albania severed relations with the U.S.S.R. in December 1961.

### The Constitution

According to the constitution adopted in 1946 and amended in 1950, Albania is a People's Republic. The original constitution of 1946 was formed on the model of Stalin's 1936 constitution for the Soviet Union; the amendments made in 1950 brought it into closer conformity with that Soviet constitution—the aim being to duplicate the Soviet system. This constitution proclaims that power belongs to the people, who delegate it to the People's Assembly. But since the assembly nationalized every item of economic importance in the country—its mineral resources, rivers, lakes, springs, forests and farmland, all channels of communication, factories, government services and banks—it placed total control of the country in the hands of the Politburo, which is the central administrative body of the Communist party.

#### PEOPLE'S ASSEMBLY

Nominally, the People's Assembly is the supreme organ of state power. But no candidate for the assembly who does not subscribe to the tenets of Communism and is not a member of the party (the Albanian Labor Party, as it is called) or one of its front organizations, is permitted to stand for election. In practice, no voter who opposes the "agreed list" presented by the Communists is safe to proceed with his ordinary life.

The People's Assembly is elected

*Tirana, the capital and largest town of Albania, is situated in the middle of a fertile depression. It was founded in the early 17th century by the Turkish soldier of fortune, Suleiman Pasha, who named it Teheran (later corrupted to the present Tirana) for a victory he had won in Persia.*

*A stretch of the high and rocky coast in the southern part of Albania. The 50-mile highway connecting the naval bases of Valona and Sarandë runs for long stretches with the rocky coast on one side and steep cliffs on the other. Although this is a major highway, it has a dirt surface—a clear indication of Albania's generally primitive conditions.*

the chairman of the State Planning Commission and various secretaries.

The council formulates all decrees, regulations and ordinances for the observance of internal law; it coordinates the work of ministers and controls the budget and general economic state planning. It is responsible for defense and foreign affairs.

Effective power is held by the Politburo, which has seven members, three deputy members and a large secretariat.

### LOCAL ADMINISTRATION

Albania is divided into five economic regions, which are further subdivided, for administrative purposes, into 27 *rrathe* (districts).

## The Judiciary

The judiciary of the Albanian state consists of, from the highest to the lowest, the Supreme Court, the People's Tribune of the Prefecture and the People's Tribune of the Sub-Prefecture. In addition there are military tribunals which deal with crimes committed by members of the armed forces.

In theory the function of the Supreme Court should approximate to that of the United States Supreme Court; the People's Tribune of the Prefecture should deal with crimes and major social offenses, while the People's Tribune of the Sub-Prefecture should deal with local and minor offenses.

## Language

The Albanian language derives from the dialects spoken by the ancient Illyrians and Thracians who inhabited a large area adjacent to the Danube. It is a member of the Indo-European language group and is spoken not only in Albania but also by minority groups in Yugoslavia, Greece and Italy.

There are two main Albanian dialects: Gheg, which is spoken in the north, and Tosk, which is spoken in the south. No common literary language exists in Albania; indeed, no common alphabet had been worked out before 1908, when one was established at a meeting of scholars who agreed upon a Latin alphabet. In

every four years, when all citizens over 18 years of age vote. At the 1962 election, 208 deputies (that is, one deputy for every 8000 inhabitants) were elected from this single list.

All legislation must be given the formal assent of a majority vote by the assembly, at which a majority of members is present. Any amendments to the constitution or to bills require a two-thirds majority of votes from the assembly. Such amendments may be proposed by the Presidium, the government, or by two-fifths of the members of the assembly.

### THE PRESIDIUM

The Presidium, like the assembly, has the function of giving formal assent to all legislation, coupled with the duty of formally proclaiming and promulgating all legislation passed by the government and of ratifying international treaties. It also nominates, after sanction by the government, diplomatic representatives for foreign posts, and it formally receives the

diplomatic representatives of foreign powers. It holds office for the term of the assembly which has elected it.

The Presidium comprises the president, three vice-presidents, a secretary and ten members.

### THE EXECUTIVE

The executive and administrative body of the republic is the Council of Ministers, which nominally is responsible to the assembly by which it is nominated. According to the constitution it can at any time be removed from office. In fact, however, it controls all power in Albania in concert with the Central Committee of the Albanian Labor Party.

The Council of Ministers comprises the first secretary of the Central Committee of the Communist party, the Presidium, the premier and five vice-premiers, the ministers of Foreign Affairs, Interior, National Defense, Education and Culture, Industry and Mines, Trade, Agriculture, Finance, Communications, Public Health and Justice. It also includes

1952 the Albanian Writers' Union decided that the Tosk dialect should be universally used in publications.

### Religion

The Albanian Constitution proclaims freedom of religion for all citizens and establishes a clear separation between church and state. By far the greatest number of Albanians are Moslem (65 per cent); there are also minorities belonging to the Orthodox Church of Albania (23 per cent) and the Roman Catholic Church (11 per cent). In 1951 the Albanian government banned all relations between the Roman Catholic Church within the country and the Vatican.

### Education

While education is both compulsory and free for all children between the ages of six and 13 years in Albania, the country has the great problem of school building and the education of teachers to overcome. In 1956 there were 303 kindergarten schools, 2095 primary schools, serving 185,000 pupils, 25 high schools, with 2762 pupils, and 13 technical high schools. In 1957 a university was established at Tirana and there are agricultural, technological, medical and teachers' training colleges and an institute of science. During the 1959-60 period there were 3890 students at the university and college level; of these 18 per cent were women.

### Currency and Measures

The unit of currency is the *lek,* which is divided into 100 *quintars.* It replaced the Albanian gold franc *(franc ar)* in 1947. At current rates of exchange, there are approximately 50 *leks* to the U. S. dollar.

The metric system is used for weights and measures.

### PHYSICAL GEOGRAPHY

### Relief

ALBANIA IS PREDOMINANTLY MOUNtainous, with two-thirds of its area lying above the 3000-foot contour line. The remainder comprises the low hills of the coastal regions and the lower reaches of the valleys opening onto the coastal plain. This physical structure has been a major factor in the economic and cultural separation of the lowland from the upland population. Although the pattern of Albania's relief is complex, the country can be divided broadly into four natural regions: the North Albanian Alps, the Central Mountain Region, the Southwest Highlands and the Coastal Lowlands.

#### THE NORTH ALBANIAN ALPS

This spur of the Dinaric system (locally called the Great Mountains) stretches in a northeasterly arc of about 60 miles along the Albanian-Yugoslavian border, from the basin of Lake Scutari to the Yugoslavian plains of Kosovo and Metohija. The chain is largely formed from strata of calcareous rock and magnesium lime. The rugged landscape has been accentuated by glacial erosion, which has made the valleys deeper and wider. The slopes are thickly wooded and the plateaus consist of alpine meadows. The highest peak is Djaravica (9524 feet), on the Yugoslavian side of the border.

#### THE CENTRAL MOUNTAIN REGION

This covers a large area of central Albania, extending from the valley of the Drin (in the stretch between the town of Kukës and the Adriatic in the north) to the Greek frontier in the southeast. It includes three mountain ranges, which lie roughly parallel in a south-north direction, increasing in size and height from west to east. Between these ranges is a series of depressions.

Of the three mountain clusters, the most important is the eastern group, which forms part of the border with Yugoslavia. It also forms the divide between the basin of the Drin River in Albania (emptying into the Adriatic) and that of the Vardar River in Yugoslavia (emptying into the Aegean). Because these mountains consist chiefly of paleozoic rock, they may be considered to belong to the Macedonian system, of which they are the forward western front.

#### THE SOUTHWEST HIGHLANDS

The Southwest Highlands are formed by parallel ranges which follow the direction of the Dinaric Alps—northwest to southeast—and extend from the Adriatic, where they form the peninsula ending at Cape Linguetta, to the interior of Albania.

#### THE COASTAL LOWLANDS

This is the sloping, flat region which extends along the coast from north to south.

A large part of the coastal area

*The North Albanian Alps are bounded in the south by the depression of Lake Scutari and the Drin River; to the northwest, however, they link up with the plateaus of Montenegro in Yugoslavia. Many of the peaks rise above 8000 feet.*

# GREECE AND ALBANIA

## GREECE
### Principal Cities

Agrínion..........C 3
Aitolikón..........C 3
Aíyina (Aegina)...D 4
Aíyion..........C 4
Akharaí..........g11
Alexandroúpolis....B 5
Alistráti..........B 5
Almirós..........C 4
Amaliás..........D 3
Amaroúsion........g11
Ámfissa..........C 4
Árgos..........D 4
Árgos Orestikón...B 3
Argostólion........C 3
Arta..........C 3
Asprópirgos........g11
Atalándi..........C 4
Athens
  (Athínai)...C 4, h11
Ayía Paraskeví.....C 6
Ayiássos..........C 6
Áyios Dhimítrios...g11
Dhidhimótikhon....B 6
Dráma..........B 5
Edhessa..........B 4
Ekhínos..........B 5
Elassón..........C 4
Elevsís (Eleusis)...g11
Erithraí........C 4, g10
Fársala..........C 4
Filiatrá..........D 3
Flórina (Phlorina)...B 3
Gargaliánoi........D 3
Glifádha..........h11
Grevená..........B 3
Ierápetra..........E 5
Ioánnina..........C 3
Iráklion (Candia)...E 5
Istiaía..........C 4
Kalámai..........D 4
Kalampáka........C 3
Kálimnos..........D 6
Kallithéa..........h11
Kardhítsa..........C 3
Karlóvasi..........D 6
Karpenísion........C 3
Kastoría..........B 3
Kástron..........C 5
Kateríni..........B 4
Katoúna..........C 3
Kaválla..........B 5
Kérkira (Corfu)....C 2
Khalkís
  (Chalcis)...C 4, g11
Khaniá (Canea)....E 5
Khíos (Chios).....C 6
Khrisoúpolis........B 5
Kifisiá..........g11
Kilkís..........B 4
Kími..........C 5
Kiparissía..........D 3
Komotiní..........B 5
Kórinthos
  (Corinth)...D 4, h 9
Koropí..........h11
Kós (Cos)..........D 6
Kozáni..........B 3
Kranídhion........D 4
Lamía..........C 4
Langadhás..........B 4
Lárisa (Larissa)...C 4
Lávrion..........D 5
Leonídhion........D 4
Levádhia......C 4, g 9
Levkás (Leucas)...C 3
Límni..........C 4
Litókhoron........C 4
Loutrá Aidhipsoú...C 4
Loutrákion........h 9
Mándra........C 4, g11
Markópoulon......h11
Mégara......C 4, g10

Conic Projection

SCALE 1:4,000,000   1 Inch = 63 Statute Miles

consists of marshy, malarial lands which have been only partially reclaimed; for this reason the coast has hindered, rather than helped, communications with the West. This is the most heavily populated region of Albania.

### Climate

The chief factor governing Albania's climate is the predominance of mountains. The mitigating influence of the sea is felt only along the coast and on the plains of lower Albania.

In the coldest months the average coastal temperature is 50° F. but this falls rapidly toward the interior, even falling below freezing point on higher ground. The average temperature of the hottest months is about 77° F. on the coast and in enclosed basins; even at heights of 1650 feet the average is still 68° F.

The winds are governed by the

*The urban and economic development of Tirana dates from 1920, when it became the capital of Albania. Many of its older buildings clearly show the Turkish architectural influence. Tirana is also the educational and cultural center of Albania, with a university, teachers' training college, art and music schools and agricultural colleges.*

Mediterranean Sea and the Balkan land mass. The southerly Mediterranean winds bring rain in winter, while northerly winds from the interior produce clear, dry skies.

Precipitation is heaviest in the north, around Lake Scutari, where the average is about 110 inches of rain a year. Mountainous areas, such as the North Albanian Alps, receive considerable snowfall in winter and heavy rain in summer. Other areas with high rainfall are the mountainous areas of Krujë and Tirana, where it is more than 99 inches, and the southern part of the country between the Aoos River and the Bay of Valona. Lesser amounts fall in the enclosed basins of the interior, where the fall is less than 32 inches, and between the mouth of the Shkumbi River and that of the Seman River, where it is between 32 and 39 inches.

### Hydrography

Because they rise at great heights, most Albanian rivers, including the Drin, reach the lowland area in mountain torrents. In mountain areas the rivers cut deep channels in the soft sandstone of the valleys, forming gorges with nearly vertical walls, which sometimes stand 300 feet above the streams.

#### MAIN RIVERS

The flow of Albania's rivers is most irregular, especially in the south. During the rainy winter months, parts of the lowlands are inundated for weeks at a time, with the result that communications and economic activi-

ties are at a virtual standstill.

The Bojana, a short navigable river (25 miles), flows out of Lake Scutari in a generally southward direction along the Albanian Yugoslavian border to the Adriatic.

The Drin, the longest river of Albania (95 miles), is formed by the confluence of the Black Drin and the White Drin at Kukes and flows generally west through the plain of Scutari, where it changes direction and flows south to enter the Adriatic (through a delta) in the Gulf of Drin. The Black Drin (80 miles) rises in the Yugoslavian part of Lake Ochrida at Struga and flows northwest to Kukes. The White Drin (80 miles) rises north of Pec in Yugoslavia and flows south through Metohija to Kukes. The Via Zenta, an ancient highway built by Ragusan merchants who wished to trade with the old Serbian Empire, runs into the valley of the Drin.

The Mat (60 miles) rises southeast of Klos and flows northwest then west to enter the Gulf of Drin, nine miles southwest of Lesh.

The Arzen (50 miles) rises 15 miles east of Tirana, flows northwest and enters the Adriatic nine miles north of Durazzo.

The Shkumbi (90 miles) rises just west of Lake Ochrida and flows northwest and west to enter the Adriatic 20 miles south of Durazzo. The Via Egnatia, which runs in the valley of the Shkumbi, was built by Rome to link the Balkan provinces with Italy. On the collapse of the Roman Empire, this highway fell into disuse. The Durazzo-Elbasan railroad runs along the lower valley of the river. The Shkumbi forms a language border : Tosk is spoken to the south of it and Gheg to the north.

The Seman (50 miles) is formed by the confluence of the Devoll and Osum rivers eight miles northwest of Berat. It flows generally west to the

*Durazzo. A view of the city and port from the Venetian castle whose ruins dominate the residential area from the hill. An important port and commercial center since Roman times, when it was called Dyrrachium, the city has been ravaged in the course of its history by fires and wars. Today, it is the most important port in Albania and is connected with the main inland centers by railroad and highway.*

Adriatic, which it enters through a delta south of Kravasta Lagoon.

The Aoos (125 miles, locally called the Vijose) rises in the Pindus Mountains of Greece near Metsovon and flows generally northwest past Konitsa, Permet and Tepelene to the Strait of Otranto.

### LAKES

The many small lakes of Albania are of glacial origin, while the larger are of tectonic origin (formed by movements of the earth's crust).

Most of Lake Scutari, in the northwest, is in Yugoslavia. In the summer the average depth is 20 to 23 feet, but with the coming of winter rains it rises by seven to ten feet. This is accompanied by an increase in area from about 146 square miles to about 205 square miles. In the southwest there are several deep whirlpools.

The Albanian part of Lake Scutari has three ports, Vir, Plarnica and Scutari, at which small steamers call. Fishing is an important industry. The lake is rarely frozen and even then only along the northern shore; it is drained by the Bojana in the southeast and the Moraca in the northwest.

Lake Ochrida, like Lake Scutari, lies mostly in Yugoslavia. With a maximum depth of 938 feet, it is the deepest lake in the Balkan Peninsula. The area is 134 square miles. Fishing is a prosperous industry at Ochrida.

Lake Prespa, at an altitude of 2798 feet, is the highest lake in the Balkan Peninsula. It lies in Albania, Greece, and, for the largest part, in Yugoslavia.

With a maximum length of 18 miles and a maximum width of eight, it has an area of 112 square miles, and at its deepest is 177 feet. Little Lake Prespa, lying almost wholly in Greece, is to the southeast of Lake Prespa, from which it is separated by a sandpit one-and-a-half miles wide.

### Flora and Fauna

Albania has a varied landscape, as a result of its altitude and distance from the sea. The coastal zone is characterized by Mediterranean woods and *maquis,* which are followed higher up and toward the interior by forests of broad-leaved trees.

First, a forest of oaks stretches up to a height of 3300 feet in the Albanian Alps and up to 3900 feet in the mountains of the Upper Shkumbi; then, still higher, is beechwood, which covers large areas, principally in the Albanian Alps. The elevated plains are covered with conifers. Above that is the grazing zone which sometimes has been artificially extended at the expense of the wooded zone. The woods have an upper limit that varies from 6000 to 6500 feet.

Bears and wild boars still survive, mainly in the mountain areas of the Aoos, where they have been driven by hunters. Wolves and jackals, on the other hand, are found not only in the mountains, but also in the plains. The chamois is found in the Albanian Alps. Small mammals, such as the hare, rabbit and marten, are found throughout the country. Bird life is plentiful, particularly in the marshy coastal zone.

---

### HUMAN GEOGRAPHY

### Distribution of Population

THE LATEST ESTIMATE (1963) SHOWS that Albania had a population of 1,800,000 on its 11,024 square miles —giving a density of approximately 163 people per square mile, one of the lowest in Europe. This popula-

tion, for economic and topographic reasons, is unevenly distributed. The coastal plains have more people than the mountain regions: for example, the plain of Koritsa, the best cultivated in the country, had about 240 people to the square mile in 1949, while in parts of the Albanian Alps there are fewer than six people to the square mile.

There are large settlements of Albanians in Yugoslavia (750,000 in 1948), Greece (60,000) and Italy (250,000). The total number of Albanians living in other countries is estimated at 3,000,000.

### Principal Cities

According to the census taken in 1960, only five cities, Tirana, Durazzo, Koritsa, Scutari and Valona have more than 30,000 people each.

### TIRANA (TIRENE) *(pop. 136,300)*

Tirana, the capital, stands on a fertile plain 19 miles from the port of Durazzo, with which it was linked by rail in 1951. It was founded in the early 17th century by a Turkish general, Barkinzadeh Suleiman Pasha, who named it Teheran because of a Turkish victory in Persia.

A large part of the city still retains its Oriental character, but recent alterations and new buildings have given it a more Western and modern appearance. Under King Zog (ruled

*A street in Argyrokastron (from the Greek meaning "silver castle"), a city (also called Gjinokastër) of southern Albania on the Drin River. Dating from about the 4th century, the city has seen many foreign rulers: Venetians, Turks, Italians and, during World War II, Germans. It is now a thriving commercial center, specializing in dairy products, tobacco, wine-growing and silver-smithing.*

1928-39) and with the help of Italian architects, large government offices were built round Scanderbeg Square. There are many mosques in the town, the most famous being the Etehem Bey (completed in 1819), in which Suleiman Pasha is buried. Places of learning include a university, a tea-cher-training college, an agricultural college and art and music schools.

In 1920 a congress of patriots chose Tirana as the capital. During World War II the town was occupied by Italian and later by German for-

ces. There, on Jan. 11, 1946, the country was proclaimed a People's Republic.

## DURAZZO (DURRES) (pop. 40,000)

Durazzo, situated on the northern end of the Adriatic bay of the same name, is the country's chief port and commercial and communications center. It was founded about 627 B.C. as a joint colony by Corinthians and Corcyraeans, who named it Epidamnus. In 312 B.C. it was captured by Glaucias, the Illyrian king. After 229

B.C. it came under Roman rule and was named Dyrrachium (from which the present name is derived). Under the Romans it became the western terminal of the Via Egnatia, which linked Italy with Salonika and Byzantium. In 48 B.C., Pompey made his last successful stand against Julius Caesar here.

In the Middle Ages, Durazzo came under various rulers and was destroyed by an earthquake in 1273. During World War II, with all of Albania, it was occupied by Italian and, later, by German forces. The retreating Germans completely destroyed the harbor installations which, earlier, had been partially crippled by heavy Allied bombings and shelling. Since World War II, the harbor has been rebuilt and enlarged with the help of other Communist countries.

Olive oil, grain, hides and skins and tobacco are exported through Durazzo, which also has a small ship-building yard.

Places of interest include a former royal villa and a large mosque.

## ELBASAN (pop. 29,800)

Elbasan is on the northern bank of the Shkumbi, 20 miles southeast of Tirana, to which it is linked by highways. It is the terminal of the railroad from Durazzo and stands on the ancient Via Egnatia.

Olives, corn and tobacco form agricultural produce, while industrial products consist of olive oil, soap and processed timber.

## KORITZA (KORCE) (pop. 39,400)

Koritza is a major cultural center, with various schools and an important library, situated 70 miles southeast of Tirana, not far from the Greek border. It is also an important agricultural center, producing grain and sugar beet, and manufacturing beer, liquor and knitwear.

## SCUTARI (SHKODER) (pop. 43,200)

Scutari, the capital of ancient Illyria, stands on the southeast shore of Lake Scutari, where the Bojana River leaves the lake, 55 miles northwest of Tirana.

In 168 B.C. it became a Roman colony and in 395 A.D. came under the Byzantines.

This important industrial and commercial center produces textiles, building materials, cigarettes and tobacco.

Its chief buildings and places of interest include a Jesuit college, town gardens, several mosques and a Roman Catholic cathedral.

## VALONA (VLORE) *(pop. 41,300)*

Valona, 70 miles southwest of Tirana, is a seaport on the northeast end of the Bay of Valona.

Cement-making and rice-husking factories were built after World War II, augmenting the existing industries of fishing and canning; olives and olive oil play an important part in the economy. Major exports are crude oil and bitumen.

Valona was the scene of the declaration of Albanian independence in 1912.

## ECONOMIC GEOGRAPHY

BECAUSE OF HISTORICAL FACTORS (particularly the Turkish rule which isolated Albania from the rest of Europe), its mountainous character, the unhealthy climatic conditions of the low-lying, marshy plains and the inaccessibility of the coastline, the Albanian national economy lags far behind that of other European countries. Up to the beginning of World War II, the economy depended heavily on herdsmanship and on an agriculture practiced with traditional methods, which resulted in low productivity. The exploitation of mineral resources had scarcely begun and organized manufacturing industry was almost non-existent, except for self-employed artisans who met the needs of their localities.

After the serious destruction caused by the war, the first attempts at reconstruction were made under two Two-Year Plans, the first financed by Yugoslavia, the second by the Soviet Union. These, however, proved unsuccessful, and in 1951, a Five-Year Plan was launched, aimed at bringing industrial production to a higher level. Since the break in relations with the European Communists, the Chinese have given economic aid to Albania.

### Agriculture and Stockbreeding

In 1945 the large private estates and farms were expropriated and about 400,000 acres of land were distributed among 75,000 smallholders who had formerly been landless. At the same time an attempt was made to develop collectivization by coercing smallholders to enter agricultural cooperatives similar to the Soviet *kolkhoz*. The state then nationalized all forests and grazing lands and also preserved a part of the expropriated lands for the creation of manufacturing plants belonging to the state.

### INCREASE IN OUTPUT

In 1953 the area of cultivated land has increased by 64 per cent over that of 1938, from about 606,000 acres to about 995,000 acres. Irrigated land, which was 40,000 acres before the war, had increased to 124,000. Corn continues to be the most widely cultivated cereal, as it is the staple of the Albanian diet. Wheat comes next, followed by oats, barley, rye and rice, in that order. The cultivation of rice has increased considerably. Industrial crops, particularly cotton—whose cultivation area had risen from 1000 acres in 1930 to 30,000 in 1950 and to 74,000 in 1955—have received most attention.

The breeding of livestock has also increased, particularly the breeding of pigs, which, thriving on corn, numbered 15,000 in 1938 but reached 130,000 in 1960. Cattle, including buffaloes, increased from 134,000

*The market place of Krujë on the spur of a 2000-foot mountain above the Ishm river valley, 12 miles north of Tirana. Krujë is a very old Moslem city with historical and religious associations. Among its places of interest is a 14th-15th-century fortress, used by the Albanians during their resistance against the Turks.*

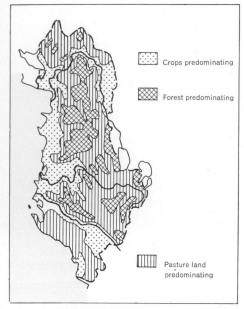

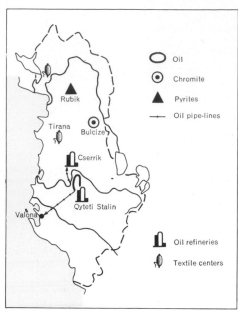

*Left: Map showing utilization of soil in Albania. Right: Map showing the location of Albania's mineral resources and principal industries.*

## ALBANIA
## AREA AND POPULATION

| REGION | AREA | POPULATION |
|---|---|---|
| | (Sq. miles) | (1958) |
| Scutari or Northern | 2551 | 225,000 |
| Tirana-Durazzo | 2308 | 487,500 |
| Elbasan-Berat | 2640 | 430,000 |
| Valona or Southwestern | 2186 | 250,000 |
| Koritsa | 1339 | 201,500 |
| TOTAL | 11,024 | 1,594,000 |

in 1938 to more than 400,000 in 1960.

## Industry

Lack of capital and skilled technicians and workmen hindered earlier development of Albanian industry, although the country has considerable natural resources, especially mineral wealth, which the Italians had started to develop. A modern and properly equipped industry is just beginning to exist. In the post-war years, first with Yugoslavian and Soviet aid and, more recently, with Chinese aid, industrialization has developed.

The petroleum reserves of the principal oil-bearing region in the southwest are estimated at between 11 and 14 million tons. The production of petroleum, which was about 100,000 tons in 1938, had increased to almost 650,000 tons in 1961. The most important oil-field is at Qyteti station (formerly Kucove) on the Devoll River.

### COAL AND ELECTRICITY

Albania's coal deposits consist of high quality lignite and are estimated at more than 10 million tons. The major coal-producing mines are at Memaliaj, Krrabe and Priske.

After the recent building of hydro- and thermoelectric power stations, production reached 120 million kwh. in 1955 and 217 million in 1961. Albania has a considerable hydro-electric potential (estimated at nearly 3 million kw.), of which only a very small part has been developed.

The country has substantial deposits of chromium, copper and iron; exploitation of these resources, started by the Italians, is now being increased.

The textile industry has been extensively developed not only in order to increase production but also to absorb the formerly independent cottage-weaver type artisans into the centralized Communist state system.

### Communications

In Albania, railroads, except the narrow-gauge line, have been built only since 1947 and in 1963 had a total length of 104 miles. The most important of the country's three lines is the 19-mile stretch connecting Tirana, the capital, with the port of Durazzo.

In 1954 the merchant navy of Albania amounted to 16 motor boats totaling 3830 tons. The Albanians placed orders for a number of ships to be built in Poland but these were not delivered because of the break with the Soviet bloc in 1961.

*Picking cotton by hand. The cultivation of this industrial crop shows considerable growth each year, in accordance with government plans. However, there is one setback: the government cannot yet afford complete mechanization of agriculture and so certain operations which in many countries are now done by machinery still depend on human labor which would otherwise be released for urban industrial development.*

*A group of teen-age boys gaze quizzically into a camera at Berat in south-central Albania. The boys are typically Albanian, with Turkish, Serbian and Italian features apparent. Berat is a commercial center, producing and processing cereals, wine, tobacco, fruit and olives. It contains many fine old churches and a 15th-century mosque. Part of it, the "upper town," is a 13th-century citadel.*

pecially after World War II, to giving Albania a more modern look have not yet entirely, in the mountainous areas of the interior, changed its traditional appearance.

### Oriental Influences

Various ancient elements of Mediterranean, Balkan and Central European origin have contributed to form the Albanian cultural heritage. Successive Slav influences have left a few traces in the north, while the Turkish influence is met in the religion and some typical Oriental institutions, such as the bazaar, which survives in many Albanian cities.

The capital, Tirana, among many buildings in reinforced concrete, still keeps its bazaar in the center of the city. In this intricate network of ways and alleys and low, one-story buildings, dozens of the most varied kinds of shops are jumbled together.

### The Tribal Family

The basic core of communal life is still the family, which has always been very important in Albania. The large family was still a fact of life until recent years. An Albanian family is in fact a small tribe. Often it is made up of 30 to 40 people, because custom demanded that the male child remain in the family house even after marriage.

The large family was a survival of the country's tribal life and until the first years of the 20th century, Albania still was divided into tribes. The tribe was directed by the assembly of the fathers, among whom a few chiefs were dominant.

The *miku* (guest) was welcomed with all honors; for him the best lamb would be slaughtered, for him the most comfortable bed prepared. It is an ancient tradition, still kept up today in the mountain villages, that the women of the household wash the guest's feet with hot water when he has barely crossed the family threshold.

#### MUTUAL SLAUGHTER

The *gjaku* (vendetta), was an obligation for honor which passed from

According to an Albanian legend, the Eternal Father decided one day to visit the world he had created and see what was going on. He traveled from one country to another in search of some trace of the world he remembered. There was none; all had changed. Disillusioned and sad, the Eternal Father was about to return to Heaven, when he arrived in Albania, where he sighed with relief. "Now I get my bearings," he said. "This world is still the one I created!"

### THE TRIBES AND THE LAW

THE TALE HAS A CERTAIN TRUTH. Albania is the one European country where the primitive and patriarchal ways of life have in many instances survived. The energies dedicated, es-

father to son. It involved mutual slaughter organized by families who considered themselves slighted by each other, and it continued from generation to generation. Until a few years ago it constituted one of the principal duties of every Albanian. Blood called for other blood, and if the murderer could not be killed, the avenging hand fell implacably upon his relatives. In the north it was a social scourge, and claimed a large number of victims every year, forcing many to live in a state of permanent war. Often the men of a murdered man's family devoted themselves to the total slaughter of the opposed family and did not return home until they had wiped out their adversaries.

Fortunately there remained the women. The vendetta was a male occupation and women were never involved.

## MARRIAGE AND FUNERALS

ALBANIAN WOMEN THUS ACQUIRED A primary role in the family circle, and also in the economy of the community. When men gave themselves over to butchery, the women assumed responsibility for the family and took on agricultural and craft work which the men had abandoned.

Women enjoyed great consideration, and on marriage the husband acquired his wife as, among other things, a worker. Women led a very retired life and until recently 14-year-old girls were shut away at home. At that time they said goodbye to childish games and gave themselves to domestic chores under the guidance of their mother or sister.

In recent years customs have been modified but Albanian women have in no way lost this sense of retirement and discretion, which has for centuries been one of their greatest qualities and is common both to Christian and Moslem. The latter never leave home except for *ramadan,* the month-long religious festival, when they are allowed to pass the evening with a relative.

### Moslem Marriage

Moslem marriage is celebrated before the *cadi,* who receives from the husband a sum of money, which he holds in trust to give to the wife in case (as sometimes occurs) there should be a divorce.

In the villages, marriage has kept the character of a contract and the husband must pay to the parents of the woman he has chosen a sum which varies according to the wealth of the two families.

### Christian Marriage

Among Christians, the most interesting marriage rites are observed in northern Albania, where the usual custom is that the parents of bride and groom draw up a marriage contract.

Parents often promise their children in marriage while the latter are infants, sealing the promise with a lock of hair from each of the two children. But in most homes they have recourse to a mediator or marriage broker, who has the task of establishing the girl's price, fixing the date of the engagement and the marriage and ensuring the money is paid over to the girl's parents.

#### FEE FOR THE MEDIATOR'S SHOES

For this work the mediator is given an extra fee "for wearing out his shoes," which implies that the work of a mediator may be tiring. The mediator must also make sure that no impediments exist to the marriage.

#### CONCLUDING THE ENGAGEMENT

When all moral and financial difficulties have been smoothed out, the engagement ceremony gets under way. The mediator and the husband's father are guests and the main hosts are the father or elder brother of the bride. The mediator sits near the hearth, scatters the ashes from it and then speaks, setting out the terms of the contract. All sit down at table and at the end of the meal the husband's father consigns the agreed sum to the mediator for the pledging of the daughter-in-law and the engagement ring. The ceremony ends without the girl ever making an appearance.

Once decided, the date of the wedding cannot be changed for any reason, except the death of a member of the family, and the marriage

*A young Romeo regards his Juliet with an affectionate smile in southern Albania. By contrast with the lady's costume, the man's is austere but it is traditional: the white shirt and white skirt (or kilt) he wears are of very ancient origin. The cloak is more often worn in winter. The exquisite lace bodice worn by the girl over a beautiful brocade dress represents perhaps generations of fine needlework. These young people are Orthodox Christians.*

ceremony is fixed by law in the smallest particulars. The following persons must take part: 12 male matrimonial agents and one female; messengers, who are those bringing the wedding invitations; servants, who include the women who bake the bread, dancers and singers and those who bring sheep; the godfathers of the couple and their relatives; and the guests.

The guests' order of arrival varies according to their wealth. Marriages are performed on a Sunday and the married daughters and nephews of the families arrive on the Thursday before. On the Friday evening the recipients of invitations, the women who make bread, those who bring sheep and the matrimonial agents, all arrive.

### THE WEDDING OX IS SLAUGHTERED

On Saturday morning the wedding ox is slaughtered and finally a long cortege is formed, which moves toward the bride's house. The 12 male matrimonial agents head the column, then come the woman matrimonial agent, behind her the bridegroom's father, who holds a horse by the bridle, and finally the guests and players.

### THE WEDDING FEAST

The law also fixes the quantities and quality of food for the marriage feast. The food includes the marriage ox, corn flour, grain flour, coffee, sugar, rice, honey, cheese, butter, olive oil and, finally, brandy. At the end of the meal, every matrimonial agent makes his gift, which is a coin thrown onto the unbroken bread that remains on the table.

The day after the wedding everyone again goes to the husband's house, where the festivities continue with sumptuous meals, dances and songs.

### THE PENITENT BRIDE

On her wedding day, the bride goes on her knees before her parents and brothers and asks pardon for any of her acts which may have displeased them. She receives the parental blessing and then with her husband goes to celebrate the marriage rite, which is performed first before the civil authorities, and then in church. Rejoicings continue for the day until at midnight the bride is taken to the nuptial bedroom and left alone with her husband.

At dawn the husband leaves the room to summon relatives and women friends, who kiss his wife. Again songs start but they do not continue for long, because the marriage is completed.

### Death in Albania

Albanian funeral rites have also kept their traditional character, especially in the mountain villages. When a person dies, the women announce the death with loud shouts and the deceased is dressed in his best clothes and placed in the center of the house with his face turned to the east. A large, black silk handkerchief is draped over his face. Around the corpse mourners sing death songs, while others sob, all accompanied by the rhythmic clapping of hands. One mourner shouts praise of the deceased in a loud voice, accompanied at intervals by the others.

When the family can afford such luxuries, it hires the *vajtojce* (professional mourners), who join in the chorus of lamentations and beg of the newly dead to carry to those who preceded him to the next world the greetings of the living. A salute to the dead man is given by the womenfolk and the men join together in a nearby room, somber-faced and silent, because tears are not becoming to warriors.

### A MOSLEM FUNERAL

Among Christians it is the custom to keep the body in the house for at least a day, but Moslems scarcely wait until the dying man has stopped breathing before they wash and cover him with a sheet. Immediately he is taken to the cemetery on one of many stretchers which are kept for this purpose in the mosques. The stretcher is placed near a grave previously dug. Before the corpse is lowered, those present answer the ritual question, "Has this man been good or bad?" All reply "Good!": then the body is lowered into the grave.

---

## DANCES

---

DANCES AND SONGS ACCOMPANY ALL the important moments in the life of

*These Albanians are not fighting: they are performing a step from a peasant ritual dance. Each wears the traditional white fez, which varies in height in different parts of the country. The use of swords in the dance is typical of a country where fighting was considered the only activity worthy of men—the work of supporting and raising children being left to the women. The "peacock" stance of the dancers implies the romantic attitude of the Albanian male to militarism.*

the Albanians. The most popular dance is the *valle*, which is executed in a circle or semicircle like the dances of other Balkan peoples. But there are many types of dance which differ from each other in form, kind and content.

Solo performances are the most typical kind of female dance in northern Albania. They are performed with simple movements and with great composure, accompanied by gentle movements of the hands and the body. They embody ancient mimicry unknown in other parts of the country.

### Communal Dances

The most usual kinds of communal dance are performed by two rows of men placed one in front of the other. The dance is accompanied by song: the first chorus is sung by the first row, which advances toward the second with rhythmical and measured paces. There are many movements and turns, and the performers are linked together by means of handkerchiefs, or by the arms.

### Water and Warrior Dances

In some dances acrobatic elements are included, as in the "vase dance" of the Tirana region, in which the men put vases filled with water or some other liquid on their heads and dance, taking care not to spill it. Warrior dances express strength and virility. Once widespread, they can still be found in regions of the interior. The dancers proceed in single file. Each in turn takes the head of the line, puts his knees to the ground and jumps with a great shout.

The traditional musical instruments are the *lahuta* with one string, furnished with a long handle and a small, round box, which is played with a bow; and the archaic *fyelli*, the flute, which accompanies the dirges of the peasants and shepherds.

---

## RELIGION AND PAGAN RITUALS

TWO-THIRDS OF THE ALBANIANS ARE Moslems; the rest are Christians, Orthodox and Catholic. Officially, the country enjoys freedom of religion and the differences of faith do not have the same importance in Albania as in other Balkan countries. Nor are there striking differences in customs; quite often the only distinguishing feature between Moslem and Christian communities are the mosques and churches.

*A peasant craftsman at work in Krujë in north-central Albania. Krujë is famous for the fine work which goes into the national costumes which are made there, and also for its fine craftsmanship in metals, pottery and wood carving. The people are now mostly Moslems but in the 14th and 15th centuries the fortress in the town fiercely withstood the Turkish invaders.*

### VAMPIRES, WITCHES, FAIRIES AND PROPHETS

Ancient superstitions still remain quite widespread. A popular tradition holds that the *dreqci* (demon) enters into the bodies of people who live bad lives; when they die they are forced to wander shouting and terrorizing the living. Vampires are condemned souls who suck blood from the living when they sleep. *Shtrigat* (witches) are let loose in the month of March. To fight them, the young men light resin torches on Easter eve and, waving them, go in procession through the villages. They then throw their torches in the river, shouting, "Witches, we throw you in the river like this torch, so that you can never return."

The people also believe in *zanat* (good fairies), who inhabit woods and mountains, and in *shtoizavallat*, mysterious beings who have the infallible gift of prophecy.

### The Christian Feasts

Traditionally, spring is celebrated by the Christians on St. George's Day, April 24, the most venerated holiday in Albania.

An established part of the festival amusements, especially for country girls, is swinging. A thick, looped cord is tied to a beam in a house or from the branches of a tree and a cushion is placed in the loop. A girl takes her place on it, surrounded by her friends, who swing her and sing three-line poems in chorus.

On the last day of carnival, revelers swarm through the steets and enter the homes, where they are welcomed and are given coffee, wine, spirits, beer or, if very young, money.

St. Mark's day, April 25, and St. Michael's Day, September 29, are celebrated with shots from guns and small mortars, much drinking and lavish eating. A whole sheep, goat or calf is roasted on a spit over a fire.

### CELEBRATING EASTER

Easter is celebrated in Albania with great solemnity. The ceremonies begin on Holy Saturday afternoon, when

every family carries a tart or a cake to church. These cakes are made from eggs, flour, milk and butter. In church the priests bless them. The tart or cake is eaten on Easter Sunday morning, when the family returns home from Mass. The formula with which the Albanians exchange Easter greetings is traditional: "Me schdet, me zener te mire per shum mot!" which means "With health and with joy for many years!"

### THE FRIENDLY SAINT

On St. Nicholas' day, December 6, an enormous candle is lit in front of every house in honor of the saint who is the patron of mariners, students, merchants and, of course, children—he is the original Santa Claus. The duty of honoring him is omitted by none in Albania; even the Moslems light the candle before their houses, and make the same show of devotion and faith.

### CHRISTMAS AND CHESTNUTS

On Christmas Eve, Albanians get together around enormous log-fires and sing and talk cheerfully, eat chestnuts and drink wine and spirits. At midnight when church bells sound, everyone makes the sign of the cross: then the men shoot their guns into the sky as a sign of joy. The ashes of the biggest Yule log are scattered over the fields to make them fertile.

### NEW YEAR FOR THE CHILDREN

New Year is passed in the countryside without ceremony. But in the city, the children, beginning at dawn, holding little baskets, go from door to door wishing all a happy new year, and asking for gifts. Their request is stated in poetry: "Good morning, we are here for the gift!/ Come with a bowl full of good things!/ Happy New Year!/ Good morning, today!/ Come outside, O lady of the house/ With your husband's purse/ That you in the year to come may have a fine little son./ Come outside, then, or we'll go away!" But they do not go away, and if the door is not opened, or the gift is not considered generous, the blessings and good wishes quickly turn to insults.

### The Moslem Feasts

For the Moslems, the principal religious feast is *ramadan,* the month of fasting prescribed by the Koran.

During the whole month, no Moslem may drink, smoke or eat during the day. Food is taken at *yftaar* (sundown) and *syfyr* (dawn). Each day a cannon or musket shot announces sundown. Then the *muezzin* calls from the minaret: "Allah hypber! Allah hypber! La eu in Allah! Mohammed Rasul Allah! Ja el sela, ja el sela! Allah hypber!" which means "God is great! God is great! Mohammed is his prophet! Come, good and evil, to prayer! God is great!"

When the prayer ends, the faithful drink a glass of fresh water or *hardic* (a liquid made with juniper berries). Then they eat. By day *ramadan* dislocates the normal flow of Moslem activity: fasting diminishes the energies of the faithful. They walk slowly in the streets or over carpets in their rooms, deep in prayer. But by night some become gluttons and they emerge at dawn dazed. The month of *ramadan* sometimes has consequences which last for a considerable time. In recent times a tendency has developed to relax rigid enforcements of the commandment of the Koran, so that the good Moslem is not forced to change his normal ways for almost a whole month.

### TOMB OF THE PROPHET

After *ramadan* come the three days of *bajram,* when pilgrims travel to the tomb of the Prophet, in Mecca. Those who can afford to keep to the rule of the Koran are few and many pay a deputy who takes the journey on their behalf and makes sacrifice for them. But all good Moslems aspire to visit Mecca and pray there before they die.

---

## CRAFTS AND COSTUMES

---

THE OFTEN TRAGIC CONDITIONS OF life in Albania have not taken from the Albanian people their traditional love of beauty. From the cradle to the grave they are accompanied by art.

### Cradles and Shrouds

The wooden cradle which receives the newborn baby is carved or painted with great taste; the shrouds which cover the Albanian dead are embroidered with fine designs; even tombstones are artistically sculpted.

The objects in daily use—wooden utensils, crockery, cloths—are decorated with geometrical, animal or human shapes.

### Metalwork

The passion of the Albanians for arms has inspired native goldsmiths. Weapons are inlaid with finely worked precious metals. Sword and pistol grips, worked in chiseled or engraved silver, are works of art.

### Folk Costume

Many rural Albanians still wear picturesque traditional folk costume.

*Old and new blend in this scene in an Albanian bazaar in Tirana. The coat worn by the man is a relic of World War II (it is a type worn by British officers in the desert), while his headdress is of a kind worn by Arabs and adopted by the British—Lawrence of Arabia wore such a headdress, bound, similarly, with a cord. The white kerchiefs worn by the women in the foreground indicate that they are married. Albanian women wear more colorful costumes than men and love to festoon themselves with beads and jewelry.*

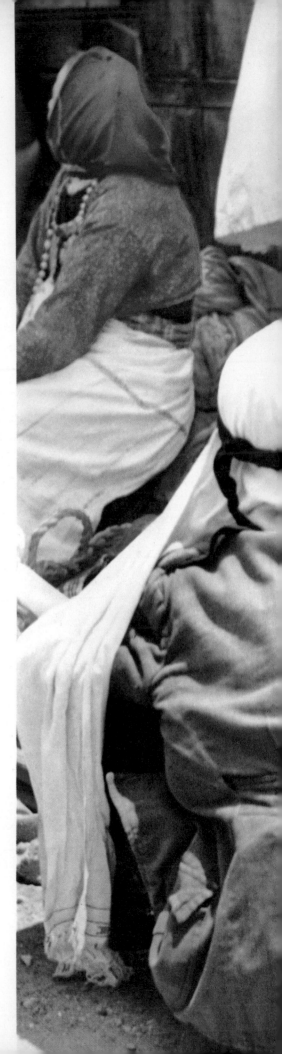

The men wear the *gylaf* or *geleshe*, a white fez, which varies from region to region only in its height.

In the south they wear knee-length trousers with woolen stockings. The shirt is of white linen, embroidered and bound close to the waist with a wide, richly ornamented belt.

### KILTS AND RED WAISTCOATS

In the past, Albanians also wore the *fustan*, a skirt (or kilt) made from pieces of embroidered cloth; this may have been inherited from their Illyrian ancestors. In the north the men wear more varied costumes, the trousers being long and narrow, almost always white, edged with black for summer wear, and with gray or brown for winter.

In summer they wear *zhurdu*—red and yellow waistcoats, decorated with epaulettes. In winter heavy jackets and large cloaks are worn.

### WHITE SHIRTS AND WIDE TROUSERS

Women's clothing is richer in color and design. A long, white shirt with wide sleeves is common to all. But Christian women wear a red vest

*A group of peasants subscribing to a national loan. The great majority of Albanians work on the land. As in Soviet Russia, the Communists started by expropriating large estates and distributing the land among the peasants and then adopted a policy of collectivization. At least 85 per cent of the land is now farmed in this way.*

*The sheep is the basis of Albania's agricultural economy. All Albanians eat mutton, cooked in a variety of ways, and all wear woolen garments. In the mountains shepherds are often isolated for many weeks with their flocks; and often they have to rescue them in winter from deep snow drifts. The cheerful Albanian shepherd in this picture is characteristic of shepherds throughout all Europe, from Scotland's far north to the Ukraine—he is a man at home with his flock.*

above it, pleated and ornamented with lace, while their Moslem sisters wear wide trousers which taper to the ankles, where they are bound tight. Women of both religions wear head cloths of many colors; married women cover their heads with a white cloth, called a *kesa*.

---

## FOOD

---

ALBANIAN COOKING IS SIMPLE AND the Albanians are distinguished for their sobriety.

### MUTTON, THE MAIN DISH

The staple national meat is mutton. Grazing sheep were, in the past, the basis of the country's economy.

Mutton is prepared in many ways. *Jahni* is baked mutton flavored with much paprika. *Japrak* is minced mutton finely minced and mixed with rice, small pieces of onion and parsley and the whole wrapped in cabbage leaves or vine leaves. *Mish te ziem* is simply boiled mutton.

Meals generally begin with a plate of salad. Between the two servings of meat which generally form the basis of the meal, rice is served, either cooked with meat sauce, tomatoes, pine seeds, chestnuts and dry grapes, or in the form of a minestrone soup, bitter or sweet, called *ciorba*.

### Circassian Chicken

Many Albanian dishes show Turkish or Greek influence. *Cerkas* is chicken cooked in the Circassian way, boiled, boned and flavored with nut sauce. Egg plants *à la Turque* are cooked with chilies.

*Beyrek* is puff pastry which encloses chicken, spinach or cheese in layers, and resembles a similar dish found in Genoa and Sicily.

Eggs are often cooked with ginger.

### 'CADAIF' AND COFFEE

The most popular Albanian sweet is *cadaif*, which is made by draining off a liquid paste of sweetened milk and flour into a kind of heated can. The liquid immediately congeals and forms the confection.

An Albanian meal always ends with a cup of coffee. There are no distinctively good native wines and spirits.

*Remains of the theater at Apollonia. Founded as a colony of Corcyra (Corfu) in 588 B.C., Apollonia fell into Roman hands, along with its parent city-state, in 299 B.C. It was important as a seaport for the export of wheat, and as a center on the route to the Orient, until the Barbarian invasions, when it declined.*

## THE HISTORY

### Under Greece and Rome

THE ALBANIANS ARE THE OLDEST OF all the Balkan peoples. Their ancestors were already settled in that part of the world when the Greeks came, and in classical times they were the troublesome northern neighbors the Greeks knew as Thracians, Macedonians and Illyrians. But although small pockets of these peoples remain in Greece, successive waves of Slav tribes pushed most of them west toward the Adriatic, and they are now concentrated in Albania and southern Serbia, apart from a sizable colony in southern Italy, to which many of them fled after the Turkish conquest.

### GREEKS ON THE SEABOARD

The Greeks founded several colonies on the Albanian seaboard, the most important, Epidamnus (Durazzo), established about 627 B.C. as a joint colony of Corinth and Corcyra (Corfu); but the Greeks had little influence on the Albanians until the time of Philip II of Macedon (reigned 359-336 B.C.), father of Alexander the Great, whose army subjugated part of their country.

In the middle of the 3rd century B.C. the kingdom of Illyria was formed, its capital being Scodra (the modern Scutari or Shkodër). The piratical forays of its inhabitants into the Adriatic and Ionian seas brought the wrath of Rome onto its head and in 167 B.C. the Romans conquered the country.

### VITAL LINK IN THE ROMAN EMPIRE

The great Roman road to the East, the Via Egnatia, was built through Albania, and was for more than five centuries a vital link in the Roman Empire. When the empire finally split into two parts (395 A.D.) Albania found itself in the Eastern or Byzantine Empire; but during the next thousand years it was often under the sway of invaders from the north — Huns, Ostrogoths, Serbians, Croatians and Bulgarians. The imperial rule was also disputed by the Normans, then holding southern Italy, in the late 11th century, by the Venetians in the early 13th century, and by the Angevin kings of Naples from the late 13th to the late 14th century.

### SERBIANS AND TURKS

For a short time, too, Albania was part of the empire of the Serbian conqueror Stephen Dushan (c. 1308-55), but on his death his empire broke up and Albania was sundered by the rivalry of its feudal lords. The Venetians took the opportunity to seize the coastal towns of Durazzo, Scutari and Alessio (Lesh), and in 1385, in blind pursuit of his ambitions, one of the Albanian lords appealed to the Ottoman sultan, Murad I, to aid him against a rival. The Turks swept into the country and one by one the Albanian native chieftains were forced to pay them tribute.

### Turkish Colony

The Turks garrisoned the main towns and built a number of fortified

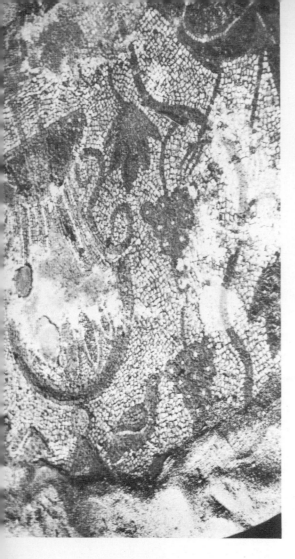

citadels, but they used the Albanian lords to keep the mountain tribes in order. The lords were allowed to keep their feudal positions in return for supplying troops to the Turks, but their sons were taken as hostages to the sultan's court.

One of these hostages, George Castriota (c. 1403-68), was to become Albania's greatest national hero. Taken by the Turks when he was still a boy, he was brought up as a Moslem and trained as a soldier. The Turks called him Iskander (Alexander) Bey, from which came his popular name of Scanderbeg, and he became a noted military commander.

### HOLY WAR

In 1443 a Turkish army was defeated by the forces of the great Hungarian leader János Hunyadi at Nis in Serbia. At the same time,

*A 16th-century Venetian map of Albania. In the center is Croia (Krujë), the fortress from which Scanderbeg led the Albanians in their struggle against Turkish domination. The engraving also shows cities held by the Venetians until they were driven out by the Turks.*

Scanderbeg, who was taking part in the campaign, heard that his countrymen had risen. He left the army and returned to Albania, where he proclaimed himself a Christian and declared a Holy War against the Turks.

Under Scanderbeg, the Albanians held the Turks at bay for 24 years, although in 1541, Scanderbeg felt obliged to recognize King Alfonso I of Naples as his overlord, in order to secure his aid. The struggle continued after Scanderbeg's death from fever in 1368, but the Turks gradually reconquered Albania. With the evacuation of Durazzo by the Venetians in 1501, the whole of the country was in their hands.

### Albania Under the Turks

Only the highlanders retained any vestiges of independence. As in the other Ottoman dominions, the secret of advancement for the few, and of some easing of their burdens for the many lay in embracing Islam, and although there were some forced conversions, most of them were brought about by such pressures. By the 19th century two-thirds of the inhabitants were Moslems. Just as the Illyrians had risen to high positions (even to that of emperor) under the

Romans, so Albanians became prominent in the Ottoman Empire. One Albanian family, the Bushatis, became so powerful in north and central Albania that the sultan eventually, in 1831, waged war against it to reassert his authority.

The re-emergence of a strong movement for national independence was provoked by Russia's victory over Turkey in the war of 1877-78, which resulted in the enlarging of all her neighbors — the principality of Montenegro, the kingdom of Serbia, and Greece — at Albania's expense. The Serbians occupied the territories granted to them under the peace treaties, but under the banner of the Albanian League, the Albanians successfully resisted the encroachments of Montenegro until the great powers forced them to comply by sending warships to the Adriatic.

### LANGUAGE UNITES THE ALBANIANS

The League was proscribed by the Turkish government in 1881, but Albanian nationalism continued to grow. While religion divided the Albanians into two Moslem sects (the Sunnites and the Bektashi) and two Christian Churches (Orthodox and Catholic), their common language, distinct from that of their Slav and Greek neighbors, proved a strong unifying force, despite rivalry between speakers of the two main dialects, Tosk and Gheg.

Linguistic congresses were held in in 1895 and 1897, and members of the Albanian communities in Italy played an important part at them. In 1908, emigrants joined with delegates

*George Castriota, known as Scander-beg, (c. 1403-68) is Albania's greatest national hero. A hostage of the Turks from his boyhood, he was brought up as a Moslem and trained as a soldier. In 1443 he proclaimed himself a Christian and for 24 years, until his death, he led a Holy War against the Turks.*

began. The rapid collapse of the Turkish armies before the Greeks, Serbians, and Montenegrins seemed to leave the Albanians at the mercy of their covetous neighbors. Nevertheless, on Nov. 28, 1912, an assembly of national leaders at Vlore (Valona) proclaimed Albania's independence, which was recognized by the great powers at the conference convened in London to stop the war from spreading. The frontiers finally agreed on substantially satisfied Albanian aspirations, although a few places with a majority of Albanian inhabitants, notably Prizren, were left outside them.

An International Control Commission was appointed by the great powers to administer Albania, and they nominated Prince William of Wied as the country's constitutional head. But intrigue and insurrection forced him to leave Albania in September 1914, only six months after his arrival.

### Member of the League of Nations

Although she declared herself neutral, Balkan rivals and the great powers fell on Albania during World War I. At the end of the war Italy, Greece, and the new state of Yugoslavia tried to dismember her. In January 1920, with the fate of its country still undecided, a representative congress met at Lushnje and resolved to form a national government. The Italian army of occupation was forced to withdraw by a rising in Vlore, and in December 1920, Albania was admitted to the League of Nations.

### DISSENSION AND DICTATORSHIP

Internally, however, the country was rent by the personal rivalry of its political leaders and by dissension over questions of reform and Westernization. Ahmed Bey Zogu (1895-

*Ali Pasha (1741-1822), the brigand chieftain who became a Turkish despot. Appointed governor of Janina in 1788, his sway eventually extended over southern Albania and northern Greece. He refused to recognize the authority of the sultan and intrigued with the British and French until he was deposed and shot in 1822.*

1961), who had been prime minister from December 1922 to February 1924 and continued to dominate the political scene after his resignation, was driven from the country in June 1924 by a military revolt instigated by the Opposition party led by the radical Orthodox bishop, Fan S. Noli. Six months later, backed by wealthy landowners, highland chieftains and the Yugoslavian government, Zogu returned to power. A purge of his opponents followed, and he was given wide powers as president of the new republic.

### KING ZOG

King Zog I (as he became in 1928) used his dictatorial powers to reform the administration and to organize improvements in the country's system of communications, but modernization was not matched by social reform and poverty remained widespread. Zog allied Albania with Mus-

from the homeland in adopting a common Latin alphabet at a congress at Bitolj (Monastir).

### THE YOUNG TURKS

At the same congress, a national committee was formed to press for Albanian autonomy within the Ottoman Empire. The Young Turks' movement for reform had just overthrown the autocratic government and it was thought that the new regime would look favorably on this demand, especially as Albanians had played an active part in the revolution. But it soon became clear that the Young Turks were no more in favor of self-government for the separate nationalities within the empire than their predecessors had been. A series of revolts broke out and on Sept. 4, 1912, the Turkish government yielded to practically all the Albanian demands.

### Independent Albania

Hardly had this settlement been reached when the first Balkan War

solini's Italy, and so complete did Italian control of her economy become that Albania was now virtually a vassal state.

### The Italian Occupation

In April 1939 Italian troops occupied Albania and King Zog went into exile. Mussolini's intention was to turn the country into a base for an attack on Greece, which was launched on Oct. 28, 1940. But the Greek forces drove the Italians back and by March 1941 were occupying about a quarter of Albania. Only the German *blitzkrieg* through Yugoslavia into Greece in April rescued the Italians from their predicament.

The Italians tried to win over Albanian nationalists by incorporating those parts of Yugoslavia with large Albanian populations into Albania and by giving the country some semblance of autonomy, but with little success. The resistance movement grew in strength, though its effectiveness was greatly diminished by the fratricidal strife between the National Liberation Movement controlled by the Communists and the *Balli Kombëtar* (National Front), whose program advocated social democracy. From this strife, which finally assumed the proportions of a civil war, the Communist front organization emerged victorious.

### Communist Albania

When the German forces withdrew from Albania in the fall of 1944, the Communists were already in effective control, and their leaders dominated the government formed at Berat on October 22 and installed in the capital, Tirana, on November 28.

#### PERSECUTION AND PURGES

Many of the leaders of *Balli Kombëtar* fled to Italy. Others were tried as "war criminals" or simply as "enemies of the people," a fate which also befell many landowners, members of the bourgeoisie and Roman Catholic clergy.

#### SPLIT WITH TITO

Until June 1948, when the Yugoslavian Communist party was expelled from the Cominform (successor to the Communist International) for "deviationism," Albania was dominated by Marshal Tito's regime. There were even plans for the country's incorporation into Yugoslavia as a federal republic. But the section of the Albanian Communists which took Russia's part in the dispute with Yugoslavia, led by the premier Enver Hoxha (1908-    ), came out on top and its opponents were purged. Foremost among them was Koci Xoxe, who, as Minister of the Interior and chief of the secret police, had himself been largely responsible for earlier purges.

#### BREAK WITH RUSSIA

Until Stalin's death Albania was noted as Soviet Russia's most loyal satellite, but when the official Russian policy was to a certain extent liberalized under Khruschev's leadership, Albania clung to the old Stalinist ideas. The rift between the two countries became so wide that in December 1961 diplomatic relations were severed, and since the drying up of economic aid from Russia, Albania has turned more and more to China for support.

### Industrial Planning

There has been considerable development of industry since the war and the Communists' third Five-Year Plan, for 1961-65, aims to raise the country's industrial production to more than 50 per cent of the total value of her production. However, most of the people still work on the land, some 85 per cent of which had been collectivized by 1962.

In 1954, Enver Hoxha relinquished the premiership to Mehmet Shehu, formerly successor to the purged Minister of the Interior, Koci Xoxe. However, Hoxha retained his key post as party chief.

*Partisans parade through the streets of the capital, Tirana, in November 1944, where, on the 28th of that month, the new national government was installed. By the time the German forces were withdrawn from Albania the Communists had already virtually eliminated all the rival resistance movements in a civil war.*

*The Oxen Gate (4th century A.D.) at Buthrotum. Erected and carved during the first period of Byzantine rule over Albania, the Oxen Gate is an example of the early Byzantine style which prevailed throughout the territory during the 4th century, and again, in a more advanced form, from the 6th to the 14th century. Byzantine features include the flat rendering of the beast and the abstracted plant motif which the animal holds in its mouth. Buthrotum is also the site of a 4th-century Byzantine baptistry which is enhanced with a mosaic pavement decorated in a similar, but more sophisticated style.*

## THE FINE ARTS

THE HISTORY OF ALBANIAN ART reflects the country's geographical position, as Albania has formed the crossroads for several civilizations. The art also reveals the number of foreign states which have dominated the territory since prehistoric times. Preserved in museums and in archaeological sites are remains from Greek and Roman antiquity and from the Byzantine and Venetian Middle Ages. There are also indications of the four centuries of Turkish rule, from the 15th to the 18th century, and traces of Western European, especially Italian and Soviet, styles.

### Prehistoric Art

#### THE STONE AGE

There is evidence that art was produced in the territory of present-day Albania during the late Stone Age (20,000-2500 B.C.). Fragments of painted pottery have been unearthed near Sarandë, in the southern tip of Albania.

#### THE BRONZE AGE AND EARLY IRON AGE

The Indo-Europeans, among the earliest invaders of the Balkans, arrived during the Bronze Age (2500-1000 B.C.). Some formed the kingdom of Illyria, while others moved into the southern areas of the Balkans.

The Indo-Europeans brought their advanced form of design from the East; characterized by flat, abstract patterns reminiscent of Oriental styles, this formed the foundation for the art produced in the territory of Albania, during the Bronze Age and early Iron Age (beginning 1000 B.C.).

### Greek Settlements

Due to commerce and trade, Greek settlements were established on the coast of Illyria as early as the 7th century B.C. The colonies were settled mainly by people from Corcyra (now Corfu) and Corinth. Among the major Greek centers which were rich in artistic creations, the more important were Apollonia, Butrinto (Buthrotum) and Epidamnus (Durazzo).

#### APOLLONIA

Apollonia was founded in 588 B.C. as a colony of Corcyra; it thrived as a Greek center up to the 3rd century B.C., and some of the walls, built in a triangle around the ancient city, still remain.

Among the sculpture from Apollonia, carved between the 6th and 4th centuries B.C., are: the *Satyr Anapauomenos* (Paris, Louvre Museum), the *Head of Ares* (Vienna, Museum of Art) and the *Head of Meleager* (Tirana Library).

#### BUTRINTO

The ancient Greek city of Butrinto was founded during the 6th century B.C. Among the outstanding Greek remains are the 16-foot-high walls which surround the acropolis and the seven entrance gates to the old city. Most remarkable of these portals is the bent-entrance gate, similar to the bent-axis approach in the palace of Cnossus on the island of Crete. Notable, too, are the monumental

*Seacoast Gate* and the *Lion Gate*, adorned with bas-relief sculpture representing a lion eating a bull.

#### EPIDAMNUS

Durazzo is the site of the ancient Greek city of Epidamnus, founded as a colony of Corinth and Corcyra in 627 B.C. Although no major excavations have been performed at Durazzo, pieces of pottery and sculpture, dating from the 7th century B.C., have been found.

Of greatest importance are archaic stone carvings which include a 6th-century-B.C. torso of a *kouros* (a nude male figure probably used as a votive offering) and fragments of sculptural decoration from the treasury of Olympia.

### Roman Rule

During the 3rd century B.C., the Romans conquered various cities in Illyria and in 168-167 B.C., the territory became a Roman province. Known as Illyricum, it remained under Roman rule through most of the 3rd century A.D.

Artistically, the more important Roman centers, captured from the Greeks, were Apollonia, Buthrotum and Durazzo.

#### ROMAN APOLLONIA

The Romans added architecture to the Greek acropolis at Apollonia and to the surroundings areas. Still remaining are ruins of the temple, built in the Roman Corinthian order, the gymnasium, the Roman bath, the triumphal arch and the theater, all built between the 1st century B.C. and 1st century A.D.

In the field of sculpture, the Romans left behind several 2nd-century B.C. steles.

#### ROMAN BUTHROTUM

Buthrotum is the site of an important Roman center which thrived from the 3rd century B.C. to the 5th century A.D. The Romans rebuilt

ince. During the 4th and 5th centuries, however, the territory was overrun by the Goths, but the Roman Emperor Justinian (438-567) reconquered the area in 535. Parts of it remained under Byzantine rule up to the 14th century.

During the same period, from the 3rd to the 14th century, various parts of Albania were invaded by many peoples, of which the most important in the history of Albanian art were the Venetians.

The earliest extant Byzantine structures in Albania date from the 4th century. They include the circular baptistry at Buthrotum (c. 360), built over a Roman bathing pool, part of a bath. The floor is decorated with richly colored mosaics, embellished with flat, circular designs, typically early Christian in style.

There is also a Byzantine portal at Buthrotum, the *Oxen Gate,* decorated with a flat relief carving (see page 211).

Argyrokastron, now known as Gjinokastër, was founded during the 4th century as a center of the Eastern Orthodox faith. All that remains of the early Byzantine ecclesiastical structures are foundations indicating the ground plans. These include the Greek Cross type (where four arms of equal length project from the nave or central chamber) and the basilican type (made up of a long nave culminating in an apse, and two aisles, one on each side of the nave) with the addition of a dome, placed over the nave.

## Late Byzantine Art

During the second period of Byzantine dominance over Albania, there was a great deal of building, especially in the southern part of the province. A number of 6th- to 15th-century Byzantine structures have survived, though many have been converted into mosques.

the stage of the Greek theater and added decorative sculpture to its exterior and interior. Among the carvings which are still extant are the so-called *Goddess of Buthrotum* (Rome, Terme National Museum), which is a 4th-century Roman copy of an earlier Greek work of art (see above), and a head which actually represents Apollo, but which was placed in error on the torso of a draped female figure.

### ROMAN DURAZZO

Durazzo, known as Dyrrachium during the period of Roman occupation, is rich in Roman remains.

Besides the ruins of an aqueduct, a library and an amphitheater, there is a temple dedicated to Minerva. These structures were built between 229 B.C. and the 3rd century A.D.

The most typical piece of Roman sculpture unearthed at Durazzo is the low-relief carving of *Victory Standing between Trophies of War and Barbarian Prisoners* (Paris, Louvre Museum), from a 3rd-century triumphal arch.

## Early Byzantine Art

When the Roman empire was divided during the 3rd century A.D., Illyricum became a Byzantine prov-

In general, the Albanian Byzantine churches show affinities with the Macedonian, Serbian and Rumanian variants of the style, as well as with Byzantine structures at Mt. Athos and Corfu. The churches are usually of the basilican type, and often have an independent square bell tower.

An exception is the late-10th-century church of Mesopotamo, near Sarandë, which is an example of the central type of church in Albania (see below).

## Venetian Colonies

Scutari, Lesh and Durazzo, among others, came under Venetian rule during the 13th and 14th centuries. In general, the Venetian churches built in Albania were of the Latin Cross type (a basilican church with transepts projecting from the eastern end of the nave). Most of the surviving castles and citadels in Albania are of Venetian origin.

### SCUTARI

The Venetians dominated Scutari from 1396 to 1779 and left behind the 14th-century citadel of Rosafat, based on an elliptical (oval) ground plan, and surrounded by three walls, integrated with nine bastions.

Scutari and its environs preserve a number of Catholic churches built during the 15th century in the Venetian-Gothic style. Most important of these is the Church of the Virgin of the Good Counsel (1476), the largest Catholic church in Albania.

### LESH

The 13th-century Romanesque church of St. Nicholas, one of the most beautiful and best-preserved Venetian structures in Albania, is located at Lesh, a Venetian colony from 1396 to 1478.

### DURAZZO

Durazzo, a Venetian center from 1392 to 1501, preserves the Venetian town walls and large cylindrical bastions, built in a Gothic style. The Venetian-Gothic castle (1447) is now in ruins.

## Turkish Rule

Turkish rule over Albania began in about 1478 and lasted until 1912. During this period of cultural isolation from Western Europe, many Byzantine and Italian churches were destroyed or converted into mosques simply by the addition of minarets. Of the mosques that were constructed, more than 1000 have survived.

The most outstanding Turkish structure in Albania is the mosque (constructed 1791-1819) of Etehem Bey at Tirana, which consists of the building proper with a shallow dome above it, a colonnaded portico on two of its sides, and a minaret at the back. Rich decorations, which adorn the exterior and interiors, include elaborate, low-relief carvings at the tops of columns and bas-reliefs set into the walls.

### MOSQUE DECORATIONS

During the 19th century and first decade of the 20th century, interiors of 16th- and 17th-century mosques were decorated with Byzantine-style paintings often placed over frescoes. At the same time, large decorative carvings were executed in a flamboyant Turkish style. This is exemplified by the cupola in the 15th-century mosque at Koritsa.

## The Twentieth Century

In 1913, Albania became a sovereign state, and a cultural contact was established with the Western world. This was severed, however, in 1949, when Albania became subservient to the U.S.S.R.

The art and architecture produced in Albania from 1912 up to the present reveals the country's varying political positions.

Many of the 20th-century buildings in Albania resemble 19th-century Italian monumental architecture. Tirana, Albania's most modern city, contains early-20th-century structures erected by Italian architects and post-World War II buildings which resemble the Soviet style.

*The church of Mesopotamo, near Sarandë, built during the latter part of the 10th century. Based on a central type of plan, the style of this ecclesiastical building was derived from the Byzantine churches at Mt. Athos and Corfu. Placed over the central chamber is a cupola of the Eastern Orthodox type. Both church and cupola are decorated with bricks and stones arranged to create abstract patterns, as well as painted tiles and low-relief carvings of fantastic animals. The church of Mesopotamo is one of the few Byzantine structures which was not converted into a mosque by the Turks, who dominated Albania from the 15th to the 19th century.*

*Naïm Frásheri (1846-1900), the outstanding literary figure in the 19th-century movement for the creation of an Albanian national culture. Frásheri wrote didactic, lyrical and epic poems which include the large-scale work* Istoria e Skënderbeut *(The Story of Scanderbeg) 1898, an epic biography of the national hero who fought for Albanian independence in the 15th century.*

## THE LITERATURE

### The Albanian Language

THE COURSE OF HISTORY HAS BEEN unfavorable to the development of a body of national literature in Albania. This is partly due to the unsettled political history of the country and to the division of the spoken language between the two main dialects of Gheg, spoken in the north, and Tosk, spoken in the south, as well as a number of minor dialects. In addition, an official system of written Albanian, based on the Latin alphabet, did not come into force until the early years of the present century, Greek, Cyrillic and Arabic-Turkish characters having also been previously used.

#### FOLK LITERATURE

The traditional folk literature of the Albanian people was transmitted orally up to the present century, though it has now been collected. Much of it is in verse, and it is in ballads that the true spirit of the Albanian people is best expressed. The Albanians have often had to struggle for their liberty and independence, and this has given rise to a tradition of epic songs, notably the many ballads which center around the exploits of the national hero, Scanderbeg.

As well as heroic themes, there are also lyrical songs, forming a body of verse impressive in its variety, its forceful expression and the richness of its imagery. Vigorous and forthright sentiments are a common quality in Albanian folk literature, as might be expected from a tough and hardy race in a small, mountainous country.

### Religious Texts and Poetry

The earliest survivals of written Albanian are found in a few religious works of the 15th century, the earliest being a baptismal formula inserted into a pastoral letter in Latin in 1462. The 16th and 17th centuries are richer in early texts, which are in a language which differs little from modern spoken Albanian.

In 1555, Bishop Gjon Buzuki published a *Missal* in northern Albania. This was the first in a series of religious, etymological and grammatical works in the northern dialect (Gheg) published up to the end of the 18th century, though these works are of historical rather than literary importance. Notable, however, was the collection of sacred poems by the Italian-Albanian ecclesiastic Jul Variboda, published in 1762.

### The Nineteenth Century

As has been mentioned above, the production of books in Albanian was actively discouraged during the years of Turkish rule; until the early years of the present century printing in Albanian was forbidden, only the clergy of Scutari, in the north, enjoying partial exemption. For this reason, the main Albanian literary movements of the 19th century were centered outside the country around exiled writers.

One of the major Romantic poets was Girolamo Rada (1813-1903), active in Italy, whose early lyrical works and later verse narratives had a nationalistic appeal which inspired other Italian-based writers. Among these were the dramatist Anton Santori (1819-94) and the lyric poet Zef Srembe (1843-91). Konstantin Kristoforidhi (1827-95), a noted translator and linguist, attempted to unify the Albanian literary language by popularizing the Elbasani dialect of Albania in place of Gheg and Tosk.

The major figure of the 19th century was, however, Naïm Frásheri (1846-1900), a member of a prominent literary family. Frásheri, a Moslem and the master of a number of Oriental languages, wrote lyrical and epic poetic works in Tosk, among them *The Story of Scanderbeg*, 1898

### The Twentieth Century

Like the writers of the 19th century, Albanian writers at the beginning of the 20th century mainly wrote outside their country, although with the growing movement toward independence their work took on new nationalistic fervor. Among them were the patriotic poet Anton Zako-Cajupi (1886-1930), active in Egypt; the lyric poet Aleksander Sotir Drenova (called Asdreni, 1872-1945), active in Rumania; the folklorist and poet Zef Schiro (1865-1927), in Italy; the essayist and critic Fajk Kontiza (1875-1942), in Belgium, England and America; and the versatile Fan Noli (1881-    ), the Bishop of the Albanian Orthodox Church in America, a writer of drama and history and a translator of the Spanish and Russian classics.

With the achievement of independence, Albanian writers were able to work in their own country. The period between the two world wars, which saw a period of Italian dominance (1928-45), produced a number of notable writers, among them the dramatists Mihal Grameno (1878-1931) and Kristo Floqi; the poets Luigi Gurakuqi (1879-1925), Nore Mjedja (1866-1937) and Fishta (1871-1940); and the prose writers Midhat Frásheri (1880-1949), Ernest Koliqi (1903-    ) and Etem Hashiademi (1902-    ).

The period of World War II, with the culmination of the long struggle against Fascism in the founding of the present Communist state, saw the emergence of a number of young writers, many of whom were much influenced by the heroic folk tradition. Among these were the poets Shefqet Muraraj (1914-    ), Aleks Caci (1916-    ) and Llazar Siliqi (1924-    ); and the prose writers Zihni Sako (1913-    ), Dimitir Shuteriqi (1915-    ) and Fatmir Gjata (1922-    ).

In recent years, Albania's growing isolation from both Western Europe, as a Communist state, and from Eastern Europe, through the Albanian separation from Soviet Russia, has meant that little Albanian writing has penetrated into the outside world.

*A scene from the opera* Russalka *(1856) by the Russian composer Aleksandr Dargomyzhski (1813-69); the story is adapted from the work by the great Russian poet A.S. Pushkin (1799-1837). The performance shown here is by the Albanian Philharmonic at Tirana, the center of Albanian musical life.*

## THE THEATER

DURING THE FOUR CENTURIES OF Turkish rule, it was illegal for Albanian subjects to read, write or perform plays in their native tongue. Theater thus, developed very late in Albania, gaining strength only after the end of Turkish rule in 1912.

The first attempts at serious drama were made during the decades that preceded the collapse of the Ottoman Empire ; they represented one aspect of the national longing for independence. The Turks' opposition to any manifestation by which the Albanians might feel aware of their common traditions caused drama to find expression outside the country, chiefly in the Albanian colonies of Italy.

Two representatives of this phase in the development of Albanian theater were Girolamo de Rada (1813-1903) and Anton Santori (1819-94), both Italians of Albanian parentage, whose works found their way secretly into Albania.

### DRAMA IN SCUTARI

An exception to the otherwise rigid ruling against Albanian cultural activity was found in Scutari, capital of northern Albania, where the Roman Catholic clergy enjoyed special privileges. This accounts for the appear-ance of the first playwright to write on Albanian soil, Pasko Vasa Pasha (1827-92). His name is linked with the production of *The Jew's Son*, that inaugurated theatrical activity at the Xaverian College in Scutari in 1879.

Two Roman Catholic priests who took advantage of the conditions in Scutari to write plays were Stefan Gjeçov (1874-1929), the author of several historical dramas ; and one of the most authoritative personalities on the history of the Albanian theater, Gjergji Fishta (1865-1941). Fishta wrote several plays which criticized the social conditions under Turkish rule ; three examples are *St. Francis of Assisi* (1909), *The Uncivilized Albanian,* and *Iphigenia in Aulis*.

### Toward Independence

The partition of Albanian territories by the Congress of Berlin (1878) precipitated a movement toward political and cultural unity. An attempt to standardize the Albanian language, using the Latin alphabet, gathered support under the leadership of the writer Sami Bey Frásheri. A noted patriot, Frásheri was largely responsible for the wave of national consciousness that swept the country at the turn of the century. His play *Besa* (The Pledge of Honor), a story of the Albanian highlanders, written originally in Turkish, was translated into Albanian and published in Sofia in 1901.

Once independence had been achieved in 1912, the Albanian language was purified of all Turkish, Slav, German and Italian elements, and the output of original Albanian plays increased considerably; it was also matched by notable translations from the great European playwrights.

### AMERICAN ALBANIAN

One Albanian writer who has achieved a considerable reputation abroad is the Orthodox bishop, Fan S. Noli (1881-     ). For a short time, Noli was prime minister of his country, but, forced to leave in the 1920s, he settled in the U.S.A., where he had studied earlier, and is now an American citizen. Noli, an excellent translator, is the author of several philosophical plays, including *Israelite and Philistine* (1907), which emphasizes the need for an independent Albania.

### Between the Wars

Some notable young playwrights emerged between world wars. The work of Etëhem Haxhiademi is remarkable for its classical precision of style, revealed in *Ulysses* (1924), *Achilles* (1926), *Pyrrhus* (1931) and *Skanderbeg* (1935). The novelist, Foqion Postoli, has also written several dramas, including the rather sentimental *The Mother's Duty* (1925).

More recent is the work of Aleks Çaçi (1916-   ) and Koli Jakova, but the present regime in Albania, separated from Western Europe because of its Communist principles and from Eastern Europe because of ideological disagreement with Russia, has made the country culturally isolated and little is known about recent developments.

Theaters were established after 1945 in Koritsa, Argyrokastron, Tirana and Durazzo. The first national people's theater, founded in Tirana in 1944, under Soviet direction, is used largely as an instrument of propaganda.

## THE MUSIC

MANY RELICS OF ANCIENT CULTURE survive in the music of the Albanian region. The country's colonization by successive migrant waves has led to the existence of several different types of popular music in Albania today. These reveal different idioms, none of which fit the European classical system.

### Folk Tradition

The type of music considered the most ancient is the *olkanje,* a vocal style, the instrumental accompaniment to which is played on a *roja,* a kind of bagpipe.

In the cities there are instrumental groups, for strings plucked or used with a bow, which play a very ornate type of music, with strong Turkish elements.

In the mountains, men's dances have a solemn and forceful quality, emphasized by the accompanying instrument, a large tambourine-like instrument, the *tupan.* The player carries the instrument on his chest, plucking it with his right hand while his left hand rubs it with a short bow, thus producing quite complex rhythmic patterns. In the north the people sing to the sound of a *lahuta* (lute).

Many Albanians left their country in the 12th century, to avoid living under Turkish rule. Some settled in Calabria and Sicily and created communities where, even today, early Albanian musical traditions may be found.

### The Twentieth Century

It was only at the beginning of the 20th century that systematic musical forms began to evolve. The first public performances took place in Scutari and Koritsa, when D. Michele Koliqi added a musical commentary to the dramatic poems of D. Andrea Zaděja (1890-1945). The latter wrote the music as well as the text of *Rozafa,* which may be considered a real opera.

### Current Trends

At the present time all musical production is subject to Communist control, and because of the desire for art forms which promote the party political cause, propagandist songs are the most favored form of musical expression. Among the foremost Albanian composers, Kristo Kono has written many songs, including *Albanian Fantasies*, and *Agimi* (The Dawn) (1954). The work of Konstantin Trako is also very popular.

Young musicians are now being trained at the state musical academy at Tirana.

## THE FILM

VERY LITTLE IS KNOWN ABOUT THE film industry in Albania since none of its products are shown in international film festivals, nor do any films from the West achieve showings on Albanian circuits.

In 1941 an Italo-Albanian company, known as *Tomorrifilm,* was formed in Tirana; it produced mainly documentary films, notably *Meeting on the Lake.*

A studio opened in Tirana in 1952 now produces two or three films a year.

*A group of Albanian girls in southern Italy, where many Albanian communities are found, the largest being a colony in Sicily. At one time, under Turkish repression and until the coming of their country's independence, Albanians were allowed no proper expression for their native art; and only those living abroad could carry on its traditions.*